Institutional Interaction in Global
Governance

Global Environmental Accord: Strategies for Sustainability and Institutional Innovation
Nazli Choucri, series editor

A complete list of books published in this series appears at the back of the book.

Institutional Interaction in Global Environmental Governance

Synergy and Conflict among International and EU Policies

edited by Sebastian Oberthür and Thomas Gehring
with a Foreword by Oran R. Young

The MIT Press
Cambridge, Massachusetts
London, England

MIT Press books may be purchased at special quantity discounts for business or sales promotional use. For information, please e-mail special_sales@mitpress.mit.edu or write to Special Sales Department, The MIT Press, 55 Hayward Street, Cambridge, MA 02142.

This book was set in Sabon on 3B2 by Asco Typesetters, Hong Kong and was printed and bound in the United States of America. Printed on recycled paper.

Library of Congress Cataloging-in-Publication Data

Institutional interaction in global environmental governance : synergy and conflict among international and EU policies / edited by Sebastian Oberthür and Thomas Gehring ; with a foreword by Oran R. Young.
    p.   cm.
Includes bibliographical references and index.
ISBN 0-262-05115-X (alk. paper)—ISBN 0-262-65110-6 (pbk. : alk. paper)
1. Environmental policy—International cooperation. 2. Environmental policy—European Union countries. 3. Environmental law, International. I. Oberthür, Sebastian. II. Gehring, Thomas, 1957–
GE170.I53   2006
363.7'0526—dc22   2005052121

10 9 8 7 6 5 4 3 2 1

Contents

Series Foreword

A new recognition of profound interconnections between social and natural systems is challenging conventional constructs and the policy predispositions informed by them. Our current intellectual challenge is to develop the analytical and theoretical underpinnings of an understanding of the relationship between the social and the natural systems. Our policy challenge is to identify and implement effective decision-making approaches to managing the global environment.

The series Global Environmental Accord: Strategies for Sustainability and Institutional Innovation adopts an integrated perspective on national, international, cross-border, and cross-jurisdictional problems, priorities, and purposes. It examines the sources and the consequences of social transactions as these relate to environmental conditions and concerns. Our goal is to make a contribution to both intellectual and policy endeavors.

Nazli Choucri

Foreword

First published in 1999, the Science Plan of the long-term research project on the Institutional Dimensions of Global Environmental Change (IDGEC) states that "the effectiveness of specific institutions often depends not only on their own features but also on their interactions with other institutions" (Young et al. 1999, 49). This observation, which gave rise to the development of an analytic theme known to the IDGEC community as the problem of interplay, struck a responsive chord and launched what has become an important stream of research on interactions between and among distinct institutions that influence the course of human-environment relations. We can say with some certainty at this stage that the results of this stream of research will make up a significant component of IDGEC's scientific legacy.

No one has made a larger contribution to this line of inquiry than Thomas Gehring and Sebastian Oberthür, two German political scientists who have addressed the problem of interplay in a number of individual papers and who have now joined forces in producing this major contribution to the literature on institutional interplay. Funded by the European Commission and endorsed by IDGEC, *Institutional Interaction in Global Environmental Governance* brings together a sizable collection of case studies of interplay occurring both at the international level and at the European Union level and subjects the findings from the cases to rigorous comparative analysis. The result is a book that sets the standard for all those seeking to produce new insights pertaining to the dynamics of institutional interactions.

Three things make this volume especially noteworthy. First, Oberthür and Gehring adopt what amounts to a reductionist approach to the study of institutional interplay. Thus, they disaggregate interplay to focus on a single source institution, a single target institution, and a unidirectional causal pathway as their basic unit of analysis. They argue that the route to understanding institutional interactions lies in this reductionist approach. Once we understand interplay in its simplest form, we can proceed to build up an understanding of more complex interactions featuring two-way flows and more than two institutions. Others have argued that we need to focus directly on the more complex forms of interaction on the assumption that some of the things we want to understand arise as emergent properties of institutional complexes. We do not know at this stage what approach to institutional interplay will ultimately prove most fruitful. But Oberthür and Gehring have done us all a distinct service by flagging this issue and laying out their own approach in a clear and rigorous manner.

A second distinctive feature of the volume is its sustained examination of causal mechanisms. What is at stake here is an effort to identify the pathways and mechanisms through which interactions between distinct institutions can affect the course of human-environment relations. Using the familiar distinction among outputs, outcomes, and impacts, Oberthür and Gehring began by differentiating among several causal mechanisms in constructing the analytic framework for this project. They devoted particular attention to cognitive interaction, which highlights interinstitutional learning; interaction through commitment, which features the effects of commitments on the part of members of the source institution on the preferences of those associated with the target institution; and behavioral interaction, which centers on ways that behavior taking place within the source institution affects the operation of the target institution. Of course, exploring the nature of these causal mechanisms is a priority concern. But equally important in the context of institutional analysis is the fact that they spelled out these mechanisms in considerable detail in advance of the project's empirical phase. As a result, the mechanisms function as theoretically derived expectations to be tested or at least explored systematically through the case studies conducted by all the participants in the project.

Third, as Gehring and Oberthür point out, there is a need to think more carefully about the circumstances under which institutional interplay produces synergistic outcomes in contrast to disruptive or conflict-ridden outcomes. Without doubt, many of those who have become interested in institutional interplay have been concerned about the potential for interference associated with institutional interaction. The contributors to this volume do not deny that interference does occur or that it may sometimes be serious in terms of its consequences. But their studies provide evidence that synergistic interactions are common, perhaps more common than disruptive interactions. This is especially true when the relevant institutions operate within the same policy field. The results are certainly not all in with regard to the incidence of synergistic and disruptive interactions. But the findings reported in this volume regarding the importance of synergy certainly constitute food for thought.

The study of institutional interplay remains an infant industry. The findings we have been able to generate so far are only first steps toward an understanding of this pervasive phenomenon; much work remains to be done. Nevertheless, we have already learned some important things about institutional interplay. Equally important, the research conducted so far has established this subject as a fruitful area for institutional analysis. No one deserves more of the credit for achieving these results than the leaders of the project whose findings are presented in this volume.

Oran R. Young
Chair, Scientific Steering Committee
Institutional Dimensions of Global Environmental Change

Reference

Young, Oran R., Leslie A. King, Arun Aggarval, Arild Underdal, Peter H. Sand, and Merrilyn Wasson. 1999. *Institutional Dimensions of Global Environmental Change (IDGEC): Science Plan*. Bonn: International Human Dimensions Programme on Global Environmental Change.

Acknowledgments

This book is the result of a collaborative European research project that involved four institutes from three countries: Ecologic—Institute for International and European Environmental Policy in Berlin, Germany; the Foundation for International Environmental Law and Development (FIELD) in London, UK; the Fridtjof Nansen Institute in Lysaker, Norway; and the Institute for European Environmental Policy (IEEP) in London, UK. The project, titled "Institutional Interaction—How to Prevent Conflicts and Enhance Synergies between International and EU Environmental Institutions," was conducted between the end of 2000 and the beginning of 2003. More information about the project and its results can be found at http://www.ecologic.de/projekte/interaction.

We are particularly grateful to the European Community for providing funding for our project under the Specific Research and Technological Development Programme "Energy, Environment and Sustainable Development" of the Fifth Framework Programme for Research (Contract no. EVK2-CT2000-00079). We are also thankful for the endorsement of the project by the Institutional Dimensions of Global Environmental Change (IDGEC). This volume is intended to make a contribution to this long-term international research project, which operates under the auspices of the International Human Dimensions Programme on Global Environmental Change (IHDP). The editors would like to extend special thanks to Ecologic—Institute for International and European Environmental Policy and the Otto-Friedrich University Bamberg for enabling us to continue working on the book after the official end of the research project cofunded by the European Community.

We also owe special thanks to the members of the project team for patiently responding to recurring requests for revisions. Furthermore, we are indebted to a number of individuals who have helped bring about this book in a number of ways. Oran R. Young and two anonymous reviewers provided helpful comments on the manuscript. The series editor, Nazli Choucri, gave valuable and encouraging guidance for the revision and finalization of the manuscript. Kristina Vesper provided invaluable assistance in the conduct of the project throughout its lifetime. Philipp Bleninger and Sebastian Krapohl have earned our gratitude by providing important assistance in and advice on the handling of our database of cases of institutional interaction reflected in the appendix to this volume and its evaluation contained in chapter 13. Thanks are also due to Ulrich Pilster for his tireless assistance in producing the final manuscript.

Finally, we would like to express our appreciation to The MIT Press for their excellent cooperation in producing this volume. Needless to say, responsibility for the contents remains solely with the authors.

Sebastian Oberthür and Thomas Gehring
Bamberg, Germany

List of Contributors

Clare Coffey
Institute for European Environmental Policy
(IEEP)
Brussels, Belgium

Beatrice Chaytor
Foundation for International Environmental
Law and Development (FIELD)
London, UK

Andrew Farmer
Institute for European Environmental Policy
(IEEP)
London, UK

Thomas Gehring
Otto-Friedrich University Bamberg
Bamberg, Germany

Ingmar von Homeyer
Ecologic-Institute for International and
European Environmental Policy
Berlin, Germany

John Lanchbery
Royal Society for the Protection of Birds/
BirdLife International
Sandy, UK

Sebastian Oberthür
Ecologic-Institute for International and
European Environmental Policy and Otto-
Friedrich University Bamberg
Berlin and Bamberg, Germany

Alice Palmer
Foundation for International Environmental
Law and Development (FIELD)
London, UK

G. Kristin Rosendal
Fridtjof Nansen Institute
Lysaker, Norway

Jon Birger Skjærseth
Fridtjof Nansen Institute
Lysaker, Norway

Olav Schram Stokke
Fridtjof Nansen Institute
Lysaker, Norway

Jacob Werksman
Foundation for International Environmental
Law and Development (FIELD)
London, UK

Jørgen Wettestad
Fridtjof Nansen Institute
Lysaker, Norway

List of Abbreviations

APEC	Asia-Pacific Economic Cooperation
BAT	Best available technique/technology
BREF	BAT Reference Document
CAC	Codex Alimentarius Commission
CAEP	Committee on Aviation Environmental Protection
CAFÉ	Clean Air for Europe
CAP	Common Agricultural Policy (of the European Union)
CBD	Convention on Biological Diversity
CCD	Convention to Combat Desertification
CCAMLR	Convention on the Conservation of Antarctic Marine Living Resources
CCMV	Convention for the Conservation and Management of the Vicuña
CFP	Common Fisheries Policy (of the European Union)
CITES	Convention on International Trade in Endangered Species of Wild Fauna and Flora
CLRTAP	Convention on Long-Range Transboundary Air Pollution
CMS	Convention on Migratory Species of Wild Animals
COP	Conference of the Parties
CTE	Committee on Trade and Environment
DRD	Deliberate Release Directive
EC	European Community
ECJ	European Court of Justice

EU	European Union
FAO	Food and Agriculture Organization of the United Nations
FD	Framework Directive
GATT	General Agreement on Tariffs and Trade
GEF	Global Environment Facility
GHG	Greenhouse gas
GMO	Genetically modified organism
ICAO	International Civil Aviation Organization
ICCAT	International Commission for the Conservation of Atlantic Tunas
ICES	International Council for the Exploration of the Sea
IMO	International Maritime Organization
INSC	International North Sea Conference
Interpol, ICPO	International Criminal Police Organization
IPCC	Intergovernmental Panel on Climate Change
IPOA	International Plan of Action
IPPC Directive	Integrated Pollution Prevention and Control Directive
IPPC	International Plant Protection Convention
IPR	Intellectual property rights
IUCN	World Conservation Union (previously: International Union for the Conservation of Nature and Natural Resources)
LCP	Large combustion plants
LMO	Living modified organism
MEA	Multilateral Environmental Agreement
MEPC	Marine Environment Protection Committee
NAFO	Northwest Atlantic Fisheries Organization
NATO	North Atlantic Treaty Organization
NEC	National Emission Ceiling
NGO	Nongovernmental organization
OECD	Organization for Economic Cooperation and Development
OSPAR	Oslo and Paris Conventions for the protection of the Northeast Atlantic

OSPARCOM	OSPAR Commissions
PCB	Polychlorinated biphenyl
PD	Pesticides Directive
PPM	Process and production method
SAC	Special Area of Conservation
SCM Agreement	Subsidies and Countervailing Measures Agreement
SPA	Special Protection Area
SPS Agreement	Agreement on Sanitary and Phytosanitary Measures
TAC	Total allowable catch
TBT Agreement	Agreement on Technical Barriers to Trade
TRAFFIC	Trade Records Analysis of Fauna and Flora in Commerce
TRIPS Agreement	Agreement on Trade-Related Aspects of Intellectual Property Rights
UNCED	United Nations Conference on Environment and Development
UNECE	United Nations Economic Commission for Europe
UNEP	United Nations Environment Program
UNFCCC	United Nations Framework Convention on Climate Change
UPOV	International Union for the Protection of New Varieties of Plants
WCMC	World Conservation Monitoring Centre
WCO	World Customs Organization
WHO	World Health Organization
WIPO	World Intellectual Property Organization
WTO	World Trade Organization
WWF	World Wide Fund for Nature

1

Introduction

Thomas Gehring and Sebastian Oberthür

International and EU environmental governance is affected by the interaction of numerous sectoral legal instruments. International environmental regimes and EU environmental instruments do not exist in isolation from each other or from institutions in other policy fields. While they are usually targeted at specific issue areas, their effects are not limited to their own domains. Frequently, they exert influence on the development and effectiveness of other policy instruments, and are themselves influenced by other such instruments, both within the same policy field and beyond ("institutional interaction"). This influence may create synergy by supporting the policy of the affected institution or it may undermine and disrupt its effectiveness. Hence, interinstitutional influence may be employed to enhance international and EU environmental governance, but it also aggravates the difficulties of governance.

This book seeks to understand how institutional interaction can occur and what its governance effects are. It is based on a coherent analytic approach to the relatively novel subject of institutional interaction and explores interaction phenomena in international and EU environmental governance from a comparative perspective. We focus on the investigation of the causal mechanisms that drive individual cases of interaction in which one international institution or EU legal instrument affects another's effectiveness or institutional development. Our empirical investigation covers a broad range of interaction phenomena in EU and international environmental governance and reaches beyond the ad hoc study of individual cases or limited "nests" of interacting institutions prevailing in the field to date.

The Relevance of Institutional Interaction

The heavily fragmented institutional structure of international environmental governance has contributed to an increasing political salience of issues of interinstitutional coordination and cooperation. Over the last decades, states have entered into a growing number of international environmental agreements, and they have tended to establish them separately from each other. To date, more than two hundred agreements have been concluded. While on average one treaty was adopted per year until the 1970s, this number has grown to five since the 1980s (Beisheim et al. 1999). Whenever a new international treaty is adopted, it enters an institutional setting that is already densely populated. The growing number of separately established international environmental institutions suggests the rapidly increasing relevance of institutional interaction. Accordingly, conferences of parties of multilateral environmental agreements increasingly address issues of interinstitutional coordination and cooperation. Problems of institutional interaction support suggestions to "cluster" multilateral environmental agreements—that is, to integrate groups of such agreements or certain of their parts (Oberthür 2002), as discussed within the framework of the UN Environment Program (UNEP). Calls for the creation of a "world environment organization" have partly been justified with reference to an increasing demand for interinstitutional coordination within the field of the environment and beyond, and to a growing potential for duplication of work (German Advisory Council on Global Change 2001; Biermann and Bauer 2005).

Likewise, EU environmental policy consists of a patchwork (Héritier 1996) of numerous instruments with diverse regulatory approaches, which has reinforced efforts at improved policy integration. To date, the EU has produced more than two hundred environmental legal instruments, primarily directives and regulations (Krämer 1999; Haigh 2003). Some of them set quality standards, while leaving the mode of implementation to the member states. Others envisage emission control limits and detailed technical regulations. Yet others prescribe particular procedures for the assessment of environmental risks and impacts, or establish crosscutting mechanisms such as environmental liability. In any given problem area, environmental governance rests on several of these instruments and is also influenced by instruments from other policy fields. Enhancing synergies and coherence between different policy instruments has therefore been a central element in the debate launched by the European Commission's White Paper on European Governance (European Commission 2001) as well as in discussions on an EU Sustainable Development Strategy started in 2001. Since 2003, the European Commission is required to examine all significant economic, social, and environmental impacts of a proposed measure, both within and beyond the EU's borders (European Commission 2002; in general, Haigh 2003; Wilkinson 1998; Lenschow 2002).

We find both synergistic and disruptive cases of institutional interaction in international and EU environmental governance. The global regime on the transboundary movement of hazardous wastes has been strengthened as a result of the establishment of a number of regional regimes addressing the same environmental problem (Meinke 2002). And the EU Nitrates Directive has contributed to the implementation of the North Sea Declarations. This "surprisingly effective" relationship has allowed the EU to act as an international leader in this area (Vogler 1999, 24). In contrast, incentives for establishing fast-growing monocultural tree plantations provided by the 1997 Kyoto Protocol to the UN Framework Convention on Climate Change in order to maximize carbon sequestration from the atmosphere are potentially at odds with the 1992 Convention on Biological Diversity (CBD) that aims at preserving the biological diversity of forest ecosystems (Pontecorvo 1999).

Institutional interaction also occurs across the boundaries of policy fields. Perhaps the most prominent example in international environmental governance concerns the relationship between the World Trade Organization (WTO) that promotes free international trade and several multilateral environmental agreements that establish new trade restrictions, such as the 1973 Convention on International Trade in Endangered Species of Wild Fauna and Flora (CITES) and the 1987 Montreal Protocol on Substances That Deplete the Ozone Layer. The WTO has constrained the options available to environmental policymakers in these cases and may have limited the effectiveness of the environmental agreements concerned (chapter 8). Also, the EU Structural Funds that provide financial support to economic development projects have undermined the effectiveness of EU nature conservation policies enshrined, in particular, in the EU Habitats Directive. In this case, Structural Fund rules have been revised so as to provide incentives for the implementation of the Habitats Directive (chapter 10).

Political actors increasingly recognize the constraints, and employ the opportunities, arising from the growing institutional density and interdependence at both the international and EU levels. On the one hand, institutional interaction provides opportunities for forum shopping and purposive policy development (Raustiala and Victor 2004). It may also be employed to overcome obstacles that hinder policy development within another institution. The International North Sea Conferences were exclusively established to enhance the momentum of pollution-abatement activities in an area already governed by an existing international institution with very similar membership (chapter 5). On the other hand, environmental policymakers are utterly aware of the constraints imposed by WTO rules and have adapted relevant multilateral environmental agreements to make them WTO-compatible. The tensions between the world trade system and various multilateral environmental agreements are addressed in the Doha Round of trade negotiations launched in 2001 (chapter 8).

Issues of institutional interaction have increasingly attracted the attention of the scientific community. Whereas the analysis of international institutions has for a long time started from the fiction that institutions exists in isolation from and do not significantly interfere with the performance of each other (Keohane 1984; Rittberger 1993), research on the broader consequences of international institutions has intensified more recently (Gehring 2004). As part of this shift in perspective, initial steps have been made to examine the side effects of international institutions beyond their own issue areas. Contributions have particularly built on the analytic framework established to assess the effectiveness of international institutions (Young et al. 1999; Young 2002; Underdal and Young 2004; Stokke 2001a). Legal scholars and political scientists have identified a risk of "treaty congestion" (Brown Weiss 1993, 679) and a growing "regime density" (Young 1996). Empirically, much of the increasing literature on the phenomena of institutional interaction has focused on instances of interinstitutional conflict that had raised political interest, while cases resulting in synergy have received far less attention (e.g., Rosendal 2000, 2001; Andersen 2002; Chambers 1998, 2001; Oberthür 2001; Stokke 2001b). Institutional interaction has also been identified as a key issue for future research—for example, by the Institutional Dimensions of Global Environmental Change (IDGEC) project of the International Human Dimensions Programme on Global Environmental Change (IHDP) (Young et al. 1999) and by the Concerted Action on the Effectiveness of International Environmental Agreements sponsored by the EU (Breitmeier 2000).

A diversity of terms is employed in the literature to denote phenomena of interinstitutional influence, including *interplay, linkage, interlinkage, overlap,* and *interconnection* (e.g., Herr and Chia 1995; King 1997; Young 1996, 2002; Young et al. 1999; Chambers 1998; Stokke 2001b). The term *interaction* appears to us particularly suitable because it emphasizes that interinstitutional influence is rooted in decisions taken by the members of one of the institutions involved. It is thus action that triggers interaction.

The present volume attempts to generate a more comprehensive picture of the largely uncharted territory of institutional interaction in international and EU environmental governance by presenting the results of a large comparative exploration of relevant interaction phenomena. It intends to advance our knowledge about institutional interaction by focusing on the causal influence of governance institutions on each others' normative development and performance. Empirically, it analyzes a wide range of interaction incidents of varying political salience, different outcomes, and distinct causal pathways in different areas of environmental governance beyond the nation-state.

Conceptual Foundations

The development of the conceptual foundations for the investigation of institutional interaction is at an early stage. Existing approaches mainly constitute typologies and attempts to categorize phenomena of institutional interaction, which differ significantly in form and substance (see Stokke 2001a, 1–8). They do not provide a sufficient basis for the systematic analysis of the causal mechanisms and driving forces of institutional interaction. The concept of institutional interaction on which the present volume rests, relies on the following three components. Accompanied by an overview of existing approaches, it is fully elaborated in chapter 2.

The Notion of International and EU Institutions   The inquiry of the present volume focuses exclusively on negotiated sectoral legal systems because we are generally interested in capturing institutions that are established for the purpose of governance. Only negotiated institutions may be used instrumentally to bring about collectively desired change in the international system. Scholars exploring the effectiveness of international institutions have focused their attention on such negotiated institutions (e.g., Haas, Keohane, and Levy 1993; Young 1999; Miles et al. 2002). International institutions can be defined as "persistent and connected sets of rules and practices that prescribe behavioral roles, constrain activity, and shape expectations" (Keohane 1989, 3). Usually they include a separate communication and decision-making process from which their norms and rules emerge (Gehring 1994). Both international regimes based on international treaties and international organizations qualify as specific international institutions.

We identify EU legal instruments, in particular directives and regulations, as the suitable functional equivalent of specific international institutions at the EU level. Like international institutions, they constitute distinct systems of norms negotiated to balance the interests of the member states and other actors involved. They also focus on limited functionally defined issue areas and possess separate communication processes. EU member states and the European Commission decide on their establishment and development separately from other instruments. Frequently, so-called comitology committees related to a particular instrument prepare amendments of that instrument or take implementing decisions. This is not to deny that the EU has a particularly sophisticated overarching institutional framework for lawmaking and implementation, which includes the EU and EC Treaties as well as the European Court of Justice, the European Commission, and the European Parliament. Whereas this framework has to be taken into account, EU legal instruments are sufficiently similar to international institutions so as to serve as functional equivalents in our study of institutional interaction.

Specific international institutions (international regimes and specific international organizations) and EU legal instruments (directives, regulations, decisions) constitute the prime governance instruments in international and European affairs. The choice of these institutions as the principal units of institutional interaction relates the inquiry of this volume to the extensive literature on international and European governance. It also provides a suitable foundation for investigating the ramifications of institutional interaction for the system of international and EU governance.

The Meaning of Institutional Interaction   Generally, institutional interaction will exist, if one institution affects the institutional development or the effectiveness (performance) of another institution. In essence, *institutional interaction* refers to a causal relationship between two institutions, with one of these institutions ("the source institution") exerting influence on the other ("the target institution"). In the absence of causal influence, we would be faced with mere coexistence of two or more institutions. In studies on the emergence and development of institutions, the institution constitutes the dependent variable to be explained. In studies on institutional effectiveness, it constitutes the independent variable that explains observed effects. In the case of institutional interaction, both the independent and the dependent variables are institutions.

Our concept of institutional interaction does not imply that influence runs back and forth between the institutions involved. On the contrary, causal influence implies that influence runs unidirectionally from the source to the target. Accordingly, a causal relationship between the institutions involved will be established, if we identify (1) the source institution and, more specifically, the relevant rules/decision(s) from which influence originates; (2) the target institution and, more specifically, the relevant parts of the institution itself or the issue area governed by it that are subject to the influence of the source institution; and (3) a unidirectional causal pathway connecting the two institutions.

This concept of institutional interaction requires that complex interaction situations are analytically disaggregated into a suitable number of individual cases so that clear causal relationships between pairs of institutions can be identified. In real-world situations, a clear-cut causal relationship between two institutions may be difficult to identify—be it because interaction involves more than two institutions, or because influence runs back and forth between two institutions, or because two institutions influence each other in various ways. Complex situations are difficult to analyze rigorously unless we disaggregate them into a suitable number of cases comprising a single source institution, a single target institution, and a single, clearly identifiable causal pathway. Emergent properties of more complex situations are then expected to result from particular forms of the coexistence of, and interplay between, several cases of interaction. They may be examined by carefully recombining the individual cases.

This concept expands the study of the effectiveness of environmental institutions to the investigation of institutional interaction. We share with the established research on the effectiveness of international institutions the interest in cases in which the "output" of an institution (i.e., its norms and decisions) results at least potentially in behavioral changes of relevant actors ("outcome")—changes that have actual or potential effects on the environment or another target of governance ("impact"; on these categories of effectiveness, see Underdal 2004). In the present volume, we do not examine cases of institutional interaction with little or no implications for the performance of the institutions involved, such as attempts to increase the bureaucratic efficiency of institutions, for example through streamlining or coordinating reporting requirements.

Causal Mechanisms of Institutional Interaction   Causal mechanisms help us understand how, and under which conditions, governance institutions are capable of exerting influence on each other. They elucidate the driving forces of institutional interaction beyond a mere description of coevolution processes or of the density of institutional settings in particular areas such as marine pollution or nature conservation. Causal mechanisms not only structure the multifaceted realm of institutional interaction and explain variations in cases, but also demonstrate which actors are indispensable for the emergence of interinstitutional influence. The empirical analysis of the present study relies on three of four causal mechanisms that were derived from theories of international institutions, cooperation theory, and negotiation theory and that we believe are exhaustive. The way the target institution is affected by a decision of the source is particularly important for the identification of the causal mechanisms, because no interaction occurs without a noticeable effect on the target institution or the issue area governed by it. Causal mechanisms of interaction identified on this basis differ in particular with respect to how source and target are linked.

In two of the four causal mechanisms, interaction affects the decision-making process of the target institution. First, a case of interaction may be based on a transfer of knowledge (Cognitive Interaction). This causal mechanism follows from the complexity of the world and the fact that actors have limited information and information processing capacities at their disposal. Cognitive Interaction may occur between any two institutions, since "learning" can take place without any overlap in issues or in the memberships of the institutions involved. Moreover, it can be triggered by states and nonstate actors, such as nongovernmental organizations and secretariats of international institutions. Second, a case of interaction may also be based on commitments agreed on within the source institution that affect the constellation of interests and the decision-making process within the target institution by influencing the payoffs of available options (Interaction through Commitment). In this case, conditions are much more restrictive. The issues dealt with by the institutions involved must overlap somewhat, because otherwise commitments under one institution could not affect options considered in the other institution. Memberships of the institutions must also overlap somewhat, because otherwise no participant in the policymaking process within the target institution would be subject to the commitments of the source institution. It follows that member states are the most important actors for Interaction through Commitment.

In the other two causal mechanisms, interaction affects the effectiveness of the target institution within its own domain. First, the source institution may induce behavioral changes of actors within its own issue area that are relevant for the effectiveness of the target institution within its issue area (Behavioral Interaction). Such interaction occurs outside the decision-making processes of the two interacting institutions and usually involves nonstate actors such as companies and citizens that are active within the issue areas concerned. It affects the performance of the target institution directly without requiring a decision from the latter. Finally, a case of interaction may be based on effects on an institution's ultimate target of governance (such as international trade or the ozone layer) induced by the source institution at the impact level (Impact-Level Interaction). In this case, the effect on the target is a direct spillover of the effects of the source institution on its target of governance that may occur due to the "functional interdependence" (Young 2002, 23) of the issue areas concerned.

Apart from their value as a basis for systematic and meaningful research and accumulation of knowledge, the causal mechanisms of institutional interaction help distinguish between different conditions of governance existing in the realm of institutional interaction. They differ with respect to the actors who might initiate them and the purposes for which they might be employed, as well as the forums in which options to enhance synergy or mitigate conflict might primarily be pursued. A careful analysis of the underlying causal mechanism of a case of interaction will therefore also facilitate systematic thinking about effective policy options so as to enhance international and European governance.

The Design of the Empirical Investigation

Our empirical analysis of institutional interaction starts from eleven environmental or environmentally relevant international regimes and environmental EU directives. The analysis explores the cases of interaction in which these "core institutions" are involved and investigates how each core institution interacts with other international institutions and pieces of EU legislation. Three criteria guided the selection of the core institutions. First, we aimed at covering varying environmental media or policy areas at both the international and the EU level (i.e., atmosphere, protection of biodiversity, marine pollution/water policy, management of living resources). Second, we focused on institutions with a demonstrated political relevance for international or EU environmental governance. Third, we selected institutions that could, according to preliminary expert judgment, reasonably be expected to interact with other international and EU institutions in significant ways. We believe that our selection of core institutions covers a broad range of international and EU environmental governance.

Chapters 3–8 each start from an environmental or environmentally relevant international institution. The climate change regime based on the UN Framework Convention on Climate Change and its Kyoto Protocol serves as the core institution of institutional interaction explored by Sebastian Oberthür in chapter 3. In chapter 4, G. Kristin Rosendal takes the Convention on Biological Diversity as the point of departure for her investigation. Jon Birger Skjærseth analyzes in chapter 5 the institutional interactions in which the international regime for the protection of the

Northeast Atlantic has been involved. Olav Schram Stokke and Clare Coffey examine in chapter 6 the global fisheries regime composed, in particular, of the UN Fish Stocks Agreement and a number of FAO regulations. Chapter 7, authored by John Lanchbery, is devoted to the examination of institutional interactions involving the Convention on International Trade in Endangered Species of Wild Fauna and Flora (CITES). In chapter 8, Alice Palmer, Beatrice Chaytor, and Jacob Werksman explore the interactions between the World Trade Organization and a number of multilateral environmental agreements.

Environmental EU directives serve as core institutions of chapters 9–12. In chapter 9, Andrew Farmer covers the institutional interactions of the EU Water Framework Directive and the Directive on Integrated Pollution Prevention and Control (IPPC Directive) related to industrial plants. Chapter 10, authored by Clare Coffey, explores the manifold interactions in which the EU Habitats Directive on nature conservation is involved. Ingmar von Homeyer discusses in chapter 11 interactions with the EU Deliberate Release Directive on genetically modified organisms. Finally, in chapter 12, Jørgen Wettestad investigates institutional interactions of the EU Air Quality Framework Directive.

Reflecting the first step of the empirical analysis in our project, each chapter attempts to provide a comprehensive overview of the most significant cases of institutional interaction in which each of the core institutions has been involved. Authors searched for empirical cases of interaction irrespective of their political salience and were thus able to ascertain cases that may not have caught the attention of policymakers. This approach promises to elucidate the network of institutional interactions in which the core institutions are involved. Networks of interaction relate both to horizontal interaction between international institutions or between EU legal instruments (depending on the core institution) and vertical interaction between international institutions and EU legal instruments.

Of particular relevance for the identification of cases of institutional interaction is the problem of remote causation and long causal chains (Underdal 2004). In our project, we prioritized obvious cases of interaction with short causal chains over less obvious ones with longer causal chains. Thus, we focused on cases in which influence runs directly from the source institution to the target institution, not on constellations in which it passes through numerous intermediate steps. Moreover, we concentrated on identifying cases driven by three of the four general causal mechanisms mentioned above, namely, Cognitive Interaction, Interaction through Commitment, and Behavioral Interaction. The empirical analysis does not consider

Impact-Level Interaction because it is frequently based on complicated natural science links and requires investigation of long causal chains with many intervening variables.

In the second step, each chapter examines a smaller number of cases of interaction in more detail. The in-depth analysis especially focuses on elucidating the causal influence exerted by the source institution on the target institution, and on investigating the causal mechanism driving the case of interaction in question and examining its momentum and effects. Cases for in-depth analysis were selected so as to ensure that horizontal interaction at the international level, horizontal interaction between EU legal instruments, and vertical interaction between international institutions and EU instruments were roughly equally represented.

In the third step, we engage in a comparative analysis of institutional interaction. Case-study authors were asked to codify the cases according to a number of criteria presented in chapter 13. The resulting database covering all identified 163 cases of interaction is reflected in the appendix to this volume. It provides a comparatively broad picture of the diversity and variety of institutional interaction in international and EU environmental governance. The database enabled us to aggregate data on individual cases and to identify dominant patterns of institutional interaction. Inductively derived patterns provided the basis for elaborating Weberian ideal types of institutional interaction that follow distinct rationales. These ideal types further differentiate our general causal mechanisms and may provide a kit of standard forms of interaction (see also Gehring and Oberthür 2004). Chapter 13 provides a comparative evaluation of our codification data and elaborates ideal types of institutional interaction.

Empirical Findings and Conceptual Development

Our analysis of institutional interaction leads to a wealth of general and case-specific findings. In this section, we highlight findings relating to two complexes, namely, the empirical analysis of our sample of more than 150 cases of institutional interaction, and the development of Weberian ideal types of institutional interaction designed to fine-tune the general causal mechanisms. The general results are elaborated in more detail in chapter 13.

Empirical Findings   The comparative examination of a larger set of cases of interaction enables us to derive aggregate insights about the patterns of institutional interaction and thus supports the generation of policy-relevant knowledge. Given the methodology of case selection, we are confident that our results at least roughly reflect the overall situation in international and EU environmental governance, although figures may be expected to differ to some extent for other samples. The empirical conclusions constitute inductively generated hypotheses, which might be tested against other samples of cases. However, we caution that the sample is not statistically representative and therefore does not allow for the generalization of insights to other populations of cases. In particular, we do not claim that the empirical results hold for interaction phenomena beyond international and EU environmental governance.

All three general causal mechanisms on which the empirical inquiry was based were represented in our sample, but distribution varies considerably. Cognitive Interaction was comparatively rare, whereas Behavioral Interaction accounted for about half and Interaction through Commitment for about 40 percent of all cases. Cases of Cognitive Interaction may be underrepresented in our sample because "learning" may be a tacit process, which is not easy to detect. However, we see that institutional interaction is a multifaceted phenomenon that cannot be reduced to a single causal mechanism.

A clear majority of the cases of interaction identified by us created synergy, while only about one-quarter resulted in disruption. Whereas disruption was somewhat more frequent at the international level, synergy dominates at all levels, namely, in horizontal interaction between international institutions, in horizontal interaction between EU legal instruments, and in vertical interaction between international and EU instruments. This finding contrasts with conventional wisdom. Much of the existing literature has focused on the problems arising from institutional interaction. According to our sample, this focus does not provide a full picture of the interaction phenomenon. It may be a consequence of the fact that conflict attracts significantly higher political and scientific attention than harmonious or synergistic situations, because people react more strongly to the risk of losses (conflict) than to the promise of additional benefits. This finding further suggests that institutional interaction may not primarily be a bad thing that ought to be diminished as far as possible. The prevailing institutional fragmentation of international and EU environmental governance as well as substantive overlap do not predominantly result in conflict or undesirable "duplication of work." They may provide a valuable asset for skillful policymaking to enhance environmental governance. Policies to minimize allegedly undesirably interaction could risk sacrificing this asset.

Disruption prevails in interaction across the boundaries of policy fields, while synergy dominates within the field of environmental policy. Interaction staying within environmental affairs has supported the effectiveness of governance in more than 80 percent of the relevant cases in our sample, whereas conflicts prevailed in interaction with institutions from other policy fields. Most cases of disruption in our sample related to interaction across policy fields, and a majority of cases of interaction across policy fields resulted in disruption. Once again, this pattern holds true for horizontal interaction between international institutions and between EU instruments as well as for vertical interaction. This finding might not come as a surprise because institutions belonging to different policy fields will frequently have considerably diverging objectives and may be supported by different constituencies.

Whereas more than a third of the unintentionally triggered cases of interaction in our sample resulted in disruption, intentionally triggered cases of disruption appear to be particularly rare. It may not be surprising that disruptive interaction is virtually absent from the environmental policy field; we may expect that it plays a more prominent role in more competitive policy fields such as security affairs. It is more noteworthy that disruptive interaction is occasionally employed intentionally even in environmental governance to bring about change within other institutions, in particular those belonging to other policy fields. It is also remarkable that roughly half of our synergistic cases were unintentionally triggered. Moreover, a majority of the disruptive cases have been responded to, whereas roughly 80 percent of the synergistic cases have not drawn a collective political response. This may be explained by the fact that conflicts leave some actors aggrieved who may then struggle for improvement, whereas synergy tends to be simply "consumed." Overall, significant opportunities exist for enhancing international and EU environmental governance by an intensified political management and use of institutional interaction.

Weberian Ideal Types of Institutional Interaction   Our sample of cases also provided a solid basis for the development of Weberian ideal types of institutional interaction, which subdivide and specify the general causal mechanisms and elaborate their distinctive features. Thus, we move beyond the three basic causal mechanisms and develop a more sophisticated framework for the analysis of individual cases of interaction so as to be able to better explain and understand the strikingly different properties of cases of interaction driven by the same causal mechanism. Ideal types are abstract and deductively generated models, which reflect mutually exclusive rationales inherent in different social-interaction phenomena, to which real-world cases can be compared. We identified two ideal types of Cognitive Interaction and three types of Interaction through Commitment, while we were unable to identify ideal types of Behavioral Interaction.

Intentionality is the crucial distinction between the two types of Cognitive Interaction. While "learning" cannot be imposed, it may or may not be intentionally triggered by the source institution. If Cognitive Interaction is not intended, members of the target institution use an institutional arrangement or policy idea of the source institution as a policy model. For example, the compliance system under the Montreal Protocol for the protection of the ozone layer influenced the negotiations on the compliance system under the Kyoto Protocol on climate change because it provided a model of how to supervise implementation and deal with cases of possible noncompliance. If Cognitive Interaction is intentionally triggered, the source institution largely frames the learning process by requesting assistance from the target, ultimately in order to trigger a feedback case of Behavioral Interaction furthering its own effectiveness. For example, the Convention on International Trade in Endangered Species of Wild Fauna and Flora (CITES) requested assistance from specialized international institutions such as the World Customs Organization (WCO) and Interpol because it expected this assistance to facilitate the effective implementation of CITES obligations (chapter 7).

The three ideal types of Interaction through Commitment are characterized by a key difference in the objectives or memberships or means of governance of the institutions involved. Cases of Interaction through Commitment that are driven by differences in objectives create a demand for jurisdictional delimitation. Due to their underlying rationale, they will usually cause disruption and restrain the effectiveness of both institutions involved. Consider that international trade is regulated within the WTO with the purpose of liberalizing trade and thus removing obstacles to international trade. At the same time, the Cartagena Biosafety Protocol to the Convention on Biological Diversity (CBD) governs international trade in genetically modified organisms (GMOs) predominantly with the purpose of protecting the environment of the importing countries. In this situation of contentious interdependence, the governance challenge consists in arriving at a delimitation of jurisdictions. However, it might occasionally prove useful as a political strategy to deliberately raise (potential) jurisdictional conflict.

Interaction through Commitment may also take place between two institutions that differ exclusively with respect to their membership, while pursuing identical objectives and employing the same means. Under these circumstances, interested actors may promote governance by establishing a smaller "pilot" institution in order to affect decision making in a larger institution addressing a similar range of issues. For example, the establishment of the Natura 2000 system of nature conservation sites under the EU Habitats Directive led to the creation of the similar Emerald network under the pan-European Bern Convention. In such cases, interaction relies on the fact that agreement reached within the smaller institution significantly changes the situation and interest constellation facing actors in the larger institution. If rules are applied regionally, the leading coalition within the broader institution will be strengthened and acceptance costs will decrease so that opposition against equivalent measures may wane—a mechanism that may be purposefully exploited by political actors.

Skillful reinforcement of international or European governance through institutional interaction will also be promising, if interested actors manage to activate additional means to realize their desired objectives. Frequently, international and EU institutions do not control the full spectrum of possible governance instruments but differ in the means available to them. Interaction will regularly raise the effectiveness of both institutions involved if the diffusion of an obligation from one institution to another one with identical objectives and memberships activates an additional means of implementation. For example, the ministerial North Sea Conferences were established in the 1980s in order to reinforce the existing OSPAR Convention for the protection of the Northeast Atlantic. They raised the political salience of the issues at stake, but resulted in "soft-law" agreements. Transformation into binding international law under the OSPAR Convention and into EU supranational law subsequently increased the originally low degree of obligation and mobilized additional enforcement mechanisms that enhanced the effectiveness of all institutions involved (chapter 5).

Obviously, this volume does not resolve all issues of institutional interaction; it may even raise more questions than it was able to answer. An important area for future research is the systematic analysis of more complex settings of institutional interaction. Eventually, we will not be content with knowing how and why a particular case of institutional interaction matters. The conceptual framework of this volume can be employed and further developed to systematically explore more complex settings and their emergent properties by recombining individual cases. We identify two particular ways individual cases might be recombined so as to account for more complex interaction situations. Cases of interaction may form sequential chains so that an individual case gives rise to a subsequent case that feeds back on the original source institution or influences a third institution. Cases of interaction may also cluster around certain issues and institutions, so that a number of institutions jointly address a particular problem and contribute to the effectiveness of governance of a certain area. Whereas our study has hardly been able to delve into pertinent aspects of these more complex interactional situations, it has made a start that demonstrates the potential of the effort. On this basis, we may over time be able to gain a clearer picture of the interlocking structure of international governance institutions and EU legal instruments.

References

Andersen, Regine. 2002. The Time Dimension in International Regime Interplay. *Global Environmental Politics* 2 (3): 98–117.

Beisheim, Marianne, Sabine Dreher, Gregor Walter, Bernhard Zangl, and Michael Zürn. 1999. *Im Zeitalter der Globalisierung? Thesen und Daten zur gesellschaftlichen und politischen Denationalisierung.* Baden-Baden: Nomos.

Biermann, Frank, and Steffen Bauer, eds. 2005. *A World Environment Organization: Solution or Threat for Effective International Environmental Governance?* Aldershot: Ashgate.

Breitmeier, Helmut. 2000. "Complex Effectiveness": Regime Externalities and Interaction (Working Group III). In Jørgen Wettestad, ed., *Proceedings of the 1999 Oslo Workshop of the Concerted Action Network on the Effectiveness of International Environmental Regimes,* 45–48. Oslo: Fridtjof Nansen Institute.

Brown Weiss, Edith. 1993. International Environmental Issues and the Emergence of a New World Order. *Georgetown Law Journal* 81 (3): 675–710.

Chambers, Bradnee W., ed. 1998. *Global Climate Governance: Inter-Linkages between the Kyoto Protocol and Other Multilateral Regimes.* Tokyo: United Nations University.

Chambers, Bradnee W., ed. 2001. *Inter-Linkages: The Kyoto Protocol and the International Trade and Investment Regimes.* Tokyo: United Nations University Press.

European Commission. 2001. *European Governance: A White Paper.* Doc. COM(2001) 428 final, 25.7.2001. Brussels: European Commission.

European Commission. 2002. *Communication from the Commission on Impact Assessment.* Doc. COM(2002)276 final, 5.6.2002. Brussels: European Commission.

Gehring, Thomas. 1994. *Dynamic International Regimes: Institutions for International Environmental Governance.* Frankfurt/Main: Peter Lang.

Gehring, Thomas. 2004. Methodological Issues in the Study of Broader Consequences. In Arild Underdal and Oran R. Young, eds., *Regime Consequences: Methodological Challenges and Research Strategies,* 219–246. Dordrecht: Kluwer.

Gehring, Thomas, and Sebastian Oberthür. 2004. Exploring Regime Interaction: A Framework for Analysis. In Arild Underdal and Oran R. Young, eds., *Regime Consequences: Methodological Challenges and Research Strategies,* 247–269. Dordrecht: Kluwer.

German Advisory Council on Global Change. 2001. *World in Transition: New Structures for Global Environmental Policy*. London: Earthscan.

Haas, Peter M., Robert O. Keohane, and Marc A. Levy, eds. 1993. *Institutions for the Earth: Sources of Effective International Environmental Protection*. Cambridge, MA: MIT Press.

Haigh, Nigel, ed. 2003. *Manual of Environmental Policy: The EU and Britain*. Leeds: Maney Publishing and Institute for European Environmental Policy.

Héritier, Adrienne. 1996. The Accommodation of Diversity in the European Policy-Making Process and Its Outcomes: Regulatory Policy as a Patchwork. *Journal of European Public Policy* 3 (2): 149–167.

Herr, Richard A., and Edmund Chia. 1995. The Concept of Regime Overlap: Toward Identification and Assessment. In B. Davis, ed., *Overlapping Maritime Regimes: An Initial Reconnaissance*, 11–26. Hobart: Antarctic CRC and Institute of Antarctic and Southern Ocean Studies.

Keohane, Robert O. 1984. *After Hegemony: Cooperation and Discord in the World Political Economy*. Princeton, NJ: Princeton University Press.

Keohane, Robert O. 1989. *International Institutions and State Power: Essays in International Relations Theory*. Boulder, CO: Westview.

King, Leslie A. 1997. Institutional Interplay: Research Questions. Paper Commissioned by Institutional Dimensions of Global Environmental Change and International Human Dimensions Programme on Global Environmental Change. Burlington VT: Environmental Studies Programme, School of Natural Resources, University of Vermont.

Krämer, Ludwig. 1999. Bilanz und Perspektiven der europäischen Umweltpolitik unter besonderer Berücksichtigung der Erweiterung, Presentation at the Forum Constitutionis Europae of the Humboldt University Berlin on July 15, 1999 (FCE 6/1999). Available at http://www.rewi.hu-berlin.de/WHI/deutsch/fce/fce699/index.htm.

Lenschow, Andrea, ed. 2002. *Environmental Policy Integration: Greening Sectoral Policies in Europe*. London: Earthscan.

Meinke, Britta. 2002. *Multi-Regime-Regulierung: Wechselwirkungen zwischen globalen und regionalen Umweltregimen*. Darmstadt: Deutscher Universitäts-Verlag.

Miles, Edward L., Arild Underdal, Steinar Andresen, Jørgen Wettestad, Jon Birger Skjærseth, and Elaine M. Carlin. 2002. *Environmental Regime Effectiveness: Confronting Theory with Evidence*. Cambridge, MA: MIT Press.

Oberthür, Sebastian. 2001. Linkages between the Montreal and Kyoto Protocols: Enhancing Synergies between Protecting the Ozone Layer and the Global Climate. *International Environmental Agreements: Politics, Law and Economics* 1 (3): 357–377.

Oberthür, Sebastian. 2002. Clustering of Multilateral Environmental Agreements: Potentials and Limitations. *International Environmental Agreements: Politics, Law and Economics* 2 (4): 317–340.

Pontecorvo, Concetta Maria. 1999. Interdependence between Global Environmental Regimes: The Kyoto Protocol on Climate Change and Forest Protection. *Zeitschrift für ausländisches öffentliches Recht und Völkerrecht* 59 (3): 709–749.

Raustiala, Kal, and David G. Victor. 2004. The Regime Complex for Plant Genetic Resources. *International Organization* 58 (2): 277–309.

Rittberger, Volker, ed. 1993. *Regime Theory and International Relations.* Oxford: Clarendon Press.

Rosendal, G. Kristin. 2000. *The Convention on Biological Diversity and Developing Countries.* Dordrecht: Kluwer Academic.

Rosendal, G. Kristin. 2001. Impacts of Overlapping International Regimes: The Case of Biodiversity. *Global Governance* 7 (1): 95–117.

Stokke, Olav Schram. 2001a. The Interplay of International Regimes: Putting Effectiveness Theory to Work. FNI Report 14/2001. Lysaker, Norway: Fridtjof Nansen Institute.

Stokke, Olav Schram, ed. 2001b. *Governing High Seas Fisheries: The Interplay of Global and Regional Regimes.* Oxford: Oxford University Press.

Underdal, Arild. 2004. Methodological Challenges in the Study of Regime Effectiveness. In Arild Underdal and Oran R. Young, eds., *Regime Consequences: Methodological Challenges and Research Strategies*, 27–48. Dordrecht: Kluwer.

Underdal, Arild, and Oran R. Young, eds. 2004. *Regime Consequences: Methodological Challenges and Research Strategies.* Dordrecht: Kluwer.

Vogler, John. 1999. The European Union as an Actor in International Environmental Politics. *Environmental Politics* 8 (3): 24–48.

Wilkinson, David. 1998. Steps towards Integrating the Environment into Other EU Policy Sectors. In Timothy O'Riordan and Heather Voisey, eds., *The Transition to Sustainability: The Politics of Agenda 21 in Europe*, 113–129. London: Earthscan.

Young, Oran R. 1996. Institutional Linkages in International Society: Polar Perspectives. *Global Governance* 2 (1): 1–24.

Young, Oran R., ed. 1999. *The Effectiveness of International Environmental Regimes: Causal Connections and Behavioral Mechanisms.* Cambridge, MA: MIT Press.

Young, Oran R. 2002. *The Institutional Dimensions of Environmental Change: Fit, Interplay, and Scale.* Cambridge, MA: MIT Press.

Young, Oran R., Leslie A. King, Arun Aggarval, Arild Underdal, Peter H. Sand, and Merrilyn Wasson. 1999. *Institutional Dimensions of Global Environmental Change (IDGEC): Science Plan.* Bonn: International Human Dimensions Programme on Global Environmental Change.

2

Conceptual Foundations of Institutional Interaction

Sebastian Oberthür and Thomas Gehring

This chapter introduces the shared conceptual framework of the contributions to this volume in five steps. First, a brief review of existing approaches to institutional interaction demonstrates that the conceptual development of the systematic study of institutional interaction is still at an early stage. Existing approaches cannot readily guide the empirical study of interaction between international and EU environmental institutions, but provide a starting point for developing a suitable conceptual foundation to that end.

Second, we identify international and EU institutions as the units of interaction. In contrast to research on European integration, scholars of international relations have developed a particular concept of issue-area specific governing institutions that has been fruitfully applied to the study of international regimes. We identify single legal instruments such as directives and regulations as the functional equivalents to these institutions at the EU level that are most appropriate for the empirical analysis of institutional interaction.

Third, we develop a notion of institutional interaction that is based on the identification of a causal relationship between two interacting institutions. A case of interaction thus comprises a source institution from which influence originates, a target institution that is affected, and a causal pathway through which influence runs from the source to the target. Complex interaction situations are analytically disaggregated into individual cases with a single source institution, a single target institution, and an identifiable causal pathway.

Fourth, we derive deductively from various theories of institutions, as well as from negotiation theory and from cooperation theory, four general causal mechanisms that may drive institutional interaction. A source institution may exert influence directly on the rule-making process of the target institution in two different ways. It may either trigger a learning process that leads to purely voluntary adaptation by the target institution (Cognitive Interaction). Or it may commit its members to an obligation that changes their preferences on matters negotiated within the target institution (Interaction through Commitment). A source institution may also affect the effectiveness of the target institution within its issue area in two different ways. It may either exert influence on the behavior of states and nonstate actors that is relevant for the implementation of the target institution (Behavioral Interaction). Or it may directly affect the ultimate target of protection of the target institution (Impact-Level Interaction). Three of these mechanisms serve as theoretical points of reference for the empirical case studies contained in this volume.

Fifth, we spell out the tasks faced in the ensuing empirical investigation.

Existing Approaches to the Study of Institutional Interaction

Much of the empirically founded research on institutional interaction has so far been motivated by concern about the detrimental impact of this interaction on the effectiveness of the institutions involved, in particular in the field of environmental protection. This literature constitutes an offspring of the research on the effectiveness of international institutions that flourished in the 1990s (Haas, Keohane, and Levy 1993; Victor, Raustiala, and Skolnikoff 1998; Young 1999; Miles et al. 2002). Like effectiveness research, it is interested in identifying successes and failures of deliberate policymaking in order to draw lessons for global governance. Most prominent is the empirical analysis of single problematic cases of institutional interaction (e.g., Chambers 1998; Stokke 1999; Rosendal 2000, 2001; Oberthür 2001; Andersen 2002). Raustiala and Victor (2004) expanded the research focus and explored the "regime complex" in the area of plant genetic resources composed of five "elementary regimes." They put forward conjectures about how actors can use different institutions in the same policy field to pursue their interests, as well as about the impact of institutional interaction on the evolution of regulatory approaches and legalization in international relations.

In a series of contributions, Oran Young has put forward a number of analytic concepts and categories that constitute the single most important attempt to provide a basis for systematic research on institutional interaction. In an influential article, he put forward a taxonomy of four different types of interaction (Young 1996). *Embeddedness* refers to the relationship of a governance institution to overarching principles and practices such as sovereignty. *Nestedness* denotes the relationship of a smaller institution to a functionally or geographically broader institution such as the nesting of the Multi-Fiber Agreement within the General Agreement on Tariffs and Trade (GATT; now incorporated into the World Trade Organization, WTO) (Aggarval 1983). *Clustering* refers to the deliberate combination of different institutions such as the linkage of a wide variety of issues in the law of the sea convention. Finally, *overlap* constitutes "a separate category of linkages in which individual regimes that were formed for different purposes and largely without reference to one another intersect on a de facto basis, producing substantial impacts on each other in the process" (Young 1996, 6). Later, Young proposed to distinguish between horizontal interaction between institutions at the same level of social organization and vertical interaction between hierarchically ordered units at different levels of social organization from the local to the international (Young et al. 1999; Young 2002, 113–132). This approach to the study of institutional interaction provides an idea of the wide variety of possible subjects of inquiry and is useful in identifying areas of particular interest. However, its overall research focus is so broad that the categories and distinctions are too unspecific to guide a multicase empirical investigation of interaction involving international and EU institutions.

Young and a program group of the Institutional Dimensions of Global Environmental Change (IDGEC) project in the framework of the International Human Dimensions Program (IHDP) also put forward a distinction between two different drivers of institutional interaction (Young 2002, 23; Young et al. 1999, 50). Functional linkages will exist "when substantive problems that two or more institutions address are linked in biogeophysical or socioeconomic terms" (Young 2002, 23, also 83–109). Based on this particular form of interdependence, they reflect "facts of life" because "the operation of one institution directly influences the effectiveness of another through some substantive connection of the activities involved" (Young et al. 1999, 50). For example, chlorofluorocarbons (CFCs) functionally link the international regime for the protection of the ozone layer and the regime on global climate change because they have ozone-depleting properties and are at the same time potent greenhouse gases. Action taken within the ozone regime is immediately relevant for the climate change regime. In contrast, political linkages "arise when actors decide to consider two or more arrangements as parts of a larger institutional complex" (Young et al. 1999, 50). In this case, actors deliberately design the relationship between different institutions.

This classification is compelling at first glance, but at closer inspection it creates considerable analytic difficulty. In particular, the two categories do not denote mutually exclusive types. For example, Young et al. (1999, 53) take the protocols on

SO_2, NO_X, and VOCs of the international regime on transboundary air pollution as an example for a functional linkage. However, these protocols are undoubtedly parts of a larger institutional complex, since they all belong to one convention managed under the UN Economic Commission for Europe (Levy 1993). They may be linked "functionally" and "politically" at the same time, with no clear cause-effect relationship apparent between both types of linkage.

Based on a series of studies on international resource management (Stokke 1999, 2000, 2001a), Stocke (2001b) distinguishes between four different forms of institutional interaction. *Ideational interplay* (previously referred to as *diffusive interplay*) relates to "processes of learning" (Stokke 2001a, 10) and implies that the substantive or operational rules of one institution serve as models for those negotiating another regime. This may, for example, help us understand the rapid spread of general normative principles such as sustainability, precaution, and ecosystem management. *Normative interplay* refers to situations where the substantive or operational norms of one institution either contradict or validate those of another institution (e.g., in the case of the relationship of the WTO and multilateral environmental agreements). *Utilitarian interplay* relates to situations where decisions taken within one institution alter the costs and benefits of options available in another. *Interplay management*, finally, relates to the political management of interinstitutional influence, including the deliberate coordination of activities under separate institutions in order to avoid normative conflict or wasteful duplication of programmatic efforts. Stokke's taxonomy constitutes an attempt to derive causal mechanisms of institutional interaction from theoretical approaches such as organizational learning (diffusion), legitimacy (normative interaction), and utilitarian cost-benefit analysis rather than inductively from empirical cases. It has provided valuable input for the conceptual framework presented in this chapter.

To summarize, conceptual work on interaction between international and EU institutions is still at an early stage. While research on European integration and policymaking does not have concepts at its disposal to systematically analyze interaction phenomena, the limited conceptual work by international relations scholars has not yet produced an encompassing framework (for an overview see Stokke 2001b, 1–8). Existing approaches mainly constitute attempts to categorize and systematize phenomena of institutional interaction, which differ significantly in form and substance. Rather than providing a ready conceptual foundation for a comparative empirical investigation of interaction phenomena, they provide a starting point and basis for our efforts to develop such a foundation in the following pages.

International and EU Institutions as the Interacting Units

In the present volume, we focus exclusively on deliberately established ("negotiated") systems of norms, because they may be used to bring about collectively desired change within the international system. This delineation of the research area is in line with much of the literature on institutional institutions and their effectiveness (e.g., Keohane 1993; Victor, Raustiala, and Skolnikoff 1998; Miles et al. 2002). From a governance perspective, deliberately established institutions receive primary attention in the research, because they are employed instrumentally to bring about change. Likewise, deliberately established governance arrangements attract much interest in the literature on policymaking within the European Union (see generally, Scharpf 1999; Jachtenfuchs 2001). We recognize that systems of norms can also emerge spontaneously as the result of uncoordinated behavior of actors in the international system (Young 1982; Axelrod 1984). However, spontaneous institutions such as international customary law (Hurrel 1993) and sovereignty are not part of our research focus because they are merely suited to stabilize existing behavior and cannot be created and developed purposefully as governance instruments. We would also like to point out upfront that our use of the term *institution* diverges from usage in the literature on European integration, where it predominantly denotes the supranational bodies of the EU such as the European Commission, the European Parliament, and the European Court of Justice. This is further discussed below.

Relevant international institutions have two components. First, they encompass substantive rules and obligations that indicate socially desirable behavior. These norms are the principal instruments of governance that may affect the behavior of addressees and have an impact within the issue area governed. Second, "negotiated" institutions are distinguished from other types of institutions, such as spontaneous institutions, by the particular decision-making processes from which their norms and behavioral guidelines emerge. Generally, they include their own decision-making apparatuses (see Levy, Young, and Zürn 1995). The importance of negotiations and collective decision making has been increasingly acknowledged (Young 1994; Morrow 1994; Fearon 1998; Victor, Raustiala, and Skolnikoff 1998). The procedural arrangements for the making of collective decisions enable actors to adapt and develop international regimes dynamically and use them as flexible instruments of international governance (Gehring 1994). Where the same problem area is governed by several systems of norms, institutions are best identified according to their distinct decision-making processes.

Both formal international organizations and more loosely institutionalized regimes qualify as relevant international institutions (Simmons and Martin 2002). Issue-area specific international regimes that are usually based on one or several international treaties have been a major subject of inquiry for more than two decades (Keohane 1984; Rittberger 1993; Miles et al. 2002). In contrast, formal international organizations, such as the Food and Agriculture Organization of the UN (FAO), the WTO, and the International Maritime Organization (IMO), have attracted far less scientific attention (but see Abbott and Snidal 1998; Barnett and Finnemore 1999). They are usually defined by reference to their secretariats and their ability to enter into legal contracts (e.g., Young 1994, 163–183; Keohane 1989, 3–4). Frequently, international organizations are issue-area specific arrangements that closely resemble international regimes (e.g., the WTO). At times, they fulfill functions within regimes and thus become part of them. In other cases, international regimes are embedded in international organizations. Regularly, international organizations develop procedures for elaborating collectively binding decisions, and many have elaborate legislative programs (Keohane 1989, 5; Abbott and Snidal 1998, 15–16).

Because our research subject includes institutional interaction at the EU level, we must identify EU equivalents of international regimes and organizations. The organizational actors that are usually denoted as "European institutions" such as the European Commission, the European Court of Justice, and the European Parliament do not qualify. Although they play an important role in EU policymaking, they do not represent systems of norms, rules, and related decision-making processes that are deliberately established to govern a given area of European relations. In particular they lack substantive rules designed to guide actors' behavior. Given that the EU at large is occasionally conceptualized as a highly developed international institution (Keohane and Hoffmann 1991; Moravcsik 1998; Gehring 2002), it might be considered a suitable equivalent of relevant international institutions. Alternatively, one could take the different EU policies, such as environmental, agricultural, or single-market policy as EU institutions. However, both the Union at large and the policies themselves consist of numerous structured and institutionalized communication processes, which characterize international regimes and organizations. They display considerable internal differentiation of instruments, policy approaches, and processes. Neither the EU at large nor its policy areas thus seem to constitute functional equivalents of international regimes and organizations.

EU legal instruments such as directives and regulations (in some cases also decisions) can be considered functional equivalents of specific international institutions.

Despite the specific conditions of EU policymaking, such EU legal instruments share the fundamental characteristics of specific international regimes and organizations. Their substantive norms and obligations are also designed and adopted to guide and influence the behavior of relevant addressees. Like international obligations, they are decided on with strong intergovernmental participation, and they are usually addressed to the respective member states. Moreover, EU legal instruments are usually negotiated separately from each other rather than in comprehensive packages. We even find decision-making processes that are specific to particular EU instruments in the form of so-called comitology committees attended by representatives of the member states and the European Commission (Joerges and Vos 1999; Pollack 1997). These committees monitor the implementation of the instruments and collaborate with the Commission on the development and adoption of secondary legislation.

However, we must take into account that international institutions and EU legal instruments differ in important respects. While the decision-making processes of separately established international institutions are formally independent from each other, the decision-making processes of EU directives and regulations are embedded in an overarching and integrated institutional framework. EU legal instruments are the result of the regular EU lawmaking processes involving the European Commission, the Council of Ministers, and the European Parliament as supranational bodies. The Commission enjoys the right to initiate legislation and deals with issues of implementation, secondary decision making, and enforcement, and it generally occupies a much stronger role than the secretariats of international institutions. The apparatus of regular EU decision making fulfills functions similar to the "machinery" of international regimes and organizations, but it does so in specific ways. Moreover, EU legislation has a supranational character. It does not require national ratification to take effect and the EU has a particularly strong enforcement system at its disposal, which includes the Commission as a "prosecutor" and the European Court of Justice, whose decisions are binding and can be enforced through a system of penalty payments. Due to the comprehensive institutional framework, it will frequently be much easier to adopt an EU directive than to establish an international regime. Moreover, EU policymaking is embedded in, and relies on, broader programs and policy processes more often than policymaking at the international level (on EU policymaking see, for example, Hix 2005; Nugent 2003).

To conclude, we identify as relevant institutions for the purpose of this volume international regimes and organizations as well as EU legal instruments, in particular directives and regulations, always including the associated decision-making processes. Without denying important differences, we argue that the particularities of the EU decision-making process do not render EU directives and regulations fundamentally different from international governance institutions. This delineation of our area of research excludes two sorts of phenomena from our inquiry in institutional interaction. We do not focus on interaction between a specific international or EU institution and broad or unspecific entities such as "the UN system." The interplay between different instruments of a single regime or organization is also beyond our research focus. For example, interaction between the UN Framework Convention on Climate Change and its Kyoto Protocol is considered part of the development *within* an international regime rather than interaction *between* institutions, even though the analytic framework developed here may easily be employed to investigate such intraregime influence (Gehring 2004).

The Concept of Institutional Interaction

In this section, we develop a concept of institutional interaction (see also Gehring and Oberthür 2004). The analysis of institutional interaction requires establishing a clear-cut cause-effect relationship between the institutions involved and disaggregating complex situations into a suitable number of cases of interaction.

Establishing a Cause-Effect Relationship between Institutions

Institutional interaction relies on a cause-effect relationship between two institutions. Interaction will occur if one institution affects the development or performance of another institution (Breitmeier 2000). Thus defined, institutional interaction is clearly distinguished from developments that occur in the presence of other institutions but without their causal influence.

Conceptualizing institutional interaction as a matter of causal influence between institutions relates our concept to existing research on the establishment and effectiveness of international institutions. Exploration of causal influence constitutes the core of this branch of research that has been fruitful for many years. In traditional regime analysis, the emergence and design of international regimes have been attributed to different constellations of interests (Oye 1985; Martin 1993). Research on the effectiveness of institutions is ultimately interested in whether, how, and to what extent institutions affect the state of the environment or other targets of governance (Underdal 1992).

To establish a case of institutional interaction, we must explore the influence exerted by one international or EU institution on another international or EU institution. For the exploration of cause-effect relationships, it is generally indispensable to identify factors from which influence originates, and factors affected by such influence. In the case of institutional interaction, both the independent variable and the dependent variable are institutions. Accordingly, establishing a case of institutional interaction requires careful identification of (1) the source institution and, more specifically, the relevant rules/decision(s) from which influence originates; (2) the target institution and, more specifically, the relevant parts of the institution itself or the issue area governed by it that are subject to the influence of the source institution; (3) a unidirectional causal pathway connecting the two institutions. Causation requires that influence runs unidirectionally from the source to the target. Hence, our understanding of the term *inter*action does not imply that influence runs back and forth between the institutions involved.

This approach implies that there cannot be a case of interaction without an observable effect in the target institution (or the issue area governed by it). Without any effect on the target side, there would be no detectable influence, and thus no case of interaction. However, observable changes on the target side of the interaction may be the result of action of the source institution that is only anticipated. An institution may adapt its own rules in reaction to the development (rather than the adoption) of new rules by another institution. For example, the Convention on Biological Diversity reacted to the negotiations on the WTO Agreement on Trade-Related Aspects of Intellectual Property Rights (TRIPS Agreement) by adapting its provisions on equitable sharing of benefits from genetic resources (chapter 4).

The effect in the target institution that forms a necessary part of any case of interaction must be carefully distinguished from additional response action, which is not a necessary part of a case of interaction. Consider that the Kyoto Protocol provides incentives for carbon sequestration, which might induce states and nonstate actors to plant fast-growing trees and encroach on established habitats protected under the Convention on Biological Diversity (CBD) (Pontecorvo 1999). Ideally, the case will be complete, if there are observable—in this case detrimental—effects on habitats protected by the CBD. In response, the actors operating within either institution might adopt new rules to mitigate this undesired effect. This response action would be additional to the case of interaction, because interinstitutional influence would be observable even in its absence. This even holds true for cases in which response action occurs in response to interinstitutional effects that are only anticipated. Thus, actors may anticipate adverse effects of the climate change regime on biodiversity and may respond to them before they materialize because the climate change regime establishes incentives that can be expected to lead to relevant behavioral changes. Response action would then indicate effects that are not yet empirically observable, but sufficiently well established to provide the foundation for additional decisions.

Identifying a causal relationship between two international or EU institutions is, at least implicitly, based on counterfactual arguments. Generally, institutional interaction requires that observed changes in the target institution are caused by the source institution. Establishing causal influence in the social sciences must not be confused with accounting for all possible factors contributing to the occurrence of an observable event. In the case of institutional interaction, it (merely) requires proving that the observed changes within the target institution or the issue area governed by it could not be expected to have occurred in the absence of the source institution or its relevant parts (King, Keohane, and Verba 1994, 75–85). The construction of counterfactual scenarios addresses the hypothetical question of how the target institution and the issue area governed by it would have developed in the absence of the source institution. This is an important and well-known method for establishing causality in the social sciences (Tetlock and Belkin 1996; Bierstecker 1993).

However, the usefulness and reliability of counterfactual scenarios decrease sharply with the length of the causal chains in question because of the increasing number of intervening factors that have to be taken into consideration. Consider that the creation of the North Atlantic Treaty Organization (NATO) arguably contributed to the bipolar stability of the world order between 1950 and 1990, facilitating prosperous economic development in particular in the OECD part of the world. As a side effect, this economic development aggravated a number of environmental problems, including global climate change, which has since been responded to by the creation of an international regime. Does it follow that NATO has contributed to the emergence of the international climate change regime? As a first consequence of this so-called problem of "Cleopatra's nose," we might prioritize obvious cases of interaction with short causal chains over less obvious ones with longer causal chains. Second, counterfactual analysis may be complemented by the exclusion of alternative explanations (Bernauer 1995), that is, by exploring the question of whether factors other than the source regime might convincingly explain the observed result in the target institution. These methods are well established and widely employed in the literature on the simple effectiveness of international regimes (Underdal 2004).

Dealing with Complexity: Identifying "Cases" of Interaction

Serious causal analysis of institutional interaction requires disaggregation of a complex situation into an appropriate number of *cases of interaction*. Frequently, real-world situations comprise more than two institutions and develop over a longer period of time; influence may run back and forth between the institutions involved (Young 2002, 111–138; Raustiala and Victor 2004). Such complex interaction situations must be disaggregated into a suitable number of "cases" to allow for identifying clear causal relationships of the institutions involved encompassing a single source institution, a single target institution, and a unidirectional causal pathway connecting the two. In particular, three types of complex interaction phenomena require disaggregation.

Disaggregation will be necessary, if two institutions interact in more than one way at the same time. This may in particular be expected to be the case for complex international and EU institutions such as the WTO, the regime for the protection of the Baltic Sea, or the EU Directive on Integrated Pollution Prevention and Control (IPPC Directive), all of which govern broad issue areas. However, even an allegedly single-purpose institution such as the regime for the protection of the ozone layer comprises a number of different components and includes auxiliary arrangements such as a funding mechanism (DeSombre and Kauffman 1996) and a system for implementation review (Victor 1998). As a consequence, two institutions can be involved in numerous cases of interaction at the same time. For example, the Montreal Protocol for the protection of the ozone layer indirectly promotes the use of certain greenhouse gases (hydrofluorocarbons, HFCs), thus undermining the objective of the Kyoto Protocol to the UN Framework Convention on Climate Change. At the same time, it mandates the phaseout of CFCs that are also potent greenhouse gases, thus reinforcing efforts under the international climate change regime. Moreover, the Montreal Protocol's noncompliance procedure provided a precedent for the elaboration of a similar component within the climate change regime (Oberthür 2001). Although the situation involves only two institutions and influence runs exclusively from the ozone regime to the climate change regime, the three instances of interaction follow different causal pathways and have different properties. Each is best analyzed as a separate case of interaction.

Disaggregation will also be useful, if an interaction situation involves more than two institutions. For example, EU policy on industrial installations is made up of a number of different directives. While the IPPC Directive provides an integrative framework, other directives, such as the Air Quality Framework Directive and related daughter directives, contain relevant quality standards, and yet others—for example, the Large Combustion Plants Directive—set relevant emission standards (see chapter 9). To investigate causal influence, such complex situations must be disaggregated into pairs of interacting institutions with clear-cut cause-effect relationships that can be analyzed separately. Accordingly, we would have to investigate whether, and how, the development and performance of the IPPC Directive was affected by the Air Quality Framework Directive, and separately whether, and how, it was influenced by the Large Combustion Plants Directive, and so forth. In addition, we would have to investigate separately how the IPPC Directive influenced the development and performance of each of these instruments.

Disaggregation will also be appropriate, if two or more institutions coevolve over time. If coevolution involves feedback processes, neither of the institutions in question would exist in its current state without the existence of the other (Meinke 2002). Moreover, influence will be bidirectional. However, the observation that two or more coevolving institutions are mutually constitutive does not explain how these regimes exert influence on each other. Analytic disaggregation of the complex coevolution process into a suitable number of cases of interaction with a single direction of influence enables us to examine when, how, and why influence actually runs back and forth (rather than repeatedly in the same direction). The principal strategy is to analytically divide a coevolution process into different phases over time (Archer 1985; Carlsnaes 1992). In doing so, we assume for the purposes of our analysis that there was a point in time when neither of the institutions in question was influenced by the other. While it may not be possible to identify any such moment empirically, we will not expect that *a particular decision*, or set of decisions, may cause effects prior to its adoption (or at least prior to the anticipation of its adoption). For example, the EU Habitats Directive and the 1979 Bern Convention on the Conservation of European Wildlife and Natural Habitats codeveloped for almost twenty-five years and appear to have been mutually reinforcing (chapter 10). The adoption of the Bern Convention can then be seen as triggering the first case of interaction that caused EU member states to develop and adopt the Habitats Directive. Incidentally, the EU Habitats Directive installed a more thorough protection scheme than the Bern Convention. In the second phase, the EU scheme thus exerted influence on the Bern Convention that subsequently adopted the more stringent EU model. Influence in this second case is also clearly directed, but it runs from the EU Habitats Directive toward the Bern Convention. Hence, "coevolution" of the two institutions involved a feedback loop and may be analyzed as a sequence of two cases with reverse direction of influence.

The strategy of disaggregating complex situations into a suitable number of clear-cut cases is based on the assumption that complex patterns of interaction can be reduced to their component cases. While it might miss properties that are not inherent in the individual cases but emerge only from the complexity of the situation or from the combination of cases, this approach allows for a clear causal analysis and appears to cover all major incidents of institutional interaction discussed in the existing literature. Moreover, it does not preclude that we recombine cases to gain a more complex picture. Coevolution processes such as the one between the Bern Convention and the Habitats Directive can be analyzed and understood as a causal chain in which one case of interaction triggers the next. Other complex situations appear to be made up of clusters of parallel cases of interaction. For example, the IPPC Directive demonstrates that an institution may be concurrently affected by different source institutions in similar ways, while it may generate, as a source institution, parallel effects on a number of other institutions (chapter 9). Given the limited conceptual maturity of the analysis of institutional interaction at present, emerging properties of complex situations do not constitute the focus of the present volume. The possibilities of recombining connected cases of institutional interaction and of analyzing complex interaction situations on the basis of our concept are further explored in chapter 13.

Causal Mechanisms of Institutional Interaction

At the current stage of research on institutional interaction, it is too early for the development of a full-fledged, deductively derived theory of its driving forces and effects. However, the rigor of empirical analysis as well as the significance of its results will be greatly enhanced by a reliable theoretical conception of the causal mechanisms that might drive particular cases of institutional interaction. In this section, we first explore the general concept of causal mechanisms of institutional interaction. Subsequently, we develop two causal mechanisms in which the source institution directly affects the rule-making process of the target institution through its influence on the preferences of relevant actors within the target institution. Moreover, we present two causal mechanisms in which the source institution affects the performance of the target institution within the latter's own domain. We claim that each of these causal mechanisms derived from various theories of international institutions as well as from negotiation theory and cooperation theory has its own logic that clearly distinguishes it from the other three mechanisms. Whereas other mechanisms might be constructed, they are of a rather hypothetical nature. It is highly improbable that they gain relevance in practice.

The Concept of Causal Mechanisms

Exploration of the causal mechanisms of institutional interaction is intended to elucidate how causal influence travels from the source institution to the target institution. A causal mechanism is a set of statements that are logically connected and provide a plausible account of how a given cause creates an observed effect (Schelling 1998). It opens the black box of the cause-effect relationship between the institutions involved in a case of institutional interaction (Elster 1989, 3–10; King, Keohane, and Verba 1994, 85–87; Hedström and Swedberg 1998).

Causal mechanisms of institutional interaction reveal how actors matter. The search for causal mechanisms raises the question of how developments located at the systemic level of the institutions are related to developments located at the actors' level. Like any other theory in the social sciences, a concept of institutional interaction requires a reliable micro-macro link (Buzan, Jones, and Little 1993, 104; Alexander and Giesen 1987). In the bulk of traditional analyses of international and EU institutions, the micro-macro link is quite obvious, because causes and effects are located at different levels (on the discussion of the agent-structure relationship, see Wendt 1987; Carlsnaes 1992). If we want to explain the establishment and design of an international or EU institution, the dependent variable is located at the macro-level, while the explanatory variable—namely, the relevant group of actors, their perceptions, interests, and so on—is located at the microlevel. Most effectiveness research examines the reverse direction. A given institution as the independent variable is located at the macrolevel, while the dependent variable, namely effects caused by the institution such as changes of behavior of relevant actors, is located at the microlevel. In cases of institutional interaction, the micro-macro link is not as obvious because both the independent and the dependent variables (the source institution and the target institution) are located at the macrolevel. Yet it is difficult to imagine that an institution could influence another institution directly without intermediate (changes of) action by relevant actors.

A causal mechanism of institutional interaction consists of three separate stages. In the first stage, the source institution, or a relevant component of it, will affect the preferences or behavior of relevant actors within its own domain. Influence originates from the structural level and is directed at the actors' level. This stage is thus driven by a logic of the situation. In the second stage, this effect must lead to a change of preferences or of individual behavior of actors relevant to the target institution. Hence, the causal mechanism comprises a theory of action that tells us why actors behave as they do. In the third stage, individual action must produce the

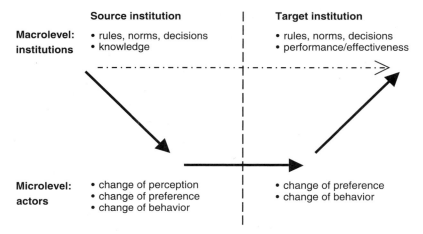

Figure 2.1
The logic of causal mechanisms

effect observed within the target institution or its issue area. The causal mechanism therefore also comprises a logic of aggregation. The analytic concept of the causal mechanism, as illustrated in figure 2.1, is well established in the social sciences (Coleman 1990, 1–23; Hedström and Swedberg 1998, 21–23).

The approach may be illustrated by the interaction regarding forest management between the two international regimes on global climate change and on biodiversity (Pontecorvo 1999; Jacquemont and Caparrós 2002). To establish the causal relationship between the two regimes, one would have to demonstrate (1) that relevant actors react to the adoption of the Kyoto Protocol in the form of increasing carbon sequestration in forests (or can be expected to react in this way); (2) that these behavioral changes encroach on biodiversity-rich habitats such as tropical rainforests; and (3) that the Convention on Biological Diversity is (at least potentially) affected by this change because its performance is undermined.

A causal mechanism provides an abstract model of the actual causal pathway that a case of institutional interaction follows. Being deductively derived, such a model must be theoretically coherent, but it cannot be empirically right or wrong (Snidal 1985). It may or may not fit a given case of interaction. A causal mechanism points to the steps of the causal chain leading from the source institution to the target institution and highlights how institutional interaction can ideally take place. It draws attention to the actors and their behavior that are indispensable or possibly relevant for cases of interaction that fit their inherent rationale.

Whereas the concept of causal mechanism points to the fact that actors are indispensable transmitters of influence, the precise role of actors is far from obvious. The same actors might be active in both institutions, but this is not a necessary condition. Moreover, different types of actors and behavior may be involved. Effects observed within the target institution will frequently be attributable to changes in the behavior of key states, because states are the members of both international and EU institutions and institutional obligations are primarily addressed at states. However, other types of actors, like nongovernmental organizations, industry, the secretariats of international institutions, or the European Commission, may play an important role (see also Selin and VanDeveer 2003).

To identify relevant causal mechanisms of institutional interaction, we follow the distinction of three levels of effectiveness of governance institutions, namely output, outcome, and impact. This distinction has been introduced and widely employed in research on the effectiveness of international regimes (Underdal 2004). No international or EU institution may directly affect the state of the environment or another ultimate target of governance. It merely produces collectively agreed-on knowledge or norms prescribing, proscribing, or permitting behavior, as its immediate *output*. To become effective, this output of an institution must generate some form of behavioral *outcome*. It must result in an observable influence on the behavior of relevant states and/or substate actors such as affected industries or private households. Finally, a behavioral outcome may or may not result in an *impact* on the targeted part of the environment or other ultimate target of governance. The three levels of effectiveness are hierarchically ordered: impact requires outcome and outcome requires output. It should be noted that the output is a property of the institution in the narrow sense, whereas outcome and impact occur within the issue area governed by the institution.

Institutional interaction can occur at various levels. If an institution exerts influence on another institution, such influence must originate from its output (norms, including institutional arrangements and decisions as well as knowledge), from the outcome within its own domain (influence on behavior of relevant actors), or from the impact on its ultimate target of governance (e.g., influence on the global climate). And vice versa: the target institution may be affected by the source institution at the output level (influence on its decision-making process), at the outcome level (influence on the behavior of relevant actors within its domain), or at the impact level (direct influence on its ultimate target of governance).

A causal mechanism of institutional interaction has to clarify in particular how a given event within a source institution or its issue area can affect the target institution. The effect on the target is not only constitutive of a case of interaction, but it is also more selective than the causal event originating from the source institution. While an institution generates numerous effects that might potentially trigger interaction, only a minority of them results in actual institutional interaction. The key to deriving causal mechanisms of institutional interaction lies, therefore, in answering the question of how, and under which circumstances, the output, outcome, or impact of the target institution can be influenced by a source institution. Hence, to identify relevant causal mechanisms, we start reasoning from the target side.

Interaction Influencing the Decision-Making Process of the Target Institution

Interaction influencing the decision-making process of the target institution can be driven by two distinct causal mechanisms. One is related to the knowledge of actors operating within the target institution, while the other is related to the commitments of actors entered into within the source institution. An institution will influence the output of another institution if it affects the preferences of relevant actors within the target institution. It is evident that interaction of this sort cannot occur against the will of the members of the target institution. No institution, however powerful in comparison, has a direct grip on the decision-making process of another institution. While the source institution might affect the preferences of the members of the target institution, the latter must decide and can thwart institutional interaction by deciding not to adapt. Hence, establishing a causal relationship between source and target requires demonstrating that the members of the target institution would have decided differently in the absence of the relevant decision of the source institution.

Cognitive Interaction   The decision-making process of an international institution will be influenced if information, knowledge, or ideas (Haas 1992; Risse-Kappen 1994; Yee 1996) produced within another institution modify the perception of relevant decision makers. For example, the adoption of an innovative noncompliance procedure under the Montreal Protocol influenced the deliberations on a similar arrangement within the climate change regime. It provided a policy model that actors to some extent followed and that served as a starting point for their deliberations (Werksman 2005), whereas no actor was in any way committed or obliged to adopt the model.

Cognitive Interaction is based on the premise that actors must aim at reducing "analytic uncertainty" (Keisuke 1993) and will be prepared to adapt their perceptions to new information. These perceptions then shape their interests (Checkel 1998; Risse 2000). In real-world situations, the rationality of actors is usually "bounded," either because the actors do not have all relevant information available or because their information processing capacity is limited (Keohane 1984, 100–115; Simon 1972). If relevant actors operating within the target institution were fully informed rational utility maximizers, as is frequently assumed in rational-choice cooperation and regime theory (see Keohane 1984; Hasenclever, Mayer, and Rittberger 1997), Cognitive Interaction could not be expected to occur.

Cognitive Interaction passes through the following steps. First, the source institution must produce some new information such as a report revealing new insights on a scientific or technological problem or an institutional arrangement solving a particular regulatory problem. Note that new information has to emerge from the collective decision-making process of the source institution. If it were merely presented by some actors individually, it would not qualify as an output of the institution. Second, the information must be picked up by some actors capable of feeding it into the decision-making process of the target institution. This may be done by member states, nongovernmental organizations, or the secretariats of the institutions involved. Third, the information obtained from the source institution must change the order of preferences of actors relevant to the target institution, be they member states and their representatives or nongovernmental organizations capable of influencing member states. Finally, the modification of the preferences of some actors must have an impact on the collective negotiation process of the target institution and its output.

Cognitive Interaction is purely based on persuasion and may be conceived of as a particular form of interinstitutional learning. It is similar to the "ideational interplay" referred to by Stokke (2001b, 10) and can occur between any two institutions whether or not their memberships or the subjects regulated overlap, as long as there is a similarity of problems that allows for learning across institutional borders. The source institution does not exert any pressure on the decision makers of the target institution. However, once sufficiently relevant actors adapt their preferences to new information, the decision-making process of the target institution will be affected. This effect will be felt even by participants in the process that have not been convinced.

Interaction through Commitment   Institutional interaction directed at the decision-making process of the target institution can also occur if commitments entered into by some members of the source institution affect the preferences of actors related to the target institution. For example, the EU distributed its joint commitment to reduce the emission of greenhouse gases among its member states by assigning differentiated targets to them in a "Burden-Sharing Agreement." Since emission increases were granted to EU laggard countries, these states lost their potential interest in securing less demanding obligations internationally and joined the whole of the EU in requesting stringent emission targets in the international negotiations. The Burden-Sharing Agreement thus enabled the European Union as a bloc to pursue and eventually secure comparatively stringent emission reductions internationally in the Kyoto Protocol (chapter 3). This case of interaction does not touch on the outcome or impact levels of either of the two institutions, but is confined to the output level.

Interaction through Commitment is based on the desire of member states to avoid mutually incompatible obligations, or on their desire to broaden the geographic scope of such obligations. Cooperative arrangements regularly promise cooperation gains to their members in exchange for their commitment to a particular way of action, so that noncompliance with the commitments endangers the gains from cooperation. In a Prisoner's Dilemma situation, for example, actors frequently set up institutional arrangements to supervise, and possibly enforce, cooperative behavior in order to avoid free riding and achieve cooperation (Martin 1993). Hence, once sincere cooperators have entered into an obligation within one institution, they become interested in avoiding incompatible decisions in other forums, because otherwise they might not be able to comply with their commitments. They will endeavor to preserve a reputation of keeping their promises because possible future cooperators might otherwise be less inclined to enter into agreements with them (Keohane 1984, 105–106; Young 1992, 75–76). Moreover, a commitment already subscribed to within one institution can easily be accepted within another institution because it does not produce additional costs of adaptation. Actors may also be expected to actively promote the transfer of a commitment to another institution, if this results in additional benefits such as the extension of the commitment to potential competitors. Being aware of the binding force of obligations, actors may also wish to adopt commitments in one institution in order to frame the policy choices available in another institution.

Members of the target institution may less easily avoid Interaction through Commitment than Cognitive Interaction. While the latter is purely based on persuasion, the former is based on a modification of preferences of relevant actors motivated by substantive costs and benefits. The mechanism relates to Stokke's "normative" and "utilitarian" interplay (Stokke 2001b). Interaction through Commitment adds a new dimension to the insight of negotiation analysis that the order of preferences of the participants of negotiations within the framework of institutions as well as the resulting constellation of preferences may be influenced by adding or subtracting issues and/or parties, even if no single actor has changed its general interests (Sebenius 1983, 1992). Other international institutions may also influence the preferences of relevant actors and the ensuing preference constellation. They can constitute an important determinant of negotiations, if they commit actors in the target institution in ways that influence the range of options acceptable to them.

Interaction through Commitment evolves in the following steps. First, members of the source institution agree on an obligation that might be relevant for the target institution. Second, this obligation actually commits one or more states that are members of both institutions. Third, the commitment accepted by these member states induces one or more of them to modify their preferences related to the target institution. Fourth, the modified preferences influence the collective decision-making process of the target institution and its output. Ideally, Interaction through Commitment will take place when actors who are already bound to an obligation originating from the source institution participate in a subsequent decision-making process of the target institution on a related subject. However, anticipated commitments to be entered into within the source institution may trigger the mechanism, if an actor participates in concurrent decision-making processes, so that coevolution of the norms of two institutions may pertain to this category.

Interaction through Commitment requires a certain overlap of both the memberships and the issue areas of the interacting institutions. Without a jurisdictional overlap of issue areas, neither inconsistent commitments nor side benefits of extending commitments to potential competitors could occur. Without overlapping memberships, the target institution would remain unaffected because none of its members would be subject to relevant commitments. Except for rare cases in which nonstate actors enter, formally or informally, into commitments within the framework of international and EU institutions, this mechanism commonly relies on state action because only states decide on, and are directly bound by, obligations in the framework of these institutions.

Possible Further Causal Mechanisms   It is difficult to imagine that an international or EU institution affects another institution by means other than knowledge and commitment. Hypothetically, a potential source institution might employ other means at its disposal such as financial transfers or the threat of sanctions. However, to influence the decision-making process of the target institution directly, actors operating within the latter would have to be bribed or forced to change their voting or negotiating behavior according to the policy of the former. While this cannot be excluded, we are not aware of anything coming close to it in contemporary international relations. To our knowledge, nothing of this kind has been reported even in the case of the rather tense relations between international environmental regimes and the WTO, or between adverse military alliances such as NATO and the Warsaw Pact.

Furthermore, we can hardly imagine that the decision-making process of an international or EU institution is *directly* affected by events occurring at the outcome or impact levels of another institution. We cannot expect, for example, that the members of the regime for the protection of the ozone layer will adapt the rules of their institution because the WTO triggers behavioral changes within its own issue area (e.g., the reduction of trade barriers by member states), if there are no immediate or anticipated effects of these behavioral changes on the performance of the ozone regime. If the performance of the ozone regime was affected, however, we would be faced with a case of Behavioral Interaction influencing the outcome level of the target institution (see below). We also cannot expect the members of the ozone regime to react to the impact of the WTO on its ultimate target, namely increased international trade, if there is no immediate impact on the state of the ozone layer. If the ozone layer were affected, however, we would be faced with a case of Impact-Level Interaction (see below).

Interaction Influencing the Target Institution at the Outcome Level: Behavioral Interaction

The target institution may also be influenced by the source institution at the outcome level, if the latter triggers behavioral effects within its own domain that become relevant for the former. All international governance institutions are designed to influence the behavior of relevant actors in order to achieve their objectives such as protecting the environment or liberalizing international trade (Levy, Young, and Zürn 1995; Young 1992). In some cases, behavioral effects in one issue area affect the implementation of another institution. Consider again the interaction between the Kyoto Protocol on climate change and the Convention on Biological Diversity (CBD). The Kyoto Protocol creates incentives for interested states and nonstate actors to engage in forestry activities that threaten to undermine the performance of the CBD. Interaction of this type influences the target institution through changes of behavior of states and nonstate actors relevant to its implementation. The rules of the target institution may remain totally unaffected, and if they are modified, this adaptation occurs as an additional response to the original effect.

The causal mechanism of Behavioral Interaction is composed of the following steps. First, the source institution produces an output with a potential effect on the behavior of relevant actors outside the decision-making process, such as behavioral prescriptions or proscriptions, behaviorally relevant knowledge, an offer of financial assistance, or a decision to impose sanctions for noncompliance. Second, relevant actors such as the member states of the source institution, other states, or nonstate actors (e.g., companies polluting the environment or nongovernmental organizations advocating human rights) adapt their behavior significantly in response to the output by acting differently from what we would have expected in its absence. Relevant behavioral changes include unforeseen side effects and deviating behavior, such as increased smuggling in response to trade restrictions to protect endangered species or to stabilize the coffee price at the world market. Third, the behavioral changes triggered by the source institution within its own issue area are either also directly relevant for the performance of the target institution or prompt further behavioral changes that affect the target's outcome level. Fourth, the behavioral effect within the issue area of the target institution affects the performance and effectiveness of the target institution.

Behavioral Interaction is characterized by a high ability of the source institution to influence the target institution unilaterally. In contrast to interaction directed at the decision-making process of the target institution, Behavioral Interaction does not depend on a decision within the target institution, because it occurs as the aggregate result of the uncoordinated behavior of actors operating within the two issue areas involved. The effect on the target institution might even come about unnoticed by the members of the institutions involved. A collective decision by the target institution or the source institution, or a "political linkage" (Young et al. 1999, 50) between them, may occur in response to the behavioral interaction, but such interaction "management" (Stokke 2001b) is not an essential element of this causal mechanism.

Interaction influencing the behavioral performance of the target institution will always originate from the behavioral effects of the source institution. Effects of an institution on the behavior of actors outside its issue area are always a secondary effect of behavioral effects within its own domain, irrespective of whether the interaction is intentionally created or not and whether it is anticipated or not. Other hypothetical causal pathways are hardly relevant in reality. In particular, we might speculate, and cannot exclude, that the members of an institution make decisions that *directly* induce behavioral effects in the issue area of the target institution without prior behavioral effects within its own domain. However, it seems a rather remote possibility that, for example, the international ozone regime would pass international trade rules unrelated to the protection of the ozone layer. Nothing of that kind has been reported in the literature so far. On the one hand, all international and EU sectoral institutions are predominantly established to govern their own issue areas. They do not enact rules, norms, or other decisions that are directed at issue areas exclusively governed by other institutions. On the other hand, it is difficult to see why actors involved in international trade should adapt their behavior in response to rules created within the ozone regime, if these rules do not address ozone protection and thus first trigger behavioral changes within the domain of the latter. Likewise, effects at the impact level within one institution cannot directly affect the behavior of actors governed by another institution. If they were also relevant for the target institution, we would be faced with a case of Impact-Level Interaction.

Interaction Influencing the Impact Level of the Target Institution

Principally, an institution may also be affected by another institution at the impact level. In this case, its ultimate target of governance, such as international trade or the ozone layer, is directly influenced by side effects originating from the ultimate target of governance of another institution. A stylized example that we owe to Arild Underdal may illustrate this least intuitive causal mechanism. Consider that protection of the stocks of cod and herring are the ultimate targets of two separate international institutions. Because cod eats herring, successful protection of cod, resulting in a growing population of this species, will unintentionally decrease the population of herring. In this case, the two institutions involved are not linked at the level of output (neither the norms nor knowledge produced within the cod regime influence the norms protecting herring), nor through behavioral changes (decreased fishing of cod does not directly influence the fishing activities related to herring). They are "functionally linked" (Young et al. 1999; Young 2002) at the impact level because the effect of the source institution on its ultimate regulatory target (increased population of cod) directly influences the ultimate regulatory target of the target institution (decreasing the population of herring).

Impact-Level Interaction is characterized by the following causal chain. First, the source institution produces an output, which might trigger behavioral effects.

Second, states and nonstate actors operating within the issue area governed by the source institution adapt their behavior in response to this signal. Third, these behavioral changes have an impact on the ultimate target of governance of the source institution. Fourth, this impact affects the target institution's ultimate target of governance. Fifth, this impact on the target institution's ultimate target of governance is relevant for the performance and effectiveness of the target institution. For the same reasons as in the case of Behavioral Interaction, Impact-level Interaction is characterized by a high ability of the source institution to influence the target institution unilaterally. Possible interaction "management" (Stokke 2001b) by the institutions involved—be it separate or in the form of a "political linkage" (Young et al. 1999, 50) between them—is not an essential part of the causal mechanism.

Interaction exerting influence on the impact level of the target institution has to run through the impact level of the source institution. The output of the source institution cannot directly affect the target institution's ultimate target of governance, because neither norms nor knowledge nor financial assistance nor sanctions can directly affect any ultimate target of governance such as the state of the ozone layer or free trade without intermediate behavioral changes of relevant actors. It is also difficult to see how behavioral effects of an institution within its own domain could directly affect another institution's ultimate target of governance. They must first create behavioral effects within the issue area of the target institution that subsequently affect the target's ultimate target of governance—as is the case in the example of biodiversity-relevant forestry activities induced by the Kyoto Protocol. In this case, the effect on the target institution's ultimate target of governance (the earth's biological diversity) follows from a case of Behavioral Interaction.

Concluding Remarks

Figure 2.2 illustrates the four general causal mechanisms of institutional interaction. They differ from each other by their underlying rationale. The bold arrows indicate the principal course of influence. In cases of Cognitive Interaction (1) and of Interaction through Commitment (2), influence originates at the output level of the source institution and directly affects the output level of the target institution. In cases of Behavioral Interaction (3), an output of the source institution changes the behavior of relevant actors within the issue area of the source institution, before it can exert influence on the behavior of actors relevant for the effectiveness of the target institution. In cases of Impact-Level Interaction (4), an output of the source institution creates effects at the behavioral and impact levels of that institution, before it directly

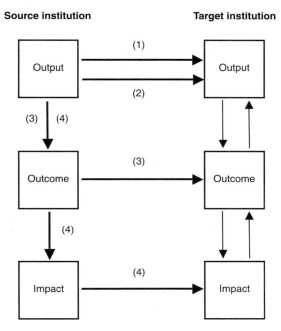

Figure 2.2
Four general causal mechanisms of institutional interaction

affects the impact level of the target institution. Hence, all causal mechanisms ultimately start with a significant output of the source institution, but the link between
the domains of the source institution and the target institution is located at different
levels of effectiveness. The relatively modest number of causal mechanisms is due
to the fact that all causal mechanisms are located at one level of effectiveness,
whereas cross-level interaction is either theoretically impossible or empirically highly
improbable.

The thin arrows at the right side of figure 2.2 indicate possible secondary effects
of institutional interaction in the target institution. They may follow from the
respective causal mechanisms, but they are not part of these mechanisms, because
interaction will take place even in their absence. Rules of the target institution that

are modified upon Cognitive Interaction or Interaction through Commitment may subsequently affect the outcome and, thereby, ultimately the impact of the target institution. Behavioral Interaction may be responded to at the output level of the target institution and may lead to subsequent effects at the impact level. If Impact-Level Interaction is recognized, actors whose behavior is relevant to the effectiveness of the target institution may adjust their behavior, and the rules of this institution may be adapted at the output level. Possible response action occurring within the domain of the source institution is not illustrated.

Consequences for the Empirical Investigation of Institutional Interaction

Three of the four general causal mechanisms developed in the preceding section provide the theoretical point of reference for the empirical investigation of institutional interaction in this volume. We focus on Cognitive Interaction, Interaction through Commitment, and Behavioral Interaction. Empirical case studies do not consider Impact-Level Interaction because it is rarely as limited and focused as in the hypothetical example of the regulation of cod and herring given above. In the real world, Impact-Level Interaction is diffuse and difficult to analyze. Frequently, it is based on complicated natural scientific links and requires investigation of long causal chains with many intervening variables. For example, establishing Impact-Level Interaction between the international regime for the protection of biodiversity and the international regime on climate change would require demonstrating both that the international climate change regime has actually slowed down climate change and that this effect has led to an increase in, decrease in, or stabilization of biological diversity (for illustrations of the complexities involved, see IPCC 2002; CBD 2003). It should be noted that the difficulties in exploring Impact-Level Interaction are exclusively of an empirical, not of a conceptual nature.

In line with the literature on the effectiveness of institutions, we exclusively examine cases of interaction that affect, or have the potential to affect, the issue areas governed by the institutions involved. Generally, research on the effectiveness of institutions is interested in whether, how, and to what extent institutions affect the state of the environment or other ultimate targets of governance (e.g., Young 1999; Haas, Keohane, and Levy 1993; Wettestad 1999). Thus, we are not interested in interaction cases that are limited to efficiency gains without significant effects in the domains of the institutions involved—for example, minor changes in reporting or organizational structure.

The first major task of the following empirical investigation of institutional inter-action is to explore whether, and to what extent, the three general causal mechanisms are relevant in practice in the field of international and EU environmental policy. So far, we do not know, for example, whether actual interaction cases are evenly distributed, or whether they concentrate on one or two of these mechanisms, and if yes, on which ones and why. For this purpose, case-study authors compiled inventories of identifiable cases of institutional interaction, in which their respective core institutions have been involved either as the source institution or as the target institution. The following chapters thus provide an overview of the network of interinstitutional relations in which the respective core institutions are embedded.

The second major task is to explore empirically how exactly institutional interaction operates in particular cases. We wish to know whether each of the cases examined fits one of our three general causal mechanisms, and vice versa, whether our three models reflect the basic properties of the empirical cases. For this reason, case-study authors explore in depth selected cases of interaction involving their core institutions. Together, cases were selected so as to cover a broad variety of phenomena of institutional interaction. The case studies demonstrate both the usefulness of our theoretically derived causal mechanisms and the empirical variety of actual cases of interaction. Examples of all three causal mechanisms are examined. Moreover, case studies address the three different dimensions in which international and EU institutions can interact. An international institution may interact *vertically* with an EU institution. It may also interact *horizontally* with another international institution. Finally, an EU institution may interact *horizontally* with another EU institution. Because of the relatively sophisticated overarching institutional framework of the EU (see above), we may expect the two forms of horizontal interaction to differ significantly.

The third major task of the following empirical investigation is to examine the effects of cases of interaction for international governance. Effects are assessed in terms of their compatibility with the policy direction *of the target institution*. The policy direction indicates the direction of collectively desired change or the objective of maintaining a desired status quo against some collectively undesired change (Gehring 1994, 433–449). It has generally been the major yardstick in the literature on regime effectiveness. Note that the policy direction is a property of the institution that may not be fully supported by all of its members. While the climate change regime is aimed at halting global climate change, some of its members may reject the adoption of measures to implement this objective. In contrast, conformity with the policy direction of the source institution is conceptually less relevant. The primary effects of institutional interaction occur in the target institution and thus outside the source institution. We may also assume that interaction effects will to a large extent be in line with the objectives of the source institution, because they ultimately resulted from the source institution's decisions.

The effects of a case of institutional interaction may be beneficial, adverse, or neutral for the target institution. Beneficial effects will create *synergy* between the two institutions because the policy direction of the target institution is supported by measures originating from the source institution. For example, the EU IPPC Directive creates synergy with other environmental EU directives, including those on waste and water management, because it supports the achievement of their objectives (chapter 9). Adverse effects will result in *disruption* of target-institution policies because measures originating from the source institution thwart or undermine the effectiveness of the target institution's own measures, or they force the target institution to adopt unwanted rules. Consider that the objective of the WTO to promote free world trade and reduce trade obstacles creates the potential for disruption of the policies of several environmental regimes that restrict trade in certain goods in order to achieve their objectives (chapter 8). Finally, effects on the target institution may also be indeterminate or neutral. If Interpol and the World Customs Organization adapt to the needs of the Convention on International Trade in Endangered Species of Wild Fauna and Flora (CITES) on the latter's request, this effect is neither detrimental to, nor supportive of, the policy directions of the target institutions (chapter 7).

Based on our theoretical approach, the empirical investigation of institutional interaction creates a wealth of empirical insights about single cases of interaction and enables us to further advance our understanding of the operation of the causal mechanisms of institutional interaction. In chapter 13, we further differentiate our general causal mechanisms by developing a number of Weberian ideal types of institutional interaction based on distinct rationales and deriving hypotheses about their effects on the target institution.

References

Abbott, Kenneth W., and Duncan Snidal. 1998. Why States Act through Formal International Organizations. *Journal of Conflict Resolution* 42 (1): 3–32.

Aggarwal, Vinod K. 1983. The Unraveling of the Multi-Fiber Arrangement, 1981: An Examination of International Regime Change. *International Organization* 37 (4): 617–646.

Alexander, Jeffrey, and Bernhard Giesen. 1987. From Reduction to Linkage: The Long View of the Micro-Macro Link. In Jeffrey Alexander, Bernhard Giesen, Richard Münch, and Neil J. Smelser, eds., *The Micro-Macro Link*, 1–42. Berkeley: University of California Press.

Andersen, Regine. 2002. The Time Dimension in International Regime Interplay. *Global Environmental Politics* 2 (3): 98–117.

Archer, Margaret S. 1985. Structuration versus Morphogenesis. In Shmuel N. Eisenstadt and Horst-Jürgen Helle, eds., *Macro-Sociological Theory: Perspectives on Sociological Theory Vol. 1*, 58–88. London: Sage.

Axelrod, Robert. 1984. *The Evolution of Cooperation*. New York: Basic Books.

Barnett, Michael N., and Martha Finnemore. 1999. The Politics, Power, and Pathologies of International Organizations. *International Organization* 53 (4): 699–732.

Bernauer, Thomas. 1995. The Effect of International Environmental Institutions: How We Might Learn More. *International Organization* 49 (2): 351–377.

Bierstecker, Thomas J. 1993. Constructing Historical Counterfactuals to Assess the Consequences of International Regimes: The Global Debt Regime and the Debt Crisis of the 1980s. In Volker Rittberger, ed., *Regime Theory and International Relations*, 315–338. Oxford: Clarendon.

Breitmeier, Helmut. 2000. "Complex Effectiveness": Regime Externalities and Interaction (Working Group III). In Jørgen Wettestad, ed., *Proceedings of the 1999 Oslo Workshop of the Concerted Action Network on the Effectiveness of International Environmental Regimes*, 45–48. Oslo: Fridtjof Nansen Institute.

Buzan, Barry, Charles Jones, and Richard Little. 1993. *The Logic of Anarchy: From Neorealism to Structural Realism*. New York: Columbia University Press.

Carlsnaes, Walter. 1992. The Agent-Structure Problem in Foreign Policy Analysis. *International Studies Quarterly* 36 (3): 245–270.

CBD. 2003, October. Ad hoc Technical Expert Group on Biological Diversity and Climate Change. *Interlinkages between Biological Diversity and Climate Change: Advice on the Integration of Biodiversity Considerations into the Implementation of the United Nations Framework Convention on Climate Change and Its Kyoto Protocol*. Montreal: Secretariat of the Convention on Biological Diversity.

Chambers, Bradnee W. ed. 1998. *Global Climate Governance: Inter-Linkages between the Kyoto Protocol and Other Multilateral Regimes*. Tokyo: United Nations University.

Checkel, Jeffrey T. 1998. The Constructivist Turn in International Relations Theory. *World Politics* 50 (3): 324–348.

Coleman, James S. 1990. *Foundations of Social Theory*. Cambridge, MA: Belknap Press of Harvard University.

DeSombre, Elisabeth R., and Joanne Kauffman. 1996. The Montreal Protocol Multilateral Fund: Partial Success. In Robert O. Keohane and Mark A. Levy, eds., *Institutions for Environmental Aid: Pitfalls and Promise*, 89–126. Cambridge, MA: MIT Press.

Elster, Jon. 1989. *The Cement of Society: A Study of Social Order*. Cambridge: Cambridge University Press.

Fearon, James D. 1998. Bargaining, Enforcement, and International Cooperation. *International Organization* 52 (2): 269–305.

Gehring, Thomas. 1994. *Dynamic International Regimes: Institutions for International Environmental Governance*. Frankfurt/Main: Peter Lang.

Gehring, Thomas. 2002. *Die Europäische Union als komplexe internationale Organisation: Wie durch Kommunikation und Entscheidung soziale Ordnung entsteht*. Baden-Baden: Nomos.

Gehring, Thomas. 2004. Methodological Issues in the Study of Broader Consequences. In Arild Underdal and Oran R. Young, eds., *Regime Consequences: Methodological Challenges and Research Strategies*, 219–246. Dordrecht: Kluwer.

Gehring, Thomas, and Sebastian Oberthür. 2004. Exploring Regime Interaction: A Framework for Analysis. In Arild Underdal and Oran R. Young, eds., *Regime Consequences: Methodological Challenges and Research Strategies*, 247–269. Dordrecht: Kluwer.

Haas, Peter M. 1992. Introduction: Epistemic Communities and International Policy Coordination. *International Organization* 46 (1): 1–35.

Haas, Peter M., Robert O. Keohane, and Marc A. Levy, eds. 1993. *Institutions for the Earth: Sources of Effective International Environmental Protection*. Cambridge, MA: MIT Press.

Hasenclever, Andreas, Peter Mayer, and Volker Rittberger. 1997. *Theories of International Regimes*. Cambridge: Cambridge University Press.

Hedström, Peter, and Richard Swedberg. 1998. Social Mechanisms: An Introductory Essay. In Peter Hedström and Richard Swedberg, eds., *Social Mechanisms: An Analytical Approach to Social Theory*, 1–31. Cambridge: Cambridge University Press.

Hix, Simon. 2005. *The Political System of the European Union*. 2nd edition. London: St. Martin's.

Hurrel, Andrew. 1993. International Society and the Study of Regimes. A Reflective Approach. In Volker Rittberger, ed., *Regime Theory and International Relations*, 49–72. Oxford: Clarendon Press.

IPCC. 2002, April. *Climate Change and Biodiversity*. IPCC Technical Paper V. Geneva: Intergovernmental Panel on Climate Change.

Jachtenfuchs, Markus. 2001. The Governance Approach to European Integration. *Journal of Common Market Studies* 39 (2): 245–264.

Jacquemont, Frédéric, and Alejandro Caparrós. 2002. The Convention on Biological Diversity and the Climate Change Convention 10 Years After Rio: Towards a Synergy of the Two Regimes? *Review of European Community and International Environmental Law* 11 (2): 139–180.

Joerges, Christian, and Ellen Vos, eds. 1999. *EU Committees: Social Regulation, Law and Politics*. Oxford: Hart.

Keisuke, Iida. 1993. Analytic Uncertainty and International Cooperation: Theory and Application to International Economic Policy Coordination. *International Studies Quarterly* 37 (4): 431–457.

Keohane, Robert O. 1984. *After Hegemony: Cooperation and Discord in the World Political Economy*. Princeton, NJ: Princeton University Press.

Keohane, Robert O. 1989. *International Institutions and State Power: Essays in International Relations Theory*. Boulder, CO: Westview.

Keohane, Robert O. 1993. The Analysis of International Regimes: Towards a European-American Research Programme. In Volker Rittberger, ed., *Regime Theory and International Relations*, 23–45. Oxford: Clarendon Press.

Keohane, Robert O., and Stanley Hoffmann. 1991. Institutional Change in Europe in the 1980s. In Robert O. Keohane and Stanley Hoffmann, eds., *The New European Community: Decisionmaking and Institutional Change*, 1–39. Boulder, CO: Westview.

King, Gary, Robert O. Keohane, and Sidney Verba. 1994. *Designing Social Inquiry: Scientific Inference in Qualitative Research*. Princeton, NJ: Princeton University Press.

Levy, Mark A. 1993. European Acid Rain: The Power of Tote-Board Diplomacy. In Peter M. Haas, Robert O. Keohane, and Mark A. Levy, eds., *Institutions for the Earth: Sources of Effective International Environmental Protection*, 75–132. Cambridge, MA: MIT Press.

Levy, Marc A., Oran R. Young, and Michael Zürn. 1995. The Study of International Regimes. *European Journal of International Relations* 1 (3): 267–330.

Martin, Lisa L. 1993. The Rational State Choice of Multilateralism. In John Ruggie, ed., *Multilateralism Matters: The Theory and Praxis of an Institutional Form*, 91–121. New York: Columbia University Press.

Meinke, Britta. 2002. *Multi-Regime-Regulierung: Wechselwirkungen zwischen globalen und regionalen Umweltregimen*. Darmstadt: Deutscher Universitäts-Verlag.

Miles, Edward L., Arild Underdal, Steinar Andresen, Jørgen Wettestad, Jon Birger Skjærseth, and Elaine M. Carlin. 2002. *Environmental Regime Effectiveness: Confronting Theory with Evidence*. Cambridge, MA: MIT Press.

Moravcsik, Andrew. 1998. *The Choice for Europe: Social Purpose and State Power from Messina to Maastricht*. Ithaca, NY: Cornell University Press.

Morrow, James D. 1994. Modelling the Forms of International Cooperation: Distribution versus Information. *International Organization* 48 (3): 387–423.

Nugent, Neill. 2003. *Government and Politics of the European Union*. 5th edition. Durham, NC: Duke University Press.

Oberthür, Sebastian. 2001. Linkages between the Montreal and Kyoto Protocols: Enhancing Synergies between Protecting the Ozone Layer and the Global Climate. *International Environmental Agreements: Politics, Law and Economics* 1 (3): 357–377.

Oye, Kenneth A. 1985. Explaining Cooperation under Anarchy: Hypotheses and Strategies. *World Politics* 38 (1): 1–24.

Pollack, Mark A. 1997. Delegation, Agency, and Agenda Setting in the European Community. *International Organization* 51 (1): 99–134.

Pontecorvo, Concetta Maria. 1999. Interdependence between Global Environmental Regimes: The Kyoto Protocol on Climate Change and Forest Protection. *Zeitschrift für ausländisches öffentliches Recht und Völkerrecht* 59 (3): 709–749.

Raustalia, Kal, and David G. Victor. 2004. The Regime Complex for Plant Genetic Resources. *International Organization* 58 (2): 277–309.

Risse, Thomas. 2000. "Let's Argue!" Communicative Action in World Politics. *International Organization* 54 (1): 1–39.

Risse-Kappen, Thomas. 1994. Ideas Do Not Float Freely: Transnational Coalitions, Domestic Structures, and the End of the Cold War. *International Organization* 48 (2): 185–214.

Rittberger, Volker, ed. 1993. *Regime Theory and International Relations*. Oxford: Clarendon Press.

Rosendal, G. Kristin. 2000. *The Convention on Biological Diversity and Developing Countries*. Dordrecht: Kluwer Academic.

Rosendal, Kristin. 2001. Impacts of Overlapping International Regimes: The Case of Biodiversity. *Global Governance* 7 (1): 95–117.

Scharpf, Fritz W. 1999. *Governing in Europe: Effective and Democratic?* Oxford: Oxford University Press.

Schelling, Thomas. 1998. Social Mechanisms and Social Dynamics. In Peter Hedström and Richard Swedberg, eds., *Social Mechanisms: An Analytical Approach to Social Theory*, 32–44. Cambridge: Cambridge University Press.

Sebenius, James K. 1983. Negotiation Arithmetics: Adding and Subtracting Issues and Parties. *International Organization* 37 (2): 281–316.

Sebenius, James K. 1992. Challenging Conventional Explanations of International Cooperation: Negotiation Analysis and the Case of Epistemic Communities. *International Organization* 46 (1): 323–365.

Selin, Henrik, and Stacy D. VanDeveer. 2003. Mapping Institutional Linkages in European Air Pollution Politics. *Global Environmental Politics* 3 (3): 14–46.

Simmons, Beth A., and Lisa L. Martin. 2002. International Organizations and Institutions. In Walter Carlsnaes, Thomas Risse, and Beth Simmons, eds., *Handbook of International Relations*, 192–211. London: Sage.

Simon, Herbert A. 1972. Theories of Bounded Rationality. In Charles B. McGuire and Roy Radner, eds., *Decision and Organization*, 161–176. Amsterdam: North Holland.

Snidal, Duncan. 1985. The Game Theory of International Politics. *World Politics* 38 (1): 25–57.

Stokke, Olav Schram. 1999. Governance of High Seas Fisheries: The Role of Regime Linkages. In Davor Vidas and Willy Østreng, eds., *Order for the Oceans at the Turn of the Century*, 157–172. The Hague: Kluwer Law International.

Stokke, Olav Schram. 2000. Managing Straddling Stocks: The Interplay of Global and Regional Regimes. *Ocean and Coastal Management* 43 (2–3): 205–234.

Stokke, Olav Schram. 2001a. Conclusions. In Olav Schram Stokke, ed., *Governing High Seas Fisheries: The Interplay of Global and Regional Regimes*, 329–360. Oxford: Oxford University Press.

Stokke, Olav Schram. 2001b. The Interplay of International Regimes: Putting Effectiveness Theory to Work. FNI Report 14/2001. Lysaker, Norway: Fridtjof Nansen Institute.

Tetlock, Philip E., and Aaron Belkin, eds. 1996. *Counterfactual Thought Experiments in World Politics: Logical, Methodological, and Psychological Perspectives*. Princeton, NJ: Princeton University Press.

Underdal, Arild. 1992. The Concept of Regime "Effectiveness." *Cooperation and Conflict* 27 (3): 227–240.

Underdal, Arild. 2004. Methodological Challenges in the Study of Regime Effectiveness. In Arild Underdal and Oran R. Young, eds., *Regime Consequences: Methodological Challenges and Research Strategies*, 27–48. Dordrecht: Kluwer.

Victor, David G. 1998. The Operation and Effectiveness of the Montreal Protocol's Non-Compliance Procedure. In David G. Victor, Kal Raustiala, and Eugene B. Skolnikoff, eds., *The Implementation and Effectiveness of International Environmental Commitments: Theory and Practice*, 137–176. Cambridge, MA: MIT Press.

Victor, David G., Kal Raustiala, and Eugene B. Skolnikoff, eds. 1998. *The Implementation and Effectiveness of International Environmental Commitments: Theory and Practice*. Cambridge, MA: MIT Press.

Wendt, Alexander. 1987. The Agent-Structure Problem in International Relations Theory. *International Organization* 41 (3): 335–370.

Werksman, Jacob. 2005. The Negotiation of a Kyoto Compliance System. In Olav Schram Stokke, Jon Hovi, and Geir Ulfstein, eds., *Implementing the Climate Regime: International Compliance*. 17–38. London: Earthscan.

Wettestad, Jørgen. 1999. *Designing Effective Environmental Regimes: The Key Conditions*. Cheltenham: Edward Elgar.

Yee, Albert S. 1996. The Causal Effects of Ideas on Politics. *International Organization* 50 (1): 69–108.

Young, Oran R. 1982. Regime Dynamics: The Rise and Fall of International Regimes. *International Organization* 36 (2): 277–297.

Young, Oran R. 1992. The Effectiveness of International Institutions: Hard Cases and Critical Variables. In James N. Rosenau and Ernst-Otto Czempiel, eds., *Governance without Government: Order and Change in World Politics*, 160–194. Cambridge: Cambridge University Press.

Young, Oran R. 1994. *International Governance: Protecting the Environment in a Stateless Society*. Ithaca, NY: Cornell University Press.

Young, Oran R. 1996. Institutional Linkages in International Society: Polar Perspectives. *Global Governance* 2 (1): 1–24.

Young, Oran R. 2002. *The Institutional Dimensions of Environmental Change: Fit, Interplay, and Scale*. Cambridge, MA: MIT Press.

Young, Oran R. ed. 1999. *The Effectiveness of International Environmental Regimes: Causal Connections and Behavioral Mechanisms*. Cambridge, MA: MIT Press.

Young, Oran R., Leslie A. King, Arun Aggarval, Arild Underdal, Peter H. Sand, and Merrilyn Wasson. 1999. *Institutional Dimensions of Global Environmental Change (IDGEC): Science Plan*. Bonn: International Human Dimensions Programme on Global Environmental Change.

3

The Climate Change Regime: Interactions with ICAO, IMO, and the EU Burden-Sharing Agreement

Sebastian Oberthür

Reflecting the vast scope and complexity of the climate change challenge, the international regime on climate change is one of the broadest and most complex international governance systems in the field of the environment and beyond. Representing the biggest environmental challenge at the beginning of the twenty-first century, climate change has a variety of impacts on the natural environment and on human society. Various human activities and sectors of society contribute to the problem and will, therefore, be influenced by any effective policy response (IPCC 2001a, 2001b). Consequently, the climate change regime is one of the politically most important international environmental institutions and spans an enormous scope. Since international negotiations on a UN Framework Convention on Climate Change began in 1991, the growth in the number, detail, and complexity of the relevant international rules has become particularly apparent with the adoption of the 1997 Kyoto Protocol and the subsequent elaboration of its provisions, including a number of innovative elements such as emissions trading and opportunities to take credit for forestry activities (e.g., Oberthür and Ott 1999; Yamin and Depledge 2004).

Given its enormous scope, it is hardly surprising that the climate change regime interacts with a great number of other international institutions and EU legal instruments, as further detailed in this chapter. The chapter first briefly introduces the main elements of the international regime on climate change. This is followed by an overview of the major interactions of the climate change regime with other international institutions and EU legal instruments. The chapter then focuses on the interaction with three other institutions in more detail. The interaction with the International Maritime Organization (IMO) and the International Civil Aviation Organization (ICAO) exemplifies the at times problematic relationship of the climate change regime with institutions from other policy fields. The climate change regime's request to the IMO and ICAO to restrict greenhouse gas emissions from international transport raised the issue of which of the institutions involved should possess regulatory authority in this respect. The request has largely failed to draw an effective response to date, because the requested restrictions are not in the immediate interest of the target institutions. Similar issues arise more frequently especially between environmental and economic institutions. Subsequently, the chapter analyzes the climate change regime's interaction with the agreement on differentiated emission limitation and reduction commitments of EU member states ("Burden-Sharing Agreement"). This interaction provides an example of how EU legal instruments can facilitate and strengthen international environmental governance. This rather positive perspective on the EU Burden-Sharing Agreement contrasts with the harsh criticism by several non-EU countries. The concluding section summarizes the findings.

The International Regime on Climate Change

The international regime on climate change is built on two international treaties, the UN Framework Convention on Climate Change (UNFCCC) of 1992 and its Kyoto Protocol adopted in 1997 (Bodansky 1993; Oberthür and Ott 1999). The rules under the Kyoto Protocol were further specified in agreements reached in 2001 (Bail, Marr, and Oberthür 2003). As of mid-2005, the Convention had 189 parties and the Protocol had been ratified by 150 countries and the EU. The EU and its member states are all parties to both the Convention and the Protocol.[1] The Kyoto Protocol entered into force in February 2005. However, the new U.S. President George Bush in March 2001 decided not to ratify the Kyoto Protocol.

The Convention established the regime by defining the principles that guide its development (Art. 3) and its ultimate objective: to stabilize atmospheric concentrations of greenhouse gases (GHGs) "at a level that would prevent dangerous anthropogenic interference with the climate system" (Art. 2). It also established the soft aim that industrialized countries would strive to return their GHG emissions to 1990 levels by 2000. It covers all GHGs "not controlled by the Montreal Protocol" for the protection of the ozone layer and establishes that removals by sinks such as forests are to be taken into account.

The Kyoto Protocol for the first time establishes legally binding emission-reduction commitments for industrialized countries. These differentiated commitments must amount to an overall reduction of at least 5 percent from 1990 levels by 2008–2012 (the "commitment period"). The commitments cover carbon dioxide (CO_2), methane (CH_4), nitrous oxide (N_2O), and three (groups of) fluorinated gases, namely hydrofluorocarbons (HFCs), perfluorocarbons (PFCs), and sulfur hexafluoride (SF_6). Removals and emissions of GHGs from afforestation, reforestation, and deforestation are to be accounted for (Art. 3.3). In addition, parties agreed in 2001 that forest management and agricultural activities (cropland management, grazing-land management, and revegetation) could be taken into account as additional sink categories under Article 3.4 of the Protocol (Bail, Marr, and Oberthür 2003).

The Protocol furthermore establishes three innovative "Kyoto Mechanisms" that allow countries to meet their emission obligations by acquiring emission credits from abroad. An emissions-trading system allows industrialized countries with excess emission allowances to transfer them to other countries in need of such allowances (Art. 17). Under the "Joint Implementation" (JI) scheme according to Article 6 of the Protocol, an investor and a host industrialized country can generate additional emission reductions by implementing a suitable project jointly, with the investor receiving (part of) the resulting emission credits. Similarly, industrialized countries can invest in emission-reduction projects (including sinks projects) in developing countries to earn additional emission credits under a Clean Development Mechanism (CDM, Art. 12). Further rules and guidelines on the operation of the Kyoto Mechanisms form part of the agreements reached in 2001 (Bail, Marr, and Oberthür 2003).

The institutional structure of the UNFCCC and the Kyoto Protocol are closely related. The Conference of the Parties (COP), which usually meets once a year, is the supreme decision-making body of the Convention. It is assisted by two standing subsidiary bodies, the Subsidiary Body for Scientific and Technological Advice (SBSTA) and the Subsidiary Body for Implementation (SBI). The Convention furthermore establishes a financial mechanism to assist developing countries in their implementation, which is operated by the Global Environment Facility (GEF), and a secretariat (located in Bonn). It also acknowledges the role of the Intergovernmental Panel on Climate Change (IPCC) established by the WMO and UNEP in 1988 to provide scientific advice to its parties. Since no rule on voting could be agreed, all decisions under the Convention have so far required consensus. Until the entry into force of the Protocol in February 2005, the development of the regime occurred in the framework of the Convention. Whereas the Subsidiary Bodies and the financial mechanism of the Convention as well as the secretariat are also adapted to serve under the Protocol, the COP sessions concurrently serve as the meeting of the parties to the Protocol (COP/MOP). In addition, parties to the Protocol have elaborated detailed rules on reporting, monitoring, and review of information as well as a compliance system to determine and address cases of noncompliance (Bail, Marr, and Oberthür 2003; Yamin and Depledge 2004).

The Climate Change Regime as Source and Target of Institutional Interaction

The climate change regime interacts with many other environmental and nonenvironmental international institutions and EU legal instruments. Twenty-four specific cases of horizontal and vertical institutional interaction are listed in table 3.1. This list is not necessarily exhaustive. Not included are numerous cases in which a specific interaction has not occurred yet and/or the causal pathway leading from one institution to the other is rather long. For example, trade liberalization advanced by the World Trade Organization (WTO) may lead to rising GHG emissions due to induced growth in international trade, as may the EU Single Market. Furthermore, effective climate protection may prevent the spreading of health diseases (relevant to the World Health Organization, WHO), help efforts to preserve biological diversity (Convention on Biological Diversity, EU Habitats Directive) and wetlands (Ramsar Convention) and combat desertification (Convention to Combat Desertification), and so on (see IPCC 2001a). In other instances, a potential for the emergence of future interaction exists, for example between the Kyoto Mechanisms and the WTO (e.g., Chambers 1998, 2001; Charnovitz 2003). In these cases, the interaction has so far remained rather indirect and unspecific. Furthermore, more EU legal instruments affect GHG emissions, but including them would have been beyond the scope of this study.

All major causal mechanisms of institutional interaction are represented in the twenty-four cases. Cognitive Interaction is apparent from the model function that the compliance procedure of the Montreal Protocol has performed in the elaboration of the compliance system of the Kyoto Protocol. The Montreal Protocol has also served as a model that was not accepted (due to a blocking minority) with respect to the establishment of technology and economic assessment panels. Other international institutions have also served as templates of various elements of the climate change regime, but including them would have been beyond the scope of this chapter.

In other instances, the commitments entered into under the climate change regime have affected the rules of other international institutions and EU legal instruments (Interaction through Commitment). Thus, the GEF operates the financial mechanism

Table 3.1
Interactions of the Climate Change Regime

Montreal Protocol on Substances That Deplete the Ozone Layer	• Has served as a model in several respects (e.g., compliance procedure) Has served as a model that was blocked by a minority with respect to the establishment of technology and economic assessment panels • Has helped phase out ozone-depleting substances that are also potent GHGs • Has supported use of fluorinated GHGs regulated under the Kyoto Protocol (while the latter has provided a disincentive for such use to replace ozone-depleting substances)
Convention on Biological Diversity	• May suffer from establishment of monocultural tree plantations induced by climate change regime
Ramsar Convention on Wetlands	• May benefit from additional resources for wetland management or suffer from conversion of wetlands for carbon sequestration induced by climate change regime
Convention to Combat Desertification	• May benefit from forestry activities promoted under the climate change regime that help combat desertification
International Civil Aviation Organization	• Was asked by climate change regime to act on GHG emissions from international aviation
International Maritime Organization	• Was asked by climate change regime to act on GHG emissions from international shipping
World Trade Organization	• Is used as a major argument against elaboration of trade-relevant climate-protection measures ("chill effect")
World Bank	• Has greened its policies to some extent in response to the climate change regime
Global Environment Facility	• Has been asked to operate the financial mechanism of the climate change regime
EU Landfill Directive	• Results in reductions of methane emissions and thus helps implement the Kyoto Protocol
EU Renewable Energy Directive	• Is to result in increasing use of non-GHG-emitting energy sources and thus helps implement the Kyoto Protocol
EU Directive on the Internal Market for Electricity	• Is expected to result, inter alia, in lower energy prices counteracting efforts to save energy and reduce GHG emissions
EU Directives on car emission standards	• Require cars to be equipped with catalytic converters, leading to increases of GHG emissions

Table 3.1
(continued)

EU GHG monitoring	• Responds to international reporting and monitoring requirements under the Kyoto Protocol
EU Burden-Sharing Agreement	• Facilitated agreement on and strengthened targets under Kyoto Protocol • Was codified in supranational EU law in response to Kyoto Protocol • Helps implement the Kyoto Protocol by strengthening enforcement in the EU
EU Regulation and Directive on fluorinated greenhouse gases	• Was triggered by the Kyoto Protocol • Is expected to lead to reductions of emissions of fluorinated GHGs
EU Emissions Trading Directive	• Was triggered by the Kyoto Protocol • Is expected to result in reductions of GHG emissions

of the climate change regime and the World Bank has to some extent made its policies more climate-friendly. As discussed further in the next section, ICAO and IMO have initiated some activities to address GHG emissions from international transport in response to a request by the Kyoto Protocol. Furthermore, the climate change regime has shaped the EU's legislation implementing the Kyoto Protocol, including the EU GHG monitoring mechanism, the EU regulatory framework on fluorinated GHGs, the codification of the EU Burden-Sharing Agreement, and the EU Emissions Trading Directive. The climate change regime has also been the target of Interaction through Commitment. For example, free-trade commitments under the WTO (chapter 8) have contributed to preventing elaboration of trade-related climate protection measures. In contrast, the EU's commitment to its Burden-Sharing Agreement facilitated and strengthened the Kyoto Protocol, as analyzed further in this chapter.

The climate change regime has also served as a source and a target of Behavioral Interaction. The EU Landfill Directive, the Renewable Energy Directive, the Emissions Trading Directive, EU rules on the internal market for electricity, the directives on car emission standards, the EU Burden-Sharing Agreement, the EU regulatory framework on fluorinated GHGs, the IPPC Directive (chapter 9), and other EU legal instruments affect the level of GHG emissions within the EU. The Montreal Protocol has had synergistic and disruptive effects by phasing out ozone-depleting substances such as chlorofluorocarbons (CFCs) that are also potent GHGs, while encouraging the use of other fluorinated GHGs (Oberthür 2001). The Kyoto Protocol, in turn, provides incentives for forestry activities that are expected to support the objectives of the Convention to Combat Desertification (CCD). In contrast, the Protocol is likely to have a disruptive effect on the Convention on Biological Diversity (CBD) by providing incentives for investments in fast-growing monocultural forest planta-tions (Pontecorvo 1999; see also chapter 4). It may also violate the prohibition of dumping at sea under the OSPAR Convention for the protection of the Northeast Atlantic by providing an incentive to sequester CO_2 in North Sea oil fields (chapter 5). Due to scientific uncertainties, uncertain behavioral effects, and unknown appli-cation of rules in practice, the behavioral effects of the climate change regime are not always unambiguously synergistic or disruptive. For example, whether and to what extent wetland conservation and management regulated under the Ramsar Conven-tion on wetlands will benefit from additional resources made available through the climate change regime or may be harmed by conversion of wetlands for carbon se-questration depends heavily on the future development and application of relevant rules.

The relations of the climate change regime with nonenvironmental institutions have been disruptive more frequently than those with other environmental institu-tions. Of the five identified environmental-economic interactions with ICAO, IMO, the WTO, the World Bank, and the EU electricity market, all except the one con-cerning the World Bank have been disruptive. In contrast, only five of the about twenty interactions with other environmental institutions have resulted in disrup-tions (including the interaction with the OSPAR Convention; see chapter 5).

Political decision making can lead to improvements. For example, some decisions have been made in the framework of the climate change regime to mitigate the disruptive effect on the CBD (Jacquemont and Caparrós 2002). The relationship be-tween the climate change regime and the CBD as well as the Convention to Combat Desertification and the Ramsar Convention and others are also actively managed to enhance synergy. Since most cases have a potential for further improvement, the situation may change in the future.

Requesting Change from Unfriendly Institutions: Regulatory Competition between the Kyoto Protocol and ICAO and IMO

Although climate change is not among their main concerns, ICAO and IMO started to address GHG emissions from international transport in response to a request contained in the 1997 Kyoto Protocol. Both organizations have, however, been far from enthusiastic about the newly acquired task. The limited action they have taken has mainly been driven by the threat of regulation by the climate change regime and of unilateral action by major players. A more elaborate analysis of this case of Interaction through Commitment can be found in Oberthür 2003.

Structure and Objectives of ICAO and IMO

ICAO and IMO are the prime international organizations responsible for international aviation and shipping, respectively. Their major objectives are the promotion and enhancement of these modes of international transport. Shipping and aviation interests (owners, builders, operators) are their main stakeholders. As of mid-2005, ICAO had 188 and IMO 165 member states (http://www.icao.int; http://www.imo .org).

IMO possesses an Assembly of all parties, a Council with a limited membership elected by the Assembly, and various committees. Its supreme governing body is the Assembly. In between its biennial meetings, the Assembly's functions are largely performed by the Council. However, with respect to the central task of IMO—the elaboration of international agreements (Art. 3(b), IMO Convention)—the Council may not recommend adoption of regulations or amendments to such regulations on behalf of the Assembly. IMO agreements become binding on parties subject to their ratification (http://www.imo.org).

While ICAO also possesses an Assembly, a limited-membership Council, and various committees, its supreme governing body is the Council. The Assembly meets once every three years and provides general policy guidelines for the work of the other ICAO bodies framed in "Assembly Resolutions." The Council governs the organization in the interim. In addition to passing resolutions and recommendations, it adopts legally binding standards and recommended practices that are included in annexes to the ICAO Convention. An international standard adopted by the Council immediately binds all ICAO members that do not explicitly decide to deviate from the standard. Member states undertake to comply with the organization's regulations, which also apply over the high seas (Art. 12, ICAO Convention; see Buergenthal 1969; http://www.icao.int).

Both organizations have assumed at least partial competence for regulating environmental matters relating to their mode of international transport. In the case of IMO, such authority is an explicit part of its mandate. According to Article 1(a) of its Convention, the purposes of IMO include "to encourage the general adoption of the highest practicable standards in matters concerning maritime safety, efficiency of navigation and the prevention and control of marine pollution from ships." Among the five open-ended committees of the organization is a Marine Environment Protection Committee (MEPC) that is primarily concerned with adopting and amending the organization's environmental conventions and reports to the Council and the Assembly. IMO has adopted a number of conventions addressing marine pollution and oil spills, most importantly the International Convention for the Protection of the Marine Environment from Pollution by Ships of 1973/78 (MARPOL 1973/78).

In contrast, environmental protection is not among the explicit objectives of ICAO (compare Art. 3, IMO Convention, and Art. 44, ICAO Convention). However, according to Article 44(d) of the ICAO Convention, the organization aims at, inter alia, meeting "the needs of the peoples of the world for safe, regular, efficient and economical air transport." The Convention allows for the establishment of committees as appropriate (Diederiks-Verschoor 1993, 36–40). The Committee on Aviation Environmental Protection (CAEP) that was established by the ICAO Council in 1983—superseding two committees on aircraft noise and aircraft engine emissions created in the 1970s—prepares the Council's decisions on environmental matters. ICAO has elaborated a limited number of environmental standards, most importantly regarding nitrogen oxide emissions of aircraft.

The Trigger of the Interaction: The Request by the Kyoto Protocol

A request of the climate change regime to ICAO and IMO marks the beginning of the interaction (figure 3.1). Article 2.2 of the Kyoto Protocol implicitly contains this request by committing industrialized countries to "pursue limitation or reduction of emissions of greenhouse gases not controlled by the Montreal Protocol from aviation and marine bunker fuels [i.e., the fuel sold to and burned by aircraft and ships in international transport], working through the International Civil Aviation Organization and the International Maritime Organization, respectively." It was the result of a political deadlock during the elaboration of the Kyoto Protocol. In protracted discussions, the parties to the UNFCCC were unable to reach agreement on how to deal with GHG emissions from international transport. Consequently, such emissions are not subject to the emission targets agreed on in Kyoto, and the parties decided to turn to ICAO and IMO (Oberthür 2003, 193).

International transport contributes a significant and growing share to global GHG emissions. According to the available data, international aviation and shipping

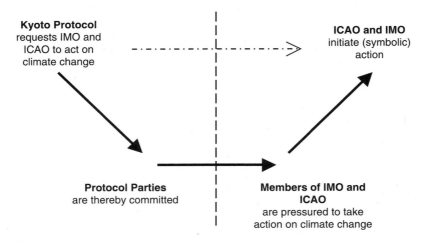

Figure 3.1
Kyoto Protocol triggers action by IMO and ICAO

account for about 4 percent of global CO_2 emissions in total. This is in the range of German CO_2 emissions in the 1990s. The IPCC has estimated the share of international aviation to have amounted to about 2 percent in 1992. Aviation's overall contribution to radiative forcing even amounted to 3.5 percent due to other factors (buildup of ozone, contrails, and so on). International shipping has been found to have been responsible for about 1.8 percent of global CO_2 emissions in 1996 (while accounting for a much larger volume of freight than air transport). While CO_2 emissions from aviation were set to increase dynamically by about 3 percent per year between 1990 and 2015, shipping emissions are to increase by at least 1–2 percent per year (IPCC 1999; IMO 2000; WBGU 2002; UNFCCC 2002). On the basis of these growth rates, emissions from international transport would double around 2020.

The request of the Kyoto Protocol increased the pressure on IMO and ICAO to address GHG emissions from international transport. The Protocol committed its parties (in particular industrialized-country parties) to take action on GHG emissions from international transport. Because of the large overlap in membership, this commitment essentially concurrently extended to most member states of IMO and ICAO. Furthermore, the commitment contained the implicit threat that restrictions on GHG emissions from aviation and marine bunker fuels could in principle be imposed under the climate change regime, which would be of immediate relevance to air and sea transport fostered by ICAO and IMO. The regulatory competition with the climate change regime has been an important motivation for both organizations' efforts to deal with climate change. Thus, the ICAO Assembly called on the ICAO Council not to leave the initiative on aviation matters related to the environment "to other organizations" (Abeyratne 2001, 38). Less strongly, the IMO Assembly declared that IMO "should take the lead in developing GHG limitation and reduction strategies and mechanisms for international shipping" (IMO 2003). Overall, the case for taking action on climate change within both organizations was strengthened.

The threat of regulatory competition has, however, remained weak. First of all, the Kyoto Protocol only entered into force in 2005. In the interim, regulation of GHG emissions from international transport had basically fallen off the agenda of the UNFCCC for several years after Kyoto. Activities within the UNFCCC focused on, and remained confined to, improving the informational basis. Initiatives by the EU and others regularly failed to significantly advance the issue due to resistance in particular by the United States and oil-producing countries (Oberthür 2003, 199).

Another potential driving force, the threat of unilateral action, has also remained weak. Transnational aviation and shipping interests at times prefer uniform international regulation to a disparate regulatory environment with widely varying national standards. Norway introduced taxation of kerosene in spring 1999 but was forced to abandon the tax when international airlines complained and refused to pay (Oberthür and Ott 1999, 112). The EU has also considered introducing an emission charge/levy for (international) air transport for several years (European Commission 1999). In 2001, the EU Environment Council declared that the EU should take action if no concrete measures were agreed on within ICAO by 2002 (Council of the European Union 2001, para. 5). However, no specific action was in sight as of the end of 2004. Shipping has received less attention mainly due to the fact that it is considered relatively environmentally friendly as compared with air transport. Although the EU announced that the European Commission would identify and undertake specific actions to reduce GHG emissions from shipping if no such action was agreed on within IMO (ECON 2003, 19), no initiative has resulted yet.

The Response by ICAO and IMO: Slow with Uncertain Results

Although they had recognized the problem of climate change before, both ICAO and IMO started to consider effective action on GHG emissions primarily in response to the Kyoto Protocol. ICAO had emphasized the need for further study of the problem in the early 1990s (Crayston 1993, 53) and requested the afore-mentioned Intergovernmental Panel on Climate Change (IPCC) in 1996 to prepare what became the IPCC Special Report on Aviation and the Global Atmosphere (IPCC 1999). Referring to the Kyoto Protocol, the thirty-second ICAO Assembly in 1998 then asked the CAEP "to study policy options to limit or reduce the green-house gas emissions from civil aviation, taking into account the findings of the IPCC special report and the requirements of the Kyoto Protocol" (ICAO 1998, Appendix F; see also Crayston and Hupe 2000, 32). IMO first addressed the issue in September 1997 when the Kyoto Protocol was already looming. An IMO conference called on the organization to undertake a study of CO_2 emissions from ships and the MEPC to identify feasible CO_2-reduction strategies. In November 1998, the MEPC decided to commission a study on GHG emissions from ships, noting explicitly that IMO had the mandate from the Kyoto conference to address the issue (Fayette 2001, 204–208). The study was presented in mid-2000 (IMO 2000).

Both organizations originally considered a similar range of measures (including levies and charges, voluntary measures, technical and operational measures, emission standards, and emissions trading), and they have reached similar conclusions on a number of them. The potential of voluntary measures is rather limited in both international aviation and shipping, given that governments lack a stick to move industry beyond "business as usual" (ECON 2003, 26–27, 36; IMO 2000; Bode et al. 2002, 175–176). Realization of technical and operational improvements is further considered and promoted by both ICAO and IMO (ICAO 2004, Appendix H; IMO 2003), but is either expected to occur regardless of further action in the foreseeable future (IPCC 1999) or hinges on provision of appropriate incentives for shipbuilders and shipowners (IMO 2000). Finally, both organizations have in effect dismissed emission standards and *internationally coordinated* levies or charges as impractical or unwarranted (despite continuing proposals for their introduction: e.g., WBGU 2002). The abandonment of emission standards is particularly note-worthy in the case of the IMO, because of the organization's experience with such standards. In particular, it had been considered that GHG emission standards could become part of Annex VI of the IMO-administered MARPOL Convention on air pollution from ships that was elaborated in the 1990s (Fayette 2001) and currently contains standards for emissions of sulfur dioxide and nitrogen oxides (Pisani 2002).

ICAO has been particular in its discouragement of the unilateral introduction of levies by individual countries. An ICAO recommendation on reciprocal tax exemptions for foreign aircraft has become the norm in international air transport by its incorporation into most bilateral air transport agreements between states. While introducing an emission charge might in principle still be possible, it is difficult to design such a charge so that it would not be considered taxation. In addition, ICAO has defined rather restrictive guidelines for emission-related levies. Accordingly, "The funds collected should be applied in the first instance to mitigating the environmental impact of aircraft engine emissions" (addressing specific damage, funding research). Furthermore, such charges should not serve any fiscal aims, should be related to costs, and "should not discriminate against air transport compared with other modes of transport" (ICAO 1996; see also Abeyratne 2001). While this policy is not legally binding on members and leaves some room for interpretation, the ICAO Assembly mandated further work on the issue by 2007 and, in the interim, urged countries to refrain from unilateral action (ICAO 2004, Appendix I).

Despite the similarities mentioned above, ICAO and IMO have headed off in different directions. The ICAO Assembly assigned priority to the development of "open emissions trading for international aviation" by the Council (ICAO 2001, Appendix I). An "open" emissions-trading system could be connected to the emissions-trading system under the Kyoto Protocol and would thus allow aviation to trade emission permits with other sectors. To implement such a system, a cap on emissions from aviation would need to be defined and the resulting amount of emission allowances allocated to the aviation industry. Given the inconclusiveness of many years of discussions on the allocation of emissions from international transport under the UNFCCC, resolving this issue will represent a major challenge for ICAO. The ICAO schedule originally aimed at finalizing related proposals to the UNFCCC by 2003 (Abeyratne 2001). In 2004, however, the ICAO Assembly endorsed the further development of an open emissions-trading system for international aviation and repeated its previous instruction to the ICAO Council "to develop concrete proposals and provide advice as soon as possible to the Conference of the Parties of the UNFCCC" (ICAO 2004, Appendix I).

While it had originally also put emphasis on emission standards and emissions trading (MEPC 2002; UNFCCC 2002; ECON 2003, 12–13), IMO has shifted its focus toward "GHG emission indexing." GHG emission indexing refers to the determination of a set of environmental criteria (emission standards, technological and operational measures) that can be used to give an index to each vessel indicating its GHG emission performance. It can provide a basis for differentiating taxes, port dues, and charges or insurance rates, but had not received a particular blessing in the aforementioned IMO study of 2000 (IMO 2000, 150–151). GHG emission indexing grants particular flexibility to shipowners/operators, since they can choose between different components of the index for achieving any required improvement. At the end of 2003, the IMO Assembly adopted a resolution on "IMO Policies and Practices Related to the Reduction of Greenhouse Gas Emissions from Ships" that had been prepared by a Correspondence Group established by the MEPC (MEPC 2002; UNFCCC 2002). The resolution in particular mandates the MEPC to develop GHG emission indexing further. The resolution also allows further work on emissions trading by calling for the evaluation of "market-based solutions" (IMO 2003). In 2004, the MEPC further developed a CO_2-indexing scheme and asked members to apply it in a trial period (http://www.imo.org). The work has, however, not resulted in any binding measures yet.

Conclusions and Outlook

ICAO and IMO have started consideration of action on GHG emissions from aviation and maritime transport, but have not gone beyond "symbolic" action yet. More than seven years after the adoption of the Kyoto Protocol, neither of the organizations has agreed on any tangible measures, and it is doubtful whether this situation will change in the foreseeable future. On the one hand, climate change does not belong to their core concerns, contributing further to an already heavy workload, and mitigating emissions from international aviation and shipping may even be considered incompatible with the organizations' main objective of furthering these sectors. On the other hand, the threat of regulatory competition by the climate change regime, the EU, and individual countries has remained rather weak. Furthermore, disagreement over whether any measures would have global coverage or should only apply to industrialized countries has delayed progress.

In the case of IMO, the slow progress is also due to two other factors. First, IMO has perceived sea transport as part of the solution rather than as part of the problem. Shipping is seen as a comparatively environmentally friendly transport mode and its contribution to climate change as "relatively small" (MEPC 2002; see also IMO 2000, 169; UNFCCC 2002). Second, IMO has stressed that placing an additional burden on shipping requires similar measures to be taken with respect to other modes of transport (i.e., aviation). Otherwise, shipping might become uncompetitive, which would lead to a modal shift to less environmentally friendly modes of transport (IMO 2000; UNFCCC 2002).

The lack of coordination between ICAO, IMO, and the climate change regime provides a further indication of the current stalemate. The demand for coordination is apparent not only because there is a need to ensure that international aviation and shipping contribute their fair share to the overall endeavor. A particular demand for coordination exists with respect to an open emissions-trading system envisaged by ICAO because it requires compatibility with the system of emissions trading under the Kyoto Protocol. To date, however, members of the three institutions have responded to this demand for coordination primarily by exchanging information through mutual participation in meetings and reporting on relevant developments and decisions by the respective secretariats. In reality, reports have triggered little substantive debate and have resulted in very limited follow-up. As a result, members of the climate change regime may identify insufficiencies and incompatibilities of any measures only after ICAO and IMO have elaborated them (see in more detail Oberthür 2003, 200–202).

On the basis of the preceding analysis, we can identify in particular three options for enhancing the willingness and ability of ICAO and IMO to take effective action in the future:

1. Since the potential regulatory competition by the climate change regime has already been a significant driving force in the past, continuing work on measures to limit and reduce GHG emissions from international transport within the climate change regime could help keep up the pressure on ICAO and IMO. The entry into force of the Kyoto Protocol in early 2005 may improve this prospect.

2. The implementation of domestic action by individual states could enhance the willingness of aviation and shipping interests as well as state governments to accept effective international regulation. Because the EU is the biggest contributor to bunker-fuel emissions by contributing a good third of reported emissions of this source from industrialized countries, it is less constrained by considerations of competitive disadvantages than others and appears particularly suited to taking such action. Other OECD countries in favor of effective action to address, in particular, GHG emissions from aviation (e.g. Norway, Switzerland, New Zealand) could be expected to get on the EU "bandwagon" by taking equivalent action.

3. Through their deliberation, ICAO and IMO may "learn" that effective action on climate change is compatible with and may even be supportive of their general objectives. Controlling GHG emissions may not appear to be immediately and directly supportive of the orderly development of international shipping and air transport. However, GHG emission control may well increase its legitimacy and

acceptance, and can thus contribute to achieving the core objectives of ICAO and IMO. Public-awareness campaigns about the environmental impacts of international transport may further such a learning process.

Potential for creating synergy between the climate change regime and IMO and ICAO thus exists. Should ICAO and/or IMO fail in their efforts, however, GHG emissions from international transport may have to be addressed by the climate change regime. Even if the targeted organizations took action, measures under the UNFCCC and its Kyoto Protocol could complement such regulation.

Facilitating and Strengthening International Cooperation on Climate Change: The EU Burden-Sharing Agreement

On the basis of an agreement on differentiated targets of the then fifteen EU member states reached in March 1997, the EU constituted the major leader in the Kyoto negotiations. Without this Burden-Sharing Agreement, a similar leadership coalition could not have emerged. Consequently, the Agreement facilitated and strengthened the commitments agreed to in Kyoto (Interaction through Commitment). Subsequently, the Kyoto Protocol prompted the codification of the burden sharing in EU law, which strengthened the Protocol's implementation by subjecting compliance of EU member states with their quantitative emission commitments to the special enforcement powers of the EU.

Strengthening and Facilitating Agreement in Kyoto

The EU member states reached a first Burden-Sharing Agreement about nine months prior to the Kyoto conference in March 1997. It foresaw differentiated targets for the individual member states ranging from +40 percent for Portugal to −30 percent for Luxembourg and amounted to an overall GHG emission reduction of 9.2 percent. The Agreement remained conditional on an acceptable outcome of the international negotiations. It was a consequence of the EU's long-established objective to act jointly in international climate policy, because competence in this area is shared between the EU and its member states (Oberthür and Ott 1999, 141–142). Table 3.2 provides the differentiated targets under the Burden-Sharing Agreement of 1997 together with the figures as adapted to the outcome of the Kyoto negotiations in 1998 and subsequently codified in EU law in 2002.

The Agreement of 1997 committed the EU member states to a common position and thus established the EU as a powerful leading coalition favoring stringent emis-

Table 3.2
The EU Burden-Sharing Agreements of 1997 and 1998/2002

Member state	1997: emission reduction by 2010	1998/2002: emission reduction by 2008–2012
Luxembourg	−30%	−28%
Denmark	−25%	−21%
Germany	−25%	−21%
Austria	−25%	−13%
United Kingdom	−10%	−12.5%
Belgium	−10%	−7.5%
Netherlands	−10%	−6%
Italy	−7%	−6.5%
Finland	0%	0%
France	0%	0%
Sweden	+5%	+4%
Ireland	+15%	+13%
Spain	+17%	+15%
Greece	+30%	+25%
Portugal	+40%	+27%
EU-Total	**−9.2%**	**−8%**

Note: While targets of 1997 relate to CO_2, CH_4 and N_2O, targets of 1998/2002 relate to all GHGs regulated under the Kyoto Protocol.

sion reductions in the negotiations on the Kyoto Protocol (figure 3.2). It took the form of Council conclusions that do not bind member states legally but entail a strong political commitment. The differentiated targets of EU member states under the Agreement of 1997 are indicative of the range of positions of individual member states. However, several EU member states had to make concessions so that the Agreement went significantly beyond the original aggregate of the positions of individual EU member states (e.g., Ringius 1999). In the absence of the Burden-Sharing Agreement, member states would thus have pursued widely diverging interests (table 3.2), with some of them probably favoring even less stringent targets. Overall, the Agreement created an otherwise unlikely coalition of fifteen industrialized countries in the Kyoto negotiations.

First of all, acting as a united coalition, the EU facilitated reaching agreement in Kyoto by reducing the number of negotiating parties. The trilateral negotiations between the United States (with an emission share of 36.1 percent), Japan (8.5

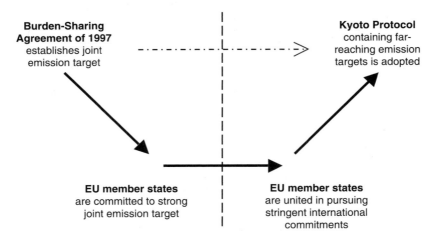

Figure 3.2
EU Burden-Sharing Agreement facilitates and strengthens Kyoto Protocol

percent), and the EU (24.2 percent) in Kyoto covered more than 68 percent of industrialized countries' CO_2 emissions in 1990. Reaching a similar coverage without the EU acting in unity would have meant increasing the number of negotiating parties at least to eight (United States, Japan, Germany, United Kingdom, Canada, Italy, Poland, France)[2] or, alternatively, seventeen (if all EU member states had been involved separately). Such an increase would have placed a considerable burden on the negotiations and would have increased the likelihood of failure, because it is "almost axiomatic that the more parties (and issues), the higher the costs, the longer the time, and the greater the informational requirements for a negotiated settlement" (Sebenius 1983, 308–309). It would have added to an already very high complexity and great time pressure (on the negotiations in Kyoto, see Oberthür and Ott 1999, chap. 7). In addition, it would have been difficult to establish which countries were to participate in the core negotiations without the EU acting in a unitary fashion, since there is no clear line between countries such as France (2.7 percent), the United Kingdom (4.3 percent), Canada (3.3 percent), and Italy (3.1 percent) (emission shares according to the Appendix of the Kyoto Protocol).

The EU acting in unity was also instrumental in achieving concessions from Japan and the United States and thus in strengthening the targets agreed on in Kyoto. In the political bargaining process with the United States and Japan—which was complemented by pledges of other industrialized countries—the EU, based on its

Burden-Sharing Agreement, supported the deepest GHG emission cut of 15 percent. In the absence of a common EU position, stringent targets would have received far less international support because only some member states would have supported them. The United States (stabilization) and Japan (small reduction) would have found it much easier to defend their positions because they would have been neatly in the middle of other countries. Accordingly, Australia, which demanded a growth target for itself, unsuccessfully tried to establish the differentiated targets of EU member states as the reference point in the international negotiations by proposing that industrialized countries' targets should be within a range of −30 percent to +40 percent (Oberthür and Ott 1999, 144). But compared with the common position of the EU, the other major players came under pressure. They eventually accepted targets close to the EU's (EU: −8 percent; United States: −7 percent; Japan: −6 percent) (on the negotiations see Oberthür and Ott 1999, chaps. 4–7). Accordingly, there is broad agreement in the literature that without the EU, the commitments by the United States and Japan would have been lower.

The Revision of the Burden-Sharing Agreement: Supporting Effective Climate Protection

The first interaction between the EU Burden-Sharing Agreement and the Kyoto Protocol resulted in two follow-up cases. First, the Kyoto Protocol triggered the revision of the Burden-Sharing Agreement and its codification in supranational EU law (Interaction through Commitment). Second, as a result of this codification, the supranational enforcement mechanisms of the Union provide a particular incentive to EU member states to comply with their Kyoto targets and thus support the effective implementation of the Protocol (Behavioral Interaction).

While there was no time in Kyoto to fix targets for each EU member state, Article 4 of the Kyoto Protocol allowed any group of countries to fulfill their commitments under the Protocol jointly and, to this end, to redistribute their emission allowances among them.[3] After notification of the secretariat at the time of ratification, the redistribution cannot be further modified. EU member states had an obvious interest in using Article 4, which had been included at the EU's request. Given the internal differences in starting points and positions, the then fifteen EU member states and the EU itself could only become parties to the Kyoto Protocol if they redistributed their common target of −8 percent under Article 4. It is worth highlighting that, by means of Article 4, the Kyoto Protocol in fact delegated the task of fixing targets for individual EU member states to the EU itself. The Kyoto Protocol thus indirectly made use of the comparatively sophisticated framework of decision making of the EU to reach binding agreement between member states, which is the daily bread of the Union. As a result, the international negotiations were relieved of the burden of establishing targets for fifteen states.

EU member states agreed on a revised Burden-Sharing Agreement in mid-1998 and codified it under supranational EU law in 2002. The Agreement of 1997 needed adaptation in light of the outcome of the Kyoto negotiations. While the 1997 Agreement had been related to three GHGs (CO_2, CH_4, N_2O), the Kyoto targets also included fluorinated GHGs. The Kyoto Protocol established a commitment period of 2008–2012, whereas the 1997 Agreement referred to 2010 as a single target year. Finally, the latter amounted to overall reductions of 9.2 percent, while the common EU target under the Kyoto Protocol was −8 percent. Targets of individual member states under the revised Burden-Sharing Agreement range from +27 percent for Portugal to −28 percent for Luxembourg (table 3.2). The 1998 Agreement became legally binding in spring 2002 as part of the Council Decision to ratify the Kyoto Protocol (European Union 2002). The UNFCCC Secretariat was notified on ratification of the Protocol on May 31, 2002.

The codification of the Burden-Sharing Agreement in supranational law has created an additional incentive for EU member states to comply with their commitments under the Protocol and thus supports climate protection. It hardened the international commitments of EU member states to limit and reduce GHG emissions. By means of the Council Decision, the Agreement became part of the supranational law of the EU and is thus subject to the supranational adjudication and enforcement mechanisms of the Union. In particular, the European Commission will monitor EU member states' compliance with their targets and may initiate infringement proceedings, if required. As a result, noncompliant member states may be brought before the European Court of Justice (ECJ), which issues binding rulings and may even authorize financial penalties to be imposed by the Commission. While a similar enforcement mechanism does not exist for any other party to the Kyoto Protocol, it provides a powerful additional incentive for EU member states to comply with their Kyoto targets and thus enhances climate protection.

Conclusions

Reflecting climate change's manifold causes and consequences, the international regime on climate change influences and is influenced by a great number of other international institutions and EU legal instruments. A considerable potential exists for further interactions that may materialize in the future. Institutional interactions of the climate change regime cover all three major causal mechanisms. On some occasions, they have resulted in synergy, while leading to tensions on others, in particular if involving institutions from other policy fields. In many cases, there is potential for creating or enhancing synergy.

The horizontal interaction with ICAO and IMO followed the causal mechanism of Interaction through Commitment and exemplifies the at times problematic relationship between the climate change regime and economic institutions. The Kyoto Protocol's request to ICAO and IMO committed the members of the climate change regime (in particular industrialized countries) to addressing GHG emissions from international transport. The request created pressure on both organizations and empowered the proponents of action on GHG emissions among their members because it carried the implicit threat of regulatory action under the climate change regime, if ICAO and IMO failed to take action. In response, both organizations have begun to address the issue. However, coordination between them and with the climate change regime has barely occurred yet. Furthermore, the objectives of ICAO and IMO to enhance international air and sea transport hardly led them to advance their efforts of their own accord. In addition, the threat of regulatory competition by the climate change regime and individual actors has remained weak. As a result, neither of the organizations has gone beyond "symbolic" action, and little progress in addressing GHG emissions from international transport has been achieved to date. Under the circumstances, the future success of the interaction is also in doubt. Progress may in particular be driven by (1) a strengthened threat of regulatory action within the climate change regime, (2) domestic action by the EU and other countries, and (3) a learning process within ICAO and IMO. In any event, the request of the Kyoto Protocol begs the question of which of the institutions involved will regulate GHG emissions from international aviation and shipping (and to what extent).

The vertical interaction with the EU Burden-Sharing Agreements of 1997 and 1998/2002 demonstrates the potential of the EU to promote the development and implementation of international institutions. The Agreement of 1997 triggered a case of Interaction through Commitment, facilitating and strengthening agreement on the Kyoto Protocol. By committing EU member states to a stringent joint target, the Agreement united the EU to form a leadership coalition pushing for strong emission limitation and reduction targets in the Protocol negotiations. This coalition even included EU member states that would not have requested strong commitments on their own. As a result, the EU was able to secure more stringent commitments from its negotiating partners in Kyoto than would otherwise have been the case. Furthermore, getting to agreement in Kyoto was significantly facilitated primarily because the number of core negotiating partners was reduced to three.

As a follow-up, the Kyoto Protocol in effect delegated to the EU itself the distribution of the EU target to individual member states. The international process was thus relieved of this task and the advanced decision-making capacity of the EU employed to this end. The resulting Burden-Sharing Agreement of 1998/2002 in turn supported the implementation of the Protocol by subjecting EU member states to the particular enforcement powers of the European Union. In case of noncompliance, EU member states may face financial penalties authorized and enforced by the European Court of Justice. In this way, the Burden-Sharing Agreement significantly hardens the quantitative emission commitments for EU member states. This finding contrasts starkly with persistent allegations by other OECD countries and the United States in particular that the allowance to fulfill their commitments jointly represents an unjustified preferential treatment of EU member states (Oberthür and Ott 1999, chap. 12).

Under certain circumstances, the EU can thus help advance international negotiations decisively and can strengthen the implementation of international commitments. EU member states could credibly commit to the targets of the Burden-Sharing Agreement because the supranational structure of the EU facilitates concluding binding agreements (which is the daily bread of EU policymaking). The EU provides a forum for twenty-five countries at present to coordinate their position and to share and implement their international commitments by employing the supranational powers of the EU. It may also be possible to take advantage of the particularly high "problem-solving capacity" of the EU more frequently in other contexts in which it can be left to the EU to share/implement a joint international commitment.

Notes

1. Legally, the European Community (EC), not the EU, is a party to both the UNFCCC and the Kyoto Protocol, in addition to the member states. I nevertheless refer to the EU throughout this chapter for ease of reference.

2. Based on the assumption that Russia would also not have participated under these circumstances; for the percentage figures see the Appendix of the Kyoto Protocol.

3. While the Agreement facilitated the negotiations on targets, the issue of how to design the resulting Article 4 of the Kyoto Protocol placed an additional burden on negotiators; see Oberthür and Ott 1999, chap. 12.

References

Abeyratne, Ruwantissa. 2001. ICAO: Some Recent Developments in Aviation and Environmental Protection Regulation. *Environmental Policy and Law* 32 (1): 32–40.

Bail, Christoph, Simon Marr, and Sebastian Oberthür. 2003. Klimaschutz und Recht. In Hans-Werner Rengeling, ed., *Handbuch zum europäischen und deutschen Umweltrecht*, vol. 2, 254–304. Cologne: Carl Heymanns.

Bodansky, Daniel. 1993. The United Nations Framework Convention on Climate Change: A Commentary. *Yale Journal of International Law* 18 (2): 451–558.

Bode, Sven, Jürgen Isensee, Karsten Krause, and Axel Michaelowa. 2002. Climate Policy: Analysis of Ecological, Technical and Economic Implications for International Maritime Transport. *International Journal of Maritime Economics* 4 (2): 164–184.

Buergenthal, Thomas. 1969. *Law-Making in the International Civil Aviation Organization*. New York: Syracuse University Press.

Chambers, W. Bradnee. 1998. International Trade Law and the Kyoto Protocol. In W. Bradnee Chambers, ed., *Global Climate Governance: Inter-Linkages between the Kyoto Protocol and Other Multilateral Regimes*, 39–58. Tokyo: United Nations University, Institute of Advanced Studies.

Chambers, W. Bradnee, ed. 2001. *Inter-Linkages: The Kyoto Protocol and the International Trade and Investment Regimes*. Tokyo: United Nations University Press.

Charnovitz, Steve. 2003. *Trade and Climate: Potential Conflict and Synergies*. Washington, DC: Pew Center on Global Climate Change.

Council of the European Union. 2001. *Climate Change: Preparation of COP 7 in Marrakesh from 29 October to 9 November 2001*. Council Conclusions. Available at http://register .consilium.eu.int/pdf/en/01/st13/13439en1.pdf.

Crayston, John. 1993, January–June. Civil Aviation and the Environment. *UNEP Industry and Environment*: 51–53.

Crayston, John, and Jane Hupe. 2000, October–December. Civil Aviation and the Environment. *UNEP Industry and Environment*: 30–32.

Diederiks-Verschoor, Isabella H. P. 1993. *An Introduction to Air Law*. Deventer: Kluwer Law and Taxation.

ECON. 2003, January. *GHG Emissions from International Shipping and Aviation*. Report 01/03. Oslo: ECON Centre for Economic Analysis.

European Commission. 1999, December 1. *Air Transport and the Environment: Towards Meeting the Challenges of Sustainable Development*. Communication from the Commission to the Council, the European Parliament, the Economic and Social Committee, and the Committee of the Regions. Doc. COM (1999) 640 final. Brussels: European Commission.

European Union. 2002. Council Decision 2002/358/EC of 25 April 2002 Concerning the Approval, on Behalf of the European Community, of the Kyoto Protocol to the United Nations Framework Convention on Climate Change and the Joint Fulfilment of Commitments thereunder. *Official Journal of the European Communities* L 130/1, 15 May 2002.

Fayette, Louise de La. 2001. The Marine Environment Protection Committee: The Conjunction of the Law of the Sea and International Environmental Law. *International Journal of Marine and Coastal Law* 16 (2): 155–238.

ICAO. 1996, December 9. Council Resolution on Environmental Charges and Taxes. Resolution adopted by the Council at the 16th Meeting of its 149th session.

ICAO. 1998. Resolution A32-8: Consolidated Statement of Continuing ICAO Policies and Practices Related to Environmental Protection. Resolutions adopted at the 32nd session of the Assembly, Provisional Edition.

ICAO. 2001. Resolution A33-7: Consolidated Statement of Continuing Policies and Practices Related to Environmental Protection. Resolutions adopted at the 33rd session of the Assembly, Provisional Edition.

ICAO. 2004. Resolution A35-5: Consolidated Statement of Continuing ICAO Policies and Practices Related to Environmental Protection. Resolutions adopted at the 35th session of the Assembly, Provisional Edition.

IMO. 2000, March 31. *Study of Greenhouse Gas Emissions from Ships*. Issue no. 1. London: International Maritime Organization.

IMO. 2003. Resolution A.963(23) adopted on December 5, 2003: IMO Policies and Practices Related to the Reduction of Greenhouse Gas Emissions from Ships. IMO Doc. A 23/Res.963, March 4, 2004. London: International Maritime Organization.

IPCC. 1999. *Aviation and the Global Atmosphere: A Special Report of IPCC Working Groups I and III*. Cambridge: Cambridge University Press.

IPPC. 2001a. *Climate Change 2001: Impacts, Adaptation, and Vulnerability*. A Report of Working Group II of the Intergovernmental Panel on Climate Change. Geneva: Intergovernmental Panel on Climate Change.

IPCC. 2001b. *Climate Change 2001: The Scientific Basis*. Cambridge: Intergovernmental Panel on Climate Change.

Jacquemont, Frédéric, and Alejandro Caparrós. 2002. The Convention on Biological Diversity and the Climate Change Convention 10 Years After Rio: Towards a Synergy of the Two Regimes? *Review of European Community and International Environmental Law* 11 (2): 139–180.

MEPC. 2002. MEPC, 47th session, March 4–8, 2002. Marine Environmental Protection Committee. Available at http://www.imo.org/Newsroom/mainframe.asp?topic_id=109&doc_id=175.

Oberthür, Sebastian. 2001. Linkages between the Montreal and Kyoto Protocols: Enhancing Synergies between Protecting the Ozone Layer and the Global Climate. *International Environmental Agreements: Politics, Law and Economics* 1 (3): 357–377.

Oberthür, Sebastian. 2003. Institutional Interaction to Address Greenhouse Gas Emissions from International Transport: ICAO, IMO and the Kyoto Protocol. *Climate Policy* 3 (3): 191–205.

Oberthür, Sebastian, and Hermann E. Ott (in collaboration with Richard G. Tarasofsky). 1999. *The Kyoto Protocol: International Climate Policy for the 21st Century*. Berlin: Springer.

Pisani, Christian. 2002. Fair at Sea: The Design of a Future Legal Instrument on Marine Bunker Fuels Emissions within the Climate Change Regime. *Ocean Development and International Law* 33 (1): 57–76.

Pontecorvo, Concetta Maria. 1999. Interdependence between Global Environmental Regimes: The Kyoto Protocol on Climate Change and Forest Protection. *Zeitschrift für ausländisches öffentliches Recht und Völkerrecht* 59 (3): 709–749.

Ringius, Lasse. 1999. Differentiation, Leaders, and Fairness: Negotiating Climate Commitments in the European Community. *International Negotiation* 4 (2): 133–166.

Sebenius, James K. 1983. Adding and Subtracting Issues and Parties. *International Organization* 37 (1): 281–316.

UNFCCC. 2002. Subsidiary Body for Scientific and Technological Advice. *Emissions Resulting from Fuel Used for International Transportation: Activities of IMO on Prevention of Air Pollution from Ships; Information by the IMO Secretariat.* Sixteenth session, Bonn, June 3– 14 (on file with author).

WBGU. 2002. *Entgelte für die Nutzung globaler Gemeinschaftsgüter.* Politikpapier 2. Berlin: Wissenschaftlicher Beirat der Bundesregierung Globale Umweltveränderungen.

Yamin, Farhana, and Joanna Depledge. 2004. *The International Climate Change Regime: A Guide to Rules, Institutions and Procedures.* Cambridge: Cambridge University Press.

4

The Convention on Biological Diversity: Tensions with the WTO TRIPS Agreement over Access to Genetic Resources and the Sharing of Benefits

G. Kristin Rosendal

Biological diversity is a broad concept that has been used to embody the variability among all living organisms, including diversity within species (genetic diversity), among species, and among ecosystems. The issue of biological diversity constitutes one of today's greatest challenges, for several reasons. There is an increased awareness and scientific agreement that the current rate of species extinction is extremely high compared to the natural average rate (Wilson 1988; Heywood 1995, 232). As the new biotechnologies greatly enhance the potential utility areas of the world's genetic resources, the economic interests linked to these resources are soaring.[1] One combined effect of these two trends has been a greatly enhanced interest in intellectual property rights and in access to genetic resources and associated technologies.

Among the international instruments that deal with the various facets of biodiversity management, the central treaty is the Convention on Biodiversity (CBD) that was signed in Rio de Janeiro in 1992 and provides an overall legal framework for the issue area. The CBD is not the first international treaty to address species or habitat conservation, but it is the first to comprehensively address conservation, sustainable use, and equity issues related to biological diversity worldwide. Because of the CBD's broad scope, it is hardly surprising that it interacts with a great many other international institutions and EU legal instruments relating to other aspects of nature conservation but also to economic issues (in particular patenting and intellectual property rights).

This chapter explores the institutional interactions of the CBD in general and analyses in detail the way the CBD and the Agreement on Trade-Related Aspects of Intellectual Property Rights (TRIPS Agreement) under the World Trade Organization (WTO) have influenced each other's implementation and performance. To this end, first the general features of the CBD are briefly introduced. Then, an overview of pertinent interactions between the CBD and other international institutions as well as one EU legal instrument is provided. The main analysis of the chapter concerns diverging incentives for behavioral activities stemming from the CBD and the TRIPS Agreement. It examines the claim that both regimes may undermine each other's implementation by inducing behavioral changes that run counter to the objectives of the other institution. This case of interaction is not only of interest because of the salience of the underlying political conflict. It also provides an interesting example in which influence runs both ways and the two institutions involved concurrently undermine each other in an "arms race" fueled by different actors pursuing their interests based on the diverging norms emanating from the two regimes.

The Convention on Biological Diversity

The CBD entered the international negotiation arena in 1989, was signed at the 1992 UN Conference on Environment and Development (UNCED) in Rio de Janeiro, and entered into force in December 1993. The CBD is governed by a Conference of the Parties (COP) that is supported by a Subsidiary Body on Scientific, Technical, and Technological Advice (SBSTTA). The CBD secretariat is located in Montreal and has 36 professionals and 26 support staff (2003-4). As of mid-2005, 188 states had ratified the CBD.

The Convention on Biological Diversity is built on a threefold, interacting objective: "the conservation of biological diversity, the sustainable use of its components and the fair and equitable sharing of the benefits arising out of the utilization of genetic resources" (Art. 1). To this end, the CBD introduces a number of important commitments and instruments. Parties shall develop national biodiversity strategies, integrate biodiversity conservation in all policy levels and sectors, identify and monitor biodiversity, establish systems of protected areas, and identify activities that are likely to have adverse effects on biodiversity. Moreover, the parties shall adopt economically and socially sound measures to act as incentives for conservation and sustainable use; establish programs for scientific and technical education and training for identification and conservation; and provide support for such training in developing countries. The CBD is equipped with a monitoring mechanism in the form of national reporting and an incentive mechanism in the form of the Global Environment Facility (GEF).

In several respects, the CBD constitutes a framework agreement that needs to be further developed and specified. For example, Article 19.3 commits parties to the CBD to consider the elaboration of a protocol addressing the safe transfer, handling, and use of genetically modified organisms. On this basis, the Cartagena Protocol on Biosafety was adopted in 2000 and entered into force in 2003. While this chapter does not address the Cartagena Protocol, the interaction between the Protocol and the WTO is analyzed in chapter 8.

The provisions on access to genetic resources, including the equitable sharing of the benefits of their utilization, form a central element of the CBD. The CBD defines genetic resources as genetic material of actual or potential value (Art. 2). They may be categorized as plant, animal, and microbiological genetic resources and are of fundamental importance for agriculture and a number of industry sectors, including the pharmaceutical sector. The bulk of the world's terrestrial species are found in tropical forests in the South (UNEP 1995, 749). In contrast, it is primarily the developed countries of the North that possess the technological and economic capacity to reap—assisted by intellectual property rights—the ever larger benefits from the genetic variability employed in the agribusiness and pharmaceutical industries (Kate and Laird 1999). Because these industrial actors were pushing hard for a strengthening of intellectual property rights systems within the TRIPS Agreement of the WTO (Rosendal 2000), the issue of access to and sharing of benefits from the utilization of genetic resources became central in the CBD negotiations and was linked to the responsibility for costly biodiversity conservation.

The essential agreement within the CBD is that equitable sharing of the benefits from the use of genetic resources is a precondition for their conservation and sustainable use. Largely as a response to the general developments in patent legislation, of which the TRIPS negotiations constituted a significant part, the CBD reconfirmed national sovereign rights to genetic resources (Art. 15.1) and equitable sharing of benefits from use of those resources (Art. 15.7). Access to the resources shall be based on mutually agreed terms and be subject to prior informed consent (Art. 15.4 and 15.5). This is to ensure that the providers of genetic resources get their fair share of the benefits derived from their use. Article 15.2 declares that the parties shall facilitate access to the same resources. In the last phases of negotiations, and as a direct response to the TRIPS Agreement that was being negotiated in the Uruguay Round of international trade talks, the CBD was equipped with Article 16.5, which establishes that intellectual property rights (IPR) systems should "not run counter to the objectives in the CBD." Here, the diverging objectives constituting the two regimes are explicitly referred to. At the same time, Article 16.2 states that the technology-transfer process is to be consistent with "the adequate and effective protection of intellectual property rights." Article 16.2 implies that the CBD sanctions IPR, but only on certain conditions that are further specified in Articles 15.4, 15.5, and 16.5. In sum, the CBD aims directly at the skewed distribution of biological resources and biotechnology between the North and the South by providing a legal basis for developing countries to demand a share of the benefits from the utilization of genetic resources.[2]

Institutional Interactions in Conservation and Management of Biodiversity

The CBD is a broad convention, encompassing and transcending a large number of sectors and scales. Conservation and sustainable use pertain to a large array of interrelated sectors, because the main threats to biodiversity—habitat destruction and fragmentation, overexploitation, and displacement by introduced species—are associated with extensive human activities in industry, agriculture, and forestry. As a consequence, the CBD touches on a great number of international and regional agreements. Investigating the interactions with all of them is beyond the scope of this chapter. For example, the CBD is likely to interact with international institutions aimed at fisheries management, which are not investigated here. In the following, I provide an overview of the institutional interactions with three clusters of instruments pertaining to biodiversity conservation, forest management, and access and benefit sharing relating to genetic resources. These cases of interaction are summarized in table 4.1. Interactions with the EU Habitats Directive are addressed in chapter 10.

First, the CBD interacts with a number of international institutions that share the objective of conserving biological diversity. In particular, the Convention on International Trade in Endangered Species of Wild Fauna and Flora (CITES; see chapter 7), the Ramsar Convention on Wetlands, and the Convention on Migratory Species of Wild Animals (CMS) belong to this "biodiversity conservation cluster." The CBD differs from most of the other institutions within this cluster in its strong, additional foci on sustainable use and equitable sharing (Rosendal 2001b). However, the implementation of the more specific agreements just mentioned generally contributes to the objective of conserving biological diversity enshrined in the broader CBD. To the extent that they lead to an effective implementation, CITES, the Ramsar Convention, and the CMS therefore quasi-automatically support the CBD at the outcome level (Behavioral Interaction). The institutions in this cluster attempt to further enhance synergy by developing joint working plans and memoranda of cooperation as well as cooperating on streamlining their national reporting, scientific data

Table 4.1
Interactions of the Convention on Biological Diversity

Biodiversity conservation cluster	
Convention on International Trade in Endangered Species of Wild Fauna and Flora (CITES)	• Implementation of CITES helps CBD achieve its targets.
Ramsar Convention on Wetlands	• Implementation of Ramsar Convention helps CBD achieve its targets.
Convention on Migratory Species (CMS)	• Implementation of CMS helps CBD achieve its targets.
Forest-management cluster	
UN Forum on Forests (and predecessors)	• CBD has facilitated international forest talks that could build on agreements reached under it.
Kyoto Protocol	• Protocol provides incentives for fast-growing monocultural forest plantations endangering biological diversity protected under the CBD.
Access and benefit-sharing cluster	
WTO TRIPS Agreement	• TRIPS Agreement affected negotiations of the CBD on equitable sharing/access to genetic resources. • TRIPS rules on patenting engender behavior at odds with CBD objectives on equitable sharing/access. • CBD objectives on equitable sharing/access to genetic resources lead to cumbersome patent protection at odds with TRIPS Agreement.
FAO International Undertaking on Plant Genetic Resources for Food and Agriculture (1983)	• FAO Undertaking influenced negotiations on CBD regarding property rights and access to genetic resources.
FAO Treaty on Plant Genetic Resources for Food and Agriculture (2001)	• CBD influenced FAO Treaty regarding access to genetic resources.
EU Patent Directive	• CBD objectives on equitable sharing/access to genetic resources influenced preparation of EU Patent Directive. • Patent Directive may undermine the implementation of the CBD objectives on equitable sharing/access.

collection, and information exchange (Rosendal and Andresen 2003; Stokke and Thommessen 2003).

A second cluster involves the international institutions that have a specific bearing on forest management, including in particular the UN Forum on Forests (and its predecessors) and the global climate change regime. Forest management has been part of the CBD agenda and has been discussed separately by governments, first in the context of the preparations for UNCED, then in forums under the Commission on Sustainable Development and the UN Economic and Social Council, and finally in the UN Forum on Forests. Because of the overlap of agendas, the separate forest discussions were able to benefit from agreements reached under the CBD on relevant issues, which could easily be transferred and used as a basis of the forest discussions (Interaction through Commitment). At the same time, a certain competition exists between both processes because both the UN Forum on Forests and the CBD claim authority over regulating forest management. This competition would become particularly prevalent, if the UN Forum were to result in the elaboration of a forest convention, as some actors demand. Furthermore, the regulations emanating from the Kyoto Protocol to the United Nations Framework Convention on Climate Change (UNFCCC) may have a significant negative impact on forest biodiversity because they provide incentives for establishing fast-growing monocultural forest plantations (Behavioral Interaction). From the point of view of biological diversity, however, such massive uniformity is synonymous with genetic erosion (Gillespie 1999; Rosendal 2001c; see chapter 3).

Third, several regimes are engaged in a delicate balance between the concerns for protecting inventions and encouraging innovations in agriculture and pharmaceuticals on the one hand, and environmental and distributional concerns on the other (Rosendal 2001a; Raustiala and Victor 2004). Both the International Undertaking on Plant Genetic Resources for Food and Agriculture of 1983 of the Food and Agriculture Organization of the United Nations (FAO) and the FAO Treaty on Plant Genetic Resources for Food and Agriculture of 2001 belong to this access and equitable sharing cluster. The FAO Undertaking that predates the CBD influenced its provisions regarding property rights and access to genetic resources. Subsequently, the CBD influenced the relevant provisions of the FAO Treaty (Interaction through Commitment). The objective of the WTO TRIPS Agreement is to strengthen and expand IPR systems worldwide. The negotiation processes of the CBD and the TRIPS Agreement coincided in time—between 1988 and 1993—so that what went on in one forum affected what went on in the other. In particular, the parallel TRIPS negotiations enhanced the interest especially of developing countries in protecting their claims regarding equitable sharing and access to genetic resources within the CBD negotiations (Interaction through Commitment). As a result, both agreements have been working at cross-purposes at the implementation level (Behavioral Interaction), as further detailed in the next section. It is worth mentioning that other international institutions such as the Union for the Protection of New Varieties of Plants (UPOV) and the World Intellectual Property Organization (WIPO) are also active in the field. At the regional level, the EU Directive on Patents in Biotechnology was partly influenced by the EU obligations under the CBD (Interaction through Commitment), but nevertheless draws behavior in the same direction as the TRIPS Agreement (Behavioral Interaction).

Intellectual Property Rights and Genetic Resources

Background

Some of the major ingredients in this interaction take us back to 1980. Originally, international transactions of plant genetic resources were based on the principle of common heritage of mankind. The more widely used definition of this principle implies that the resources should be freely available and accessible to all, regardless of economic and technological strength, and should hence be outside the reach of intellectual property rights (Bilder 1980). This principle was gradually undermined as patent legislation was reinterpreted to cover biological material (Mooney 1983). This was, among other things, an effect of the rapid development of new biotechnologies, which made it possible to overcome what had previously been legal and biological barriers to patenting in biotechnology (Bent et al. 1987; Crespi 1988). In the FAO Undertaking of 1983, developing countries pushed through an agreement that *all* categories of plant genetic resources should be regarded as a common heritage of mankind. They thus aimed to keep all types of breeding material within the public domain and outside the scope of patents. This was in line with the basic principle of the international gene banks—that seeds should be freely available as a source of plant breeding and food security. International gene banks were stocked with seeds from the most commonly used food plants and these seeds were primarily collected from the extensive variation found in the South. In an official interpretation agreed on at a FAO conference in 1989, however, developed countries succeeded in establishing intellectual property rights as compatible with the FAO Undertaking. This reopened the Pandora's Box of property rights to genetic resources.

At that time, the United States among other countries was becoming exasperated by the FAO negotiations on plant genetic resources. It wanted a fresh start by negotiating biodiversity conservation under the auspices of the United Nations Environment Program (UNEP). However, developing countries soon succeeded in adding sustainable use and equitable sharing to that of conservation on the CBD agenda (Pistorius and van Wijk 1999; Rosendal 1991; Svensson 1993; Koester 1997). The South abandoned the common-heritage strategy and successfully demanded reconfirmation of national sovereign rights over genetic resources. A sovereign right is not the same as a property right, because it implies that the state has the prerogative to regulate the area—for example, by establishing property-rights regimes for the resources in question. Simultaneously, in the Uruguay Round of trade negotiations leading up to the WTO and the TRIPS Agreement, the United States, Japan, and less adamantly, the EU successfully demanded that all countries should provide and respect intellectual property protection in all technical fields, including biotechnology. National sovereign rights were hence used as a compromise for accepting, on certain conditions, the expanding use of patents in biotechnology (Rosendal 2000).

If the contentious issue of property rights had been restricted to the agricultural sector, the controversial issue of access and benefit sharing relating to genetic resources might have been left to the non–legally binding FAO instruments—a Commission for plant genetic resources, a never functioning Fund, and the Undertaking. The new biotechnologies, however, also instigated rapid developments within the pharmaceutical sector. In this sector it is primarily the wild genetic resources—with tropical areas of the South as a primary source—that provide raw material for the products of biotechnology. In effect, the benefit-sharing issue came to stay with the CBD (which the United States—concerned with its large biotechnology sector—has persistently refused to ratify).

The developing countries had high expectations with regard to the CBD. After the UNCED Rio Conference in 1992 a central G77 spokesperson proclaimed: "Climate change was theirs (the developed countries)—biodiversity was ours!"[3] Ten years later, twelve countries (Brazil, China, Colombia, Costa Rica, Ecuador, India, Indonesia, Kenya, Mexico, Peru, South Africa, and Venezuela) formed the Group of Allied Mega-Biodiverse Nations to press for rules protecting their rights to genetic resources found on their land. Since equitable sharing is still far off, the Group now aims for more equal trade rules on patenting (Stevenson 2002). What caused the great expectations of the South to plummet? Is part of the answer that the TRIPS Agreement is obstructing the implementation of the CBD's objectives? The following examination of the relationship between the CBD and the TRIPS Agreement is meant to provide some answers. To this end, the TRIPS Agreement is first introduced in more detail in the following, before the largely disruptive relationship between the CBD and the TRIPS Agreement at the implementation level is examined.

The WTO Agreement on Trade-Related Aspects of Intellectual Property Rights
The TRIPS Agreement forms part of the WTO agreements concluded in 1994 as the result of the Uruguay Round of trade negotiations that had commenced in 1986. As of April 2004, the WTO had 147 member states. The TRIPS Agreement represents the third pillar of the WTO, along with the agreements on trade in goods and services (General Agreement on Tariffs and Trade, GATT, and General Agreement on Trade in Services, GATS). As such, it must be adhered to by all states wishing to join the WTO. The TRIPS Agreement embodies the basic WTO principles of nondiscrimination committing WTO parties to "national treatment" (i.e., treating one's own nationals and foreigners equally) and "most-favored-nation treatment" (i.e., equal treatment of all trading partners in the WTO) (Chaytor and Cameron 2000; see also chapter 8). The TRIPS Agreement covers questions about giving adequate protection to intellectual property rights, how countries should enforce those rights, and how to settle disputes on intellectual property between members of the WTO. Most importantly, the TRIPS Agreement is an attempt to standardize the way intellectual property rights are protected around the world and to strengthen this harmonization process in all technological fields—including biotechnology. Intellectual property includes copyright, trademarks, geographic indications, industrial designs, patents, layout designs (topographies) of integrated circuits, and undisclosed information, including trade secrets (http://www.wto.org).

As has been noted, negotiations of the TRIPS Agreement coincided in time with the negotiations of the CBD. Since both agreements aimed to regulate partially overlapping issues, it would have been surprising if they had not already influenced each other during their elaboration. For example, the discussions on intellectual property rights in the Uruguay Round had significant impact on the issues of access and benefit sharing pertaining to genetic resources as debated in the negotiations on the CBD. In turn, the principles elaborated within the CBD negotiations also affected the TRIPS agenda.

With respect to intellectual property rights to varieties of animals and plants, the final compromise embodied in Article 27 of the TRIPS Agreement closely reflects the relevant provisions of Article 53(b) of the European Patent Convention of 1973, which allowed for plants and animals to be excluded from patentability. The European Patent Convention applies primarily in the European Communities and is administered by a European Patent Office (EPO). Article 27 of the TRIPS Agreement on the one hand grants parties the right to exclude from patentability diagnostic, therapeutic, and surgical methods for the treatment of humans and animals (Art. 27.3(a)), and plants and animals other than microorganisms (Art. 27.3(b)). On the other hand, Article 27.3(b) obligates parties to also provide for protection of intellectual property rights for plant varieties, either by patents or by an effective sui generis system (a legal system of its own kind).

Article 27.3(b) of the TRIPS Agreement therefore is of particular relevance for the interaction with the CBD. In this respect, the central question is whether the TRIPS Agreement leaves it up to the parties to design their own sui generis systems, or whether they should preferably choose the breeder's rights system provided by the International Union for the Protection of New Varieties of Plants (UPOV). UPOV was established by the Convention for the Protection of New Varieties of Plants of 1961, which has been revised three times since then. Its purpose is to provide uniform and clearly defined principles for the protection of plant breeders' rights and bring them more in line with patent protection. Before the last revision in 1991, the Convention granted protection only to the final product, the variety, and not to subsequent varieties bred on the basis of the protected one. Farmers were thus free to use such seeds for next year's sowing ("farmers' privilege") and breeders and scientists could use UPOV-protected material for developing new products ("breeders' exemption"), without paying royalties. As a result of the revision of 1991, however, protection under the UPOV Convention has come to resemble patent protection on a number of dimensions, most importantly by restricting the former provisions for farmers and breeders (Walden 1995).

Implementation of the TRIPS Agreement Undermining the CBD

The TRIPS Agreement lays down the ground rules for what must be protected by national patent legislation, including plant varieties and pharmaceuticals. The changes in property-rights regimes pertaining to genetic resources originated from developments in biotechnology. They led to the successful demand by developed countries for all WTO members to provide and respect IPR protection, including in the field of biotechnology. While the TRIPS Agreement does not create a single, universal patent system, it seeks to strengthen, expand the scope for, and harmonize the domestic patent legislation in each of the member countries. Patent legislation is of a national character, and patent protection is applicable only in the country where it has been granted. National patent legislation is largely drawn from international conventions, administered by the World Intellectual Property Organization (WIPO). As multinational corporations seek patent protection around the world, they depend on each country's patent office to grant those rights. Any effect of the TRIPS Agreement on the CBD at the outcome level would thus have to result from strengthened and expanded national patent systems.

The potential for disruptive behavioral effects in the implementation of the two regimes is primarily a result of the fact that the TRIPS Agreement and the CBD pursue divergent policy objectives. While equitable sharing and conservation constitute the core norms and principles of the CBD, the TRIPS Agreement is geared to promote a time-limited exclusive right to genetic resources. The existing system of intellectual property rights and patents does not accommodate nonwestern systems of knowledge and ownership, such as community or farmers' rights. Hence, they can hardly contribute to enhancing equitable sharing and, in effect, they provide little incentive for biodiversity conservation in poor but gene-rich countries (figure 4.1).

In principle, patent protection of genetic resources, as demanded by the TRIPS Agreement, results in restricted access to these genetic resources—while such access is, subject to certain conditions, to be facilitated under the CBD. Access to a rich variety of genetic resources is essential for plant breeding and food security in all parts of the world (Kloppenburg 1988; Kloppenburg and Kleinman 1987; Berg

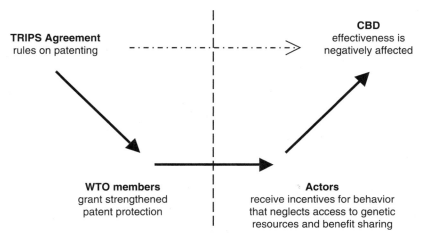

Figure 4.1
Implementation of WTO TRIPS Agreement undermines CBD

1995; Harlan 1995). Applying patents to seeds from the international genebanks is thus seen as representing a threat to the basic principle of free exchange of germ-plasm, on which these genebanks are building (Keystone 1990; Barton and Siebeck 1992). Barton and Berger (2001, 5) conclude that "it may be very expensive or dif-ficult for the public sector to gain access to patented technologies or to use protected varieties for research in developing new applications for the smaller crops or subsis-tence farmers." On the same note, the FAO Commission on Plant Genetic Resources has warned that "if the patent system is applied universally to living matter, includ-ing plants and animals, and their genetic resources, then the principle of unrestricted access will be severely eroded" (FAO 1993, 23). Developing countries maintain that without the IPRs the question of benefit sharing would not arise and all genetic mate-rial could be freely available in the same way as it was historically (Borring 2001).

Patenting may also be incompatible with the CBD objective of equitable sharing of benefits because it grants exclusive rights to only some of those who have contrib-uted to generating the benefit (Hendrickx, Koester, and Prip 1993; Crucible Group 1994; Correa 1999; Egziabher 1999). Patenting is a long and costly business that is primarily employed by large corporations. Transnational corporations hold 90 per-cent of all technology and product patents (Gleckman 1995). The developing world holds no more than 1–3 percent of all patents worldwide (WCED 1987; UNDP 2000, chap. 2). Patenting is hardly a tool for indigenous and local communities, even though these groups often harbor much knowledge about the use of biological resources. Biotechnological products in agriculture often build on local breeders' lines, which represent the end result of the work of generations of farmers. Likewise, pharmaceutical products of biotechnology often build on traditional knowledge about the medicinal traits of biological resources, such as wild plants.[4] There are, as yet, no applicable models for access and benefit sharing or alternative models to IPR laws for protection of traditional knowledge. The knowledge in its traditional form and the nonsystematically bred cultivars hardly fulfill general patent criteria, such as reproducibility, or the UPOV criteria of being "new, distinct, uniform and stable" (Art. 5.1 of the UPOV Convention).

Moreover, patenting may work indirectly to reduce genetic diversity, because patenting is largely an asset of the developed world and a handful of multinational corporations. Protected by patents, these actors dominate the seed industry and pursue their interest in promoting their products. In contrast, developing countries, where much of that diversity is found in situ, have few incentives to conserve their genetic heritage (NORD 1992; Swanson and Johnston 1999; Fauchald 2001).

A central example for the disruptive influence of the TRIPS Agreement is the EU Directive on Patents in Biotechnology that was adopted in 1998 after more than ten years of negotiations in which the CBD and TRIPS-related principles played a prominent role. The negotiation process saw the intense combat between norms associated with the CBD and the TRIPS Agreement respectively. Several EU member states, environmental and farmers' groups, as well as the European Parliament strove to bring the Patent Directive more into line with obligations under the CBD. In the end, however, the Patent Directive gave priority to patent protection for plant varieties and pharmaceuticals without ensuring equitable sharing of benefits from the utilization of genetic resources for patented products.[5] As of September 2004, eleven member states (including France, Austria, Belgium, Germany, and the Netherlands) are lagging behind in their implementation of the Patent Directive.[6] Belgium and Denmark have made specific amendments in their domestic patent legislation in order to bring it more into line with the CBD objectives.

There are also a number of related processes that support the same normative elements as the TRIPS Agreement. The so-called TRIPS plus agreements (Dutfield 2001) are bilateral trade agreements primarily between the United States or EU and a developing country or region, which include requirements for higher patent standards than what the TRIPS Agreement demands (Morin 2003). By 2004, about twenty of these agreements had been concluded. For instance, the trade agreements between the European Union and South Africa and Mexico assert that the parties "shall ensure adequate and effective protection of IPR in conformity with the highest international standards."[7] These agreements ensure implementation in advance of the timetable set up in the TRIPS Agreement and they often include the condition to implement the UPOV Convention of 1991. Although building onto the TRIPS Agreement, these "TRIPS plus" agreements represent bilateralism in contrast to the multilateral system offered by the TRIPS Agreement.

CBD Implementation Undermining the TRIPS Agreement

In contrast to the TRIPS Agreement, the CBD has spurred a great deal of domestic access legislation, in particular in the South. Several developing countries have added as preconditions for access to their genetic resources that any ensuing patent applications should include and identify the source of the genetic material and the traditional knowledge used, evidence of fair and equitable benefit sharing, and prior informed consent. For example, additional disclosure measures are found in the common regime on access to genetic resources established under the Andean Pact by Bolivia, Colombia, Ecuador, Peru, and Venezuela in 1996. This agreement requires that patent applications shall contain authorization to use traditional knowledge (Decision 391). Another example is the 1998 African Model Law for the protection of the rights of local communities, of farmers and breeders, and for the regulation of access to biological resources of the Organization of African Unity (OAU; now the African Union). This model legislation requires a permit and prior informed consent of communities, sharing of benefits from commercial products (50 percent), and community rights to control access to biological resources and knowledge. Currently, close to one hundred developing countries are in the process of making legislation and institutional arrangements to control access to genetic resources. The CBD lists twenty-eight such domestic legal frameworks.[8]

Does this legislation implementing the CBD run counter to the TRIPS Agreement? Article 27.1 of the TRIPS Agreement lists the prevalent patent criteria of novelty, inventive step, industrial application, and reproducibility. Any disclosure requirement such as prior informed consent or proof of fair and equitable benefit sharing contained in the aforementioned legislation comes on top of the TRIPS criteria. It is not clear whether the TRIPS Agreement may prohibit members from including other such requirements or if such activity would be incompatible with the TRIPS Agreement. If this legislation were to be brought to the dispute-settlement body of the WTO, it would have to address the WTO's competence to rule on domestic legislation passed to implement another international instrument—the CBD (Cannabrava 2001). So far, there has been no legal testing of the two regimes.

The proliferation of access legislation in the South has brought up questions about the effects on innovation. Some argue that the emerging legal regimes to regulate access to genetic resources in the South will be an obstacle to technological innovations based on genetic materials (Grajal 1999). To the extent that this is the case, it runs counter to the TRIPS Agreement, because the core objective of the IPR systems established under it is to create incentives for innovation (see figure 4.2). On the same note, in the eyes of the U.S. negotiation team, it was the developing countries that were trying to "hollow out" the TRIPS Agreement by using the CBD (Raustiala 1997, 47).

Assessment and Outlook

The divergent approaches of the CBD and the TRIPS Agreement to access and benefit sharing relating to genetic resources have led to the implementation of legislation in the North and the South that works at cross-purposes, and have resulted in an "arms race." The CBD rests on the principle that equitable sharing of biotechno-

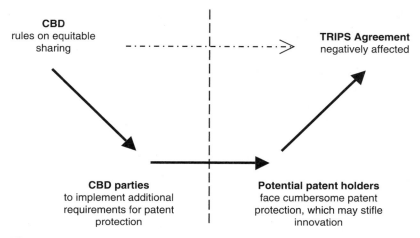

Figure 4.2
Influence of the CBD on the implementation of the WTO TRIPS Agreement

logical use of genetic resources is an essential element of biodiversity conservation and hence encourages such international benefit sharing. In contrast, the TRIPS Agreement has been set up to strengthen and harmonize intellectual property rights in all technological fields, including biotechnology. It thus is hardly compatible with the CBD as regards both equitable benefit sharing and, indirectly, the objective of conservation of biological diversity. Whereas the CBD does not embody legal and economic enforcement mechanisms, patents and intellectual property rights in general are legally enforceable under the WTO dispute-settlement procedure. At the national level, most developed countries have complied with the TRIPS obligation of a strengthened patent system, but have not established legislation for access and benefit sharing in accordance with the CBD. The EU Patent Directive is a case in point. Several newly industrializing countries have also complied with the TRIPS Agreement as part of the package of joining the WTO (Sell 2002). In contrast, the least developed countries have not yet complied with the TRIPS Agreement and many developing countries have put in place legislation to implement the requirements of the CBD concerning benefit sharing. Both sides can thus be seen to have engaged in an arms race at the implementation level (Behavioral Interaction).

There are indications that this arms race will continue and is escalating, fueled by the diverging incentives emanating from the CBD and the TRIPS Agreement. The "TRIPS plus" agreements promoted by the North provide a case in point, as does the Substantive Patent Law Treaty pursued by developed countries in the WIPO because it makes no reference to related processes dealing with traditional knowledge or with access and benefit sharing (Tvedt 2005). On the other hand, national measures to promote technology transfer under Article 16 of the CBD may raise WTO "most-favored-nation" issues if Convention parties and nonparties were treated differently. It might also raise TRIPS issues if owners of proprietary technology were compelled to license technologies on grounds other than those prescribed in the TRIPS Agreement. The regulatory controversy over whether TRIPS Article 27.3(b) allows parties to design their own sui generis systems or implies the use of the plant breeders' rights system provided by UPOV also remains unresolved. Moreover, institutional cooperation remains hampered because the CBD has still not been granted observer status under the TRIPS Agreement, in spite of repeated calls from its Conference of the Parties (COP). In the WTO TRIPS Council, the United States has repeatedly turned down these efforts on the grounds that it does not see the need for them.[9]

In this arms race, the TRIPS Agreement may be better equipped than the CBD. The WTO and its TRIPS Agreement are stronger than the CBD in terms of compliance mechanisms and in being controlled by the more powerful states. The dispute-settlement mechanism of the WTO rates among the strongest of such international instruments. In particular, if WTO members do not comply with the TRIPS Agreement, they may become liable to economic sanctions. Also, patenting in the biotechnology sector is a small part of the larger issue area of international trade and patenting in all sectors. Hence, even though the conflicts are explicitly admitted and attended to, implementation of the CBD objectives may be hampered by the stronger regulatory force of the TRIPS Agreement.

Nevertheless, there is ample evidence that the issue of the two regimes' diverging objectives is recognized in the WTO and the CBD alike, and efforts to mitigate the conflict and increase synergy have been initiated in both forums as well as in third institutions. Within the CBD, the COP has called for examination of the relationship between the CBD objectives and the strengthened IPR systems under the WTO. Moreover, the CBD established a working group on access and benefit sharing, which prepared the Bonn Guidelines adopted at its sixth COP in The Hague in 2002 and further elaborated at the seventh COP in Kuala Lumpur in 2004. The Bonn Guidelines encourage prior informed consent and mutually agreed-on terms by making concrete suggestions for how these principles could be included in bilateral bioprospecting agreements. Significantly, the Bonn Guidelines encourage disclosure of country of origin in patent applications. The Guidelines also propose a certification system for trade in genetic resources and the establishment of an international Ombudsman for monitoring infringements on bioprospecting deals. An unresolved question is how to draw the borders with respect to other international regimes, such as the TRIPS Agreement.

Efforts are also underway in the WTO. As a response to the high level of conflict associated with TRIPS Article 27.3(b), plans for its revision have been in the pipeline several times. Only the deadline for least-developed-country compliance has so far been altered by extending it from 2005 to 2016 at the WTO Doha ministerial meeting in 2001. However, an increasing number of developed and developing countries agree on the need to modify Article 27.3(b) of the TRIPS Agreement (Cannabrava 2001). The Doha Ministerial Declaration of 2001 instructed the WTO members to examine the relationship with the CBD. This has focused on the issue of disclosing the origin of genetic resources used as basis for inventions when applying for patents. In 2000, Brazil demanded that Article 27.3(b) should be amended to include as conditions for patentability (1) the identification of the source of the genetic material; (2) the related traditional knowledge used to obtain that material; (3) evidence of fair and equitable benefit sharing; and (4) evidence of prior informed consent from the government or the traditional community for the exploitation of the subject matter of the patent.[10] In addition, the EU made a turnaround on the issue by tabling a plan to the TRIPS Council in September 2002 with the key proposal to make disclosures (in a multilateral system) of geographic origin of biological material used in biotechnology inventions. Patent applications would be required to provide such disclosure, although this obligation would not constitute a "formal patentability criterion" (European Commission 2002). The EU also addressed the need to provide better protection of traditional knowledge and recognized the right of subsistence farmers in developing countries to reuse and exchange seeds, even if these seeds are covered by intellectual property rights.

Finally, a number of responses by other international forums indicate a growing legitimacy of the CBD objectives and have the potential of mitigating the tensions between the CBD and the TRIPS Agreement. First, UNESCO has addressed traditional knowledge and intellectual property by developing model provisions on the protection of folklore. Second, UNCTAD runs the Biotrade Initiative, which seeks to assist developing countries in developing, at the national level, an institutional environment to facilitate trade and investment in products and services of biological diversity, as a means to attain the objectives of the CBD (http://www.biotrade.org/).

Third, the WIPO Intergovernmental Committee on Intellectual Property and Genetic Resources, Traditional Knowledge and Folklore has yet to decide on the interrelation between access to genetic resources and disclosure requirements in intellectual property applications (Baumüller and Vivas-Eugui 2004). Another WIPO development is the General Assembly decision of October 5, 2004, to adopt a "development agenda." This includes the promotion of developing-country access to knowledge and technology, such as the World Wide Web and the Human Genome Project (Capdevila 2004). An open question is whether this may affect the WIPO negotiation process on the Substantive Patent Law Treaty, which has been insulated from links to the access and benefit-sharing debate, or whether WIPO will mimic the WTO in limiting cooperation with multilateral environmental agreements to the general forums, while not allowing them as observers on more specific topics.[11] Fourth, the FAO International Treaty on Plant Genetic Resources for food and agriculture of 2001 explicitly prohibits patenting of genetic material "in the public domain" and "in the form received" from its multilateral system of genebanks. This multilateral system is aimed at solving problems of access to plant genetic resources in agriculture to ensure that the resources are available for research and plant breeding.

Conclusion

Due to its broad scope, the Convention on Biological Diversity interacts with a great number of other international and regional legal instruments. The link is most obvious in the case of the multitude of other agreements that also pursue the goal of nature conservation, although in a more limited way than the CBD. These include in particular CITES, the CMS, and the Ramsar Convention on wetlands. Based on this commonality of objectives, the relationship with these agreements has been rather harmonious. In contrast, the relationship with a number of instruments pertaining to the use of genetic resources in biotechnology has been more problematic, including in particular regulations to protect intellectual property related to genetic resources such as the WTO TRIPS Agreement and the EU Patent Directive.

The interaction between the CBD and the TRIPS Agreement is based on different objectives and an overlap of memberships and jurisdictional scope, and it has led to disruptive effects on either side. Both regimes have a global membership and regulate the same natural resource, namely genetic resources. At the same time, they operate in different policy fields and pursue different objectives (equitable sharing of benefits versus protection of intellectual property). With both regimes ten years into their implementation phase, their interaction has led to disruptive effects in particular with regard to conservation of, access to, and equitable sharing of benefits from genetic resources. The influence is arguably unintentional, but clearly anticipated. Within both arenas, the parties acknowledge that both regimes influence each other. Most of the interaction has been handled through collective decision making in the two regimes and through behavioral adaptation in their implementation. The result of the interaction so far may to some extent be viewed as an arms race. Strengthened measures within one arena have in turn led to heavier "weapons" being applied by the other. The TRIPS plus agreements, the negotiations on the WIPO Substantial Patent Law Treaty, and legislation implementing the TRIPS Agreement in particular in the North on the one hand contrast with increasingly cumbersome access regulations emerging in many developing countries on the other. Because of the inequality of subsistence farmers and transnational corporations that has been further enhanced by new patent systems, the situation may be more problematic for the biodiversity side.

The existing tensions can be traced back to the regulatory competition between both regimes that has so far not led to a clear delimitation of their jurisdictions. The CBD agenda and the issue linking taking place in the biodiversity negotiations greatly reflected the developments in the WTO/TRIPS negotiations. This was seen most particularly in the early decision to include the issue of access to genetic resources on the CBD agenda, which established the link to domesticated biological resources and emphasized the need for equitable sharing of benefits. In contrast, in the early phases, the biodiversity issue was subordinate to the more general discussions in the WTO. Lately, however, this issue has entered the WTO equation in relation to access to raw material and technological innovation. The pressure to include links to these dimensions within the TRIPS agenda has been steadily growing.

The examination of activities suggests that the quest for enhanced synergies is hard to separate from a debate on values when different objectives clash. Policy measures may facilitate technological innovation, improve conservation, or enhance international equity. However, any one measure will hardly be able to achieve a top score on all dimensions.

Therefore a need exists to increase bridge building and restore mutual trust in this issue area. Klaus Töpfer, head of UNEP, has stated that "the interrelation between the WTO and CBD is extremely high on the agenda. We don't want to wait until we have conflicting cases. We want to do whatever is possible to solve the interrelations between them."[12] A number of relevant activities are underway, including the FAO Treaty on Plant Genetic Resources and the CBD Bonn Guidelines on access and benefit sharing that may turn out to have mitigating effects. Other constructive activities include the EU proposal to the TRIPS Council to make disclosure of origin of genetic material an obligation. This EU proposal constitutes one among the first few steps toward synergy, designed to increase mutual trust among the parties involved in transactions with genetic resources. These activities may indicate that the legitimacy of the CBD objective of equitable sharing is gaining ground. The question of how regimes develop legitimacy is crucial for future transactions with genetic material and will have implications for biodiversity conservation and biotechnological innovation alike.

Notes

1. Biotechnology traditionally includes activities such as baking bread and brewing beer, where different organisms (such as yeast and wheat) interact to create a new product. The concept of "new biotechnologies" indicates more direct dependency on human intervention (recombinant DNA techniques and genomics).

2. The concepts of developing and developed/industrialized countries, or "South" and "North," tend to obscure significant political and economic differences within the two groups. In this case, moreover, most countries are heavily interdependent in their use of genetic resources. Because large parts of the international debate on biodiversity have been formulated as part of a North-South conflict, and for simplicity, I will nevertheless keep to this admittedly simplified dichotomy. The CBD treaty makes specific use of these concepts in designating duties and rights to the parties.

3. Personal communication with Jan P. Borring, senior advisor, Norwegian Ministry of Environment and Norwegian delegation member to the CBD negotiations.

4. Screening results from Shaman Pharmaceuticals revealed that 74 percent of the samples that displayed promising chemical activity directly correlated with the original ethnobotanical use in the context of traditional knowledge (Sheldon and Balick 1995, 58–59).

5. Peter Johan Schei, special advisor to UNEP, Norwegian delegation leader, and director and chair of several working groups and scientific panels to CBD, comments: "There is indeed a conflict and the EU Patent Directive is contrary to the intentions of the CBD" (March 6, 2002, Research Council of Norway, Conference on Sustainable Development).

6. "Biotechnology: EU Countries Still Dragging Feet over Directive on Legal Protection of Inventions," *Europe Information Environment*, 307/2.12-18.2004, p. III3.

7. http://europa.eu.int/comm/trade/bilateral/mercosur/pr240702_en.htm; see also http://www.bilaterals.org.

8. See http://www.biodiv.org/programmes/socio-eco/benefit/measures.aspx, which also contains the mentioned regional measures.

9. Jan P. Borring, special advisor to the Norwegian Ministry of Environment, personal communication, April 2002.

10. Review of Article 27.3(b), Communication from Brazil, Permanent Mission of Brazil, Geneva, WTO document IP/C/W/228, November 24, 2000.

11. Interview with Aimee Gonzales, senior policy advisor, WWF, Gland, Switzerland, September 2004.

12. "Interview—Tensions Mount over Gene Rights, Trade—UNEP," *Planet Arc*, April 9, 2002.

References

Barton, John, and Peter Berger. 2001, Summer. Patenting Agriculture. *Issues in Science and Technology Online*. Available at http://www.nap.edu/issues/17.4/p_barton.htm.

Barton, John, and Wolfgang E. Siebeck. 1992. Intellectual Property Issues for the International Agricultural Research Centres: What are the Options? *Issues in Agriculture*, no. 4. Washington, DC: Consultative Group on International Agricultural Research.

Baumüller, Heike, and David Vivas-Eugui. 2004. Towards Effective Disclosure of Origin: The Role of the International ABS Regime. *Bridges* 8 (4): 21–22.

Bent, Stephen A., Richard L. Schwaab, David G. Conlin, and Donald D. Jeffery. 1987. *Intellectual Property Rights in Biotechnology Worldwide*. New York: Stockton Press.

Berg, Trygve. 1995. Kulturplanter og husdyr. In *Afrika—natur, samfunn og bistand*, edited by Nils Christian Stenseth, Kjetil Paulsen, and Rolf Karlsen. Oslo: Gyldendal, ad Notam.

Bilder, Richard B. 1980. International Law and Natural Resources Policies. *Natural Resources Journal* 20: 451–486.

Borring, Jan Petter. 2001. The International Undertaking on Plant Genetic Resources for Food and Agriculture: Is It Now or Never? *IPRGI Newsletter for Europe* (17): 5.

Cannabrava, Francisco. 2001. TRIPs and the CBD: What Language for the Ministerial Declaration? *Bridges, Between Trade and Sustainable Development*. Special Doha Ministerial Issues 5 (8): 7.

Capdevila, Gustavo. 2004, October 15. South Gains Ground in Intellectual Property Debate. Geneva: Inter Press Service News Agency. Available at http://www.ipsnews.net/africa/interna.asp?idnews=25876.

Chaytor, Beatrice, and James Cameron. 2000. The Treatment of Environmental Considerations in the World Trade Organisation. In Helge Ole Bergesen, Georg Parmann, and Øystein B. Thommessen, eds., *Yearbook of International Co-operation on Environment and Development 1999/2000*, 55–64. London: Earthscan.

Correa, Carlos M. 1999. *Access to Plant Genetic Resources and Intellectual Property Rights*. Background Study Paper No. 8. Rome: FAO Commission on Genetic Resources for Food and Agriculture.

Crespi, R. Stephen. 1988. *Patents: A Basic Guide to Patenting in Biotechnology*. Cambridge: Cambridge University Press.

Crucible Group. 1994. *People, Plants and Patents: The Impact of Intellectual Property on Biodiversity, Conservation, Trade and Rural Society.* Ottawa: International Development Research Centre.

Dutfield, Graham. 2001. Biotechnology and Patents: What Are Developing Countries Doing about Article 27.3(b)? *Bridges.* Post-Doha Ministerial Issue 5 (9): 17–18.

Egziabher, Tevolde B. G. 1999. The TRIPs Agreement of the WTO and the Convention on Biological Diversity: The Need for Co-ordinated Action by the South. *Third World Resurgence* 106: 4–7.

European Commission, Directorate-General for Trade. 2002, September 12. Communication by the European Communities and Their Member States to the TRIPs Council on Review of Article 27.3(b) of the TRIPs Agreement, and the Relationship between the TRIPs Agreement and the Convention on Biological Diversity (CBD) and the Protection of Traditional Knowledge and Folklore. A Concept Paper. Brussels: European Commission.

FAO. 1993. *Harvesting Nature's Diversity.* Rome: Food and Agriculture Organization.

Fauchald, Ole Kristian. 2001. Patenter og Allmenningens Tragedie (Patents and the Tragedy of the Commons). *Lov og Rett. Norsk juridisk tidsskrift* (Norwegian Journal of Legal Affairs) 40: 399–412.

Gillespie, Alexander. 1999. Sinks, Biodiversity and Forests: The Implications of the Kyoto Protocol upon the Other Primary UNCED Instruments. Paper presented at the International Conference on Synergies and Coordination between Multilateral Environmental Agreements, United Nations University, July 14–16, Tokyo.

Gleckman, Harris. 1995. Transnational Corporations' Strategic Responses to Sustainable Development. In Helge Ole Bergesen, Georg Parmann, and Øystein B. Thommessen, eds., *Green Globe Yearbook 1995*, 93–106. Oxford: Fridtjof Nansen Institute and Oxford University Press.

Grajal, Alejandro. 1999. Biodiversity and the Nation State: Regulating Access to Genetic Resources Limits Biodiversity Research in Developing Countries. *Conservation Biology* 13 (1): 6–10.

Harlan, Jack R. 1995. *The Living Fields: Our Agricultural Heritage.* Cambridge: Cambridge University Press.

Hendrickx, Frederic, Veit Koester, and Christian Prip. 1993. Convention on Biological Diversity: Access to Genetic Resources; A Legal Analysis. *Environmental Policy and Law* 23 (6): 250–258.

Heywood, Vernon H. 1995. *Global Biodiversity Assessment.* Cambridge: Cambridge University Press.

Kate, Keriten, and Sara A. Laird. 1999. *The Commercial Use of Biodiversity: Access to Genetic Resources and Benefit-Sharing.* London: Earthscan.

Keystone International Dialogue on Plant Genetic Resources. 1990. *Final Consensus Report.* Madras Plenary Session, February 14, Keystone, Colorado.

Kloppenburg, Jack R. 1988. *First the Seed.* Cambridge: Cambridge University Press.

Kloppenburg, Jack R., and Daniel Lee Kleinman. 1987. The Plant Germplasm Controversy. *BioScience* 37 (3): 190–198.

Koester, Veit. 1997. The Biodiversity Convention Negotiation Process and Some Comments on the Outcome. *Environmental Policy and Law* 27 (3): 175–192.

Mooney, Pat R. 1983. The Law of the Seed: Another Development and Plant Genetic Resources. *Development Dialogue* 1983: 1–2. Uppsala: Dag Hammarskjøld Foundation.

Morin, Jean-Frédéric. 2003. Le Droit International des Brevets: Entre le Multilatéralisme et le Bilatéralisme Américain. *Études internationales* 34 (3): 537–562.

NORD. 1992. *Bioteknologiska Uppfinningar och Immaterialrätten i Norden—del II* (Biotechnological Inventions and Intellectual Property Rights in the Nordic Countries—Part II). Copenhagen: Nordisk Ministerråd (Nordic Council of Ministers).

Pistorius, Robin, and Jeroen van Wijk. 1999. *The Exploitation of Plant Genetic Information.* Doctoral dissertation. Amsterdam: Amsterdam University Press.

Raustiala, Kal. 1997. Global Biodiversity Protection in the United Kingdom and the United States. In Miranda A. Schreurs and Elizabeth C. Economy, eds., *The Internationalization of Environmental Protection*, 42–73. Cambridge: Cambridge University Press.

Raustiala, Kal, and David G. Victor. 2004. The Regime Complex for Plant Genetic Resources. *International Organization* 58 (2): 277–309.

Rosendal, G. Kristin. 1991. *International Conservation of Biological Diversity: The Quest for Effective Solutions.* FNI Report: 012-1991. Lysaker, Norway: Fridtjof Nansen Institute.

Rosendal, G. Kristin. 2000. *The Convention on Biological Diversity and Developing Countries.* Dordrecht: Kluwer Academic.

Rosendal, G. Kristin. 2001a. Impacts of Overlapping International Regimes: The Case of Biodiversity. *Global Governance* 7 (1): 95–117.

Rosendal, G. Kristin. 2001b. Institutional Interaction in Conservation and Management of Biodiversity: An Inventory. Available at http://www.ecologic.de/projekte/interaction.

Rosendal, G. Kristin. 2001c. Overlapping International Regimes: The Forum on Forests (IFF) between Climate Change and Biodiversity. *International Environmental Agreements: Politics, Law and Economics* 1 (4): 447–468.

Rosendal, G. Kristin, and Steinar Andresen. 2003. *UNEP's Role in Enhancing Problem-Solving Capacity in Multilateral Environmental Agreements: Co-ordination and Assistance in the Biodiversity Conservation Cluster.* FNI Report 10/2003. Lysaker, Norway: Fridtjof Nansen Institute.

Sell, Susan K. 2002. Private Power, Public Law: The Globalization of Intellectual Property Rights. Paper presented at the International Studies Association Annual Meeting, March 24–27, New Orleans.

Sheldon, Jennie Wood, and Michael J. Balick. 1995. Ethnobotany and the Search for Balance between Use and Conservation. In Timothy M. Swanson, ed., *Intellectual Property Rights and Biodiversity Conservation*, 19–44. Cambridge: Cambridge University Press.

Stevenson, Mark. 2002, February 19. China, Brazil, India, 9 Other Nations Form Alliance against Biopiracy. *Associated Press news wire.*

Stokke, Olav Schram, and Øystein B. Thommessen, eds. 2003. *Yearbook of International Cooperation on Environment and Development 2003/04.* London: Fridtjof Nansen Institute and Earthscan.

Svensson, Ulf. 1993. The Convention on Biodiversity—A New Approach. In Svedin Sjøstedt and Hägerhäll Aniansson, eds., *International Environmental Negotiations: Process, Issues and Contexts*, 164–191. Report 93:1. Stockholm: FRN Utrikespolitiska Institutet.

Swanson, Timothy, and Sam Johnston. 1999. *Global Environmental Problems and International Environmental Agreements*. Cheltenham: Edward Elgar.

Tvedt, Morten Walløe. 2005. How Will a Substantive Patent Law Treaty Affect the Public Domain for Genetic Resources and Biological Material? *Journal of World Intellectual Property* 8 (3): 311–344.

UNDP. 2000. *Human Development Report*. New York: United Nations Development Programme.

UNEP. 1995. *Global Biodiversity Assessment*. Ed. Vernon H. Heywood and Robert T. Watson. United Nations Environment Programme. Cambridge: Cambridge University Press.

Walden, Ian. 1995. Preserving Biodiversity: Role of Property Rights. In Timothy M. Swanson, ed., *Intellectual Property Rights and Biodiversity Conservation*, 176–198. Cambridge: Cambridge University Press.

WCED. 1987. *Our Common Future*. World Commission for Environment and Development. Oxford: Oxford University Press.

Wilson, Edward O., ed. 1988. *Biodiversity*. Washington, DC: National Academy Press.

5

Protecting the Northeast Atlantic: One Problem, Three Institutions

Jon Birger Skjærseth

The North Sea has been a core area of collaboration on the protection of the Northeast Atlantic marine environment since the early 1970s. Surrounded by densely populated areas, the North Sea is an area of intense human activity. Land-based (river input and direct discharge) and ocean-based discharges (dumping and incineration at sea) of hazardous substances and nutrients as well as atmospheric fallout have been among the major sources of contaminants to the North Sea. Many of these problems have been dealt with more or less concurrently by three different types of international institutions: legal treaties on marine pollution, the "soft-law" International North Sea Conferences (INSCs), and the European Union (EU).[1] These institutions are a significant part of Europe's marine-environment management, and the thirty-year history of environmental collaboration in the Northeast Atlantic can serve as a fascinating example of a transformation from inertia to action.

Much of the literature on regime interaction or linkages tends to emphasize problems of institutional congestion and density (e.g., Weiss 1993; Rosendal 2001; Oberthür 2001; see also chapter 1). We would thus expect that a case such as this would represent a clear example of duplicated work and coordination problems leading to low effectiveness. Contrary to conventional wisdom, however, the three types of overlapping institutions covering the North Sea and the wider Northeast Atlantic have proven mutually beneficial by fulfilling different functions, all of which are needed to manage marine pollution effectively. Moreover, these functions would be difficult to manage within the same institution due to internal contradictory requirements. The synergistic result of institutional interaction in this issue area is evident in the significant overall reductions achieved in the emissions of regulated organic substances, pesticides, heavy metals, nutrients, and dumping and incineration at sea (Skjærseth 1999, 2000, 2002a, 2002b).

The collective workings of the "soft-law" INSCs, the "hard-law" Oslo and Paris Conventions (OSPAR), and the "supranational" EU have proven instrumental for the achievements reached. In the next section of the chapter, a brief introduction to the core institutions, the INSCs and OSPAR, is provided. These core institutions have also performed well with a number of other international environmental institutions. Following their introduction, a broad view is thus taken on the most relevant cases of institutional interaction in which they have been involved. Subsequently, the focus is put on the collaborative efforts of the INSCs, OSPAR, and the EU. The main argument in this respect is that the "soft-law" INSC declarations have speeded up the decision-making processes in OSPAR and the EU. Finally, the chapter analyzes how implementation has been strengthened by "hard law." The argument here is that OSPAR and the EU in turn have facilitated domestic implementation of the original INSC Declarations.

The synergistic relationship between these institutions has been enhanced by means of conscious institutional design. The cases show how the original design of the institutions "trapped" the parties in a situation of inertia. However, the parties were able to change their path through leadership by creating a new institution—the INSCs—that became linked to OSPAR and the EU water policy. The INSCs were deliberately designed to speed up the decision-making processes in these bodies. Further lessons to be learned from these synergistic processes are discussed in the concluding section of this chapter.

OSPAR and the International North Sea Conferences

The history of international cooperation among countries bordering the North Sea/ Northeast Atlantic is the story of evolution from a state of water and marine pollution "anarchy" to domestic and international "governance." In 1972, the Convention for the Prevention of Marine Pollution by Dumping from Ships and Aircraft (Oslo Convention) was established. Signed by all thirteen Western European maritime states, the Oslo Convention covers the entire Northeast Atlantic up to the North Pole. In 1974, the Convention for the Prevention of Marine Pollution from Land-Based Sources (Paris Convention) was signed in Paris by roughly the same states as the Oslo Convention. The Paris Convention allowed the EU to join as a contracting member, and water policy was the first subsector developed under EU environmental policy. The Oslo and Paris Conventions were supported by a joint secretariat, executive commissions (Oslo and Paris Commissions), and several standing and ad hoc scientific/technical bodies. Together, both instruments are referred to as "OSPAR." In 1992, the Oslo and Paris Conventions were brought together to form a single legal instrument for the protection of the Northeast Atlantic (OSPAR Convention).

The main objective of the 1974 Paris Convention on land-based sources was to take all possible steps to prevent pollution of the sea by individually and jointly adopting measures to combat marine pollution and by harmonizing the parties' policies in this regard. The Paris Commission was responsible for the supervision of the Convention. In retrospect, the Paris Commission did not even come close to realizing the aims of the Paris Convention. On average, the Paris Commission produced roughly only one legally binding decision and one recommendation each year from 1974 to 1987 (Skjærseth 2002a). Most of the recommendations and decisions adopted concerned the blacklisted substances mercury and cadmium, about which the parties were free to choose whether quality standards or emission standards should apply. In practice, quality standards—defining the minimum quality of water—gave the parties a considerable amount of leeway due to inadequate monitoring and scientific uncertainty. Moreover, the commitments were frequently softened by requiring the parties to do something "as soon as practicable" or "as soon as possible." Added to the poorly developed reporting routines, it is questionable whether the parties were actually bound to do anything at all.

The situation on reporting was somewhat better under the 1972 Oslo Convention on dumping and incineration at sea. The Convention established a permit system, which required parties to submit to the Commission records of dumping permits and approvals they had issued. Thanks to this procedure, the Commission obtained an overview of who dumped what, where, and how much. Nevertheless, the performance of the Oslo Commission was even worse than that of the Paris Commission on substantial action. By 1987, the Oslo Commission had adopted two decisions, three recommendations, and seven so-called agreements (Skjærseth 2001b). Most of these agreements were directed at establishing cooperative procedures aimed at controlling current behavior rather than changing it. In essence, the parties continued to use the North Sea as a trash can for hazardous industrial waste and sewage sludge.

The Oslo and Paris Conventions and Commissions had two deficiencies. First, although the most pressing ecological problems concerned the North Sea, the Conventions covered the entire Northeast Atlantic, and included "laggard" countries such as Spain and Portugal. The scope of the Convention hampered collective decision making and led to decisions close to the lowest common denominator. Second, the parties sought to establish a dynamic regime. Partly due to the legally binding nature of the Conventions, however, it proved static and hard to change in practice.

Spurred by dissatisfaction with existing international institutions, Germany took the initiative in arranging the first International North Sea Conference (INSC) in Bremen in 1984. This initiative reflected a combination of entrepreneurial and intellectual leadership (Underdal 1991; Young 1991). Germany showed entrepreneurial leadership by choosing an option that was particularly conducive to solving existing problems. It essentially had a choice between striving for a new convention on the North Sea (as was proposed in the European Parliament in 1983) or generating political impetus in existing conventions by convening a North Sea Conference aimed at producing "soft-law" declarations that could take immediate effect. Both options would exclude states not bordering the North Sea. The second option in addition avoided time-consuming new legal arrangements, including the need to dismantle existing conventions. Intellectual leadership was evident in the introduction of the precautionary principle ("Vorsorgeprinzip") to guide protection of the North Sea. Agreement on the precautionary principle was a precondition for the percentage-reduction targets and the phasing out of dumping at sea agreed on later. In 1980, the Council of Environmental Advisors, an independent body of experts appointed by the German government, introduced the principle in a report on environmental problems affecting the North Sea (Ministry of Environment and Energy 1995b). The Bremen Declaration subsequently hinted at the precautionary principle and the London Declaration adopted it.

While the Bremen Conference was originally conceived of as a onetime event, the conferences evolved as a more permanent institution over time by the establishment of the standing Committee of North Sea Senior Officials.[2] The Bremen Conference was followed by conferences in London in 1987, The Hague in 1990, Esbjerg (Denmark) in 1995, and Bergen (Norway) in 2002. Conference participants have been the eight North Sea coastal states and the EU, which represent a subset of the original Oslo and Paris Conventions parties. From 1990, Switzerland was also invited to participate.

The London Declaration represented a turning point because of its ambition to phase out dumping of industrial waste and incineration at sea and to achieve reductions in inputs of nutrients to sensitive areas and in total inputs of hazardous substances reaching the aquatic environment on the order of 50 percent between 1985 and 1995. The 1990 Hague Declaration clarified and strengthened the London Declaration, particularly concerning land-based sources. The Oslo and Paris Commissions (OSPARCOM) together with the EU took significant steps in the same direction in the wake of the 1987 North Sea Conference.

Synergy in Practice

The list of interactions in table 5.1 is not exhaustive, but it provides the clearest and most important cases within the environmental policy field. The interactions between the INSCs and OSPAR as well as between these institutions and various EU directives are further explored in subsequent sections of this chapter (see also chapters 9 and 10). In addition, the INSCs and OSPAR have been influenced by the Montreal Protocol for the protection of the ozone layer, the UN Framework

Table 5.1
Instances of interaction involving the INSCs and OSPAR

INSC	• Has facilitated and sped up development of OSPAR
OSPAR	• Has expanded the scope of INSCs and helped implement INSC Declarations on marine pollution
Montreal Protocol on Substances That Deplete the Ozone Layer	• Has helped implement the INSC commitments on carbon tetrachloride and methyl chloroform
UN Framework Convention on Climate Change and Kyoto Protocol	• May provide incentive for CO_2 sequestration in North Sea oil fields, which could violate OSPAR prohibition on dumping at sea
London Dumping Convention	• Benefited from OSPAR that facilitated agreement on global ban on dumping and incineration at sea within London Convention
Rhine Convention	• Helps achieve objectives of OSPAR
Convention on Long-Range Transboundary Air Pollution	• Contributes to achieving the objective of OSPAR on nutrients and eutrophication (NO_x)
EU Nitrates Directive	• Was facilitated/triggered by INSC Declaration • Helps implementation of INSC objectives on nutrients
EU Urban Waste-Water Directive	• Was facilitated/triggered by INSC Declaration • Helps implementation of INSC objectives on nutrients • Includes an obligation to phase out sewage-sludge dumping, which was facilitated/triggered by OSPAR

Source: Skjærseth 2001. Since both the INSCs and OSPAR address nutrients and hazardous substances, interaction with other international institutions or EU directives will in most cases affect both forums. For reasons of simplicity, however, only the institution (OSPAR or INSC) most directly involved is listed.

Convention on Climate Change, the Rhine regime, and the regime on long-range transboundary air pollution at the implementation level (Behavioral Interaction). Most of these interactions have created synergy in that the source institutions have led to the reduction of pollutants in support of the INSCs and OSPAR. Potential disruption occurred only with respect to the climate change regime because the latter may provide an incentive to sequester CO_2 in North Sea oil fields, which could violate the OSPAR prohibition on dumping at sea. As a source, the INSCs and OSPAR have in particular influenced the global London Convention on dumping. They facilitated global agreement on a ban on dumping at sea that was reached in 1990 because the regional ban on dumping adopted in 1987–1988 also ensured the support at the global level of previous laggard states such as the United Kingdom (Interaction through Commitment).[3]

The main conclusion to be drawn from these twelve instances of regime interaction is that the institutions governing marine pollution in the Northeast Atlantic live in harmony with each other in the sense that almost all instances of interaction have triggered higher levels of effectiveness. While OSPAR and the INSCs have proven mutually beneficial, they have also been able to benefit from the other institutions and have themselves influenced other international regimes and EU directives in a positive manner.

The positive relationships between international institutions in this issue area have most likely been facilitated by two factors. First, all the institutions share roughly the same environmental goals, in contrast to institutions dealing with, for example, trade and the environment (see chapter 8). A second probable explanation for the high level of synergy is the relatively long history of institutional cooperation on marine-pollution control. Effectiveness tends to increase along with regime "age"— at least up to a certain point (Miles et al. 2002). Most international institutions need a period of learning by doing before they mature. And most of the cases of interaction mentioned in this chapter trace their beginnings to the 1970s and 1980s. The institutions involved have thus had time to adapt and adjust.

Speeding up Decision Making by "Soft Laws"

By the early 1980s there were growing indications that specific regions in the North Sea were becoming severely polluted (Ehlers 1990). At the international level, neither the work of the Oslo and Paris Commissions nor that of the EU suggested that stringent commitments could be initiated without additional political impetus.

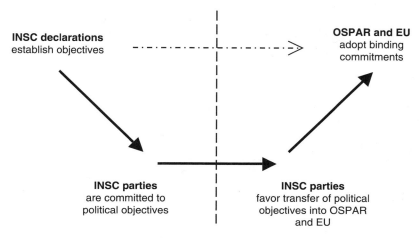

Figure 5.1
INSCs strengthen OSPAR and the EU

Against this backdrop of inertia, Germany took the initiative to arrange the first INSC at ministerial level in 1984. The INSCs turned out to have a profound impact on OSPARCOM as well as on the water- and marine-pollution policy of the EU. The causal mechanism identified is Interaction through Commitment. In this section I analyze the outcome of these INSCs, explain how the INSCs succeeded in changing OSPARCOM and EU policies, and explore the responses of OSPARCOM and the EU (see figure 5.1).

The Breakthrough: International North Sea Conference Declarations

The 1984 Bremen Declaration   The aim of the Bremen Conference was not to create a new set of international agreements, but to provide political impetus for intensifying the work of the existing international bodies. References to the Oslo and Paris Commissions and the EU are sprinkled throughout the Declaration (Ministry of Environment and Energy 1995b). Ministers of the eight North Sea coastal states—Belgium, Germany, France, the Netherlands, Norway, Sweden, Denmark, and the United Kingdom—met, together with representatives of the European Commission. The Conference Declaration did not significantly strengthen international marine-pollution commitments. As Pallemaerts (1992, 6) points out, the elasticity of phrases such as "as far as possible," "practicable," and "economically feasible" meant that the Declaration contained few substantive commitments. However, the Bremen Declaration was probably the first international text to hint at the precautionary principle: "Coastal states and the EEC must not wait for proof of harmful effects before taking action" (Ministry of Environment and Energy 1995b, 22). The Bremen Conference had initially been envisaged as a onetime event, as noted, but the ministers welcomed an invitation from the United Kingdom to host a second INSC to review implementation and adopt further measures.

The 1987 London Declaration   Particularly with respect to dumping at sea, the London Declaration represented a turning point in stringency compared to the Bremen Declaration. For the first time, it was decided to impose significant targets on dumping and incineration at sea within fixed time limits. For example, the parties aimed at phasing out the dumping of industrial wastes in the North Sea by December 31, 1989. Commitments covering land-based sources were made subject to similar targets. Eutrophication was included for the first time, and ambitious goals were agreed to for phosphorus and nitrogen substances: a substantial reduction (on the order of 50 percent) between 1985 and 1995 of inputs of phosphorus and nitrogen to those areas of the North Sea where such inputs are likely, directly or indirectly, to cause pollution. In effect, the agricultural sector was saddled with joint commitments. The commitments made with regard to hazardous substances also appear quite specific at first glance: a substantial reduction (on the order of 50 percent) between 1985 and 1995 in the total inputs to the North Sea via rivers and estuaries of substances that are persistent, toxic, and liable to bioaccumulate. However, the ministers failed to agree on specific substances beyond those already covered by international commitments. In contrast to the Bremen Declaration, the London Declaration focused squarely on domestic implementation by requiring the preparation of national action plans on implementation. The 1987 London Declaration was one of the first international environmental texts ever to explicitly incorporate the principles of precautionary action.

The 1990 Hague Declaration   The Hague Conference clarified and strengthened the London Declaration particularly concerning land-based sources. With regard to hazardous substances, the aim of reducing discharges of such substances to levels *not* "harmful to man or nature" was adopted for the first time, as a principle in Article 1 (Ministry of Environment and Energy 1995b). Against this backdrop, a list of thirty-six hazardous substances was adopted and directly linked to the 50 percent reduction target concerning hazardous substances. Moreover, the goal was changed from "of the order of 50%" to "50% or more." With regard to nutrients, measures in the municipal, industrial, and agricultural sectors were agreed on, the most specific covering the municipal sector. Targets of a 70 percent reduction of land-based and atmospheric inputs were adopted for the most dangerous substances—dioxins, cadmium, mercury, and lead. Some new obligations were also adopted at the Hague Conference. Agreement was reached on phasing out and destroying polychlorinated biphenyls (PCBs) and hazardous PCB substitutes by 1999 at the latest.

The 1995 Esbjerg Declaration The commitments adopted on hazardous substances in 1995 could symbolize the significant gains made since the 1970s. In the mid-1980s, only a few substances were under international regulation and even fewer were made subject to elimination. Only ten years later, ministers agreed to prevent the pollution of the North Sea by phasing out all hazardous substances "by continuously reducing discharges, emissions and losses of hazardous substances thereby moving towards the target of their cessation within one generation (25 years) with the ultimate aim of concentrations in the environment near background values for naturally occurring substances and close to zero concentrations for man-made synthetic substances" (Ministry of Environment and Energy, 1995a, 18). The 2002 Bergen Declaration did not introduce any new significant commitments on hazardous substances or eutrophication but focused on a number of new issue areas such as climate change, biodiversity, renewable energy, and an integrated ecosystem approach: it is too recent to have caused any significant change in target institutions.

The Causes: Changes in Membership and Institutional Setup
Why did the breakthrough on nutrients, hazardous substances, and dumping and incineration at sea take place within the INSCs and not OSPARCOM or the EU? The INSCs solved the two deficiencies of existing institutions. As noted, the Oslo and Paris Conventions covered the entire Northeast Atlantic, although the pressing ecological problems concerned the North Sea. Moreover, the Oslo and Paris Commissions and the EU lacked political momentum, though for different reasons. OSPARCOM had developed into a stagnant institution that proved hard to change. Collaborative efforts induced only low levels of participation; decision making was incremental, bureaucratic, and based on unanimity. In addition, the green movement was denied access, and actors worked together within a legally binding framework that was difficult to amend and changed very little in practice (Skjærseth

2000). The EU also embraced unanimity decision making at the time—and the environment was not included in the EC Treaty until the adoption of the Single European Act in 1986.

The INSCs solved these problems by changing *membership* and *institutional setup*. Southern European states such as Portugal and Spain were parties to OSPAR. These states frequently allied themselves with the United Kingdom to form a strong minority that was in a position to ensure that decisions reflected the lowest common denominator. In essence, the INSCs excluded the non–North Sea states and left the United Kingdom alone as the main "laggard" among the North Sea states. The position of the United Kingdom rested on its dedicated defense of environmental quality objectives, which in turn was closely linked to the fact the United Kingdom was a net exporter of marine pollution due to the counterclockwise direction of the North Sea currents. In contrast, the majority preferred uniform emission standards. Crudely put, this majority emphasized that discharges of substances known to be toxic, persistent, and bioaccumulative and listed on the blacklists should be limited as far as possible at their source, whereas the defenders of environmental-quality objectives maintained that standards set should be determined by observable negative effects in the marine environment for each particular substance.

Changes in the membership were not sufficient to reach a breakthrough since the United Kingdom remained within the INSCs. However, thanks to their soft-law qualities and political nature, the INSCs became a truly dynamic institution. First, the INSCs were based on ministerial representation, a circumstance that paved the way for political pressure to be put on the United Kingdom. Second, INSC Declarations could take immediate effect since they were based on soft law, while proposed amendments to OSPAR or EU legislation could take many years. Third, INSC Declarations were specific and visible and verification procedures and practice improved dramatically. In contrast to the Oslo and Paris Commissions, the INSCs systematically reviewed the achievements of the preceding declarations by preparing comprehensive progress reports on measures taken by each country as well as reductions in inputs from each country. This raised the level of transparency and generated pressure from environmental groups and more progressive states toward the United Kingdom. As a consequence of the increasing political costs involved, the United Kingdom accepted the precautionary principle and uniform emission standards. The change in the UK position was made explicit in a 1988 position paper that had far-reaching implications for both the United Kingdom and the North Sea/

Northeast Atlantic cooperation, particularly with regard to dumping and hazardous substances (Skjærseth 2000, 124).

Several other factors contribute to explaining the patterns witnessed but cannot fully account for them. First, there were "shocks and crises" in the North Sea in the form of the exceptional 1988 and 1989 toxic algae blooms and seal epidemics. They helped instigate the 1988 EU resolution on the North Sea (Prat 1990). But they cannot explain the 1987 INSC breakthrough because they occurred later. Moreover, their importance should not be exaggerated since their political impact faded rapidly (Skjærseth 1999).[4] Second, public opinion on environmental matters changed significantly throughout Europe in the late 1980s (Hofrichter 1991). Ministerial representation at the INSCs became important as a result. Since ministers are responsible to their domestic electorates, the "green wave" of the late 1980s could be channeled more effectively into international negotiations than the former low-level government representation in the Oslo and Paris Commissions had allowed for. In this way, the impact of the changes in level of representation became closely linked to the changes in public opinion. However, since public values and attitudes evolved most significantly after 1987, they can hardly in themselves explain the 1987 INSC breakthrough, even in connection with the algae blooms (Skjærseth 1999). Moreover, public interest in (marine) environmental questions has been on the wane in most central North Sea states since the early 1990s. Nevertheless, the 1995 INSC and OSPARCOM have continued to tighten up previous commitments, not least on hazardous substances, which shows that the dynamic impact of the institutions has continued despite fluctuations in public opinion.

While such exogenous factors contribute to our understanding of the influence of one institution on another, other potential explanations can be ruled out. Phenomena similar to the Antarctic ozone hole in 1985 were not uncovered. Uncertainty relating to the causes and consequences of marine pollution of the North Sea has receded *gradually*, so that the 1987 INSC Declaration cannot be traced back to a breakthrough in scientific knowledge comparable with the discovery of the Antarctic ozone hole. The North Sea Quality Status Reports presented in 1984 and 1987 both painted a picture of high uncertainty and "moderate" pollution levels. Moreover, the basic interests of the participating states did not change significantly, since these interests were largely linked to the counterclockwise direction of the North Sea currents that placed the states in a chainwise relationship of exporters and importers of marine pollution.

The Effects: OSPAR and the EU

Although containing far-reaching commitments, the INSC Declarations represented "soft law" that was not legally binding for the parties. Since ministers come and go as governments change, the political Declarations carried a risk of ending up as "paper tigers." This was avoided by transforming the Declarations into legally binding commitments under OSPAR and the EU.

As a consequence of the INSCs, the decision procedures within the Oslo and Paris Commissions changed from the requirement of unanimity to consensus linked to various "fast-track options." Previously, all thirteen states bordering the Northeast Atlantic had to agree on the same international regulations. The INSCs led to new procedures that allowed for differential obligations between North Sea and non–North Sea states.

The London Declaration had its strongest impact on the Oslo Commission. The first decision adopted by the Commission in 1988 stated that the riparian states of the North Sea would apply the principles on the reduction and cessation of dumping of polluting materials as set out in the INSC Declaration. This represented a sea change in dumping policies, and the collective decisions of the Oslo Commission in this period show a significant expansion in number, legal status, and content compared to previous periods (Skjærseth 1999). The Oslo Commission achieved significantly more from 1987 to 1990 than it had from 1974 to 1987. Even though the total number of commitments under the Paris Commission did not increase significantly, the parties adopted several "new" commitments, including a recommendation on the reduction of inputs of nutrients in 1988 and a coordinated program for the reduction of nutrients in 1989. The Paris Commission did not, however, act effectively to reduce discharges of hazardous substances.

EU responses to the 1987 conference related mainly to inputs of nutrients. In the fourth EU Action Program on the Environment, adopted by the EU Council of Ministers in 1987, the fight against seawater pollution from both point and diffuse sources was considered to be a matter of priority. In 1988, the Council adopted a resolution specifically related to the protection of the North Sea, requesting the European Commission to combat nutrients from different sources, particularly agriculture, and to present proposals on urban wastewater treatment. The resulting directives were to become the major means of combating eutrophication in the North Sea. Concerning hazardous substances, a proposed directive on the elimination of PCBs was directly inspired by the 1987 London Declaration (Prat 1990).

The Hague Declaration had its strongest impact on the Paris Commission. On the basis of the list of hazardous substances adopted by the Hague Conference, the Paris Commission started systematically addressing discharges from specific industrial sectors. It took action on several fronts, including best environmental practices (BEP) on diffuse sources and best available technology (BAT) on industrial point sources. In addition to the two recommendations adopted in 1988 and 1989 on nutrients, the Commission adopted Recommendation 92/7 on the Reduction of Nutrient Inputs from Agriculture.

The INSCs and OSPAR created a dumping policy for the EU. The EU had been working on regulating dumping since the early 1970s. The European Commission tabled the first proposal for a directive in 1976. However, the Council did not succeed in adopting any specific directives on dumping. The EU implemented the decision of the INSC and the Oslo Commission on phasing out sewage-sludge dumping by including this obligation in the Urban Waste-Water Directive of 1991. Moreover, the EU attended to OSPAR dumping policy by ratifying the 1992 OSPAR Convention in 1998 (Council Decision 98/249/EC (12)). Concerning nutrients, two important EU directives were adopted in 1991 based on the initiatives of the late 1980s. Besides their importance for the North Sea, the Nitrates and the Urban Waste-Water Directives reflected a slightly different approach from previous directives. Like the North Sea commitments, the new directives attacked the sources of pollution and described clear goals within given time frames, while relying less on quality objectives (Richardson 1994, 150). The Urban Waste-Water Directive set specific requirements on wastewater collecting systems to be implemented by the year 2000 or 2005 concerning nutrient discharges. The Nitrates Directive aims at supplementing these efforts by specifically addressing nutrient emissions from the agricultural sector. The agricultural sector was also made subject to a regulation on environmentally friendly production methods in 1992. These commitments overlap with both the INSC Declarations and OSPAR commitments.

The Esbjerg Declaration on hazardous substances initiated actions both within OSPAR and the EU. The political agreement to phase out hazardous substances within twenty-five years with the ultimate aim of achieving concentrations in the environment near background values for naturally occurring substances has been viewed as a breakthrough. In 1998, OSPAR copied this agreement in the so-called Sintra statement on a total phaseout of emissions of hazardous substances by 2020 (available at http://www.ospar.org/eng/html/md/sintra.htm). In 2000, the EU adopted the Water Framework Directive (Directive 2000/60/EC), which sets out its ambition "to cease or phase out discharges, emissions and losses of priority hazardous substances, with the ultimate aim of achieving concentrations in the marine environment near background values for naturally occurring substances and close to zero for man-made synthetic substances" (Art. 1; see also chapter 9).

Overall, the direct consequences of the OSPAR and EU responses to the North Sea Declarations were thus twofold. First, the North Sea Declarations were transformed into legally binding OSPAR commitments and/or EU regulations, directives, or decisions. Second, the geographic coverage of the Declarations was extended to the EU area and/or the Northeast Atlantic area.

Strengthening Implementation by "Hard Law"

In this section, we will see how OSPAR and the EU subsequently facilitated the implementation of the INSC Declarations. In particular, the hard-law nature of OSPAR and EU commitments contributed decisively to behavioral changes that improved the protection of the Northeast Atlantic and thus supported the achievement of the objectives of the INSC Declarations. This case is thus an example of Behavioral Interaction (figure 5.2).

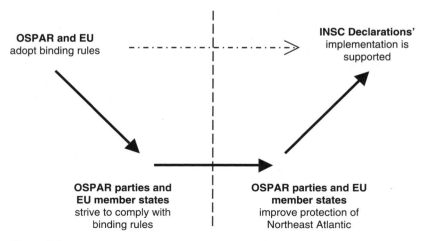

Figure 5.2
OSPAR and the EU strengthen implementation of the INSCs

OSPAR and EU Legal Instruments: Implementing INSC Declarations

The 1995 Esbjerg Declaration identified previously adopted OSPAR decisions and EU directives and regulations as the principal measures for goal attainment. While this change in focus reflects important changes in EU marine and water policy, it also reflects the fact that Norway and Switzerland were the only non-EU INSC countries as of 1995. Concerning hazardous substances like pesticides, the Declaration refers to Recommendation 94/7 of the Paris Commission on national plans for reduction of pesticides from agriculture as well as to Directive 91/414/EEC concerning the placing of plant-protection products on the market. On nutrients, the Declaration links progress directly to national action plans based on a number of OSPAR recommendations and EU directives, in particular the Urban Waste-Water and Nitrates Directives. According to the Progress Report presented to the Esbjerg Conference (Ministry of Environment and Energy 1995c, 33), "Although the North Sea Conferences have provided the political skeleton, it has been left to the established legal frameworks ... to implement Ministers' decisions by providing the necessary detailed and binding (legal) framework for the North Sea States, in particular through the medium of Decisions and Recommendations adopted by the Oslo and Paris Commissions and by EU Directives." This process of identifying previously adopted EU and OSPAR commitments continued at the INSC in Bergen in 2002 (Ministry of the Environment 2002). The conference showed that there had been progress toward achieving the targets on hazardous substances, and most North Sea states had achieved a 70 percent reduction in mercury, lead, and cadmium. The OSPAR strategy on hazardous substances and the EU Water Framework Directive were regarded as effective means for coping with the remaining implementation deficiencies and future challenges. According to the European Environment Agency (EEA), the control of hazardous substances in marine waters has been a success largely due to OSPAR (EEA 2001). The next INSC is scheduled to take place in Stockholm in 2006.

There were more problems for the North Sea states with respect to nitrogen. Lack of progress was directly related to delays in implementing the Nitrates and Urban Waste-Water Directives. In Bergen, the North Sea ministers agreed on full implementation of these directives and the Water Framework Directive as well as on reducing the use of fertilizer through Council Regulation EC/1257/1999 on support for rural development from the European Agricultural Guidance and Guarantee Fund (EAGGF).

The Causes: Institutional Authoritativeness and Enforcement

OSPAR has strengthened implementation mainly through the legally binding nature of commitments. In general, there is a conviction in the legal literature on international obligations that joint commitments should preferably be legally binding on states (Nollkaemper 1993). This view is based on the assumption that states will be more inclined to comply with legal than with nonlegal obligations. The distinction between binding and nonbinding commitments has been perceived as important by the OSPAR parties, and the legal nature of commitments has been discussed repeatedly (Skjærseth 1999). Likewise, the INSC Declarations contain several references indicating that the North Sea states considered it important that joint commitments be implemented as binding decisions within OSPAR. When it comes to enforcement, however, the distinction between binding and nonbinding obligations has little effect—if any. Enforcement has been regarded as the weakest part of international efforts to regulate marine pollution: deterrence is considered unlikely since few disputes are actually settled by international courts (Ijlstra 1986; Nollkaemper 1993). The 1992 OSPAR Convention contains detailed dispute-settlement procedures and places slightly more weight on enforcement, but it does not set out which specific steps should be taken in cases of noncompliance. Thus, it seems reasonable to assume that legally binding OSPARCOM decisions have constrained state behavior due to their authoritativeness in addition to affecting incentives.

The phasing out of dumping of industrial waste in the North Sea shows that by transforming "soft law" into "hard law," states that continued with dumping had to follow demanding, legally binding procedures. The 1987 London Conference took the decision to phase out such dumping by December 31, 1989, and the Oslo Commission followed up by translating this political agreement among the North Sea states into a legally binding decision. In this case, the EU had no competence and the Community was not a party to the Oslo Convention. There are clear indications that the United Kingdom did not seriously plan to change its behavior in accordance with the international commitments (Skjærseth 2002b). In late 1989, the UK Ministry of Agriculture, Food and Fisheries decided to support applications for licensing 50,000 tons of toxic waste through the Oslo Commission's Prior Justification Procedure. This procedure was adopted in 1988 as a direct consequence of the introduction of the precautionary principle by the 1987 INSC. It reversed the burden of proof: potential dumpers were now obliged to prove through complicated and expensive laboratory tests that substances they intended to dump *could not* harm the marine environment. Several North Sea states protested the UK decision and Greenpeace brought the case to the media's attention. An extraordinary meeting of the Oslo Commission ad hoc working group on dumping was convened. The final decision to phase out dumping of industrial waste (and sewage sludge) was made by Agriculture Minister John Gummer in 1990.

In cases of noncompliance, OSPAR has more competence than the INSCs due to its legally binding properties and the EU has more competence than OSPAR owing to its supranational attributes. When the EU acts it does so with significantly more force than traditional regimes simply because the compliance instruments at its disposal are more powerful (Tallberg 2002). Concerning enforcement, the main formal difference between OSPAR and the EU is that EU directives impose legal obligations directly on the member states (Skjærseth and Wettestad 2002). Failure to comply with EU law can be relied on in national courts required to interpret national laws in line with EU law (sympathetic interpretation). Such failure can even result in awards of damages to individuals who have suffered loss as a consequence.

The enforcement powers of the European Court of Justice (ECJ) are also unique. The ECJ has developed a number of principles affecting national law and policies as well as how EU policies apply (Haigh 2003). Since 1993, the ECJ may impose fines against member states that have failed to comply with previous rulings of the court. This provision was applied for the first time against Greece for its failure to observe a court ruling on waste management.[5] The United Kingdom was also threatened with heavy daily fines for persistent failure to comply with EU bathing-water rules.[6] Note that the threat has passed because the United Kingdom has come into compliance with regard to the specified bathing waters—if a few decades behind schedule. The ECJ has initiated legal action on a number of water directives linked to marine pollution, including the Dangerous Substances Directive, the Urban Waste-Water Directive, the Shellfish Directive, the Surface Waters Directive, the Nitrates Directive, and the Bathing Waters Directive.

The INSC obligation to reduce input of nitrogen substances in sensitive areas by 50 percent illustrates the causal mechanism of Behavioral Interaction (see figure 5.2). The INSC Declaration had scant effect on implementation. Implementation problems in the case of nitrogen have mainly been related to strong farming lobbies and conflicts of interest between environmental and agricultural authorities. The United Kingdom, for example, argued that there were no sensitive areas around its coast and did not take any significant steps to reduce nitrogen inputs.

However, the INSC obligation triggered the adoption of the EU Nitrates Directive. Even though the Nitrates Directive is an extremely poor example of "effective" EU implementation, it illustrates that the EU has more powerful tools at its disposal than OSPAR and the INSCs when states do not comply. In October 1997, EU Environment Commissioner Ritt Bjerregaard made a strong plea for better implementation of the Nitrates Directive. The EU Parliament issued a resolution in late 1998 in which it said it was "shocked by the lack of progress" in implementing the nitrate law and called for action from governments, the Commission, and farmers.[7] In 2000, thirteen out of fifteen member states were facing legal proceedings in accordance with the EU infringement procedure (table 5.2), which consists of three formal stages. First, the Commission initiates a proceeding through a letter of "formal notice." Second, the Commission's legal elaboration takes place through a "reasoned opinion" as a final warning. Third, the Commission refers a case to the ECJ for a final decision (Tallberg 2002).

Again, the example of the United Kingdom illustrates that swift enforcement action by the European Commission and the ECJ may indeed work. The United

Table 5.2
Status of Nitrates Directive infringement actions: stage of most advanced action as of April 2000

EU member state	Status of Nitrates Directive infringement action
Austria	Reasoned opinion
Belgium	**European Court**
Denmark	**No action**
Finland	Formal notice
France	**European Court**
Germany	**European Court**
Greece	European Court
Ireland	Reasoned opinion
Italy	European Court (Condemned 2001)
Luxembourg	European Court
Netherlands	**European Court**
Portugal	Formal notice
Spain	European Court
Sweden	**No action**
United Kingdom	**European Court (Condemned 2000)**

Source: ENDS, 737, 5 April 2000. "More EU countries in trouble over nitrates law". Bold entries indicate North Sea states.

Kingdom was condemned in the European Court of Justice in December 2000. Whereas the Directive requires member states to identify all surface or groundwaters polluted by nitrates or at risk of being so, and to designate all such areas as so-called vulnerable zones enjoying particular protection, the United Kingdom had only identified surface and groundwaters used as sources of drinking water. The United Kingdom announced steps to broaden its definition to substantially increase the area of land designated as nitrate vulnerable.[8] However, in October 2001 the Commission announced a repeat legal action stating that the United Kingdom still had too few areas designated. In December, the environment ministry proposed measures to bring England and Wales into compliance with the Nitrates Directive.[9]

EU members have been pulled before the court for different reasons. Germany, for example, had prepared an action plan as required by the law, but the plan was considered "insufficient" in its provisions for allowable storage capacities of livestock manure and failure to calculate maximum fertilizer application rates.[10] During 2003, the Commission continued to take action over bad application of the Directive by a number of member states. In some cases, the Commission had to open infringement procedures in order to make member states comply with earlier judgments by the Court (European Commission 2004). Time will show whether these actions prove sufficient for the North Sea ministers to conclude that the nitrogen target has been met at the upcoming North Sea Conferences.

Conclusion

Bureaucrats and lawyers defending their respective countries in the court cases related to the Nitrates Directive are probably not aware that the present problems can be traced back to a ray of optimism among eight North Sea environmental ministers in 1987. Germany's appearance in the ECJ over the Nitrates Directive can actually be traced back to the "German" precautionary principle hinted at in the first North Sea Declaration of 1984.

The interactive workings of the International North Sea Conferences, OSPAR, and the EU have proven synergistic in two ways. First, the political "soft-law" INSCs have speeded up decision making within OSPAR and the EU by Interaction through Commitment. Second, OSPAR and the EU have facilitated domestic implementation of the INSC Declarations through their institutional authoritativeness and enforcement competence by means of Behavioral Interaction.

The most robust finding in this study is that overlap between institutions does not necessarily imply duplication of work and low effectiveness. In essence, *institutional differences* between the INSCs, OSPAR, and the EU account, at least partly, for the progress in implementation witnessed. Cooperation on Northeast Atlantic environmental management shows that different types of institutions can fulfill different functions, all of which are needed to make international environmental cooperation effective. Moreover, it would be difficult to fulfill these functions within one and the same institution due to conflicting institutional requirements. For example, INSC participants had to make political decisions within a couple of days every few years, which were supposed to take immediate effect at the governmental level. This secured swift action, but created political vulnerability since governments and political priorities change. In contrast, even though the EU is in the process of expanding its array of environmental policy instruments, EU directives are developed through lengthy legislative processes and have to be transposed into national law. Most environmental directives now allow three years for their transposition, although many are transposed late. In the case of OSPAR, the adoption of new legal instruments can be even more protracted. For example, a new protocol on incineration at sea was signed in 1983 but did not come into force until 1989.

OSPAR and the EU could not match the decision-making speed of the INSCs, but were needed to keep up the pressure on implementation and compliance. Due to its legal infringement procedure, the EU possesses more power to act when the going gets tough. EU directives and regulations are more commanding than INSC or OSPAR commitments due to the "supranational" nature of the EU. EU action on the 1991 Nitrates Directive shows that EU enforcement tools in cases of noncompliance are significantly more powerful than those "traditional" regimes possess. The legally binding OSPAR also provided a legal and stable basis for the INSCs and gave authoritative force in the crucial implementation phase. Such qualities proved particularly important concerning dumping at sea where the EU had no competence.

Rather than introducing new commitments on hazardous substances or eutrophication, the 2002 Bergen Declaration set out a number of new issue areas such as climate change, biodiversity, renewable energy, and an integrated ecosystem approach. The search for new challenges indicates that the INSCs have "solved" most of the problems related to hazardous substances, nutrients, dumping, and incineration at sea through international cooperation. Further achievements now depend largely on domestic political will and the capacity to follow through. The EU will continue to have an important role to play in facilitating implementation and enforcing compliance in the future.

Notes

1. The term *European Union* will be used broadly throughout this chapter, to include the period before the Treaty of Maastricht.

2. Accordingly, OSPAR and INSC can be treated as two separate although closely related institutions. OSPAR and INSC have separate agendas, and differ in membership as well as in norms, rules, and communication processes.

3. Instances of less than harmonious collaboration can probably be found at the intersection with other issue areas, such as EU agricultural policy. Instances involving the INSCs, OSPAR, and EU directives on hazardous substances are not included. These interactions are probably not that different from cases involving nutrients, but any interaction is extremely difficult to pinpoint due to high causal complexity.

4. Important for the North Sea was that the Rhine Commission, motivated in part by the Sandoz accident, adopted the Rhine Action Program in 1987. This program addressed a number of issues, including marine issues, and included some institutional strengthening to aid compliance, thus ensuring continued action after public interest declined.

5. "EU Commission Back on the Compliance Warpath," *ENDS*, 831, September 13, 2000.

6. "UK 'to Escape Bathing Water Fines,'" *ENDS*, 1074, October 4, 2001.

7. "EU Parliament 'Shocked' by Nitrate Law Delays," *ENDS*, 401, October 21, 1998.

8. "UK Condemned over EU Water Pollution Law," *ENDS*, 891, December 7, 2000.

9. "UK Races to Comply with Nitrates Directive," *ENDS*, 1128, December 20, 2001.

10. "EU Takes Further Action on Water Law Breaches," *ENDS*, 341, July 8, 1998.

References

Cameron, James. 1994. The Status of the Precautionary Principle in International Law. In Timothy O'Riordan and James Cameron, eds., *Interpreting the Precautionary Principle*. London: Earthscan.

EEA. 2001. *Environmental Signals 2001*. Copenhagen: European Environment Agency.

Ehlers, Peter. 1990. The History of the International North Sea Conferences. In David Freestone and Ton Ijlstra, eds., *The North Sea: Perspectives on Regional Environmental Co-operation* (special issue of the *International Journal of Estuarine and Coastal Law*), 3–15. London: Graham & Trotman.

European Commission. 2004. *Fifth Annual Survey on the Implementation and Enforcement of Community Environmental Law*, 2003. Brussels: European Commission.

Haigh, Nigel. 2003. *Manual of Environmental Policy: The EU and Britain*. Leeds: Janey Publishing and Institute for European Environmental Policy.

Hayward, Peter. 1990. The Oslo and Paris Commissions. In David Freestone and Ton Ijlstra, eds., *The North Sea: Perspectives on Regional Environmental Co-operation* (special issue of the *International Journal of Estuarine and Coastal Law*), 91–101. London: Graham & Trotman.

Hofrichter, Jürgen. 1991. *Evolution of Attitudes towards Environmental Issues 1974–1991*. Mannheim: Zentrum für Europäische Umfragenanalysen und Studien, Universität Mannheim.

Ijlstra, Ton. 1986. *Enforcement of International Environmental Instruments in the North Sea: The Missing Link*. Netherlands Institute for the Law of the Sea (NILOS). Utrecht: University of Utrecht.

Miles, Edward L., Arild Underdal, Steinar Andresen, Jørgen Wettestad, Jon Birger Skjærseth, and Elaine M. Carlin. 2002. *Environmental Regime Effectiveness: Confronting Theory with Evidence*. Cambridge, MA: MIT Press.

Ministry of the Environment. 2002. *Ministerial Declaration of the Fifth International Conference on the Protection of the North Sea*. (Bergen Declaration.) Bergen, Norway, March 20–21. Oslo: Ministry of the Environment.

Ministry of Environment and Energy. 1995a. *Esbjerg Declaration*. Ministerial Conference on the Protection of the North Sea, Esbjerg, June 8–9. Copenhagen: Ministry of Environment and Energy, Danish Environmental Protection Agency.

Ministry of Environment and Energy. 1995b. *Ministerial Declarations*. International Conference on the Protection of the North Sea. Bremen, 1984, London, 1987, The Hague, 1990. Copenhagen: Ministry of Environment and Energy, Danish Environmental Protection Agency.

Ministry of Environment and Energy. 1995c. *Progress Report*. Fourth Ministerial Conference on the Protection of the North Sea, Esbjerg, June 8–9. Copenhagen: Ministry of Environment and Energy, Danish Environmental Protection Agency.

Nollkaemper, Andrè. 1993. *The Legal Regime for Transboundary Water Pollution: Between Discretion and Constraint*. London: Graham & Trotman.

Oberthür, Sebastian. 2001. Linkages between the Montreal and Kyoto Protocols: Enhancing Synergies between Protecting the Ozone Layer and the Global Climate. *International Environmental Agreements: Politics, Law and Economics* 1 (3): 357–377.

Pallemaerts, Marc. 1992. The North Sea Ministerial Declarations from Bremen to Hague: Does the Process Generate Any Substance? *International Journal of Estuarine and Coastal Law* 7 (1): 1–26.

Prat, Jean-Luc. 1990. The Role and Activities of the European Communities in the Protection and the Preservation of the Marine Environment of the North Sea. In David Freestone and Ton Ijlstra, eds., *The North Sea: Perspectives on Regional Environmental Co-operation* (special issue of the *International Journal of Estuarine and Coastal Law*), 101–111. London: Graham & Trotman.

Richardson, Jeremy. 1994. EU Water Policy: Uncertain Agendas, Shifting Networks and Complex Coalitions. *Environmental Politics* 3 (4): 139–167.

Rosendal, G. Kristin. 2001. Impacts of Overlapping International Regimes: The Case of Biodiversity. *Global Governance* 7 (1): 95–117.

Skjærseth, Jon Birger. 1999. *The Making and Implementation of North Sea Pollution Commitments: Institutions, Rationality and Norms*. Oslo: University of Oslo and Akademika, AS.

Skjærseth, Jon Birger. 2000. *North Sea Cooperation: Linking International and Domestic Pollution Control*. Manchester: Manchester University Press.

Skjærseth, Jon Birger. 2001. *The International Regime on the Protection of the North-East Atlantic: A Good Neighbour.* Oslo: Fridtjof Nansen Institute.

Skjærseth, Jon Birger. 2002a. Cleaning up the North Sea: The Case of Land-Based Pollution Control. In Edward L. Miles, Arild Underdal, Steinar Andresen, Jørgen Wettestad, Jon Birger Skjærseth, and Elaine M. Carlin, eds., *Environmental Regime Effectiveness: Confronting Theory with Evidence*, 175–197. Cambridge: MIT Press.

Skjærseth, Jon Birger. 2002b. Towards the End of Dumping in the North Sea: The Case of the Oslo Commission. In Edward L. Miles, Arild Underdal, Steinar Andresen, Jørgen Wettestad, Jon Birger Skjærseth, and Elaine M. Carlin, eds., *Environmental Regime Effectiveness: Confronting Theory with Evidence*, 65–87. Cambridge, MA: MIT Press.

Skjærseth, Jon Birger, and Jørgen Wettestad. 2002. Understanding the Effectiveness of EU Environmental Policy: How Can Regime Analysis Contribute? *Environmental Politics* 11 (3): 99–120.

Tallberg, Jonas. 2002. Paths to Compliance: Enforcement, Management and the European Union. *International Organization* 56 (3): 609–643.

Underdal, Arild. 1991. Solving Collective Problems: Notes on Three Modes of Leadership. In *Challenges of a Changing World*. Festschrift for Willy Østreng. Lysaker, Norway: Fridtjof Nansen Institute.

Weiss, Edith Brown. 1993. International Environmental Law: Contemporary Issues and the Emergence of a New World Order. *Georgetown Law Journal* 81 (3): 675–710.

Young, Oran. 1991. Political Leadership and Regime Formation: On the Development of Institutions in International Society. *International Organization* 45 (3): 281–308.

6

Institutional Interplay and Responsible Fisheries: Combating Subsidies, Developing Precaution

Olav Schram Stokke and Clare Coffey

The world's oceans have struggled for decades to sustain large-scale and increasingly invasive fishing activities. The response of governments to this situation has ranged from neglect to the establishment of regional institutions for concerted fisheries management. Where international institutions exist, they have often provided a mechanism for allocating fishing rights among members, and in some cases also cooperative means for scientific activities and compliance control (Stokke 2001). The effectiveness of such regional regimes varies considerably, however, and the overall performance of the global fisheries regime leaves much to be desired. This is partly because the underlying problem being addressed has regained much of the severity it had prior to the introduction in the mid-1970s of exclusive economic zones. Despite almost universal claims by coastal states to 200-mile fishing zones, and the concomitant "nationalization" of some 90 percent of the world's commercial fisheries, coastal states have largely failed to manage their resources sustainably. At the same time, distant-water fishing fleets have further enhanced the harvesting capacity they deploy on the high seas and in foreign fishing zones. Pushed by capital and modernization subsidies, rising competition, higher operating costs, and steadily lower-value yields, fishing companies have introduced a range of new technologies enabling them to profit from fish located in concentrations or at depths that would previously have been beyond economic or technical reach. While technology and harvesting capacity have increased, for most oceans, catches are now well below historic peak levels (FAO 2001b). Importantly, the process has also involved the gradual decline of larger, long-lived, and more valuable predator species such as tuna, cod, and haddock in the oceans—known as "fishing down marine food webs"—with significant ramifications for marine ecosystems (Pauly et al. 2002).

Efforts to strengthen international fisheries rules, regional and global, during the past decade occurred in response to these challenges. The main elements of the present global fisheries regime are introduced in the next section. This is followed by a brief overview of important cases of interaction between the global fisheries regime and other international institutions as well as the EU Common Fisheries Policy. The chapter then focuses on the interaction between the global fisheries regime and (1) the global trade regime with regard to rules on fisheries subsidies; (2) the International Council for the Exploration of the Sea (ICES) with respect to the formulation of scientific advice on fisheries management, notably the implementation of the precautionary approach; and in turn, (3) the interaction between ICES precautionary advice and the EU Common Fisheries Policy. Our focus on subsidies permits examination of cross-issue institutional interplay, whereas the precautionary approach connects activities within institutions that focus on different aspects of resource management: research and decision making. Both themes are high up on the political agenda of international environmental governance. Following a brief presentation of the broader issues involved in each case of interaction, assessments are provided of the causal relationship between source and target institutions and the adequacy of the policy responses to the set of interactions. In the last section, we draw conclusions regarding important factors that can help explain the emergence of institutional interaction and its impact on the effectiveness of the institutions involved.

The Global Regime for Fisheries

The 1990s were highly dynamic as regards international fisheries rules. The 1995 UN Fish Stocks Agreement[1] specifies the 1982 UN Convention on the Law of the Sea with regard to straddling stocks and highly migratory stocks and influences decision making within institutions that are narrower in geographic or functional terms. It strengthens and specifies the duty under international law to cooperate on all aspects of high-seas fisheries management. It provides that only states that are members of, or adhere to, regional regimes shall have access to the fishery (Art. 8) and elaborates certain basic conservation principles, including the precautionary approach to fisheries management (Art. 6, Annex II). Although the principal focus of the Fish Stocks Agreement is on high seas fisheries management, Article 7 requires that national measures concerning straddling stocks and highly migratory stocks be compatible with high seas measures, and Article 3 requires that the provisions on precautionary management also apply in national waters. As regards compliance control, the Agreement breaks new ground by creating global minimum standards that permit a broader range of compliance mechanisms than was previously the norm within regional high seas management regimes. This includes strengthened flag-state responsibilities; procedures for non-flag-state inspection, detention, and arrest on the high seas; and elaboration of certain port-state measures to enhance adherence to regional conservation and management measures (Art. 19–23). The Fish Stocks Agreement entered into force in 2001 and forms, in conjunction with the UN Convention on the Law of the Sea that came into force in 1994, the basis for the global fisheries regime.

In parallel to the Fish Stocks Agreement, a set of international instruments was negotiated under the auspices of the UN Food and Agriculture Organization (FAO). The FAO Compliance Agreement, which strengthens flag-state responsibilities with respect to vessels fishing on the high seas, was adopted in 1993. The FAO Code of Conduct for Responsible Fisheries was agreed to in 1995 and has been followed by four International Plans of Action (IPOAs) on fishing capacity, shark management, seabird protection, and illegal, unreported, and unregulated fishing.[2] The FAO Code of Conduct and its plans of action are voluntary, directed at members as well as nonmembers of the FAO, and reflect the active role of the FAO Committee on Fisheries in seeking to shape and support international fisheries rules. Alongside the UN General Assembly, which annually reviews progress under the UN Convention on the Law of the Sea, the FAO Committee on Fisheries is the only permanent international forum that, periodically and on a worldwide basis, examines major fisheries concerns and provides recommendations to governments, regional management bodies, and other stakeholders.

Institutional Interaction and International Fisheries Management

We have provided an inventory of interactions between the global fisheries regime, the EU Common Fisheries Policy (CFP), and other institutions, covering the full functional scope of resource management: science, regulation, and compliance control (Stokke and Coffey 2001). An overview of these interactions is given in table 6.1.

All three causal mechanisms investigated in this volume are represented in the inventory. The cases involving the precautionary approach (ICES and EU CFP), fisheries subsidies (World Trade Organization, the global fisheries regime, and EU), and the transparency of decision making (NEAFC) revolve around Interaction through Commitment. Here, the fact that states have assumed commitments in the context

Table 6.1
Cases of interaction of the Global Fisheries Regime

Scientific research and advice

International Council for the Exploration of the Sea (ICES)	• Has implemented the precautionary approach following its formal adoption in the global Fish Stocks Agreement (FSA) • Introduced greater safety margins in its catch recommendations and requested rapid recovery of troubled stocks and thus contributed to improved conservation in line with FSA • Is modifying its communication and terminology in response to criticism by FAO and regional regimes

Regulation

North-East Atlantic Fisheries Commission (NEAFC)	• Responded to the transparency rules of the FSA by adopting new provisions on access to meetings and reports
EU Common Fisheries Policy (CFP)	• FSA supports implementation of the precautionary approach in the CFP (through ICES), which requires preagreed decision rules within recovery/management plans • FSA rules support inclusion of management considerations in EU fish-import regulations • FAO International Program of Action on fishing capacity (IPOA-Capacity) contributes to reform of related EU rules aiming at a reduction of subsidies • IPOA-Capacity contributes to reduction of fisheries subsidies in the EU and its member states • EU fisheries subsidies still undermine conservation and management of fish stocks required by global fisheries regime
World Trade Organization (WTO)	• WTO subsidies rules improve information flows and bindingness and may therefore help reduce or limit fisheries subsidies and capacity • The global fisheries regime helped place fisheries subsidies on the formal WTO agenda (Doha Round)
Convention on International Trade in Endangered Species (CITES)	• Has contributed to emergence of FAO International Program of Action on the Conservation and Management of Sharks (IPOA-Sharks) • Benefited in its implementation from improved national reporting procedures and records of shark catches resulting from IPOA-Sharks

Compliance control

Northwest Atlantic Fisheries Organization	• Facilitated adoption of FSA provisions on inspection, detention, and arrest
Central Bering Sea Doughnut Hole Agreement	• Facilitated adoption of FSA provisions on inspection, detention, and arrest

of one regime affects decision making under another regime. The FAO-CITES case displays Cognitive Interaction: the ensuing International Plan of Action on Sharks Management (IPOA-Sharks) by the FAO did not result from commitments but from learning that was triggered by CITES activities, notably its direct requests for FAO inputs. Cognitive Interaction is also evident in the relationship between the global fisheries regime and ICES practices with respect to the involvement of and communication with stakeholders. The same is true for the two regional cases on compliance-control procedures: the more intrusive detention and arrest provisions stood out as salient in the global negotiations by having been applied successfully in earlier processes. With respect to most interacting institutions listed in table 6.1, Behavioral Interaction can also be observed: modified ICES advice has influenced fisheries management "on the ground," the EU subsidies rules have undermined sustainable use and management of fish stocks, and FAO's IPOA-Sharks help the effective implementation of CITES.

Some of the cases involve institutions with significantly different objectives, which could imply that the source undermines the target. For instance, the EU's fisheries subsidies regime has historically aimed at industrial development rather than sustainability pursued under the global fisheries regime. But whereas much of the debate on institutional interplay has focused on potentially disruptive effects, most of our cases are synergistic or have at least led to responses that reduced the level of disruption. Nevertheless, they also typically reveal ample room for further improvement.

While the general approach in this book is to identify certain dyads of institutional interaction, it is important to also consider the effects of other relevant institutions and processes when tracing the causal connection between source and target. Reduction of fisheries subsidies, for instance, is an objective of work undertaken also by the Organization for Economic Cooperation and Development (OECD), the Asia-Pacific Economic Cooperation (APEC), and the UN Commission on Sustainable Development. Similarly, in the European context, the North Sea Conferences intervened in the translation of the precautionary approach to fisheries from a global principle to regional scientific and policy approaches. Civil-society activities around these forums can also serve to link the source or target institutions and thereby influence their response action.

Capacity Control and Checks on Subsidies

This section reviews the interaction between the global fisheries regime and provisions of the World Trade Organization (WTO) relevant to fisheries subsidies, with an emphasis on the 2001 decision to place this issue on the agenda for the Doha Round of multilateral trade negotiations.

Figures on the amount of subsidies provided to the fisheries sector vary widely, a reflection partly of scattered knowledge and partly of different definitions or operationalizations of accepted definitions (Milazzo 1998; Stone 1997). Recent estimates suggest a level somewhere in the range of U.S.$7–14 billion each year (Ruckes 2000). Fisheries subsidies are politically contested. On the one hand, governments have a number of worthwhile reasons for providing them, including employment in shipbuilding, harvesting, or processing sectors, food security, or protection of settlements in sparsely inhabited or economically disadvantaged coastal regions.[3] Also, not all government financial transfers for fishing vessels or equipment are problematic from a capacity perspective. For instance, investments that improve the efficiency of vessel operations may be neutral in capacity terms if combined with buyback or scrapping schemes. On the other hand, too many vessels chasing too few fish is a fundamental impediment to responsible harvesting. Subsidies can be an important factor in generating excessive fishing capacity, especially where management policies are unsatisfactory (Hannesson 2001, 17–19), including in many high-seas areas and developing-country zones harboring distant-water fishing activity.[4] In recent years, a number of states have reduced their financial contributions to the fisheries industry (Gréboval 2000), but subsidy reduction remains an important means of controlling the buildup of vessel capacity.

Part of the Problem: Inadequate WTO Subsidies Rules

Whereas the global fisheries regime aims to ensure the sustainable use of fish stocks, the objective of the global trade regime is first and foremost to remove restrictions on international trade between its members (see also chapter 8). Potential trade distortion associated with fisheries subsidies was therefore the main rationale for raising the issue within trade-oriented international institutions in the 1960s and 1970s, especially the OECD and WTO's predecessor—the General Agreement on Tariffs and Trade (GATT) (Steenblik 1999). According to the preamble of the agreement establishing the WTO, however, the WTO is also to allow for "the optimal use of the world's resources in accordance with the objective of sustainable development," and much of the WTO debate on fisheries subsidies has therefore considered environmental as well as trade aspects.

The global trade regime, specifically the 1994 Subsidies and Countervailing Measures (SCM) Agreement negotiated under the WTO, provides rules on subsidies that are detailed, legally binding, and supported by an elaborate compliance system that includes compulsory and binding dispute-settlement procedures and authorization of countervailing trade sanctions. In spite of this no fisheries subsidy has so far been challenged under WTO rules.

Notifications to the WTO of fisheries subsidies—an obligation under Article 25 of the SCM Agreement—have been very limited in terms of the amount of subsidies reported, the range of subsidies covered, and the quality of information provided (Schorr 1998, 154–155). Part of the reason is that several key concepts in the SCM Agreement are defined in ways that make it difficult to determine whether government expenditures and other interventions in the fisheries sector fall within the domain of the agreement (Stone 1997). The definition of a subsidy as a "financial contribution" has generated a lively debate on whether public investment in fisheries management and enforcement should count as subsidies. Research, monitoring, and control activities make up a significant proportion of government financial transfers to the fisheries sector worldwide (OECD 2000). Similar questions arise where governments fail to charge for access to resources or indeed purchase access to resources in foreign exclusive economic zones on behalf of the fishing industry. Furthermore, only "specific" subsidies (i.e., those limited to an enterprise, industry, or region) are covered by the agreement, which makes it unclear whether government provision of important infrastructure, such as quays and lighthouses, should be notified.

Among subsidies that are to be reported, only those contingent on export performance or the use of domestic rather than imported goods are prohibited. Other subsidies are actionable under the SCM Agreement only if they can be shown to have adverse effects on the interests of another party.[5]

Accordingly, only a limited subset of direct or indirect financial transfers to the fisheries industry is clearly disciplined under present rules, and conceptual unclarity contributes to a lack of information on the extent, nature, and objective of subsidies. Many states have considered this situation inadequate and have requested clarification of which part of a large gray area should be disciplined under WTO rules. Key members of the so-called Friends of Fish group of countries pressing for reform of fisheries subsidies rules in the WTO (Australia, Chile, Ecuador, Iceland, New Zealand, Peru, the Philippines, and the United States), especially the United States and New Zealand, have a long track record of trying to strengthen international restrictions on subsidies in primary industries (Steenblik 1999). On fisheries subsidies, they have been heavily supported by transnational environmental organizations, especially the World Wide Fund for Nature (WWF), which sought to harness the free-trade agenda in the interest of conservation. Compared to their most outspoken opponents on the fisheries subsidies issue, including Japan, the Republic of Korea, and the European Union, the Friends of Fish countries have had relatively low levels of fisheries subsidies and would therefore be less affected by stronger rules.

Cognitive Interaction: Programmatic Work under the Global Fisheries Regime

A FAO study published more than a decade ago (FAO 1992) is widely seen as central to the comeback of fisheries subsidies on the international diplomatic agenda, after a decade of moderate interest (Stone 1997; Steenblik 1999). The new twist introduced by this report was to emphasize much more than before the linkage between subsidies and problems of resource sustainability. While subsequent examinations by international organizations such as the World Bank (Milazzo 1998), OECD (1997, 2000), and APEC (PricewaterhouseCoopers 2000) have concluded that the U.S.$54 billion estimate of fisheries subsidies—or 70 percent of world catch value—that many read into the FAO report was much too high,[6] they have nevertheless documented that current levels of subsidies are substantial and a cause of overcapacity in the fisheries sector.

In 1998, at a time when the Friends of Fish group was pushing for more work on fisheries within the WTO and other international institutions, the Sub-Committee on Fish Trade of the FAO's Committee on Fisheries decided that the FAO had a role to play in compiling and disseminating information on the impacts of subsidies (FAO 1998a, para. 17). It is notable that from the outset, the FAO opted for a supportive and complementary role to other international agencies addressing fisheries subsidies, such as the WTO and OECD, and was careful to avoid any overlap with activities taking place there (see in particular FAO, 1998a, paras. 6 and 7). This stance was not favorable to those, including the EU and the Republic of Korea, who objected to the WTO taking a more prominent role in international governance of fisheries subsidies.[7]

In its International Plan of Action for the Management of Fishing Capacity (IPOA-Capacity), the FAO pledged to "collect all relevant information and data which might serve as a basis for further analysis aimed at identifying ... subsidies which contribute to overcapacity" (Art. 45). The organization set out to prepare technical guidelines for the management of fishing capacity and organized a series of technical and expert consultations on issues related to capacity. A Task Force on Fishery Subsidies was established in the FAO Fisheries Department to serve as a focal point in subsidy matters, monitor and review discussions and contributions from other organizations, and map the various forms of fisheries subsidies.

While a first FAO expert consultation held in 2000 failed to contribute substantially to the debate on whether and how WTO disciplines should be reformed, later efforts proved somewhat more successful. The report of the Expert Consultation on Economic Incentives and Responsible Fisheries was criticized by some within the FAO Committee on Fisheries as having "raised more questions than answers," and the Committee decided that a second consultation on the issue would comprise a broader range of experts with relevant practical and multidisciplinary experience in fisheries-management and trade issues.[8] At least the expert consultation identified forms of government transfers to be prioritized in research, which were all compatible with the conventional definition of subsidies espoused by the WTO: capital expansion such as vessel purchase or modernization grants, tax waivers and deferrals, and price support.[9] Nevertheless, the inadequacy of information was presented as a key conclusion of the consultation in the WTO, and there is no indication that the subsequent discussion on fisheries subsidies in the WTO Committee on Trade and Environment (CTE) paid much attention to this particular input.[10] In the subsequent years, however, the FAO organized information-exchange meetings with other international agencies with ongoing work programs on fisheries subsidies, including the OECD, the United Nations Environment Program (UNEP), and the WTO (FAO 2001a, 2002).

On balance, programmatic efforts under the global fisheries regime have to some extent, but hardly decisively, strengthened the hand of those who favor reform of the WTO subsidies regime. Throughout the 1990s, both proponents and opponents of WTO reform have referred to the FAO as a particularly relevant source of information on the matter.[11] By attempting to develop clearer and more consensual knowledge on which types of subsidies are capacity-driving and which can be supportive of sustainable fisheries, the FAO sought to render obsolete a key argument against WTO reform in the area, namely the difficulty of separating "good" from "bad" fisheries subsidies. However, the FAO's influence may have been greatest in what it did *not* do. By not opting for a front-runner position in regulatory efforts, as it had with regard to high-seas compliance measures, but instead supporting and facilitating the fisheries subsidies initiative within the global trade regime, the FAO did not add fuel to those who argued that the WTO was a poor arena for developing criteria to separate sustainable from nonsustainable fisheries subsidies.

Interaction through Commitment: Global Fisheries Norms and the Strength of the Friends of Fish Coalition

The global fisheries regime includes legal and political commitments that are supportive of those in favor of reform of WTO subsidies. Under the Fish Stocks Agreement, coastal states and states whose vessels fish on the high seas are to "take measures to prevent or eliminate overfishing and excess fishing capacity and to ensure that levels of fishing efforts do not exceed those commensurate with the sustainable use of fishery resources" (Art. 5). There is no explicit mention of subsidies, however.

The FAO Code of Conduct encourages states to ensure that "policies, programs and practices related to trade in fish and fishery products do not result in ... environmental degradation" (Art. 6.14), and that "excess fishing capacity is avoided and ... the economic conditions under which fishing industries operate promote responsible fisheries" (Art. 7.2.2). In addition, the Code provides that "States, aid agencies, multilateral development banks and other relevant international organizations should ensure that their policies and practices ... do not result in environmental degradation" (Art. 11.2.15).

The equally nonbinding FAO IPOA-Capacity calls on states to achieve, "preferably by 2003 but not later than 2005, an efficient, equitable and transparent management of fishing capacity" (Art. 7). If excess capacity is undermining the achievement of long-term management, states should take measures to limit and progressively reduce relevant fishing capacity. National plans for the management of fishing capacity are important means for this objective and shall include assessments of "all factors, including subsidies, contributing to overcapacity" (Art. 25). Finally, "States should reduce and progressively eliminate all factors, including subsidies ... which contribute, directly or indirectly, to the build-up of excessive fishing capacity thereby undermining the sustainability of marine living resources" (Art. 26).

It is difficult to measure the influence of these fisheries-regime provisions on the process of regulating subsidies within the WTO. It is indicative of such influence, however, that those in favor of reforming the trade rules on subsidies have consistently emphasized the existence of global fisheries norms in this area and especially the Fish Stocks Agreement and the IPOA-Capacity.[12] The latter was presented to the WTO Committee on Trade and Environment (CTE) in June 1999, at a time when support for reform of fisheries-subsidies rules was growing in the Committee. FAO was invited to report to the next CTE meeting "on the main elements of an indicative work program aimed at addressing the impact of subsidies and other factors which contribute to overcapacity and unsustainability in fisheries."[13] Since then, FAO representatives have regularly attended CTE meetings, providing updates on FAO activities related to fisheries subsidies.[14]

The Outcome: Fisheries Subsidies at the Forefront of Global Negotiations

The 2001 Doha Ministerial Declaration, which provides the mandate for the new round of trade negotiations, states that "participants shall also aim to clarify and improve WTO disciplines on fisheries subsidies, taking into account the importance of this sector to developing countries." The Declaration also highlights fisheries subsidies when sketching the broader trade-environment agenda.[15]

Programmatic work under the global fisheries regime and the latter's norms contributed to this outcome by making it more difficult for opponents to reject it. Right from the outset, discussions within the WTO had focused on the need for more information on the impact of subsidies on sustainability and trade, and we have seen that activities under the global fisheries regime were significant in this regard.[16] By summer 1999, following a high-level WTO symposium on trade and development,[17] states favoring fisheries-subsidy reform presented several substantial papers at a CTE meeting. These papers pointed to the "loss-loss-loss" relationship between fisheries subsidies on the one hand, and trade, environment, and development on the other,[18] and so support for placing the issue on the Doha Round agenda grew. Already at the WTO Seattle Ministerial Conference in late 1999, the EU as one major opponent accepted that fisheries subsidies would be addressed in the next world trade round. In Doha, the EU finally also agreed that the discussions could take place under the SCM Agreement (rather than as part of the environment agenda).

More important than the interaction with the global fisheries regime, however, was probably that fisheries subsidies increasingly became a development issue. Early on in the negotiations, fisheries subsidies had been framed primarily as a trade and environmental-sustainability issue addressed, since 1997, within the CTE (Porter 2002). However, development issues gained in prominence and proved decisive in moving the subsidies issue onto the main negotiating agenda in 2001.[19] From a North-South perspective, fishing interests in developing countries had to compete at sea and on international markets with heavily subsidized counterparts from wealthier nations. There is not much to suggest that norms or activities undertaken under the global fisheries regime played any important role in the mobilization of developing countries. The work of UNEP was probably more salient in this regard. Combining research work, country studies, and policy dialogue, it convened a number of expert meetings or consultations with key officials and international institutions with particular attention to the impact of fisheries subsidies on developing countries—notably in relation to third-country fishing agreements. Several leading civil-society organizations, including WWF, have also emphasized the development aspect of fisheries subsidies.

Summary and Assessment

Fisheries subsidies surfaced on the Doha Round agenda because the interests of a coalition of countries with relatively small domestic subsidies programs coincided with the interests of developing fishing nations, as well as with those of environmental organizations in industrialized countries. As summarized in figure 6.1, this section has presented two cases of interaction.

The first causal impact of the global fisheries regime on WTO subsidies rules is cognitive in nature: the FAO has raised concern over the issue and, along with a few other international institutions, ensured for supporters and opponents of subsidies reform alike a common source of legitimate expertise on fisheries subsidies. The second case of interaction between the global fisheries regime and the subsidy segment of the WTO regime is one of commitment. The subsidy-related provisions in the Fish Stocks Agreement, the FAO Code of Conduct, and the FAO IPOA-

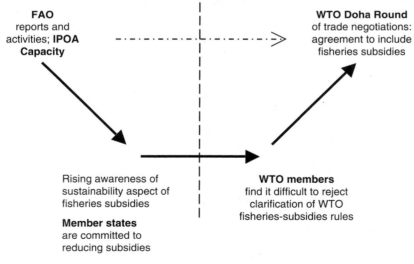

Figure 6.1
Global Fisheries Regime affects World Trade Round

Capacity supported those in the WTO who argued that fisheries subsidies are a barrier to sustainability, as well as a barrier to free trade. The provisions therefore played a part in bringing this particular issue onto the agenda for the Doha Round of global trade negotiations. Moreover, attempts to define the WTO as peripheral to the governance of fisheries subsidies and to place this issue within a forum with more fisheries expertise but less "clout"—that is, the FAO—were rejected. While the FAO has a well-established practice of mobilizing relevant fisheries expertise in the development of consensual guidelines on implementation at national levels, FAO rules, unlike WTO provisions, tend to be soft and are rarely backed up by intrusive enforcement mechanisms.

The instances of interaction described here have occurred at the level of institutional output, although this does not rule out effects at the levels of outcome (subsidies practices) or impact (on harvesting capacity). Both within the source and the target regime, the interaction has been pursued intentionally. Appreciating the significance that trade rules might assume with regard to controlling fisheries subsidies, the FAO sought to coordinate fact-finding and analytic activities relevant to the question of how subsidies influence sustainability. That said, in both regimes many of the activities relevant to fisheries subsidies were generated by internal processes and priorities, and by external pressures such as that from environmental organizations, rather than from the other regime.

Responses to the interaction have been of several kinds, although to date neither of the institutions has adapted its rules. There has been moderate interinstitutional coordination: the WTO invited the FAO to provide more specific information on available knowledge about the relationship between fisheries subsidies and sustainability problems. The FAO input provided in response has largely supported those questioning fisheries subsidies within the WTO, but it has failed to provide more than preliminary answers. Since the issue was highly controversial and FAO work is based on consensus, this is not surprising and it is doubtful whether more cross-institutional coordination could have changed the situation substantially. Adaptation to rising international attention to environmentally harmful fisheries subsidies is reflected in the fact that many governments chose to reduce their subsidies programs during the 1990s (Gréboval 2000).

Precaution, ICES, and the Common Fisheries Policy

The UN Fish Stocks Agreement contains one of the most explicit definitions provided in an international treaty of how the precautionary principle should apply in practice. Under Article 6, and applying the guidelines set out in Annex II, states are to decide on two types of precautionary reference points. First, a "limit reference point" is associated with danger: if a stock falls below this level, preagreed conservation and management action should be initiated to support stock recovery. The overall aim of management strategies is to ensure that the risk of exceeding a limit reference point is very low. Second, with respect to "target reference points," management strategies should ensure that these are not, on average, exceeded.

Based on a FAO Technical Consultation that involved fisheries experts from a wide range of organizations, a set of guidelines for implementing the precautionary approach was developed. These emphasized (1) the development of operational and measurable targets and constraints—that is, biological reference points that should (2) reflect management objectives based not only on biological but also on socioeconomic considerations and adequate stakeholder involvement, including the involvement of fishing-industry and conservation groups, and be accompanied by (3) preagreed decision rules that define what action should be taken when reference points are exceeded (FAO 1996, especially paras. 20–35).

The following assessment of how the global fisheries regime has influenced the emergence of a precautionary approach to fisheries management in the Northeast Atlantic is related to these guidelines. The first two subsections examine how the global fisheries regime has interacted with, respectively, ICES' development and communication of biological reference points. The third subsection analyzes the significance of ICES for the emergence of preagreed decision rules in the EU Common Fisheries Policy.

Interaction through Commitment: Biological Reference Points
Founded in 1902 under the Convention for the International Council for the Exploration of the Sea (last amended in 1964), ICES is an intergovernmental organization that coordinates scientific research and provides advice on fisheries management in the Northeast Atlantic. While the Fish Stocks Agreement introduces general provisions regarding the formulation and use of scientific advice at the global level, ICES has developed and implemented a specific procedure for generating advice, tailored to the relatively advanced level of knowledge about the various Northeast Atlantic fish stocks. ICES advice is not binding on governments and its influence on decision making depends largely on the organization's reputation for scientific excellence and neutrality toward the often competing claims of various stakeholders—which is widely perceived as high (Gullestad 1998). Most ICES parties are politically,

and increasingly also legally, bound by the Fish Stocks Agreement and this is an important driver of the interaction between the global fisheries regime and ICES.

The precautionary approach to fisheries management was not among the "themes" addressed at the ICES Annual Science Conferences in the years preceding the adoption of the Fish Stocks Agreement and the FAO Code of Conduct, but it has been featured repeatedly since 1997.[20] A Study Group on the Precautionary Approach to Fisheries Management was convened that year, charged with developing a form of advice that would be consistent with the precautionary approach as elaborated under the global fisheries regime.

Responding to the recommendations of the study group, the ICES Advisory Committee on Fisheries Management (ACFM) has since 1998 formulated its advice to management agencies within a framework for implementation of the precautionary approach (ICES 2000, 2001a). The advice is based on an estimate of current stock status and usually occurs in the form of catch options that should maintain the stock status inside "safe biological limits." The latter term was introduced as early as 1981 and refers to the level of the spawning stock below which there is an unacceptable probability that recruitment will be impaired (see ICES 2000, 4; 1992, 5–6). Similarly, the precautionary management strategy—or the maximum harvesting level that ICES would consider as precautionary—is identified by calculating a buffer that generates a very low probability of reaching a stock level at which recruitment will be impaired. The latter is ICES' operationalization of a limit (danger) reference point. The size of the buffer depends on the natural variability of the stock, the precision of the assessment, and the risk that management agencies are willing to accept (ICES 2000, 2).

Two specific changes are associated with the implementation of the precautionary approach: clearer articulation of the impairment risk that ICES considered acceptable (for most stocks set as low as 5 percent), and greater commitment to advise forceful rebuilding plans when stocks are depleted or overfished (compare ICES 2001b, iv with ICES 1992, 12). Since ICES used the same actual reference points after its introduction of a precautionary approach, one observer has stated that in effect, "the earlier management regime ... often remained unchanged, although the language has been given a precautionary gloss" (MacGarvin 2002, 20). That statement would surprise many nonscientist stakeholders in the region, and it underestimates the significance of the ICES decision to restrict the term *precautionary*, in cases where stocks are troubled, to conservation measures believed to rapidly rebuild the stock.

There is much to suggest that the elaboration of a precautionary approach in the Fish Stocks Agreement has galvanized scientists involved in the ICES advisory process, with their "long history of unsuccessfully trying to agree on targets with management agencies" (Hilborn et al. 2001, 100) whenever their biology-based recommendations face stakeholder complaints. A Russian request in 2000 for a change in the estimate of a precautionary reference point for Barents Sea cod, for instance, was rejected by ICES on the grounds that the data "available at present give no firm basis for revision of reference points" (ICES 2001b, 12). There is broad agreement that ICES has taken an early lead among regional scientific advisory bodies in implementing the precautionary approach (Hilborn et al. 2001, 100), particularly regarding methodologies for establishing biological reference points (Garcia 2000, 22), and the concept of precautionary management now permeates ICES activities.

While the global fisheries regime is not the only institution that has influenced ICES practices in this area, it has had the most specific effect. For instance, the precautionary approach to fisheries management was also discussed in depth during the 1997 Intermediate Ministerial Meeting on the Integration of Fisheries and Environmental Issues under the International North Sea Conferences, which involved many of the key participants in ICES. While this parallel process provided an occasion for political discussion of the subject and may have bolstered commitment to the precautionary approach and increased involvement by environmental interests, it did not advance the specification of the precautionary approach, which has largely occurred within specialized fisheries forums.[21]

Cognitive Interaction: Socioeconomic Aspects and Stakeholder Involvement

The objective pursued by ICES in the fisheries area (promotion of research and provision of scientific advice) is much narrower than that of the global fisheries regime (long-term conservation and sustainable use of fish stocks). Associated with this narrower functional scope is a significant difference in the mix of expertise mobilized under these institutions. In ICES fisheries bodies, marine biological expertise relevant to stock assessment and marine ecosystems predominates and the organization has a long tradition of advancing the research frontier in these particular areas (Stewart 1991, 2549). Such expertise is also found in the UN fisheries bureaucracy, primarily the FAO Fisheries Department, but here social scientists, economists, lawyers, and technologists are also well represented.[22] Whereas ICES is widely seen as being in the forefront of the development of biological reference points, the FAO

(1996, 16–21) has emphasized that the precautionary approach also requires mobilization of socioeconomic, technical, and institutional knowledge.

On the basis of these differences, complaints have been articulated—both within the FAO and by the regional management regimes ICES serves—that the precautionary procedure generates advice that is insufficiently sensitive to the socioeconomic costs associated with quota cuts. It has been argued from within FAO that, ideally, limit and target reference points should also be developed for socioeconomic and institutional impacts of conservation measures (Garcia 2000, 34). In the context of the EU Common Fisheries Policy, the sudden introduction of precautionary reference points and calls for recovery plans in the 1998 ICES advice left little time for discussions with industry before decisions had to be taken, while making it difficult for managers to gauge the costs and benefits of action (Brown 2000; Deas 2000). Similarly, in the years following the introduction of ICES advice based on limit and target reference points, the Norwegian-Russian Fisheries Commission chose to set quotas well above the level ICES considered precautionary (ICES 2000, sec. 3.1.2). As these examples demonstrate, complaints have easily translated into lack of acceptance of ICES recommendations.

The problem may have been exacerbated by the ways in ICES has communicated its precautionary advice, which has been criticized as difficult to understand for other stakeholders. Excessively technical language may reduce the ability of scientists to convey to industry and managers a clear picture of the biological consequences of management proposals, which is usually a requirement for obtaining their acceptance of costly restrictions on harvesting. Obscure or variant terminology may even engender suspicions that scientists "add extra (non transparent) conservatism or precaution into the estimation process" (Mace and Gabriel 1999, 69), thus trespassing into the domain of management agencies. Significant differences between the various scientific advisory bodies to North Atlantic management regimes in operational definitions of precautionary reference points (ICES 2000, 4–5) have further contributed to the problem. For instance, in contrast to the ICES practice of defining limit (danger) reference points in terms of impaired recruitment and then adding a buffer, the Northwest Atlantic Fisheries Organization (NAFO) has linked the limit reference point to the maximum sustainable yield (Garcia 2000, 24).

While ICES has never aspired to cover all relevant aspects of fisheries management, it has responded to these complaints. It is ultimately the responsibility of management agencies to ensure that they are advised by available expertise on the social, economic, and institutional effects of conservation measures—and not only on the biological impacts. Nevertheless, ICES has stepped up its efforts to improve communication with managers and industry representatives, not least about the costs and benefits of stock recovery plans.[23] To achieve a more harmonized terminology, ICES convened in 2000 an interagency meeting involving the FAO and a number of North Atlantic management bodies with a view to identifying differences and similarities in terminology and conceptual definitions, and exploring their consequences for the provision of precautionary scientific advice.[24] The ICES Advisory Committee on Fisheries Management noted that these interagency discussions "can be expected to result in further development and clarification of concepts and changes in terminology" (ICES 2001b, v), and has pledged to harmonize its use of the term limit reference point to that of NAFO (ICES 2000, 5). This reflects a general change in attitude within ICES toward the concept of maximum sustainable yield. Referring to the fact that the Fish Stocks Agreement includes this concept in its definition of the precautionary approach, ICES now pledges to "develop a balanced view on how best to interpret this reference point in a fish stock assessment context."[25]

Hence, inadequate attention to communication issues may have weakened ICES' role as an "interlocutor" between the global fisheries regime and regional management regimes. Related complaints have led to institutional learning within ICES induced, among other things, by the global fisheries regime. In the context of EU fisheries policy, some observers report that the communication between scientists and the industry has improved over time and has helped to convince parts of the fisheries sector of the benefits of the precautionary approach, not least as a means of introducing greater stability within the sector (Deas 2000). The adaptations initiated by ICES hold the same promise, although concrete results such as those in the EU have not yet materialized.

ICES and Precautionary Decision Making in EU's Common Fisheries Policy

The framework for fisheries management in the EU is set out in Regulation 2371/2002 on the Conservation and Sustainable Exploitation of Fisheries Resources under the Common Fisheries Policy (OJ L358, 31.12.2002) and its daughter regulations. Since the 1970s, a variety of instruments have been employed to curb overfishing or to prohibit damaging practices, yet a growing number of commercial fish stocks in European waters are considered to be outside safe biological limits. This is the case for some two-thirds of commercial stocks in the North Sea and the Mediterranean Sea, almost half of those in the Northeast Atlantic, and 20 percent of commercial stocks in the Baltic Sea (FAO 2001b); highly migratory species of tuna and swordfish are also overexploited.

The failure of the Common Fisheries Policy (CFP) to manage EU fish stocks is frequently blamed on the central role given to total allowable catch limits (TACs) as a management tool, and the process for setting these limits (e.g., European Commission 2000). The Council of Ministers adopts TACs each December, primarily covering commercial stocks in the Northeast Atlantic and the Baltic Sea. The Council decision follows a proposal from the European Commission. The proposals are, in turn, heavily derived from ICES advice. The annual Council negotiations over the Commission proposals are invariably politically charged, with individual fisheries ministers coming under considerable pressure to secure the best deal for their fishermen at home. Fisheries management is particularly vulnerable to such pressure precisely because of the uncertainty and ignorance about important bioecological as well as socioeconomic processes involved in fisheries (Garcia 2000). As a result, as one academic has aptly put it, "When the scientific advice has been refracted through the [EU] political process it may appear to shed little light on the final decisions" (Symes 1998, 12).

That said, the EU and several of its member states have been at the forefront of discussions on the precautionary principle. Since the Maastricht Treaty entered into force in 1993, Article 174 of the Treaty establishing the European Community states that Community environmental policy "shall be based on the precautionary principle." The EU (legally: the European Community, EC) participated actively in the negotiations on the UN Fish Stocks Agreement. And the EU is a major "client" of ICES and has benefited from, as well as contributed to, the leading role played by ICES scientists in elaborating and adapting scientific advice in line with the precautionary approach.

The challenge presented by the precautionary approach in the Fish Stocks Agreement and the FAO guidelines is to develop alternative multiannual management approaches, where decisions are based on preagreed decision rules. In other words, the precautionary approach requires adaptations not only in the generation of scientific advice but also in the decision-making process (Hanna 1999; Mace and Gabriel 1999). As Garcia (2000, 40) noted, "Alone or limited to its scientific aspects, [the precautionary approach] will only represent yet another step towards scientific sophistication along a 50-year old track which has produced large amounts of excellent science against a background of inexorably growing overexploitation, ecosystem degradation, economic dysfunction, and social stress."

As early as 1992, the CFP had provided for the adoption of "management objectives and strategies," setting the scene for a Commission proposal to this effect.[26] The proposal was the subject of some debate in the Council but discussions eventually stalled in 1995. Decisions on EU TACs were destined, for the time being, to continue to be made on an annual basis and in the absence of predetermined decision rules.

Steps were nevertheless taken to move toward the use of multiannual management plans, on a case-by-case basis, by the introduction of multiannual management strategies under bilateral agreements with Norway (several stocks, including cod) and other Northeast Atlantic states (herring and mackerel). These agreements specified that management action would be triggered when mortality or spawning stock biomass passed the precautionary reference points. Further plans were adopted within the context of the International Baltic Sea Fishery Commission (European Commission 2000, 13). These prescribed that management action should ensure a safe and rapid recovery, but without specifying exactly what this meant, or what measures were to be used to achieve it. Managers had thus agreed when to take action and certain management objectives, but had left open what action would be taken (ICES 2001c).

As detailed above, ICES presented precautionary reference points for the first time in its 1998 advice. In so doing, ICES introduced a precautionary approach "test" by stating that if a stock is regarded as depleted, or if overfishing is taking place, only an effective implementation of a rebuilding plan within a "reasonable" period would satisfy the condition for a precautionary approach. By not developing effective recovery plans in the case of depleted stocks, the EU would be failing the test.

ICES applied this approach in 1999 when it stated that "fishing mortality on cod should be reduced to the lowest level possible in 2000" (ICES 2000, part 2, 4) and should be accompanied by a recovery plan to rebuild the spawning stock. Cod is one of the EU's most significant stocks, culturally if not economically, and the ICES advice generated intense discussions in the Fisheries Council in December 1999. This led to a first set of emergency measures being adopted for Irish Sea cod in 2000, followed by longer-term measures to rebuild the stock.

Following these initial developments, efforts were redoubled to develop multiannual management plans more widely for EU fisheries. Importantly, a meeting in September 2000 showed that the need to lay down multiannual procedures that took the precautionary approach into account was now widely accepted by the member states (European Commission 2000, 13). A more concerted focus on management plans was consequently provided by a Communication of the Commission with pre-determined decision rules presented as part of such an approach. The use of such rules, according to the Commission, would end the practice that had resulted in priority being given to avoiding restrictions on fishing that were politically unpopular in the short term (European Commission 2000, 11). In December of that year, ministers agreed that conservation measures were also needed for other stocks of cod, and for hake, to be formulated within the context of multiannual recovery plans of at least five years.

These developments coincided with the Commission's preparations for the 2002 reform of the fisheries policy. In its Green Paper outlining the future direction of the CFP, the Commission referred to the measures agreed on for cod and hake as "a test case" for introducing multiannual management strategies across a range of commercial fisheries. It again supported the definition of multiannual strategies compatible with the precautionary principle (European Commission, 2001, 23). The final agreement, contained in the new basic CFP Regulation 2371/2002, states that the Council "shall adopt" multiannual plans for stocks outside safe biological limits and for other stocks, as far as necessary. Apart from biological reference points, an explicit reference is made to establishing harvesting rules laying down how annual catch or effort limits are to be arrived at. The new approach to management was accompanied by efforts by the EU to improve stakeholder communication and involvement through the introduction of regional advisory councils.

While political rather than legal, EU member states' commitment to ICES' advice regarding the management of certain critical EU fish stocks effectively put pressure on the EU to introduce recovery plans, which in turn were to provide the platform for introducing preagreed decision rules. A key provision of the Fish Stocks Agreement had thereby been translated into an EU context even before the EC and its then fifteen member states became parties to the Agreement in 2003. ICES' role as interlocutor between the UN Fish Stocks Agreement and the CFP is all but explicit in several ICES texts, including annual management advice to the EU that refers directly to provisions of the Agreement.

Summary and Assessment

This section has examined a sequence of three cases of institutional interaction on precautionary fisheries management. First, interaction between the global fisheries regime and ICES has influenced the way scientists in the Northeast Atlantic generate advice to decision makers. Partially overlapping membership is the main driver: the scientists who participate in the more specialized regional institution were bound by new global rules and responded by modifying the terms used in their advice and by placing greater emphasis on rapid recovery whenever stocks are outside safe biological limits. The effect of this interaction could be deemed synergistic, since the global fisheries regime induced ICES members to focus on a highly contentious issue—how to respond to uncertainty regarding the effects of various harvesting patterns—without disrupting their ability to come up with agreed-on recommendations. From another perspective, however, the largely natural-scientist driven implementation of the precautionary approach had tipped the fine balance between biological and social concerns and was therefore in need of remedy (Hilborn et al. 2001).

This is where the second case of interaction becomes relevant since the global fisheries regime has also influenced the way ICES advice is communicated to other stakeholders. Here, differences in the scope of objectives are the most important factor and the interaction is cognitive in nature. The FAO, which has a significant role in the implementation of global fisheries rules, has a much broader mandate than ICES. It has consistently and with some success advocated greater emphasis on nonbiological aspects of precautionary management, including socioeconomic impacts, and has also pushed for greater emphasis on the interface between scientists and other stakeholders. ICES has voluntarily responded to these considerations by attempting to improve communication and harmonize terminology, because the effectiveness of its advice depends on the voluntary acceptance by the institutions it serves.

Third, these changes in ICES practice have intervened with the reform of the EU's Common Fisheries Policy and contributed to the provisions requiring multiannual management plans and preagreed harvesting rules. The causal mechanism at work in this case is Interaction through Commitment. Although some effect flows directly from the EU's involvement in the negotiation of the Fish Stocks Agreement and its general commitment to the precautionary principle, the most specific causal signal has been the scientific advice articulated by ICES "in the shadow" of the global fisheries regime. Notably, ICES' dire advice regarding the state of EU cod and hake stocks has acted as a motor behind the emergence of rebuilding plans.

Conclusions

The global fisheries regime has developed considerably during the past decade, notably by the elaboration of a precautionary approach to fisheries management, stronger and more specific requirements for cooperation on high-seas fisheries, and more intrusive compliance-control procedures beyond national waters. Interaction with international regimes in other issue areas, and with certain particularly advanced regional fisheries regimes, has been important to this development (Stokke 2001; Stokke and Coffey 2001). This chapter has examined in detail two sets of cases where the global fisheries regime has influenced problem-solving activities under other institutions, specifically WTO regulation of fisheries subsidies, ICES' provision of scientific advice, and regulatory decision making under the EU Common Fisheries Policy (CFP).

For all of these cases, differences in means are an important driver of institutional interaction. In the subsidies case, provisions of the fisheries regime relating to subsidies are nonbinding and backed up by weaker compliance mechanisms than those of the target regime, the WTO. The fisheries regime has raised awareness of participants in the trade regime to fisheries subsidies and lent credibility to a negative framing that highlights threats to sustainability and development rather than the positive impacts that fisheries subsidies may have. Commitments of countries under the Fish Stocks Agreement and more explicitly in IPOA-Capacity worked in the same direction. The precautionary cases also display institutional Interaction through Commitment: the new binding commitments of the global fisheries regime have enhanced the compelling force of precautionary procedures in ICES and, subsequently, the EU CFP, resulting in modified scientific advice and more precautionary regulation of fisheries supported by supranational enforcement.

Differences in membership are significant to the extent that they explain differences in means. With respect to precaution, the overall format provided by the global fisheries regime has been specified and made operational within the narrower Northeast Atlantic context where membership differs notably. Furthermore, differences in the objectives of the interacting institutions have led to differences as to the bureaucratic sectors involved and the associated expertise, which has given rise to Cognitive Interaction. One reason why the WTO has been so eager to maintain cooperative links with the FAO on subsidies reform is the latter's recognized expertise in fisheries matters and its access to additional expertise at national management levels. Similarly, the broader vocational blend characteristic of the FAO as compared to ICES, especially with regard to the technological and social sciences, explains in part why this organization has given relatively more emphasis to the nonbiological aspects of precautionary management.

The overall effects of the cases of interaction examined here have been synergistic, though not always overwhelmingly so. With regard to fisheries subsidies, the global fisheries regime helped place this issue on the agenda of the new round of WTO negotiation, but it is yet unclear whether rules will actually be changed in a way that will address overcapacity in the fisheries sector. Similarly, the precautionary provisions of the Fish Stocks Agreement strengthened the hand of those within ICES and subsequently EU fisheries bodies who favored greater safety margins, long-term planning, and preagreement on recovery plans for endangered stocks. That said, the actual impacts on management are unclear, partly because precautionary advice has only recently been accompanied by regulatory decision making in favor of long-term and precautionary management.

All cases display awareness among participants in source and target regimes of the fact of interaction and also preparedness to respond to it, if necessary. Most of the response has occurred within the respective regimes, while active interinstitutional coordination has played only a moderate part. In the subsidies case, the FAO was asked by the WTO to help clarify the causal relationships between subsidies and responsible fisheries management but was unable, at least in the short term, to provide specific findings that would facilitate agreement on the issue within the WTO. There is little to suggest that more extensive cross-regime coordination would have improved this interaction, due to the high level of political controversy that surrounds the issue. The current WTO negotiations on fisheries subsidies that could generate stronger and more enforceable rules create new opportunities for the FAO and others to provide more specific inputs. As regards precautionary management, some interagency coordination on how to improve implementation has also occurred, in the form of broad expert meetings, but the higher level of conflict among various stakeholders that accompanied introduction of the precautionary approach has largely been addressed within each of the respective institutions.

The findings in this chapter confirm that institutional interaction at global and regional levels can be significant for the ability of international and European regulations to address environmental management effectively. Cross-institutional learning, by flows of concepts and ideas, is an important way such interaction occurs, as are processes of obligation in cases where the source regime is binding and the memberships partially overlap. Such impacts should not be expected to be strong in the short term because inputs from other institutions are typically filtered through the existing practices of the target regime. Accordingly, when examining how participants in the respective institutions respond to the interaction, it is vital that sufficient attention be paid to the autonomous collective decision making within the source or the target institutions (instead of focusing exclusively on interagency coordination efforts).

Notes

The authors gratefully acknowledge constructive comments from Serge Garcia, Oran Young, and our fellow contributors to this book, especially Thomas Gehring, Sebastian Oberthür, and Alice Palmer. Helpful information has been provided by Olle Hagström, Carl-Christian Schmidt, and Ronald Steenblik. The work has been supported by the European Community under the Specific Research and Technological Development Programme "Energy, Environment and Sustainable Development" (contract no. EVK2-CT2000-00079); by the Research Council of Norway (grant no. 128925/520/KS); and by the Esmee Fairbairn Foundation, UK. Parts of the material in the section "Precaution, ICES, and the Common Fisheries Policy" appeared in Stokke and Coffey 2004.

1. Agreement for the Implementation of the Provisions of the United Nations Convention on the Law of the Sea of December 10, 1982, relating to the Conservation and Management of Straddling Fish Stocks and Highly Migratory Fish Stocks, available at http://www.un.org/Depts/los/index.htm.

2. The first three were adopted in 1999, the fourth in 2001; texts are available at http://www.fao.org.

3. See, for example, WTO doc. WT/CTE/W/175, October 24, 2000, available at http://www.docsonline.wto.org/gen_search.asp.

4. Access conditions are generally believed to be the most important factor explaining cross-state variation in excess capacity (Cunningham and Gréboval 2001).

5. SCM Agreement, Articles 3, 5, and 6. Until December 31, 1999, even subsidies shown to have adverse effects were *non*actionable if they related to research activities, disadvantaged regions, or adaptation of existing facilities in response to new environmental rules; see Article 8.

6. Note that the FAO report did not actually make this claim, but much of its influence is due to the fact that many read this finding into it (Milazzo 1998; also Stone 1997); see, for example, WT/CTE/W/51, May 19, 1997, 2; also FAO 1998b, para. 8.

7. See WTO doc. WT/CTE/W/173, October 23, 2000.

8. WT/CTE/W/189, June 18, 2001, p. 1.

9. WTO doc. WT/CTE/W189, June 18, 2001.

10. *Trade and Environment News Bulletins*, TE/036, July 6, 2001.

11. WTO docs. WT/CTE/W/51 (United States), WT/GC/W/303 (Friends of Fish), and WT/CTE/W/173 (Japan).

12. See, for example, WTO docs. WT/CTE/W/121, June 28, 1999; WT/GC/W/303, August 6, 1999; WT/CTE/W/154, July 4, 2000; TN/RL/W/3, April 24, 2002.

13. See FAO 1998; WTO doc. WT/CTE/W/126, October 12, 1999.

14. See, for example, WTO docs. WT/CTE/W/135, February 29, 2000; WT/CTE/W/189, June 18, 2001.

15. Doha Declaration, paras. 28 and 31; available at http://www.wto.org.

16. See *Trade and Environment News Bulletins*, TE/018, July 1997; TE/021, December 16, 1997; TE/023, May 14, 1998; TE/028, March 31, 1999.

17. International Institute for Sustainable Development Report on the WTO's High-Level Symposium on Trade and Environment, March 15–16, 1999, available at http://www.wto.org.

18. See *Trade and Environment News Bulletins*, TE/029, July 30, 1999.

19. Compare the two 1997 documents on the issue—WT/CTE/W/51 (May 19, 1997) and WT/CTE/W/67 (November 7, 1997, pp. 33–34)—with WT/CTE/W/121 (June 28, 1999); also the report of the subsequent CTE meeting in WTO *Trade and Environment News Bulletins*, TE/031 (November 8, 1999).

20. Detailed information on the topics discussed at these conferences is available at http://www.ices.dk.

21. Compare "Statement of Conclusions from the Intermediate Ministerial Meeting on the Integration of Fisheries and Environmental Issues" (http://www.dep.no/md/nsc/Intermediate_meeting/023021-990005/index-dok000-b-n-a.html), especially sections on Guiding Principles and Strategies, with FAO 1996).

22. "FAO Fisheries Department—Staff List and Capabilities" (available at http://www.dec.ctu.edu.vn/cdrom/cd6/projects/faofish_1197/staffirm.htm).

23. "Resolutions Adopted at the 2001 Annual Science Conference," p. 14, available at http://www.ices.dk.

24. "Resolutions Adopted at the 1999 Annual Science Conference," p. 77, available at http://www.ices.dk.

25. "Resolutions Adopted at the 2000 Annual Science Conference," p. 15, available at http://www.ices.dk.

26. Proposal for a Council Regulation fixing management objectives and strategies for certain fisheries or groups of fisheries for the period 1994 to 1997, Doc. COM(93)663, in *Official Journal* C 017, 20/01/1994.

References

Brown, Sue. 2000. The Precautionary Approach: A User's View. Paper presented at ICES 2000 Annual Science Conference, September 27–30, Brugge. Copenhagen: International Council for the Exploration of the Sea.

Caddy, John. 1998. *A Short Review of Precautionary Reference Points and Some Proposals for Their Use in Data-Poor Situations*. FAO Fisheries Technical Paper 379: 30. Rome: Food and Agriculture Organization.

Cunningham, Steve, and Dominique Gréboval. 2001. *Managing Fishing Capacity: A Review of Policy and Technical Issues*. FAO Fisheries Technical Paper 409. Rome: Food and Agriculture Organization.

Deas, Barrie. 2000. Fishermen and Scientists: Collaboration as the Basis for Stock Recovery. Paper presented at ICES 2000 Annual Science Conference, September 27–30, Brugge. Copenhagen: International Council for the Exploration of the Sea.

European Commission. 2000, December 1. *Communication from the Commission to the Council and European Parliament—Application of the Precautionary Principle and*

Multi-annual Arrangements for Setting TACs. Doc. COM(2000)803. Brussels: European Commission.

European Commission. 2001, March 20. *Green Paper on a Future Common Fisheries Policy.* Doc. COM(2001)135. Brussels: European Commission.

FAO. 1992. Special Chapter: Marine Fisheries and the Law of the Sea—A Decade of Change. *The State of Food and Agriculture 1992.* Rome: Food and Agriculture Organization. Available at http://verweile.com/445_html/los-1/.

FAO. 1996. *Precautionary Approach to Capture Fisheries and Species Introductions.* FAO Technical Guidelines for Responsible Fisheries 2. Available at http://www.fao.org/DOCREP/003/W3592E/W3592E00.htm.

FAO. 1997. *Review of the State of World Fishery Resources: Marine Fisheries.* FAO Fisheries Circular 920. Available at http://www.fao.org/docrep/003/w4248e/w4248e00.htm.

FAO. 1998a. *COFI Report of the Sixth Session of the Sub-Committee on Fish Trade.* FAO Fisheries Reports R589. Rome: Food and Agriculture Organization.

FAO. 1998b. Committee on Fisheries, Sub-Committee on Fish Trade. *Fisheries Management, Subsidies and International Fish Trade.* Sixth Session, Bremen, June 3–6. Doc. COFI: FT/VI/98/4. Rome: Food and Agriculture Organization.

FAO. 2001a. *Report of the Ad Hoc Meeting with Intergovernmental Organizations on Work Programmes Related to Subsidies in Fisheries.* FAO Fisheries Reports R649. Available at http://www.fao.org/DOCREP/003/Y0999E/Y0999E00.HTM.

FAO. 2001b. *The State of the World Fisheries and Aquaculture 2000.* Available at http://www.fao.org/DOCREP/003/X8002E/X8002E00.htm.

FAO. 2002. *Report of the Second Ad Hoc Meeting with Intergovernmental Organizations on Work Programmes Related to Subsidies in Fisheries.* FAO Fisheries Reports R688. Rome: Food and Agriculture Organization.

Garcia, Serge M. 2000. The Precautionary Approach to Fisheries 1995–2000: Progress Review and Main Issues. In *Report of the CWP Intersessional Meeting.* Advisory Committee on Fisheries Management. ICES doc. CM 2000/ACFM:17, 19–46. Copenhagen: International Council for the Exploration of the Sea. Available at http://www.ices.dk/reports/acfm/2000/cwp/cwp00.pdf.

Gréboval, Dominique. 2000. The FAO International Plan of Action for the Management of Fishing Capacity. Paper presented at the Conference IIFET 2000, International Institute of Fisheries Economics and Trade, Oregon State University, July 10–15, 2000, Corvallis, Oregon. Available at http://oregonstate.edu/Dept/IIFET/2000/abstracts/greboval.html.

Gullestad, Petter. 1998. The Scope for Research in Practical Fishery Management. *Fisheries Research* 37 (1–3): 251–258.

Hanna, Susan S. 1999. Strengthening Governance of Ocean Fishery Resources. *Ecological Economics* 31 (2): 275–286.

Hannesson, Rögnvaldur. 2001. *Effects of Liberalizing Trade in Fish, Fishing Services and Investment in Fishing Vessels.* OECD Papers, 1. Available at http://www.oecd.org/dataoecd/1/11/1917250.pdf.

Hilborn, Ray, Jean-Jacques Maguire, Ana M. Parma, and Andrew A. Rosenberg. 2001. The Precautionary Approach and Risk Management: Can They Increase the Probability of Successes in Fishery Management? *Canadian Journal of Fisheries and Aquatic Sciences* 58 (1): 99–107.

ICES. 1992. *Report of the ICES Advisory Committee on Fisheries Management*. ICES Cooperative Research Report 179. Copenhagen: International Council for the Exploration of the Sea.

ICES. 2000. *Report of the ICES Advisory Committee on Fisheries Management, 1999*. ICES Cooperative Research Report 236. Copenhagen: International Council for the Exploration of the Sea.

ICES. 2001a. *Advisory Committee on Fishery Management*. Report of the Study Group on the Further Development of the Precautionary Approach to Fisheries Management. ICES Doc. CM 2001/ACFM:11. Copenhagen: International Council for the Exploration of the Sea.

ICES. 2001b. *Report of the ICES Advisory Committee on Fisheries Management*. ICES Cooperative Research Report 242. Copenhagen: International Council for the Exploration of the Sea.

ICES. 2001c. *Report of the ICES Advisory Committee on Fisheries Management*. ICES Cooperative Research Report 246. Copenhagen: International Council for the Exploration of the Sea.

Mace, Pamela M., and Wendy L. Gabriel. 1999. Evolution, Scope and Current Applications of the Precautionary Approach in Fisheries. Paper presented at the Fifth National NMFS Stock Assessment Workshop, February 24–26, Key Largo, Florida. NOAA Technical Memorandum, NMFS-F/SPO-40. Available at http://www.st.nmfs.gov/st2/nsaw5.html.

MacGarvin, Malcolm. 2002. Fisheries: Taking Stock. In Poul Harremoës, David Gee, Malcolm MacGarvin, Andy Stirling, Jane Keys, Brian Wynne, and Sofia Guedes Vaz, eds., *The Precautionary Principle 1896–2000: Late Lessons from Early Warnings*, 10–25. London: Earthscan.

Milazzo, Matteo. 1998. *Subsidies in World Fisheries: A Reexamination*. World Bank Technical Paper: Fisheries Series. Washington, DC: World Bank.

OECD. 1997. *Towards Sustainable Fisheries: Economic Aspects of the Management of Living Marine Resources*. Paris: OECD.

OECD. 2000. *Transition to Responsible Fisheries: Economic and Policy Implications*. Paris: OECD.

Pauly, Daniel, Villy Christensen, Sylvie Guénette, Tony J. Pitcher, U. Rashid Sumaila, Carl J. Walters, Reg Watson, and Dirk Zeller. 2002, August 8. Towards Sustainability in World Fisheries. *Nature* 418: 689–695.

Porter, Gareth. 2002. *Fisheries Subsidies and Overfishing: Towards a Structured Discussion*. Volume 1 in the UNEP/ETB Fisheries and the Environment Series. Geneva: United Nations Environment Program. Available at http://www.unep.ch/etu/etp/acts/capbld/rdtwo/FE_vol_1.pdf.

PricewaterhouseCoopers. 2000. *Study into the Nature and Extent of Subsidies in the Fisheries Sector of APEC Members Economies*. Prepared for Fisheries Working Group Asia Pacific

Economic Co-operation. Available at http://www.apec.org/apec/apec_groups/working_groups/fisheries.downloadlinks.0004.LinkURL.Download.ver5.1.9.

Ruckes, Erhard. 2000. International Trade in Fishery Products and the New Global Trading Environment. In *Multilateral Trade Negotiations on Agriculture: A Resource Manual*. Rome: Food and Agriculture Organization. Available at www.fao.org/DOCREP/003/X7351E/X7351E00.HTM.

Schorr, David. 1998. Towards Rational Disciplines on Subsidies to the Fishery Sector: A Call for New International Rules and Mechanisms. *The Footprint of Distant Water Fleets on World Fisheries* (a series of papers published by WWF). Godalming, UK: World Wide Fund for Nature. Available at http://www.panda.org/news_facts/publications/search.cfm?uNC=54358643.

Steenblik, Ronald P. 1999. Previous Multilateral Efforts to Discipline Subsidies to Natural Resource Based Industries. In Michael Riepen, ed., *Report of Proceedings: Workshop on the Impact of Government Financial Transfers on Fisheries Management, Resource Sustainability, and International Trade*, August 17–19, 1998, Manila, The Philippines, 39–80. Singapore: Pacific Economic Co-operation Council.

Stewart, James E. 1991. A Brief Review of the International Council for the Exploration of the Sea (ICES) on the Occasion of the Formation of the North Pacific Marine Science Organization. *Canadian Journal of Fisheries and Aquatic Sciences* 48 (12): 2543–2550.

Stokke, Olav Schram, ed. 2001. *Governing High Seas Fisheries: The Interplay of Global and Regional Regimes*. Oxford: Oxford University Press.

Stokke, Olav Schram, and Clare Coffey. 2001. *Institutional Interaction in High Seas Fisheries Management: An Inventory*. Project Deliverable No. D8 of the Project: Institutional Interaction: How to Prevent Conflicts and Enhance Synergies between International and EU Environmental Institutions. Available at http://www.ecologic.de/projekte/interaction/results.htm.

Stokke, Olav Schram, and Clare Coffey. 2004. Precaution, ICES and the Common Fisheries Policy: A Study of Regime Interplay. *Marine Policy* 28 (2): 117–126.

Stone, Christopher D. 1997. Too Many Fishing Boats, Too Few Fish: Can Trade Laws Trim Subsidies and Restore the Balance in Global Fisheries? *Ecology Law Quarterly* 24 (3): 505–544.

Symes, David. 1998. *The Integration of Fisheries Management and Marine Wildlife Conservation*. JNCC Report No 287. Peterborough: Joint Nature Conservation Committee. Available at http://www.jncc.gov.uk/marine/fisheries/reports/rpt_integFishMan.htm.

7

The Convention on International Trade in Endangered Species of Wild Fauna and Flora (CITES): Responding to Calls for Action from Other Nature Conservation Regimes

John Lanchbery

The Convention on International Trade in Endangered Species of Wild Fauna and Flora (CITES) is unusual among international environmental regimes in that its main mode of operation, the regulation of international trade, tends to drive it to interact and cooperate with a number of nonenvironmental institutions, in particular concerning trade. From its entry into force in 1975, it has thus worked not only via its parties and their domestic police and customs organizations but also directly with the World Customs Organization (WCO), the International Criminal Police Organization (Interpol), and the General Agreement on Tariffs and Trade (GATT) that later became part of the World Trade Organization (WTO).

Furthermore, CITES interacts with a number of other international regimes concerning the conservation of wildlife,[1] of which CITES is probably the leading example and has in some ways formed the center. Wildlife conservation regimes often work together as a group of treaties, assisting each other to meet common objectives. This is because they share a common, overall goal (the conservation of wild animals or plants), but differ either in the species they cover or in the way they pursue the goal. Thus, while CITES regulates international trade in endangered species, the Convention on Migratory Species of Wild Animals (CMS) provides for conservation measures "on the ground," the International Convention on the Regulation of Whaling restricts the taking of whales, and so on.

The fact that the conservation agreements are interrelated in this way is no accident. Many of them have common origins, often in the form of calls for their establishment by the World Conservation Union (IUCN), and they were often specifically designed to operate in different but complementary ways. The IUCN was the initial instigator of most of the major wildlife treaties concluded in the second half of the twentieth century, including both CITES and the CMS. Cooperation between the wildlife treaties is actively promoted by the IUCN, both directly and via the secretariats to the treaties, which it commonly provides with the United Nations Environment Program (UNEP).

This chapter focuses mainly on the interactions between CITES and two other nature conservation regimes: the CMS and the Convention for the Conservation and Management of the Vicuña (Convenio para la Conservación y Manejo de la Vicuña, CCMV). These cases of interaction were selected chiefly because they are examples of how the nature conservation treaties often act in concert and of the central role of CITES in this. In particular, they demonstrate how regimes with limited memberships have used CITES, with its larger, global membership, to assist them in meeting common nature conservation goals. CITES responded to a call for action by the CMS to protect the Asiatic subspecies of the houbara bustard, a bird recognized as endangered by both CITES and the CMS. The CCMV asked CITES for assistance in protecting the vicuña, which was again recognized as threatened by both regimes.

The chapter begins with a description of CITES, its origins, and its mode of operation. It then provides an overview of the interactions of CITES with a broad range of other international institutions and EU legislative instruments. Subsequently, the two cases of interaction with the CMS concerning the houbara bustard and the CCMV concerning the vicuña are investigated in greater detail. In each case, the other treaty is described and an account of the concrete case of interaction is provided. The chapter ends with some general conclusions.

The Convention on International Trade in Endangered Species of Wild Fauna and Flora (CITES)

CITES seeks to protect wild species by regulating trade in both the species themselves and products made from them. Its aim is to conserve endangered species, but it does so by attempting to control trade. In doing so, it implicitly recognizes that it is often hard for international regimes to effectively prescribe what their parties should do at home, whereas it can be comparatively easy to regulate an international activity, such as trade.

CITES' focus on attempting to limit trade appears to be well justified. International trade in wildlife is enormous, and controlling it to sustainable levels would undoubtedly do much to conserve many species. The Directorate General Environment of the European Commission estimates that international wildlife trade, both legal and illegal, is worth at least U.S.$10–20 billion annually. From 1995 to 1999, legal trade in CITES-listed species alone involved 1.5 million live birds, 640,000 live reptiles, about 3 million reptile skins, 150,000 furs, almost 300 tons of caviar, over 1 million pieces of coral, and 21,000 hunting trophies (Mulliken 2002).

The idea of limiting international trade in endangered species is not new. It dates back to the first decade of the twentieth century, when there was a call for a treaty limiting trade in the exotic bird feathers then used in ladies' hats (Lyster 1985). Later, the 1933 London Convention on the preservation of fauna and flora in Africa included provisions for restricting trade and also introduced the concept of having easily changeable annexes or appendixes listing endangered species (Lyster 1985; Sand 1997). Many later regional fauna and flora treaties followed the example of the London Convention, paving the way for the global CITES agreement that limits trade in species listed in exactly the same way (Lanchbery 1995).

Substantive political moves for a global agreement on trade in endangered species began in the 1950s, together with other wildlife agreements, notably the Ramsar Convention on Wetlands (Lyster 1985; Burns 1990). In 1963, the Governing Council of the IUCN called for "an international convention on regulating the export, transit and import of rare or threatened fauna and flora species or their skins or trophies."[2] Subsequent progress on negotiating a treaty was, however, slow until the 1972 Stockholm United Nations Conference on the Human Environment reemphasized the need for such an agreement. By March 1973 CITES had been negotiated and signed by its first twenty-one parties (Sand 1997). By spring 2005 it had 167 parties (http://www.cites.org), the largest membership of all wildlife conservation treaties, of which it is very much the "flagship" (Wijnstekers 2003).[3]

The main features of the mode of operation of CITES are three appendixes that are reviewed and can be changed at its Conference of the Parties (COP), which has met roughly every two years. The first appendix lists species in which trade is banned in all but the most exceptional circumstances. Appendix II includes species not necessarily threatened with extinction, but in which trade must be controlled in order to "avoid utilization incompatible with their survival" (Article II.2.a of CITES). Appendix III contains species that are protected in at least one country, which has asked other CITES parties for assistance in controlling the trade (Article II).

The treaty lays down detailed rules governing the import and export of species or products made from them. It also requires parties to establish national Management Authorities and Scientific Authorities. It further determines that the COP to CITES should meet every two years. Some operational features of the treaty have evolved considerably over time, extending and strengthening the remit of CITES over and above the provisions in the original text of the treaty (Wijnstekers 2003). It has, for example, set up a Standing Committee to oversee the operation of the agreement between COPs as well as other committees that assist the parties in making decisions on the classification of species. It has also developed a compliance and enforcement mechanism operated by the Secretariat and the Standing Committee. This mechanism includes the possibility of banning all wildlife trade with recalcitrant states. Throughout the 1990s, for example, the Standing Committee banned such trade with a number of countries, including Italy, Thailand, and Greece, until they came into compliance (Lanchbery 1995; Reeve 2002).

No description of CITES, or almost any wildlife treaty, is complete without a description of the role of the IUCN. Founded on October 5, 1948, as the International Union for the Protection of Nature (IUPN), the organization changed its name to the International Union for the Conservation of Nature and Natural Resources (IUCN) in 1956. In 1990 this was shortened to IUCN–The World Conservation Union. It called for many of the conservation agreements and helps considerably in their operation, by providing information concerning endangered species and by providing services such as secretariats, often with UNEP (Lanchbery 1995). Indeed, the IUCN's "Red Lists" of endangered species of wild animals and plants that are produced by the Species Survival Commission of the IUNC (http://www.redlist.org) largely drive the listing of species in CITES appendixes.

The IUCN is a complex and unusual international organization in that it has a large and varied membership of both states and nongovernmental organizations (NGOs). In 2002, its membership comprised 675 national NGOs, 68 international NGOs, 72 states (i.e., governments), and 107 government agencies. This unique combination of members makes it both a source of excellent, reliable information and, because of its governmental membership alone, a powerful force to be reckoned with. It has a large permanent staff, of in excess of 1,000, with 10,000 expert volunteers (http://www.iucn.org).

CITES and the other wildlife conservation treaties also have strong links with the more conventional wildlife NGOs, almost all of which are members of the IUCN. Notable among these are the World Wide Fund for Nature (WWF), the World Conservation Monitoring Centre (WCMC), Trade Records Analysis of Fauna and Flora in Commerce (TRAFFIC), and, especially in the case of treaties with a significant wild-bird interest (such as the CMS and Ramsar), BirdLife International. Both the WCMC and TRAFFIC were originally set up by WWF but are now independent of it. The WCMC has in the meantime been incorporated in UNEP.

These organizations play a key part in the operation of CITES and the CMS. Indeed, the IUCN, WCMC, and TRAFFIC are formally recognized as the "technical partners" in CITES. They provide much of the information about science and about infractions that the regime needs in order to operate effectively. The IUCN's "Red Lists" of endangered species are based heavily on information from organizations such as BirdLife International and WWF and misbehavior by parties is often reported to the CITES Secretariat by TRAFFIC (Lanchbery 1995; Reeve 2002).

Interactions and Synergies with Other Institutions

CITES has been involved in many interactions with other international institutions and EU legal instruments. Fourteen such interactions between CITES, involving seven other international institutions and the EU, are summarized in table 7.1. This list is not exhaustive but covers many pertinent cases. In most cases, extensive and lasting cooperation and exchanges between CITES and the other institutions have developed in response to the initial interinstitutional influence indicated in the table.

Horizontal Interactions with Other International Institutions
While it is hard to generalize about all CITES interactions from what is not an exhaustive list, all the horizontal interactions between international institutions were synergistic or neutral, or they were managed successfully so that tensions were prevented from turning into open conflict. The interaction with the WTO is the only one in which the underlying relationship was disruptive because the WTO promotes free trade, which is restricted by CITES. The commitments of both institutions are potentially at odds (Interaction through Commitment). This is not to say that political conflict did not occur about the political responses to interinstitutional influence. For example, a minority of parties (the remaining nations that conduct whaling) vigorously opposed the CITES decision to restrict trade in whale products in response to a request by the International Convention on the Regulation of Whaling and lodged reservations to it (for an account of the changes in the whaling regime and its impacts elsewhere, see Andresen 1998). The request as such, however, was fully in line with the conservation objective of CITES.

With the exception of the interaction with the WTO, all other cases of interaction followed the causal mechanisms of Cognitive Interaction and Behavioral Interaction. All cases in which CITES asked other institutions for support, or vice versa, constituted Cognitive Interaction because the decision on whether to respond

Table 7.1
Interactions of CITES

Convention for the Conservation and Management of the Vicuña (CCMV)	• CCMV has asked CITES for help in limiting trade in vicuña products and CITES has responded positively with a COP Resolution.
International Convention on the Regulation of Whaling (ICRW)	• The ICRW has asked for help in restricting trade in whale products and CITES has responded positively with a COP Resolution.
Convention on Migratory Species of Wild Animals (CMS)	• In response to a call for action by CMS, CITES passed a COP Resolution in support of CMS concerning the houbara bustard.
Convention on Biological Diversity (CBD)	• CITES supports implementation of the CBD; several decisions and resolutions in both institutions promote cooperation and synergy.
World Trade Organization (WTO)	• CITES restricts free trade and thus is in potential conflict with the WTO; it allows for trade with nonparties complying with its obligations.
World Customs Organization (WCO)	• CITES asked the WCO for help in implementation. • In response, WCO supports implementation of CITES by helping coordinate CITES enforcement and training via its members (national customs organizations). There is a CITES/WCO memorandum of understanding on cooperation. • CITES asked WCO to change customs codes (e.g., for shark products).
International Criminal Police Organization (ICPO, Interpol)	• CITES asked Interpol for help in implementation and enforcement. • In response, Interpol supports implementation of CITES. There is a CITES/ICPO memorandum of understanding on cooperation, a CITES/ICPO Wildlife Crime Working Group, and work on joint training.
EU Regulation on trade in endangered species	• The EU (then: the EEC) adopted a regulation to control wildlife trade in 1982 in response to CITES, although it was not a party to CITES. • CITES concerns about abolition of internal border controls caused the EU to strengthen its CITES Regulation in 1997 (revised in 2001). • CITES Regulation of the EU supports the implementation of CITES.
EU Single Market Program	• Abolition of intra-EU border controls for goods and persons endangers effective implementation of CITES trade restrictions in the EU.

favorably to the request for help was made completely voluntarily by the targets. The request as such included no substantive carrots or sticks that could have motivated the target, but drew the latter's attention to the needs of the requesting institution. The positive response of the WCO and Interpol as well as the UN Food and Agriculture Organization (FAO; see chapter 6) to the request by CITES then contributed to a more effective implementation of CITES (Behavioral Interaction). The implementation of CITES itself contributes to achieving the objective of the Convention on Biological Diversity (CBD) to protect biological diversity (see also chapter 4).

CITES has "natural" synergies with many other environmental institutions, particularly those concerning wildlife conservation. These arise from the fact that these treaties often have either the same or overlapping aims, basically to conserve wildlife and, more generally, biological diversity. These treaties include global agreements such as the Convention on Migratory Species, the CBD, and a host of regional agreements, such as that on the conservation of the vicuña. This synergy tends to be reinforced by the fact that they typically employ different means to achieve their ends: CITES restricts wildlife trade, the CMS provides for protection measures "on the ground," and so on. Rather than compete, the regimes therefore usually complement each other, often with one regime asking another to support it in attaining a particular goal, as in the case of the interactions recounted later.

That CITES has been a prominent target for requests for help from other regimes may be due to the fact that it has the largest membership, possibly the greatest influence, and certainly the highest public profile of the wildlife regimes.

The interactions of CITES with nonenvironmental institutions are quite different from those with wildlife treaties. Because CITES seeks to influence international trade it clearly should, in order to be effective, attempt not to come into conflict with and, if possible, benefit from other bodies concerning trade, notably the World Customs Organization (WCO), the International Criminal Police Organization (ICPO, Interpol), and the WTO.

Because of the institutions' different modes of operation, the potential for conflict between CITES and the WTO is greater than with the WCO and Interpol. The WCO and Interpol tend to act in many ways as trade associations whereas the WTO, like CITES, aims to regulate and control behavior—that is, international trade. The WCO and Interpol mainly aim to foster cooperation among their members, for example by providing education and training programs. The request for help in implementation originally issued by CITES to both WCO and Interpol was thus compatible with their overall aims, although it also did not promise to facilitate achieving their primary aims. Both organizations responded positively and have since supported the effective implementation of CITES, for instance by providing focused training to national customs and police officers (Reeve 2002). CITES has also long had memoranda of understanding with the WCO and Interpol, which were updated in 1999 in the drive for greater effectiveness by CITES. The CITES Secretariat sits on Interpol's Wildlife Crime Working Group.

As indicated above, the relationship between CITES and the WTO has been more problematic but has been managed successfully so as to avoid open conflict so far. Like other trade-related multilateral environmental agreements (chapter 8), CITES restricts international trade, but it promotes compatibility of its provisions with international trade rules by allowing parties to trade products regulated by CITES with nonparties that essentially comply with CITES requirements. While not all tensions may have been removed, no dispute related to CITES has yet arisen under the WTO. A cooperative and amicable relationship between both institutions is further promoted by the CITES Secretariat that sits on the WTO's Committee on Trade and Environment (CTE).

CITES has actively promoted synergy with other international agreements in order to maximize its effectiveness, and has had a formal policy of doing so since the early 1990s. The need to promote synergy, in general, was first formally raised at the ninth meeting of the Conference of the Parties (Fort Lauderdale 1994) in the Strategic Plan of the Secretariat (CITES 1994). At the tenth Conference of the Parties, this need was reiterated in the context of a review of the effectiveness of the Convention, and a decision was adopted calling for intensified and extended cooperation with other conventions (CITES Decision 10.110). This led the Secretariat to produce a document for the CITES Standing Committee at its forty-second meeting in 1999 titled *Synergy Between the Biodiversity-Related Conventions and Relations with Other Organizations* (CITES 1999), which contains various recommendations spanning a wide scope. In practice, members of the secretariats of wildlife agreements regularly attend others meetings. Also, CITES and the CMS concluded a memorandum of understanding concerning the need to work more closely together in September 2002.

Nevertheless, cooperation is often far from perfect, as the CITES Secretariat pointed out in the 1999 synergies paper:

The need now to develop synergy and provide better policy coordination among existing and future agreements is obvious. This particularly applies to the so-called biodiversity-related MEAs: CITES, the Convention on Biological Diversity (CBD), the Convention to Combat

Desertification (CCD), the Convention on Migratory Species (CMS) and the Convention on Wetlands (Ramsar). Although these Conventions address different aspects of the same issue, the risk of some overlap and duplication of effort is evident. (CITES 1999, 1)

Vertical Interactions with EU Legal Instruments

Although the EU is not a party to CITES, its legislation has interacted "vertically" with CITES in several ways. The interaction has relied on the fact that most EU member states have always been parties to CITES and have in large part relied on the EU for the implementation of their commitments. Even though CITES was officially amended in 1984 to allow for membership of regional economic integration organizations (i.e., the EU), the EU has not been in a position to join CITES because the amendment still awaits sufficient ratifications for entry into force. In the meantime, Ireland was the last EU member state to join CITES in 2000. Since all ten states that joined the EU in 2004 are also parties to CITES, all EU member states are now CITES parties.

Facilitated by the fact that (most) EU member states were committed to implementing CITES controls (Interaction through Commitment), the EU acted, synergistically, in many ways as though it were a member by implementing CITES in EU legislation. As early as 1982 it developed a Regulation (EEC No. 3626/82) for implementing CITES within the EU, which came into force in 1984. As elaborated below, it has since revised and updated this legislation to ensure compliance with CITES requirements. It set up a CITES Committee and an Enforcement Working Group and established a common reporting format. It also imposed trade sanctions against states for noncompliance with CITES, for example by banning trade in endangered species with Indonesia in 1992 (Reeve 2002, 126).

The significance of this EU implementation of CITES is that it activates the particularly effective supranational enforcement powers of the EU that subsequently support an effective implementation of CITES in the EU (Behavioral Interaction). Evidence for this synergistic effect of the EU implementation is found in enforcement activities of the European Court of Justice. In 1990, for example, the Court found that France had unlawfully issued import permits for 6,000 wildcat skins from Bolivia (Reeve 2002, 113).

Another part of the EU's "acquis communautaire," however, increasingly endangered the effective implementation of CITES since the 1980s and thus had a disruptive effect at the behavioral level. The Single European Act of 1987 introduced a legislative program that aimed at the complete abolition of internal border controls. This added to concerns raised by other parties because it would endanger an effective implementation of CITES in the EU. The effectiveness of CITES enforcement within the EU would essentially be determined by the member state with the most lax external import and export controls. CITES responded to this challenge by adopting a number of resolutions calling on the EU and its member states to ensure a more effective implementation of CITES (Reeve 2002, 112–120).

The EU's eventual response (after fifteen years) was new Council Regulation (EC) No. 338/97 and Commission Regulation (EC) No. 939/97, which came into effect on June 1, 1997. These conceded that the new regulations were needed to "adequately reflect the current structure of trade" and "cope with the abolition of internal border controls which resulted from the Single Market. The abolition of internal borders has made necessary the adoption of stricter trade control measures at the Community's external borders." In 2001 Commission Regulation (EC) No. 939/97 was replaced by Commission Regulation (EC) No. 1808/2001.

The Interaction between CITES and the CMS Concerning the Houbara Bustard

The Origins and Operation of the CMS

In the 1960s, the IUCN General Council drew international attention to the plight of many migratory animals and called for a treaty to protect them. As in the case of CITES, this call was reinforced by the 1972 Stockholm Conference, in its Recommendation 32 (CMS 2002). After a long gestation period, the treaty was concluded in Bonn in 1979 and entered into force in November 1983.

As in the case of many postwar wildlife treaties, the CMS was constructed as a framework agreement that allows its commitments to be expanded or changed over time. Like CITES, it achieves this by having two revisable appendixes that list species needing protection. Species can be listed on both appendixes. The first lists species having "unfavorable conservation status," which countries within the natural range of a migratory animal (range states) are obliged to protect. The second lists species for which completely new subagreements are required. In other words, the CMS is deliberately designed to spawn new agreements. There are now agreements on African-Eurasian migratory waterbirds, small cetaceans of the Baltic and North Seas, European bats, and the Great Bustard and six other species or sets of species (see the CMS website at http://www.cms.int for the latest information on agreements).

Originally, it was intended that only full, legally binding new subagreements (Agreements with a capital A) would be set up, but it soon became apparent that nonbinding memoranda of understanding could be usefully employed as well, and so both are now used. Which is employed is largely a practical decision. Where few parties with a record of cooperation are involved, memoranda are commonly used, because they can be agreed on more quickly and avoid the need for formal ratification.[4]

Both Agreements and memoranda are usually developed with one party taking a lead in drafting it. The party selected should be both a range state for the species involved and have knowledge of and expertise in it. In the case of the interaction covered here, the lead on the houbara bustard was taken by Saudi Arabia.[5]

In the context of this study, it is significant that the CMS has more limited participation (by states) than some other wildlife conservation agreements that are also, nominally, global in scope. Notable absentees from the list of CMS parties are the United States, Russia, Canada, Mexico, and Brazil. The reasons for lack of participation vary. The United States, for example, claims that existing arrangements with its neighbors make participation unnecessary. However, many states that are not parties to the CMS itself still participate in its Agreements and memoranda. The United States and Russia are, for example, parties to such agreements. Nevertheless, it can still assist the CMS in achieving its aims if it can elicit the support from other institutions with wider participation, such as, in this case, CITES.

The Interaction

The houbara bustard (*chlamydotis undulata*) is a rare and endangered species of large terrestrial bird (IUCN 2002). There are two subspecies: the Asiatic, which is migratory, and the North African, which is not (BirdLife International 2000). Only the former, migratory population (*chlamydotis undulata macqueenii*) therefore potentially qualifies for inclusion in the CMS although both populations are eligible for inclusion in, and are included in, the CITES appendixes. The Asiatic subspecies of the houbara bustard is included in Appendix I of CITES.

Chlamydotis undulata macqueenii breeds mainly in Central Asia and migrates to the Arabian peninsula during the period October to March. Throughout most of their vast range the houbara's numbers have long been in decline. The reasons for this decline appear to be habitat destruction, through overgrazing and intensive farming in their breeding areas, coupled with overhunting, human disturbance, and overtrapping in countries through which they migrate (BirdLife International 2001).

The Asiatic subspecies of the houbara bustard has long been on the IUCN "Red Lists" and therefore, within the CMS, it was recognized as having "unfavorable conservation status" and requiring either an Agreement or a memorandum of understanding between range states. The first institutional call for concerted action was made at the third Conference of the Parties of the CMS (COP Resolution 3.2) in 1991. The call was repeated at the fourth COP in 1994 (Resolution 4.4). CMS Resolutions are less targeted than its Decisions, and generally intended to provide long-standing guidance. They are politically important because they indicate a strong desire by the COP for parties to take action.

As a result of these Resolutions, Saudi Arabia offered to take the lead in drafting an agreement, either binding or nonbinding. Saudi Arabia is both a range state for the houbara bustard and has considerable knowledge of it. It was also the Asia representative on the Standing Committee of the CMS, which provides policy and administrative guidance between regular COPs. The Standing Committee consists of seven representatives of the main regions and includes the depositary (Germany) and the host of the next COP (http://www.cms.int). It was generally accepted that drafting an action plan would probably not be hard, given Saudi Arabia's expertise on the bustard.[6]

The status of the bustard was then raised, again, at the fifth COP of the CMS in April 1997 (Recommendation 5.4), by which time Saudi Arabia had prepared a draft agreement. Without specifically mentioning CITES, the Recommendation merely reiterated the need to conserve the bustard and for range states to assist Saudi Arabia with the agreement. In addition, IUCN's World Conservation Congress had highlighted the poor conservation status of the houbara bustard in 1996 (Recommendations 1.27 and 1.28). Recommendation 1.27 was a general call for the protection of two species of the houbara bustard and mentions the CMS and CITES in the context of many countries being obliged to protect it under these agreements (it being listed in the appendixes of both). Recommendation 1.28 specifically calls on range states to conclude an agreement under the CMS quickly and to assist Saudi Arabia in doing so.

Shortly after the CMS COP 5, CITES met for its tenth COP in June 1997. The parties to CITES were already familiar with the plight of the Asiatic species of the bustard: it had long been included in the IUCN's Red Lists and had been listed in CITES Appendix I. A number of countries that were parties to both CITES and the CMS (and the IUCN) now used the call for action passed by the CMS COP, as reinforced by the IUCN's World Conservation Congress, to raise the issue within CITES and bring it to the attention of other CITES parties. Realerted of the need for urgent action, the majority of CITES parties had no direct stake in the Asiatic houbara bustard and were thus sympathetic to further supporting its protection, as suggested by the initiators.

As a result, the CITES COP passed Resolution 10.11 on the houbara bustard that responded to the call for action by the CMS, as reinforced by the IUCN, without having been specifically asked to do so. The resolution mentioned all three of the CMS and IUCN resolutions and called on range states to take domestic action to protect the bustard. This was not particularly unusual, because CITES often echoes calls both from other nature conservation conventions and the IUCN. However, in its Resolution 10.11, CITES also "calls upon all range states of the Asiatic sub-species of the houbara bustard (chlamydotis undulata macqueenii) to review the Draft Agreement officially circulated by the Government of Saudi Arabia and communicate their comments to the National Commission for Wildlife Conservation and Development (NCWCD), Riyad, Saudi Arabia." This was a remarkable action for CITES to take because it called on CITES parties to take a highly specific action in support of a decision taken by another institution.

Following the CMS and CITES resolutions in 1997, there was a long delay and little progress was made on the CMS agreement. Indeed, in 1999, COP 6 of the CMS passed a further recommendation (6.4) on the subject. However, by COP 7, in 2002, matters were moving along more satisfactorily, as Resolution 7.7 states:

i. [The COP] *Takes note* of the information provided by the representative of the Kingdom of Saudi Arabia that an updated text of an Agreement and Action Plan on the Asiatic populations of the Houbara Bustard is ready for official dissemination and comment;

ii. *Takes further note* that an informal meeting to review the updated text will be held some time in early 2003; and

iii. *Welcomes* the information that the Kingdom of Saudi Arabia will hold a meeting of the Range States to conclude the Agreement and Action Plan in late 2003.

Discussion and Conclusions

Although the CMS had not issued a formal request for help to CITES, it was still influential in bringing about the action by CITES supporting the protection of the houbara bustard under the CMS. Having been alerted by several parties and the IUCN who employed the related CMS call for action (as reinforced by IUCN), CITES was cognizant of the CMS decisions about the houbara bustard, mentioning the most recent one in the preamble to its resolution. Even without a formal request, the knowledge about the need for urgent action as expressed in the CMS decisions changed the situation within CITES by raising awareness and enhancing support for

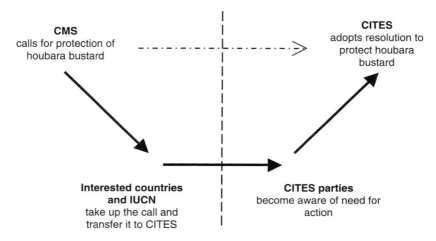

Figure 7.1
Convention on Migratory Species triggers CITES action on Houbara Bustard

action by CITES. The ensuing CITES resolution was thus a result of Cognitive Interaction (figure 7.1).

Interestingly, the CITES resolution calls on both CMS parties and nonparties (in the form of range states) to take action under the CMS, rather than CITES. In most cases of one institution assisting another, the supporting institution would call for action within its own sphere of competence or influence. CITES might, for example, call for trade sanctions in support of another regime. In this case, the houbara bustard was already subject to trade regulation (being listed in CITES Appendix I) and CITES was calling for action under the auspices of the CMS, rather than itself.

Furthermore, the interaction demonstrates the way nature conservation treaties act in support of one another, with the IUCN facilitating such support both with scientific information and via its access to both parties and institutions. It was the IUCN Red Listing that first alerted CITES and the CMS of the need for action on the houbara bustard. The recommendations of the IUCN World Conservation Congress then reinforced the calls for action of the CMS and helped transmit them to CITES, which responded by asking for action in the CMS.

The question remains, however, why CITES should bother to help the CMS in this case, when the bustard was already protected by CITES. The answer, most probably, lies in the fact that CITES has a far larger membership than the CMS. In particular, more of the range states for the Asiatic houbara bustard are parties to CITES than are parties to the CMS. Given that it is common for states that are not parties to the CMS to join Agreements or memoranda of understanding concluded under it, CITES asking for help from range states for the bustard makes considerable sense. As can be seen from table 7.2, only four of the twenty-four range states for the houbara were parties to the CMS at the end of 1997 (although several range states participate in CMS subagreements without becoming parties to the CMS itself, such as Iran, Russia, China, Oman, and Yemen). CITES membership in 1997 included more than three times as many range states (thirteen). The fact that there are so many range states for the bustard, many of which are parties to neither CITES nor the CMS and many of which are poorer developing countries with more pressing priorities than the environment, may also help to explain why it is taking so long to conclude an Agreement.

The Interaction with the Convention for the Conservation and Management of the Vicuña (CCMV)

The Vicuña and the Convention Covering It

The vicuña (*vicugna vicugna*) is the smallest species of the South American Camelidae, which include the llama, guanaco, and alpaca (Torres 1987). It lives on the high Andean plateaus. At the time of the Incas, vicuñas were an important source of wool and meat. The main product was, however, their wool and so they were normally captured, shorn, and released into the wild again, maintaining the population at an estimated 1.5 million (Grizmek 1990). Vicuña numbers dropped with the coming of the Spanish. During the nineteenth and twentieth centuries, there was a huge commercial demand for the wool, which is very soft and can be woven into delicate fabrics. Because the vicuña was then killed for its wool, rather than being "farmed" as in the time of the Incas, by 1960, vicuña numbers had fallen to only 6,000 (Torres 1987; Mendoza 1987).

Since the conclusion of the vicuña protection treaties and increased domestic efforts to conserve them in their range states, the vicuña population had risen to 125,000 by 1990 (Nowak 1991). By 2002 numbers stood at about 150,000 (http://www.iucn.org). The vicuña was until recently classified as vulnerable by the IUCN in its Red Lists but has recently been downgraded to lower risk. It was originally listed in Appendix I (endangered) of CITES although, as numbers have risen, populations have increasingly been transferred to Appendix II (threatened).

Table 7.2
Membership of Range States of the Houbara Bustard in CITES and CMS at the end of 1997

Range States of *chlamydotis undulata macqueenii* (from IUCN Red List)	Whether party to CMS	Whether party to CITES
Afghanistan	Not a party	Party
Armenia	Not a party	Not a party
Azerbaijan	Not a party	Not a party
Bahrain	Not a party	Not a party
China	Not a party	Party
India	Party	Party
Iran	Not a party	Party
Iraq	Not a party	Not a party
Israel	Party	Party
Jordan	Not a Party	Party
Kazakhstan	Not a party	Not a Party
Kuwait	Not a party	Not a party
Lebanon	Not a party	Not a party
Mongolia	Not a Party	Party
Oman	Not a party	Not a party
Pakistan	Party	Party
Qatar	Not a party	Not a Party
Russian Federation	Not a party	Party
Saudi Arabia	Party	Party
Syria	Not a party	Not a party
Tajikistan	Not a Party	Not a party
Turkmenistan	Not a party	Not a party
United Arab Emirates	Not a party	Party
Uzbekistan	Not a Party	Party
Yemen	Not a party	Party

Source: http://www.cites.org and http://www.cms.int.

The origins of the vicuña convention are in a bilateral treaty concluded in 1969 between Bolivia and Peru, in La Paz. The agreement declared that the vicuña was a "species on the way to extinction" (Preamble) and all commercial exploitation of the species or products made from it was prohibited for a period of ten years. During the following decade, Chile and Argentina joined the agreement. In October 1979 a meeting was held in Lima at which the four parties to the agreement were joined by Ecuador. On December 20, 1979, the treaty was amended to include the five countries at the meeting, whose territories include all of the current natural range of the vicuña. While the vicuña does not occur naturally in Ecuador, it was introduced later on. The agreement was also extended indefinitely and named the Convention for the Conservation and Management of the Vicuña (Torres 1987).

The treaty prohibits hunting of the vicuña and their live export, with exception of those used for scientific purposes or for display in legally established zoological gardens. It also bans trade in vicuña wool, hair, skins, and items manufactured from them and the manufacturing itself within the territories of the parties, except under special license. Licensed products nowadays bear a special CCMV logo. The parties are obliged to establish and maintain reserves and centers for raising the vicuña. In addition, they are obliged to conducting awareness raising and training activities.

As in the case of other wildlife agreements, the CCMV works closely both with environmental regimes (including CITES) and with environmental groups. Cooperation with the IUCN's Species Survival Commission Specialist Group on South American Camelids—which serves CITES as well—is particularly close.[7] The CCMV also works closely with WWF and with UNEP, which funds some of the IUCN work on vicuñas. Indeed, a compendium of resolutions of the Conference of the Parties to the CCMV has an entire section devoted to relationships with the IUCN, WWF, and TRAFFIC (Government of Argentina 2004). Over the years, the CCMV has cooperated closely with CITES. Indeed, between 1980 and 2000 the CCMV passed twenty-four resolutions concerning and involving CITES. Many of them concerned listings in the CITES appendixes, but the CCMV has also repeatedly tried to improve its effectiveness by having CITES ask its parties to restrict trade in vicuña products, particularly cloth made from vicuña wool (Government of Argentina 2004).

The Interaction
Although territories of the parties to the CCMV cover the entire natural range of the vicuña, most demand for the valuable vicuña wool, and products made from it,

comes from highly developed countries that are not parties to the CCMV. The very long, often extremely rugged borders of the CCMV parties, coupled with the fact that these countries are not wealthy, makes it hard for them to effectively control the illegal export of vicuña wool and cloth. Controlling their import into highly developed countries may provide effective complementary protection. Since the 1980s, the CCMV has thus repeatedly called on CITES to ask its members, which include all relevant importing developed countries, to help it to restrict trade in vicuña products (Government of Argentina 2004).

Interaction between the CCMV and CITES concerning vicuña wool and cloth began in 1987 when the CCMV passed Resolution 56/87. It asked the CITES Secretariat to recommend to all CITES parties that had stocks of vicuña cloth and wool to submit a list of those stocks, as soon as possible, to the CITES Secretariat, which would forward them to the CCMV. The CITES Secretariat acted accordingly by issuing a notification (number 472) to CITES parties asking them to respond. The idea was to enable an accurate assessment of globally, and legitimately, held stocks so as to better be able to track which trades were of legally held stocks and which were likely to be illegal.

This call was apparently not effective because, at its twelfth meeting in 1990, the CCMV issued a reminder to CITES about declaring stocks, CCMV Resolution 97/90. This also pointed out that all legally exported wool and cloth should bear CCMV official markings (logos). The logo was to enable a clear distinction between legal and illegal trades in wool and cloth. CITES responded by passing Resolution 8.11 concerning notification of stocks of wool and cloth, and markings, at its eighth COP in Kyoto in 1992.

This too was apparently not completely effective because in 1994 the CCMV fired off two more resolutions (133/94 and 137/94) to CITES, reminding it of CCMV resolutions 56/87 and 97/90, again concerning stocks of wool or cloth and their marking. The CCMV COP also passed two additional resolutions on listings in CITES appendixes and another on wool. The former two resulted in an amendment to CITES Resolution 8.11 at the tenth CITES COP in Harare in 1997.

Eventually, the CCMV's point about declaring stocks of wool and cloth seem to have been heeded, but the point about using the official CCMV logo on all cloth would appear not to have been acted on by all parties. At CITES COP 11 in Kenya in 2000, yet another resolution (11.6) was passed, essentially reiterating the previous resolutions. After first reminding the CITES parties of previous CCMV and CITES resolutions, it recommends that parties should "only authorize the import of vicuña cloth if the reverse bears the logotype corresponding to the country of origin and the trade mark VICUÑA—COUNTRY OF ORIGIN or if it is cloth containing pre-Convention wool of vicuña."

Discussion and Conclusion

This case shows how wildlife conservation treaties often interact so as to support each other in pursuit of common goals. The goal of the CCMV is the conservation of the vicuña and, to the extent that the vicuña is endangered or threatened as a species, this is also part of the objective of CITES. The main reason for the request by the CCMV was that the developed-country parties to CITES are the importers of vicuña products, both legal and illegal. Their controlling imports thus helps considerably in the enforcement of the CCMV, particularly because tight control over exports from the countries of origin is hard. Improving information on stocks of vicuña wool and cloth helped to clarify in which countries they had ended up after export, thereby facilitating the tracking of further trade. Gaining recognition of the CCMV logo helped in the practical enforcement of restrictions on both imports and exports.

The interaction between the CCMV and CITES followed the causal mechanism of Cognitive Interaction (figure 7.2). The requests of the CCMV were not supported by any carrot or stick so that CITES was completely free in its choice of whether and

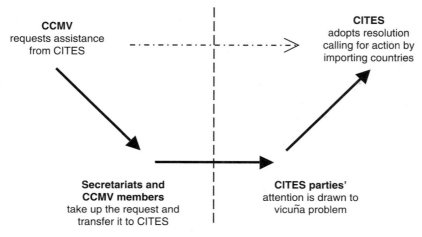

Figure 7.2
Vicuña Convention requests CITES assistance

how to respond. The request was easily brought to the attention of CITES parties because it was explicitly directed at them. The secretariats and CCMV members that were also parties to CITES transmitted the relevant CCMV decisions. These decisions drew the attention of CITES parties to the enforcement problem concerning the protection of the vicuña, which they may otherwise have ignored. Once alerted, most CITES parties had little reason to oppose the request that implied action only by a limited number of developed countries.

Ostensibly, the interaction between the CCMV and CITES appears to have been effective because assistance by CITES occurred as requested and vicuña numbers rose. However, numbers were rising prior to the interaction, and the resurgence of the vicuña appears to have been primarily due to domestic measures to protect and manage them. Having said this, the trade measures pursued by CITES in response to the CCMV have probably made a limited positive contribution, but it is hard to quantify their practical effect.

Conclusion

CITES actively and systematically strives to improve synergy with other institutions. The Convention works particularly closely with other international nature conservation regimes, as facilitated by several international and nongovernmental organizations. This is partly because the nature conservation regimes were designed to complement each other and share the common goal to conserve nature, and partly because they have evolved closer links over time. The role of the IUCN in forging these links has been considerable by, for example, providing information on which species are endangered and threatened by means of its Red Lists, which are used by all wildlife treaties.

In this study, horizontal interactions between CITES and other international institutions were either found to be synergistic or managed successfully so as to prevent tensions from turning into open conflicts. There have notably been tensions between CITES and the WTO, but CITES carefully manages its relationships so as to avoid conflict and promote synergy. This is facilitated by the fact that the overlap in membership between such large global institutions is considerable, and it seems unlikely that states would knowingly pursue one course of action in one forum and an opposing course of action in another.

There have been political conflicts between CITES and the EU, mainly as a result of CITES trying to improve enforcement. However, these conflicts have been handled in productive ways so as to eventually create synergistic effects. As early as 1982, the EU passed legislation that enhanced the effective implementation of CITES in the Union by subjecting it to the supranational EU enforcement powers. When the EU abolished internal border controls in the 1980s and 1990s, however, this potentially endangered effective implementation and enforcement of CITES restrictions on wildlife trade, leading to rising concerns of CITES and considerable political conflict. Eventually, the EU responded by strengthening its internal legislation and other implementation measures. In the end, the interaction thus produced synergistic results.

A common cause of the synergistic interactions between CITES and other wildlife treaties is that the latter try to use the greater membership of CITES to increase the effectiveness of their enforcement, as was at least partially the case in both interactions detailed here. However, in spite of the efforts by the institutions concerned, the interactions of CITES with the CMS and the CCMV demonstrate that interaction is often less successful in achieving tangible results "on the ground." It usually results in institutional action in the form of a COP decision or recommendation, but these do not necessarily have the desired practical effect.

This is because there is, perhaps, too much belief in the extent to which interactions between international regimes, or action by the regimes themselves, can achieve concrete, practical outcomes, especially regarding enforcement. This is particularly so in the case of organizations such as the WCO, which is designed to foster cooperation rather than enforcement. Ultimately, enforcement must mainly occur domestically, as seems to be demonstrated by the CITES/CCMV case concerning vicuña wool and cloth, where it appears to be domestic action—rather than regime interactions—that has caused vicuña numbers to increase.

Notes

1. Throughout this chapter, the term *wildlife* includes both wild fauna and wild flora.

2. Personal communication from Wolfgang Burhenne of the IUCN's International Law Centre in Bonn.

3. The World Heritage Convention had 177 parties in spring 2004 but is not exclusively concerned with wildlife conservation since it covers both cultural and natural heritage.

4. CMS 2002, and personal communications with Arnulf Muller-Helmbrecht, CMS Coordinator.

5. Personal communications within the BirdLife Partnership.

6. Personal communications from the BirdLife Partnership. The Saudi Arabian government representative in the CMS—the National Commission for Wildlife Conservation and Development, NCWCD—is the Saudi Arabian BirdLife Partner.

7. For more details on the group see the IUCN Species Survival Commission website at http://www.iucn.org/themes/ssc/sgs/sgs.htm#SACSR.

References

Andresen, Steinar. 1998. The Making and Implementation of Whaling Policies: Does Participation Make a Difference? In David G. Victor, Kal Raustiala, and Eugene B. Skolnikoff, eds., *The Implementation and Effectiveness of International Environmental Commitments: Theory and Practice*, 431–474. Cambridge, MA: IIASA/MIT Press.

BirldLife International. 2000. *Threatened Birds of the World*. Barcelona and Cambridge: Lynx Edicions/BirdLife International.

BirdLife International. 2001: *BirdLife's Online World Bird Database: The Site for Bird Conservation*. Version 1.0. Cambridge: BirdLife International.

Burns, William C. 1990. CITES and the International Regulation of International Trade in Endangered Species of Flora: A Critical Appraisal. *Dickinson Journal of International Law* 8 (2): 203–223.

CITES. 1994. CITES Secretariat. *Strategic Plan of the Secretariat*. 9th Conference of Parties, Fort Lauderdale, Florida, 1994. CITES Doc. 9.17.

CITES. 1999. CITES Standing Committee. *Synergy Between the Biodiversity-Related Conventions and Relations with Other Organizations*. Forty-second meeting of the Standing Committee, Lisbon (Portugal), September 28–October 1, 1999. CITES Doc. SC.42.17.

CMS. 2002. CMS Secretariat. *Guide to the Convention on the Conservation of Migratory Species of Wild Animals*, January 2002. Available at http://www.unep-wcmc.org/cms/pdf/CMS_Guide_Jan02_en.pdf.

Government of Argentina. 2004. *Resoluciones de la Comisión Técnico-Administradora del Convenio de la Vicuña, Reuniones Ordinarias (Analizadas y Extractadas) 1980–2000*. Available at http://www.medioambiente.gov.ar/fauna/programas/manejo/proyecto_vicuna/convenio/default.htm.

Grizmek, Bernhard. 1990. *Grizmek's Encyclopedia of Mammals*. Volume 5. New York: McGraw-Hill.

IUCN. 2002. *The IUCN Red List of Threatened Species*. IUCN Species Survival Commission, Gland, Switzerland: IUCN–The World Conservation Union. Available at http://www.redlist.org/search/details.php?species=4702.

Lanchbery, John. 1995. Reviewing the Implementation of Biodiversity Agreements. In John B. Poole and Richard Guthrie, eds., *Verification 1995*, 327–350. Boulder, CO: Westview Press/VERTIC.

Lanchbery, John. 1998. Long-Term Trends in Systems for Implementation Review in International Agreements on Fauna and Flora. In David G. Victor, Kal Raustiala, and Eugene B.

Skolnikoff, eds., *The Implementation and Effectiveness of International Environmental Commitments: Theory and Practice*, 57–87. Cambridge, MA: IIASA/MIT Press.

Lyster, Simon. 1985. *International Wildlife Law*. Cambridge: Grotius.

de Mendoza, Luis Hurtado. 1987. Notas Arqeológicas y Etnohistoricas acerca de la Vicuña en el Antiguo Perú (Notes about the Vicuna in Old Peru). In Hernàn Torres, ed., *Tecnicas para el Manejo de la Vicuna*, 13–23. IUCN Species Survival Commission, South American Camelid Specialist Group, UNEP. Cambridge: IUCN.

Mulliken, Teresa. 2002. Wildlife and Livelihoods. *World Conservation* 3 (special issue on "The Species Trade—CITES in the New Millennium"), 14–15.

Nowak, Ronald M. 1991. *Walker's Mammals of the World*. 5th ed. Baltimore: Johns Hopkins University Press.

Reeve, Rosalind. 2002. *Policing International Trade in Endangered Species: The CITES Treaty and Compliance*. London: Earthscan.

Sand, Peter H. 1997. Commodity or Taboo? International Regulation of Trade in Endangered Species. In Helge Ole Bergesen, Georg Parmann, and Øystein B. Thommessen, eds., *Green Globe Yearbook 1997*, 19–36. Oxford: Fridtjof Nansen Institute and Oxford University Press.

Torres, Hernàn. 1987. Preface. In Hernàn Torres, ed., *Tecnicas para el Manejo de la Vicuna*, 5–7. IUCN Species Survival Commission, South American Camelid Specialist Group, UNEP. Cambridge: IUCN.

Wijnstekers, Willem. 2003. *The Evolution of CITES: A Reference to the Convention on International Trade in Endangered Species of Wild Fauna and Flora*. 7th ed. Geneva: CITES Secretariat.

8

Interactions between the World Trade Organization and International Environmental Regimes

Alice Palmer, Beatrice Chaytor, and Jacob Werksman

The international trading regime governed by the World Trade Organization (WTO) interacts with many international environmental regimes, which also regulate international trade. The WTO is often a source of the interaction, invoking reactions from international environmental regimes in the design and implementation of rules that are responsive to WTO prescriptions. The vast number of WTO members, the institution's economic significance, and its unparalleled ability to enforce its rules through its rigorous dispute-settlement mechanism, contribute to the WTO's effectiveness as a source of interaction. Nevertheless, the WTO is also a target of influence by international environmental regimes, which are typically more proactive in seeking to inform and cooperate with the WTO. Where the WTO constitutes the source of interinstitutional influence, its primary objective of facilitating free trade has conflicted with the principal objectives of environmental regimes, which are leading to compromises in the design or implementation of the environmental regimes aimed at accommodating WTO rules. The mere possibility of a WTO challenge can inhibit negotiations and the implementation of measures under the international environmental regimes.

This chapter examines the nature and effects of interaction between the WTO and two international environmental regimes in particular: the Cartagena Protocol on Biosafety ("Biosafety Protocol") and the International Commission for the Conservation of Atlantic Tunas (ICCAT). Both the Biosafety Protocol and the ICCAT serve as valuable illustrations of the dynamics of interaction of international environmental regimes with the WTO from negotiation of commitments (Biosafety Protocol) through to their implementation (ICCAT). The chapter commences with a description of the WTO, followed by a summary of the experience of interaction between the WTO and environmental regimes in general. Subsequently, the interactions between the WTO and the Biosafety Protocol and ICCAT are studied in depth. The chapter concludes with general observations about the interaction between the WTO and the two environmental regimes.

Introduction to the World Trade Organization

The WTO is an intergovernmental organization established in 1995 to provide a common institutional framework for the conduct of trade relations formerly governed by the 1947 General Agreement on Tariffs and Trade (GATT) and related instruments (WTO 1994; Jackson 1997; Trebilock and Howse 1999). The WTO aims to liberalize markets, recognizing the need to make "use of the world's resources in accordance with the objective of sustainable development" and to "protect and preserve the environment ... in a manner consistent with [the members'] respective needs and concerns at different levels of economic development" (WTO 1994, preamble). As of early 2005, the WTO had a membership of 148 countries and customs territories (http://www.wto.org). The WTO administers the multilateral agreements regulating the international trade in goods and services and the protection of intellectual property rights and provides a forum for the negotiation of new trade rules. The WTO agreements are backed by a compulsory dispute-settlement system—whereby disputes can be referred to an ad hoc arbitration panel of trade experts and, on appeal, to a permanent Appellate Body of seven independent trade jurists—with the WTO membership having the ability to authorize bilateral trade sanctions (known as suspension of concessions).

The WTO agreements will interact with any environmental regulation that has an impact on the international trade in goods and services among its members, including those regulations enacted pursuant to multilateral environmental agreements (MEAs). The three main WTO agreements that have been of particular relevance to international environmental regimes are the General Agreement on Tariffs and Trade 1994 (GATT), the Agreement on Technical Barriers to Trade (TBT Agreement), and the Agreement on Sanitary and Phytosanitary Measures (SPS Agreement) (WTO 1994, Annex 1A). At the most basic level, all three agreements share the common purpose of ensuring that measures that affect trade in products do not discriminate on the basis of a product's country of origin (known as "national" and "most-favored-nation" treatment), and that these measures are no more trade-restrictive than is necessary to achieve the purpose for which they were designed ("proportionality," e.g., GATT Art. XX, SPS Art. 2.2, TBT Art. 2.2). Each agreement has detailed rules and a growing body of practice that develops these disciplines further.

The WTO agreements also anticipate the need to take into account other existing international agreements, such as MEAs, and other relevant state practice. Both the SPS and the TBT Agreements make reference to international standards developed by competent international organizations operating outside the WTO system. Under the SPS and the TBT Agreements, a WTO member is generally required to base its measures on international standards (SPS Art. 3.1; TBT Art. 2.4). To date, no MEA has been recognized as an "international standard" under the SPS or the TBT Agreements.

The WTO's institutional framework comprises its governing body, the General Council, and several other councils and committees that are supported by the WTO Secretariat in Geneva. The principal organ responsible for trade and environment issues at the WTO is the Committee on Trade and Environment (CTE). Since the WTO's establishment, the CTE has had the mandate to explore the relationship between the WTO and MEAs. In the CTE, and other WTO organs dealing with environmental matters, members have discussed a range of trade and environment issues. These include the application of the WTO rules to trade measures taken pursuant to MEAs (Abdel Motaal 2001); the application of WTO rules to measures based on nonproduct-related process and production methods (PPMs) (traditionally viewed as WTO-inconsistent) (Charnovitz 2002); environmental labeling (especially with respect to genetically modified organisms) (Abdel Motaal 1999); the relevance of the precautionary principle to risk assessments based on scientific evidence (particularly in the context of the SPS Agreement) (Bohanes 2002); and the environmental impacts of certain subsidies, especially fisheries subsidies (Chang 2003; see also chapter 6).

Most observers acknowledge the usefulness of the CTE's work in promoting a better understanding of the WTO-MEA relationship, and in acknowledging the legitimate role of MEAs in promoting environmental objectives. However, the CTE's work has thus far been general and inconclusive, other than recognizing that international trade rules and international environmental rules should be designed and implemented in a manner that is "mutually supportive" (WTO, 1996, para. 167). The CTE has been widely criticized for failing to produce any conclusions or recommendations of a substantive nature that would, for example, instruct the WTO's dispute-settlement system on how to deal with a conflict should one arise (Charnovitz 1997).

WTO members convene a ministerial conference approximately every two years (WTO 1994, para. 6). At the fourth WTO Ministerial Conference in Doha in November 2001, the WTO membership agreed to a new round of trade negotiations in a number of areas, including on "the relationship between existing WTO rules and specific trade obligations set out in multilateral environmental agreements (MEAs)" (WTO 2001c, para. 31(i)). The mandate is both vague and restrictive, with the negotiations being limited in scope to "the applicability of such existing WTO rules as among parties to the MEA in question" (WTO, 2001c, para. 31(i)). Nevertheless, the mandate does suggest that for the first time the WTO may produce substantive rules aimed directly and intentionally at trade-related measures contained in MEAs to which its members are also parties.

The fourth WTO Ministerial Conference also encouraged "efforts to promote cooperation between the WTO and relevant international environmental organizations" (WTO 2001c, para. 6) and launched negotiations between the members on "procedures for regular information exchange between MEA secretariats and the relevant WTO committees, and the criteria for the granting of observer status" (WTO 2001c, para. 31(ii)). The Doha mandate stems from existing practice in the CTE, which has already granted observer status to some intergovernmental environmental organizations (WTO 2004) and hosts meetings with MEA secretariats to discuss issues relevant to the WTO and MEAs (Shaw and Schwartz 2002).

WTO Interactions with International Environmental Regimes

There is a wary coexistence between the WTO and MEAs (international environmental regimes), which, like the WTO, regulate international trade (Sands 2003; Schoenbaum 2002; Nordstrøm and Vaughan 1999). The interaction between the WTO and environmental regimes is generated by differences in regime objectives and institutional features designed to achieve those objectives. The WTO is designed to promote free trade; the environmental regimes in varying degrees require or authorize trade restrictions in order to discourage the production and consumption of specific products with negative environmental consequences. The WTO agreements are backed by a compulsory dispute-settlement system with the ability to authorize bilateral trade sanctions, while the arrangements for enforcement within most MEAs are looser and less binding (WTO 2001a). Membership of the WTO and MEAs substantially overlaps since each regime aims for universal membership.

Table 8.1 contains a summary of the interactions between the WTO and five international environmental regimes: the Montreal Protocol (regulating trade in ozone-depleting substances), the Biosafety Protocol (regulating trade in "living" genetically modified organisms), the Basel Convention (regulating trade in hazardous waste), ICCAT (regulating trade in Atlantic tuna and other fish), and the

Table 8.1
Interactions between the WTO and international environmental regimes

Montreal Protocol on Substances That Deplete the Ozone Layer	• Granted exemptions from trade restrictions to nonparties complying with the Montreal Protocol, thereby avoiding WTO prohibitions on discrimination on the basis of a product's country of origin (national and most-favored-nation treatment) • Did not apply planned restrictions on trade in products produced with ozone-depleting substances partly because WTO rules have traditionally been understood to prohibit trade restrictions based on nonproduct-related process and production methods (PPMs) • Has provided a model for WTO of admissible trade restrictions for environmental purposes in a multilateral framework • Did not restrict trade in products that are obsolete because of bans on ozone-depleting substances due, to a large extent, to WTO disciplines • Was limited in its effectiveness because WTO disciplines limited Montreal Protocol parties' use of trade measures with respect to products that are obsolete because of bans on ozone-depleting substances
Cartagena Protocol on Biosafety	• Was used to block attempts to regulate biosafety under the WTO • Includes preambular language attempting to reconcile the Biosafety Protocol with the WTO Agreements • Adapts its risk-assessment procedure from WTO's SPS Agreement, which potentially constrains the use of trade measures under the Biosafety Protocol
Basel Convention on the Control of Transboundary Movements of Hazardous Wastes and Their Disposal	• Granted exemptions from trade restrictions to nonparties complying with the Basel Convention, thereby avoiding WTO prohibitions on discrimination on the basis of a product's country of origin (national and most-favored-nation treatment)
International Commission for the Conservation of Atlantic Tunas (ICCAT)	• Granted exemptions from trade restrictions to nonparties complying with ICCAT, thereby avoiding WTO prohibitions on discrimination on the basis of a product's country of origin (national and most-favored-nation treatment)
Convention on the Conservation of Antarctic Marine Living Resources (CCAMLR)	• Granted exemptions from trade restrictions to nonparties complying with CCAMLR, thereby avoiding WTO prohibitions on discrimination on the basis of a product's country of origin (national and most-favored-nation treatment)

Convention on the Conservation of Antarctic Marine Living Resources (CCAMLR) (regulating trade in Antarctic marine living resources). Chapters 3, 4, 6, and 7 of this volume address further interactions between the WTO and international environmental regimes. The WTO and the Conferences of the Parties of the various MEAs each have the mandate to act in areas that lie in the other's jurisdiction. Thus their "influence" over each other, though implicit, is as powerful as if it were expressly stated. Vertical interactions between the WTO and EU legal instruments are beyond the scope of this chapter. Some such interactions are analyzed in chapter 11 of this volume.

The GATT/WTO consistency of trade restrictions has been a concern that has constrained the respective rules and regulations of some environmental regimes (Biosafety, Montreal, ICCAT). The effect has been viewed as "chilling," disrupting or slowing negotiation processes (Montreal, Biosafety), and limiting the composition and reach of trade measures (Biosafety, Basel), and their further development and application (Montreal) (Interaction through Commitment). Although a challenge to a MEA measure has never been decided by the WTO dispute-settlement system, the threat of such a WTO challenge further influences the design of rules under the environmental regimes. The parties to MEAs remain acutely conscious of this interaction and have at times refrained from taking trade-related measures when implementing their commitments (Montreal) (Behavioral Interaction).

The response from the environmental regimes has been twofold. The first has been to deliberately avoid the possibility of conflict. Some MEAs stipulate that trade restrictions should not be imposed on nonparties where they can demonstrate compliance with the relevant MEA rules (ICCAT, Basel, CCAMLR, Montreal). Indeed, both the ICCAT and CCAMLR regimes go out of their way to provide a multistep process for nonparties to comply with their regulations before action is taken against them. On their side, some WTO members (parties or nonparties of MEAs) have chosen not to enforce their rights under the WTO where their products have been the subject of MEA-based trade restrictions (ICCAT, Montreal), implying tacit acceptance of the MEA strategies. The second response has been to initiate and maintain institutional coordination between respective secretariats. MEA secretariats (CBD, Montreal, ICCAT) have been granted observer status at meetings of the WTO's CTE, and in turn, the WTO Secretariat has attended sessions of the Conferences of the Parties of various MEAs. Since 1997, MEA secretariat representatives have participated in information exchanges in the CTE, tabling papers about trade measures used in MEAs. The process of information exchange has also involved requests by respective MEA membership for expert advice from the GATT/WTO Secretariat (Montreal) (see, in general, Shaw and Schwartz 2002).

The response from the WTO has been reflected in its "judicial" decisions, through the settlement of disputes, and in its political agenda. While there has never been a WTO decision based on a challenge to a MEA-related trade measure, the WTO's "judicial" organ—the Appellate Body—has taken into account existing international agreements and state practice when clarifying relevant provisions of the GATT. Indeed, the Appellate Body made reference to a number of MEAs when clarifying the meaning of "exhaustible natural resources" under one of the "environmental" exceptions in GATT Article XX. When analyzing this exception, the Appellate Body looked to MEAs as one source of evidence of the "contemporary concerns of the community of nations about the protection and conservation of the environment" (WTO 1998b, para. 129). The WTO's active management of the relationship with MEAs in the context of dispute settlement has been in contrast to the historically passive response of its political organs. While some environmental regimes have been cited in the WTO as examples of properly functioning, multilaterally negotiated, and narrowly drawn exceptions to free-trade rules (CCAMLR, Montreal: Cognitive Interaction) (e.g., WTO 2002, para. 5; 2000b, para. 22), no political decisions have yet been made. The new round of WTO negotiations on the relationship between MEAs and WTO rules, however, could lead to a more constructive relationship between the WTO and international environmental regimes.

WTO Interactions with the Cartagena Protocol on Biosafety

Cartagena Protocol on Biosafety

The Cartagena Protocol on Biosafety to the Convention on Biological Diversity (the "Biosafety Protocol") was adopted in 2000 and entered into force on September 11, 2003. The Protocol governs the international trade between parties in living organisms that have been genetically modified through the use of modern biotechnology ("living modified organisms" or "LMOs")—as opposed to the use of traditional or conventional techniques. LMOs are commonly referred to as genetically modified organisms, or GMOs, although GMOs could include both living and dead genetically modified organisms (Glowka, Burhenne-Guilmin, and Synge 1994, 45). The Biosafety Protocol was negotiated under the auspices of the Convention on Biological Diversity (CBD) and is served by the secretariat to the Convention in Montreal (http://www.biodiv.org/biosafety).

The Biosafety Protocol's primary objective is protection from the risks that LMOs may pose to biological diversity, and to human health (Art. 1), providing a basis for policymakers in a country of import to regulate against such risks. It puts in place standards of treatment for import, export, and shipment of LMOs that require exporting countries to ensure that importing countries are informed of a proposed transfer of LMOs, through a system of "Advance Informed Agreement." The Biosafety Protocol authorizes importers to impose greater constraints on LMOs destined for release into the environment, primarily seeds, but is less stringent with regards to LMOs destined for food or feed, or for processing ("LMO-FFPs" or "GM commodities"). With regard to LMOs destined for release into the environment, parties of proposed import may, on the basis of a risk assessment, approve the import, with or without conditions, or impose import bans (Art. 10). With regard to GM commodities, exporters are required to inform other parties of decisions to place GM commodities on their domestic markets; other parties may make decisions on the import of GM commodities in accordance with the Biosafety Protocol's objective (Art. 11).

Shipments of LMOs are subject to certain handling, transport, packaging, and identification requirements, which vary depending on the category of LMO. In particular, shipments of LMOs intended to be introduced into the environment or subject to contained use must be accompanied by documentation identifying them as LMOs and, in the case of GM commodities, accompanying documentation is required to state that the shipment "may contain" LMOs and that they are not intended for introduction into the environment (Art. 18).

A significant part of the Biosafety Protocol's rules provide standards for the conduct of risk assessment on LMOs (Art. 15 and Annex III). The Biosafety Protocol also contains numerous references to the "precautionary approach" (e.g., Art. 1) and to the use of socioeconomic data in the risk-assessment process (e.g., Art. 26). Finally, the Biosafety Protocol requires the proponent of export to pay for any risk assessment that may be demanded by the importing country if the latter so requests (Art. 15).

As an instrument that provides a legal basis for the regulation of the trade in products, the Biosafety Protocol necessarily has the potential to interact with the WTO rules. The Biosafety Protocol's Advance Informed Agreement and risk-assessment procedures and identification requirements could create trade restrictions subject to the WTO agreements (Eggers and Mackenzie 2000, 539–540; see also Charnovitz 2000; Phillips and Kerr 2000). While it is as yet unclear which of the WTO agreements might apply to a Protocol trade measure, the GATT and the TBT and SPS Agreements contain the same basic provisions that require trade measures to be nondiscriminatory, and to be no more trade restrictive than necessary to achieve their objective ("proportionate"). The TBT and SPS Agreements also require harmonization to international standards and the SPS Agreement requires trade measures to have a scientific basis.

The Interaction with the WTO

The interaction between the Biosafety Protocol and the WTO results from an overlap in means and a divergence of objectives. Both regimes seek to create international standards for the regulation of the international trade in products that are associated with risks to the environment of the importer. The regimes diverge fundamentally in their principal objectives. The Biosafety Protocol is primarily concerned with protecting the rights of the importer to be informed of and to regulate LMOs, while the WTO agreements are primarily concerned with the rights of the exporter to ensure that its products are treated in a nondiscriminatory and rational (scientifically based) manner. Interaction also occurs by virtue of overlapping memberships. As of January 2003, 98 of the 117 signatories and parties to the Biosafety Protocol were also WTO members. In addition, 10 further signatories and parties to the Protocol were also WTO observers, awaiting WTO membership (http://www.biodiv.org/biosafety and http://www.wto.org).

The relationship with the WTO was at the heart of the Biosafety Protocol negotiations and was largely responsible for the collapse of the negotiations in Cartagena during the first meeting that was intended to complete and adopt a text in 1999 (Pomerance 2000; see also Eggers and Mackenzie 2000). WTO rules were relevant to many of the areas of disagreement in the Biosafety Protocol negotiations, such as scope and GM commodities, and were considered specifically in the context of the discussions on the Protocol's relationship to other international agreements and other trade-related matters.

With respect to scope and GM commodities, there was significant discussion about the extent to which GM commodities would be covered by the Biosafety Protocol and the manner in which they should be identified (Pomerance 2000). The Miami Group (including Argentina, Australia, Canada, Chile, the United States, and Uruguay) and other LMO-exporting countries fought to exclude GM commodities from the Advance Informed Agreement procedure, arguing that the procedure should apply only to those LMOs that were intended to be introduced into the environment and therefore posed a risk to biological diversity. The Miami Group also argued that the risk-assessment requirements underlying the Advance Informed Agreement procedure should be based on "sound science" and in accordance with WTO rules, while the European Union (EU) pushed for risk assessment based on the "precautionary principle." As for identification of GM commodities, the Miami Group insisted that the identification requirement be limited to a statement that the shipment "may contain" LMOs, allowing exporters to mix LMO and non-LMO products in the same shipment (Newell and Mackenzie 2000, 315–316).

Up until and during the negotiating meeting in Cartagena, it had been proposed that the Biosafety Protocol include an article on the relationship with other international agreements (draft Art. 31). The Miami Group wanted a "savings clause" that would preserve WTO obligations and effectively subordinate the Biosafety Protocol to the WTO agreements, a position unacceptable to most developing countries and the European Union. In the course of the negotiations, the discussion of the relationship between the Biosafety Protocol and other international agreements was merged with the discussion of other "trade-related" matters concerning nonparties and nondiscrimination (UNEP 1999b). The implications of these provisions for the international trading regime established by the WTO were the principal basis for disagreement between the negotiators in Cartagena. Trade-related matters served to stall the adoption of the Biosafety Protocol as some delegations sought full debate and consideration of the implications for the WTO (Pomerance 2000, 618–619; Falkner 2002).

The influence of the trade regime on the development of the Biosafety Protocol has been felt through the direct intervention of the LMO-exporting countries, represented in large part by the Miami Group, in the negotiating process. However, it should be noted that most delegations in the Biosafety Protocol negotiations were dominated by their environment ministries, which were reluctant to defer to their trade counterparts. The influence common to both regimes was industry, which participated directly in some delegations and contributed independently to the Biosafety Protocol negotiations (personal communication with Biosafety Protocol delegate).

A WTO Secretariat representative attended negotiation meetings of the Biosafety Protocol (e.g., UNEP 2000, 6, 21). In some instances, a representative from the WTO addressed the Biosafety Protocol negotiators and informal consultations between the CBD and WTO were initiated. However, this interaction had little or no impact on the negotiations, and WTO bodies and trade-related organizations dealing with issues specific to the Biosafety Protocol were notably absent (personal communication with Biosafety Protocol delegate).

The WTO's influence on the Biosafety Protocol is apparent in the adaptation of WTO principles and conflict avoidance. The main effect is reflected in the text of the Biosafety Protocol in two main ways: (1) the risk-assessment procedures set out in Annex III of the Biosafety Protocol to a large extent follow the approach in the WTO SPS Agreement; (2) the negotiators sought, as far as possible, to direct policymakers through preambular paragraphs to avoid conflict by interpreting the Biosafety Protocol and the WTO agreements in a "mutually supportive" manner. Perhaps the most significant outcome of the interaction was the narrowing of the scope of the Biosafety Protocol's main regulatory instrument (Advance Informed Agreement procedures) from LMOs generally to only those other than GM commodities (Pomerance 2000). It appears that this has effectively carved out from the Biosafety Protocol the commodities that are most significant from an economic or trade perspective: those destined for use as food or feed, or for processing (Newell and Mackenzie 2000, 315).

Assessment and Outlook

The influence of the WTO on the Biosafety Protocol constituted Interaction through Commitment. WTO members were bound by WTO rules on nondiscrimination, proportionality, scientific basis, harmonization, and transparency. As a consequence, free-trade interests in the negotiations on the Biosafety Protocol were strengthened because they could refer to the WTO and claim consistency. As a result, the rules of the Biosafety Protocol regarding Advance Informed Agreement, risk assessment, and identification requirements were designed so as to minimize the potential for conflict with WTO rules (figure 8.1).

The potential for future interaction between the Biosafety Protocol and the WTO in the administration, implementation, and development of rules is difficult to analyze in the abstract: the Biosafety Protocol does not specify the precise products it seeks to regulate, what specific risks it is intended to guard against, and what measures it will authorize parties to take against those risks. Countries on both sides of the debate have made statements praising the Biosafety Protocol for having dovetailed neatly into existing trade rules (Phillips and Kerr 2000, 68; Falkner 2000, 311). However, recognizing that the adoption of the Biosafety Protocol is a significant step toward reconciling trade and environmental interests, many commentators

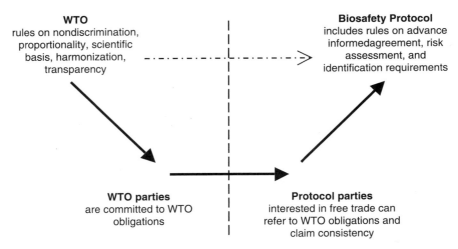

Figure 8.1
WTO influence on the design of the Biosafety Protocol

acknowledge that the preambular language and other compromises made on trade-related matters are imperfect solutions (Falkner 2000, 312–313; Eggers and Mackenzie 2000, 542–543; see also Qureshi 2000, 835, 853; Phillips and Kerr 2000, 69, 74).

Ultimately, it would appear that the terms of the Biosafety Protocol and WTO agreements do not, in and of themselves, conflict and that, with or without savings language, an international adjudicator *could* interpret their provisions to complementary effect (Safrin 2002). One important indicator of whether the Biosafety Protocol has achieved a successful accommodation of WTO rules will be the rate of ratification by major LMO exporters, represented largely by the Miami Group. It should be noted that the United States cannot become a party to the Protocol without first becoming a party to the CBD (CBD Art. 32(1)), although it is likely to voluntarily comply with the Protocol until then (Phillips and Kerr 2000, 65). The optimism and skepticism surrounding the compromise language of the Biosafety Protocol will be tested if measures justified under the Biosafety Protocol are challenged under the WTO (Eggers and Mackenzie 2000). In this respect, the outcome of the WTO complaint over the EU de facto moratorium on GMO imports initiated by the United States and other countries in 2003 may prove important—although the moratorium is technically not a Biosafety Protocol measure (see also chapter 11).

In the future, the Parties to the Biosafety Protocol are expected to consider whether and how it should cooperate with other intergovernmental organizations. There has already been a growing degree of institutional coordination, through reciprocal representation at meetings, and coincident representation at meetings in third "standard-setting" institutions relevant to LMOs (such as the Codex Alimentarius Commission, organs of the International Plant Protection Convention, and the Office International des Epizooties) (Buckingham and Phillips 2001). The WTO's mandate from the fourth Ministerial Conference to negotiate on the WTO-MEA relationship might present further opportunities for clarifying the relationship between the WTO and the Biosafety Protocol.

Finally, it is worth noting in passing that, in addition to being a source of interaction with the Biosafety Protocol, the WTO was also a target. The negotiation of the Biosafety Protocol overlapped with the WTO's third Ministerial Conference in Seattle, where some WTO members sought to create a working group on biotechnology in part to allow the WTO to seize exclusive jurisdiction over the issue (Buckingham and Phillips 2001; Falkner 2000, 305). Supporters of the Biosafety Protocol rejected the initiative, citing the ongoing negotiations under the CBD as the appropriate forum for resolving these issues (Tapper 2000; UNEP 1999a, para. 9). From the point of view of those within the WTO with expansionist ambitions, the result was disruptive.

WTO Interactions with the International Commission for the Conservation of Atlantic Tunas

International Commission for the Conservation of Atlantic Tunas

The International Commission for the Conservation of Atlantic Tunas (ICCAT) is an intergovernmental organization, consisting of over thirty contracting parties (including Canada, China, the EC, Japan, and the United States), governed by an international convention signed in 1966 (the Convention) (http://www.iccat.es). Established in Madrid in 1969 when the Convention entered into force, the Commission is responsible for the conservation of tunas and tunalike fish stocks in the Atlantic Ocean and adjacent seas, including the Mediterranean Sea. The Commission collects statistics from all tuna fisheries and conducts stock assessments, which it uses in adopting regulatory measures for the management of various stocks of tunas. Such regulatory measures include catch quotas, time/area closures, size limits, and import bans. In recent years, the Commission has focused its regulatory regime on the management of Atlantic bluefin tuna (*Thunnus thynnus*) and swordfish (*Xiphias gladius*), both of whose stocks have been overexploited.

The Commission first adopted regulatory measures (minimum size and catch limits) for the entire Atlantic in November 1975. As the depletion of the western Atlantic stock became apparent, the Commission recommended at its 1981 meeting that fishing for western Atlantic bluefin tuna be prohibited, except for a minor quantity for scientific monitoring purposes. This allowance was shared by three bluefin tuna fishing countries (Canada, Japan, and the United States) and according to ICCAT has been well monitored (UNEP 1998). In 1993, the Commission adopted a recommendation that prohibits bluefin tuna fishing by large pelagic longline fishing vessels (over 24 meters in length) during June and July (the bluefin spawning season) in the Mediterranean. In 1996, it adopted a recommendation to prohibit purse seine fishing in August in the Mediterranean Sea to protect small fish. In 1994, it recommended, for the first time, a catch reduction for the eastern stock, which entered into effect in 1995 (WTO 1998a).

Another of the Commission's priority objectives has been to stop illegal, unregulated, and unreported fishing carried out by vessels flagged by both parties and nonparties. ICCAT is particularly concerned about the fishing activities of vessels registered in countries operating "open registries" ("flags-of-convenience" states), since such vessels have traditionally had little or no control exercised by their respective flag states over their fishing activities.

The regulatory measures recommended by ICCAT are binding only on its parties (ICCAT Art. VIII.2). However, since 1995, ICCAT measures may bind a category known as "cooperating parties." These are nonparties that "voluntarily fish in conformity with the conservation decisions of ICCAT" (Resolution 94-6 and Recommendation 03-20). Such status is granted for a period of one year and is subject to annual review. In 1999, Mexico and Chinese Taipei were granted status as cooperating parties, and Mexico subsequently became a party (http://www.iccat.es).

ICCAT has passed trade measures because even stringent regulations for sustainable management of fisheries may be undermined in the absence of effective enforcement measures. International experience has shown that lack of appropriate disincentives cause irresponsible vessel operators to overfish and thereby deplete fisheries resources (Stone 1997; Downes and Van Dyke 1998). Overfishing may result in the collapse of entire fisheries. ICCAT is therefore concerned to enforce the implementation of its fisheries-management regime by both parties and nonparties, through a package of specific actions. ICCAT has recorded that the unreported catches of flags-of-convenience vessels of nonparties make its scientific studies progressively more inaccurate and difficult to carry out. In addition, the increase in such fishing operations may end up discouraging parties from effectively implementing the regulations (WTO 1998a, 3).

The Interaction with the WTO

The interaction between ICCAT and the WTO is, again, based on different objectives of the institutions involved and their overlapping memberships. ICCAT's primary aim is the conservation and sustainable management of species of tuna and other similar fish stocks in a particular geographic area. Enforcement of its management measures to serve this goal necessarily implies limits on the fishing efforts of the countries under its jurisdiction. The WTO, on the other hand, aims to remove restrictions and limits on the trade and economic activities of its members. It therefore disciplines trade restrictions such as import bans or quotas. As of January 2003, twenty-six of the thirty-four ICCAT parties were WTO members. These are particularly concerned about respecting WTO principles in the design of ICCAT trade measures. For example, both the EU and the United States, in enacting their import bans, comment on the WTO compatibility of those measures (EU Council 2000). There are also some nonparties (which are WTO members) that ICCAT considers to be key players because of their involvement in tuna fisheries. These are Turkey, Cyprus, Malta, Belize, Denmark (Faroe Islands), the Philippines, and Thailand (WTO 2001b). Turkey partially complies with ICCAT management regulations. Other countries such as Taiwan, being "cooperating parties," comply with ICCAT regulations to the same extent as parties.

While the Convention itself does not contain any specific trade measures, resolutions adopted by the Commission do contain trade restrictions. For example, ICCAT adopted two action plans for bluefin tuna, which came into force in 1995, and for swordfish, which entered into force in 1996 and were subsequently revised (Resolutions 94-3 and 95-13 replaced by 03-15). Pursuant to these action plans, the Commission will recommend that parties prohibit imports of bluefin tuna and swordfish and their products in any form, from parties or nonparties, whose vessels it is determined are fishing the species in a manner inconsistent with ICCAT's regulatory regime. Paragraph (f) in each action plan provides that "the Commission will recommend that Contracting Parties take nondiscriminatory trade restrictive measures, consistent with their international obligations." For instance, import bans with respect to bluefin tuna took effect regarding three nonparties in 1997 (Belize and Honduras: Recommendation 96-11 and Panama: Recommendations 96-12); and regarding one party in 2000 (Equatorial Guinea: Recommendation 99-10). Similarly, to make effective its Resolution Concerning Illegal, Unreported and Unregulated Catches of Tuna by Large-Scale Longline Vessels (Resolution 98-18 replaced by 03-15), ICCAT has recommended a ban on imports of tuna from several countries (e.g., Belize, Cambodia, Honduras and St. Vincent and the Grenadines: Recommendation 00-15). Furthermore, where the vessel of a nonparty has onboard species subject to ICCAT conservation measures, landings and transshipments of all its fish are subject to inspection when it voluntarily enters a port of a party. Unless the vessel establishes that the fish were caught outside the Convention Area or in compliance with the relevant ICCAT conservation measures and requirements under the Convention, its landings and transshipments of relevant species will be prohibited (Recommendation 98-11).

Under ICCAT, all parties must also require all imported bluefin tuna to be accompanied by an ICCAT statistical document that is defined by the Commission. The program has applied to frozen fish since 1993 and to fresh bluefin tuna since 1994. Document details include the name of the country issuing the document, the name of the exporter and importer, and the area of the harvest. In principle, all bluefin tuna products (not only from the Atlantic) must now be accompanied by such a document validated by a government official. This applies to products from parties and nonparties (WTO 1998a, 4). Only products accompanied by documents containing seals and signatures registered with the Commission are accepted for import.

Both the import bans implemented by ICCAT parties and the ICCAT documentation requirements are in potential conflict with WTO rules. Import bans against nonparties such as Belize or St. Vincent and the Grenadines could violate GATT and TBT nondiscrimination provisions or the GATT Article XI prohibition on the imposition of quantitative restrictions against the products of other WTO members. Technical documentation requirements might raise issues relevant to the TBT Agreement. Furthermore, the documentation requirements implicitly rest on an essential distinction between bluefin tuna fish products. Differences in the manner in which the imported and domestic products have been harvested or produced are a central concern of ICCAT's conservation measures. However, some WTO members might argue that such nonproduct-related process and production methods (PPMs) are not a legitimate basis for distinguishing between products under the WTO rules. Also, the de facto application of the discriminating measures to areas outside ICCAT's jurisdiction (tuna caught outside the Atlantic) raises further questions about their WTO compatibility, particularly where the measures are taken in relation to nonparties. Unless those countries have expressly waived their WTO rights, they cannot be said to have forgone them through their participation in the documentation program.

Finally ICCAT import bans appear to authorize a blanket ban on all target species imported from a particular country. Such import bans do not, therefore, distinguish fish caught by a vessel complying with ICCAT conservation measures from fish caught by a noncomplying vessel flying the same flag. This could be viewed as arbitrary and discriminatory under GATT rules. In the *U.S.–Shrimp* case, the WTO Appellate Body noted that the U.S. measure may have been better tailored to provide for shipment-by-shipment certification (WTO 1998b). However, ICCAT import bans are generally targeted at promoting the enforcement by a government of rules applicable to all vessels flying its flag, and in particular appear to have been designed to address the "flags-of-convenience" problem. So far the target countries for such import bans have been small developing economies that are less likely to invoke WTO dispute-settlement procedures. According to ICCAT, it will continue to use such measures "to combat the undermining of its regulatory measures in order to ensure continuous conservation of the stocks under its mandate" (WTO 2000a, para. 6).

The Effects of the Interaction

In response to the potential tensions with the WTO, ICCAT has designed its measures so as to make them WTO-consistent, which has also made them more resource-intensive to administer. For instance, ICCAT has developed a staged approach to the adoption of trade measures. With respect to its tuna and swordfish action plans, ICCAT first informs the flag state concerned of any illegal fishing carried out by its registered vessels. ICCAT then requests the cooperation of the flag state in bringing its vessels' activities into compliance with ICCAT measures. Lastly, ICCAT warns the relevant flag state that nondiscriminatory, trade-restrictive measures may be taken against it in the event of continued noncompliance. For instance, warning letters were sent to Guinea-Bissau concerning bluefin tuna catches, Sierra Leone concerning its bluefin tuna and swordfish fishing activities, and Equatorial Guinea concerning its fishing practices (WT 2001b, 12). At the Commission meeting following the issuance of a warning, where the flag state has continued to fish in contravention of ICCAT regulations, ICCAT generally recommends that parties take nondiscriminatory, trade-restrictive measures against the offending state, including prohibiting imports of its relevant tuna or swordfish products. Significant resources are also employed in identification of infractions, which involves numerous legal studies, biological analyses, gathering of trade statistics and landings data, and sophisticated monitoring of vessels' activities (WTO 1998a, 5).

ICCAT has made further efforts to enhance the chances that its import bans, quotas, and technical restrictions could be saved by the "environmental" exceptions in GATT Article XX or be found to comply with the provisions on trade-restrictive measures under the TBT Agreement. Most of ICCAT's management measures have a scientific basis, and it is careful to ensure that the trade measures it recommends to its parties are nondiscriminatory. As mentioned before, ICCAT also stresses that the trade measures implemented by its parties should be "consistent with their international obligations," which include obligations under the WTO.

Furthermore, the Commission makes conscientious efforts to achieve the cooperation of nonparties. It specifically encourages countries that are active in tuna and swordfish fisheries to accede to the Convention. In 1994, ICCAT urged nonparties fishing in the Convention area for species under ICCAT competence to become parties or "cooperating parties," and requested their observance of ICCAT's conservation measures (Resolution 94-6 and Recommendation 03-20). Also, ICCAT's use of trade measures acts as a powerful incentive to nonparties (including WTO members) to accede to the Convention. For example, after trade measures were imposed against Panama, it acceded to ICCAT and implemented stringent domestic measures, such as cancellation of all open registries of tuna fishing vessels, and started a licensing system with a strict satellite vessel-monitoring system. Based on those measures, in 1999 ICCAT recommended the lifting of the ban against Panamanian imports of tuna (Recommendation 99-9). According to the ICCAT Secretariat, as soon as strict quotas were introduced, membership of ICCAT increased (WTO 2001b, 12). Incentives to join include the right to participate in the process of establishing regulatory measures, taking part in the allocation of quotas, and obtaining a quota.

The consistency with WTO rules of ICCAT measures against nonparties (that are WTO members) is further enhanced by direct cooperation between the two institutions. ICCAT has observer status in the WTO Committee on Trade and Environment, and the WTO is notified of all its recommendations and resolutions at the same time that they are officially transmitted to ICCAT parties (WTO, 1998a, 2000a). When they enter into force, notification is again given to the WTO. In contrast, although ICCAT has consistently invited the WTO to attend its meetings, the WTO has not yet participated in any ICCAT activities. Nevertheless, ICCAT receives the reports of the CTE meetings from the WTO Secretariat.

Assessment and Outlook

There appears to be general agreement by both the WTO and ICCAT that ICCAT's trade measures do not raise conflicts with WTO rules (personal communication with ICCAT representative; WTO 2001b, 12–13). Where trade measures are considered necessary, ICCAT is careful to ensure that it advocates measures that are nondiscriminatory in effect and stresses that the measures taken by its parties should be "consistent with their international obligations." ICCAT has tried generally to incorporate WTO principles in a manner that improves the fairness and the legitimacy of its trade measures, and to date, no formal WTO dispute has arisen or been initiated. In seeking to be nondiscriminatory with regard to nonparties, and in providing repeated opportunities—particularly to developing countries—to remedy noncompliant behavior, ICCAT has made its trade restrictions more WTO compatible and generally more acceptable.

The interaction has followed the causal mechanism of Interaction through Commitment. WTO members are bound by WTO rules on nondiscrimination and proportionality. The majority of ICCAT parties have been WTO members and have thus had a significant interest in avoiding commitments that would be inconsistent with WTO disciplines. As a result, ICCAT has made particular efforts to minimize and prevent potential tensions between both regimes by designing WTO-consistent trade measures (see figure 8.2).

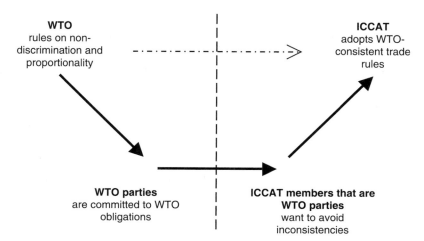

Figure 8.2
Influence of WTO rules on the design of ICCAT trade rules

The continued interaction with WTO rules may involve deeper scrutiny of ICCAT trade measures, and eventually require them to be tailored more precisely. The question could be raised as to whether trade-restrictive measures are the appropriate response to infractions by countries at low levels of economic development. Nevertheless, it is fair to say that ICCAT's trade measures are combined with supportive measures such as technical assistance to establish statistical systems; training; access to scientific research, statistical databases, and other information; and special funding arrangements.

Finally, it should be noted that the 1995 UN Fish Stocks Agreement provides added support to port-state enforcement under ICCAT. Article 21 of this agreement creates an elaborate system of regional cooperation for the enforcement of regionally agreed-on measures against vessels that are suspected of violating them. Not only may a port state (party to the Fish Stocks Agreement and ICCAT) inspect documents, fishing gear, and catch onboard a vessel that is voluntarily in its port, but pursuant to Article 23.3 of the Fish Stocks Agreement, it may also prohibit the landings and transshipment where it is established that the catch has been taken in a manner that undermines the effectiveness of ICCAT's management measures on the high seas. This type of enforcement measure is allowed regardless of whether the flag state is a member of ICCAT or not.

Concluding Observations: WTO, Biosafety, and ICCAT

The cause of interaction for both the Biosafety Protocol and ICCAT arises from overlapping memberships and jurisdictions but potentially divergent objectives with those of the WTO. The Biosafety Protocol and ICCAT, together with the WTO, regulate trade in goods but the objective of the environmental regimes—for example to protect biological diversity—is potentially at odds with the WTO's aim to liberalize markets. Measures taken under the Biosafety Protocol or pursuant to ICCAT decisions could restrict trade on a discriminatory basis—a ban on imports of living modified organisms or tuna from a specific country or countries—and the extent to which the measures restrict trade would need to be proportionate to their aim of protecting biological diversity if they are to survive a WTO challenge.

The influence of the WTO regime on the Biosafety Protocol and ICCAT has been felt at different stages in the cycle of their development. The Biosafety Protocol has experienced the weight of interaction to date in its negotiation, where the interaction was arguably disruptive. However, the resulting rules appear to largely accommodate both objectives of protecting biological diversity and promoting free trade. In contrast, ICCAT was established during GATT's lifetime but before the WTO and its agreements came into being. The opportunities for interaction have arisen in the design and implementation of measures under ICCAT instruments, where interaction seems to have been managed successfully.

The interactions of the Biosafety Protocol and ICCAT with the WTO appear to be Interactions through Commitment. Ultimately, both the Biosafety Protocol and ICCAT have adapted to and sought to avoid conflict with the WTO regime. In the case of the Biosafety Protocol, it is widely perceived as having achieved a basis on which the two regimes can be mutually supportive. However, it will be necessary to await actual implementation of the Protocol in order to assess whether this response will ensure mutual supportiveness of the two regimes. The absence of any challenge to measures taken under the auspices of ICCAT attests, to some extent, to its success in adapting to the WTO rules. However, the absence of a WTO challenge could also be due to poor compliance with ICCAT disciplines, combined with poor enforcement, leading to ineffective measures with little or no trade impact to give rise to a complaint.

Both the Biosafety Protocol and ICCAT have used observership in certain WTO bodies to promote awareness and understanding of their respective regimes within the WTO. However, this means of communication is largely one-sided. Also, the CBD and ICCAT secretariats generally only communicate information to the CTE rather than engaging in an active dialogue that results in concrete outcomes. Moreover, issues relevant to the Biosafety Protocol and ICCAT are often considered by other WTO bodies to which their responsible secretariats are not necessarily observers (e.g., TRIPS Council). Ultimately, effective responses are most likely to come in the form of specialized technical discussion and information exchange (as is the case with the Biosafety Protocol and other international institutions relevant to LMOs), as opposed to communications made to the political organs of the respective institutions.

References

Abdel Motaal, Doaa. 1999. The Agreement on Technical Barriers to Trade, the Committee on Trade and Environment, and Eco-Labelling. In Gary P. Sampson and W. Bradnee Chambers, eds., *Trade, Environment and the Millennium*, 223–239. Tokyo: United Nations University.

Abdel Motaal, Doaa. 2001. Multilateral Environmental Agreements (MEAs) and WTO Rules: Why the "Burden of Accommodation" Should Shift to MEAs. *Journal of World Trade* 35 (6): 1215–1233.

Bohanes, Jan. 2002. Risk Regulation in WTO Law: A Procedure-Based Approach to the Precautionary Principle. *Columbia Journal of Transnational Law* 40 (2): 323–389.

Buckingham, Donald E., and Peter W. B. Phillips. 2001. Hot Potato, Hot Potato: Regulating Products of Biotechnology by the International Community. *Journal of World Trade* 35 (1): 1–31.

Chang, Seung Wha. 2003. WTO Disciplines on Fisheries Subsidies: A Historic Step towards Sustainability? *Journal of International Economic Law* 6 (4): 879–921.

Charnovitz, Steve. 1997. Critical Guide to the WTO's Report on Trade and Environment: Symposium on NAFTA and the Expansion of Free Trade: Current Issues and Future Prospects. *Arizona Journal of International and Comparative Law* 14 (2): 341–379.

Charnovitz, Steve. 2000. The Supervision of Health and Biosafety Regulation by World Trade Rules. *Tulane Environmental Law Journal* 13 (2): 271–301.

Charnovitz, Steve. 2002. The Law of Environmental "PPMs" in the WTO: Debunking the Myth of Illegality. *Yale Journal of International Law* 27 (1): 59–110.

Downes, David R., and Brennan Van Dyke. 1998. *Fisheries Conservation and Trade Rules: Ensuring That Trade Law Promotes Sustainable Fisheries*. Washington: Center for International Environmental Law and Greenpeace.

Eggers, Barbara, and Ruth Mackenzie. 2000. The Cartagena Protocol on Biosafety. *Journal of International Economic Law* 3 (3): 525–543.

EU Council. 2000. Council Regulation (EC) No 2092/2000 of 28 September 2000 Prohibiting Imports of Atlantic Blue-Fin Tuna *(Thunnus thynnus)* Originating in Belize, Honduras and Equatorial Guinea. *Official Journal L* 249, 4.10.2000, 1.

Falkner, Robert. 2000. Regulating Biotech Trade: The Cartagena Protocol on Biosafety. *International Affairs* 76 (2): 299–313.

Falkner, Robert. 2002. Negotiating the Biosafety Protocol: The International Process. In Christoph Bail, Robert Falkner, and Helen Marquard, eds., *The Cartagena Protocol on Biosafety: Reconciling Trade in Biotechnology with Environment and Development?*, 3–22. London: RIIA/Earthscan.

Glowka, Lyle, Françoise Burhenne-Guilmin, and Hugh Synge (in collaboration with Jeffrey A. McNeely and Lothar Gündling). 1994. *A Guide to the Convention on Biological Diversity*. Gland, Switzerland, and Cambridge, UK: IUCN.

Jackson, John H. 1997. *The World Trading System: Law and Policy of International Economic Relations*. 2nd ed. Cambridge, MA: MIT Press.

Newell, Peter, and Ruth Mackenzie. 2000. The 2000 Cartagena Protocol on Biosafety: Legal and Political Dimensions. *Global Environmental Change* 10 (4): 313–317.

Nordstrøm, Hakan, and Scott Vaughan. 1999. *Special Studies 4: Trade and Environment*. Geneva: WTO Publications.

Phillips, Peter W. B., and William A. Kerr. 2000. The WTO versus the Biosafety Protocol for Trade in Genetically Modified Organisms. *Journal of World Trade* 34 (4): 63–75.

Pomerance, Rafe. 2000. The Biosafety Protocol: Cartagena and Beyond. *NYU Environmental Law Journal* 8 (3): 614–621.

Qureshi, Asif H. 2000. The Cartagena Protocol on Biosafety and the WTO: Coexistence or Incoherence? *International and Comparative Law Quarterly* 49 (4): 835–855.

Safrin, Sabrina. 2002. Treaties in Collision? The Biosafety Protocol and the World Trade Organization Agreements. *American Journal of International Law* 96 (3): 606–628.

Sands, Philippe. 2003. *Principles of International Environmental Law.* 2nd ed. Cambridge: Cambridge University Press.

Schoenbaum, Thomas. 2002. International Trade and Environmental Protection. In Patricia Birnie and Alan Boyle, eds., *International Law and the Environment,* 2nd ed., 697–750. Oxford: Oxford University Press.

Shaw, Sabina, and Risa Schwartz. 2002. Trade and Environment in the WTO: State of Play. *Journal of World Trade* 36 (1): 129–154.

Stone, Christopher D. 1997. Too Many Fishing Boats, Too Few Fish: Can Trade Laws Trim Subsidies and Restore the Balance in Global Fisheries? *Ecology Law Quarterly* 24 (3): 505–544.

Tapper, Richard. 2000. *Biosafety Protocol—the Outlook for Renewed Negotiations.* Available at http://www.ukabc.org/cartagena.htm#c2.

Trebilcock, Michael J., and Howse Robert. 1999. *The Regulation of International Trade.* 2nd ed. London: Routledge.

UNEP. 1998, April 3. Conference of the Parties to the Convention on Biological Diversity. *Administration of the Convention on Biological Diversity. Report by the Executive Secretary.* Doc. UNEP/CBD/COP/4/24.

UNEP. 1999a, February 15. Conference of the Parties to the Convention on Biological Diversity. *Report of the Sixth Meeting of the Open-Ended Ad Hoc Working Group on Biosafety.* Doc. UNEP/CBD/ExCOP/1/2.

UNEP. 1999b, February 21. Open-ended Ad Hoc Working Group on Biosafety. *Protocol on Biosafety—Draft Text Submitted by the Chair of the Working Group.* Doc. UNEP/CBD/BSWG/6/L.2/Rev.2.

UNEP. 2000, February 20. Conference of the Parties to the Convention on Biological Diversity. *Report of the Extraordinary Meeting of the Conference of the Parties for the Adoption of the Protocol on Biosafety to the Convention on Biological Diversity.* Doc. UNEP/CBD/ExCOP/1/3.

WTO. 1994. *Marrakesh Agreement Establishing the World Trade Organization,* 15 April 1994, in force 1 January 1995, reprinted in: International Legal Materials 33 (1994): 1144–1153. Also available at http://www.wto.org/english/docs_e/legal_e/legal_e.htm.

WTO. 1996, November 12. Committee on Trade and Environment. *Report.* World Trade Organization. Doc. WT/CTE/1.

WTO. 1998a, July 16. Committee on Trade and Environment. *Communication from the Secretariat of the International Commission for the Conservation of Atlantic Tunas.* World Trade Organization. Doc. WT/CTE/W/87.

WTO. 1998b, October 12. Report of the Appellate Body. *United States—Import Prohibition of Certain Shrimp and Shrimp Products.* World Trade Organization. Doc. WT/DS58/AB/R.

WTO. 2000a, June 29. Committee on Trade and Environment. *Conservation Measures Taken by the International Commission for the Conservation of Atlantic Tunas (ICCAT). Communication from the ICCAT Secretariat.* World Trade Organization. Doc. WT/CTE/W/152.

WTO. 2000b, September 19. Committee on Trade and Environment. *Report of the Meeting Held on 5–6 July 2000.* World Trade Organization. Doc. WT/CTE/M/24.

WTO. 2001a, June 6. Committee on Trade and Environment. *Compliance and Dispute Settlement Provisions in the WTO and in Multilateral Environmental Agreements. Note by the WTO and UNEP Secretariats,* World Trade Organization. Doc. WT/CTE/W/191.

WTO. 2001b, June 14. Committee on Trade and Environment. *Matrix on Trade Measures Pursuant to Selected MEAs.* World Trade Organization. Doc. WT/CTE/W/160/Rev.1.

WTO. 2001c, November 20. *Ministerial Declaration,* Doha, Qatar, adopted 14 November 2001, World Trade Organization. Doc. WT/MIN(01)/DEC/1.

WTO. 2002, October 3. Committee on Trade and Environment. *Submission by Japan.* Doc. TN/TE/W/10.

WTO. 2004, August 31. Committee on Trade and Environment. *International Intergovernmental Organizations—Observer Status in the Committee on Trade and Environment—Revision.* Doc. WT/CTE/INF/6/Rev.1.

9

Interactions of EU Legal Instruments Establishing Broad Principles of Environmental Management: The Water Framework Directive and the IPPC Directive

Andrew Farmer

Both the EU Water Framework Directive of 2000 and the EU Integrated Pollution Prevention and Control (IPPC) Directive of 1996 establish broad principles for environmental management, while detailed rules of implementation are developed by the member states.[1] The Water Framework Directive establishes an extensive system for the management of fresh and coastal water resources in the EU. The IPPC Directive establishes broad requirements for the regulation of industrial installations. They contrast with many other types of EU environmental legislation that set out a limited number of specific requirements, such as emission standards or quality standards relating to particular activities or pollutants, which must be implemented in the member states. Given their broad scope, both directives have extensive interactions with other EU legal instruments and with a range of international conventions.

The first section of the chapter addresses interactions related to the Water Framework Directive. It considers the range of interactions associated with the Directive and then focuses on a case of interaction with the Convention on the Protection and Use of Transboundary Watercourses and International Lakes adopted within the United Nations Economic Commission for Europe (UNECE). This interaction is of particular interest within the framework of this book, because it elucidates how EU instruments interact with multilateral environmental agreements. The UNECE area is the region with the most comprehensive regional environmental cooperative framework. Currently there are six regional environmental conventions and related protocols adopted on transboundary watercourses, water-related diseases, prevention and response to industrial accidents, air-pollution control, environmental impact assessment, and public information and participation in decision making. These instruments are supported by around 100 bilateral or multilateral agreements and by supranational law adopted within the EU. Additionally, a number of soft-law instruments (e.g., recommendations and guidelines) are developed under the UNECE to assist implementation. The Convention on Transboundary Watercourses and Lakes and its interaction with the Water Framework Directive is only one of many interactions between similar instruments (see Tanzi 2000) and may highlight processes common to other interinstitutional interactions in the region.

The second section of the chapter examines interactions related to the IPPC Directive. Following an introduction to the Directive and an overview over the range of interactions associated with it, the analysis focuses on the case of interaction with the EU Large Combustion Plant Directive. This case stands as a model for a class of interactions of the IPPC Directive with more specific EU legal instruments establishing emission limits for industrial activities. These instruments influence the IPPC Directive irrespective of whether they existed prior to its adoption and coming into force. The case study illuminates how decision makers are to take the specific requirements of such directives into account when implementing the IPPC Directive. The interaction is driven by concern over whether the IPPC Directive will properly be implemented in the member states.

Finally, the chapter draws some general conclusions from these interactions.

The Water Framework Directive

The EU Directive Establishing a Framework for Community Action in the Field of Water Policy (2000/60/EC, Official Journal L327, 22.12.2000), commonly known as the Water Framework Directive, represents a major departure for EU water policy. The Directive developed out of a much earlier discussion concerning the limitations of existing EU water legislation. Beginning in the 1980s, debates took place in various forums on the development of new EU water legislation (Stern 1995). This resulted in the adoption of some issue-specific directives in the early 1990s (e.g., on urban wastewater treatment and on nitrates). However, legislation remained largely restricted to a series of directives establishing environmental quality standards for specific water bodies (e.g., bathing waters) or emission limits for specific activities or for substances (e.g., nitrates). EU water law was criticized for being too fragmented, concentrating on specific aspects of environmental quality or specific threats to that quality. In 1994, the European Commission submitted a proposal for a directive on the ecological quality of surface waters, which, despite its broad scope, still did not provide a sufficiently comprehensive framework. The Commission, therefore, submitted a new proposal in early 1997 (European Commission 1997), which evolved into the Water Framework Directive, adopted in December 2000 (Farmer 2000, 2001a).

The scope of the Directive is extensive. It covers all freshwater resources as well as seawaters up to one nautical mile from the coast. It pursues ecological objectives, supported by chemical and hydromorphological objectives. There is a strong emphasis on developing controls of activities that have an impact on water objectives. Finally, detailed requirements on reporting, public participation, and so on are included.

The Directive requires that surface water (i.e., rivers, lakes, and coastal waters) and groundwater are to be managed within the context of River Basin Management Plans (Lanz and Scheuer 2001; WWF 2001). All waters are to be characterized according to their biological, chemical, and hydromorphological characteristics. These parameters are to be compared with an assessment of waters unmodified by human activity and classified according to different categories of ecological status. All waters are required to meet "good status," except where specific derogations apply. Member states are to achieve these objectives through the development of the River Basin Management Plans, which shall integrate existing EU measures to protect the water environment and identify all remaining human pressures, which may result in a failure to achieve "good status" (Griffiths 2002). Member states are required to establish their own programs for each river basin that spell out the measures by which they intend to achieve the objectives of the Directive (Chave 2001). Hence, the Water Framework Directive allows significant flexibility on the detailed regulations that member states might adopt.

The Directive (Bloch 2001) seeks to cluster water-protection measures within a common rule framework. It is intended not to affect adversely rules that are already established at either the EU or the international level (e.g., on nitrates or urban wastewater treatment). Conversely, it seeks to set them in a broader, integrated context to enhance implementation results, not only for those issues newly addressed in the Framework Directive, but also in older legislation (Farmer and Wilkinson 2001). Potentially, interaction between broad framework rules and specific rule approaches will become more apparent as implementation proceeds. This might in the future lead member states to seek rule changes in existing directives not necessarily to alter environmental outcomes and impact, but to alter the ways such outcomes are to be achieved. Therefore, the Water Framework Directive poses some interesting possible future interactions in relation to governance issues within the EU.

Overview of Cases of Interaction Involving the Water Framework Directive

Given its extended scope, the Directive interacts with a considerable number of other institutions. Table 9.1 identifies the most important cases of horizontal and vertical interaction in which the Water Framework Directive is involved. Indeed, the Directive itself lists a range of existing EU instruments, which are to be taken into account when implementing its obligations. These include many items of water and pollution-control legislation. Other cases will only become obvious as the complexities of implementation become clear.

Among the horizontal interactions between the Water Framework Directive and other EU legislative instruments we find several cases of Behavioral Interaction. Generally, effects of these cases are synergistic. For example, active management of water quality in water basins will almost automatically enhance the quality of bathing waters and thus help implement the Bathing Waters Directive (76/160/EEC), which defines specific quality requirements of bathing waters. In turn, more locally concentrated action to improve bathing waters will automatically contribute to implementing the overall obligations of the Water Framework Directive. Similarly, implementation of the Nitrates Directive (91/676/EEC) providing for specific limits of nitrates pollution from agricultural sources, in particular manure, helps implement the Water Framework Directive, and vice versa. In other cases of Behavioral Interaction, influence runs predominantly one way. Improvement of water quality after implementation of the Water Framework Directive will support the conservation of habitats protected under the Habitats Directive (see also chapter 10) that depend on freshwater resources or coastal waters. Finally, the Environmental Liability Directive introduces financial compensation for environmental damage and will thus add a new instrument supporting the implementation of the Water Framework Directive.

Other horizontal interactions follow the causal mechanism of Interaction through Commitment. For example, the revised Bathing Waters Directive provides stronger links with the Water Framework Directive. This will include rule changes attempting to integrate its objectives more closely with the Framework Directive, in particular requiring that monitoring and assessments are done within the system of river-basin planning and programs of measures under the Framework Directive. Some other EU environmental directives explicitly refer to the Water Framework Directive and thus provide explicit links between these instruments. Hence, the Environmental Liability Directive defines the concept of environmental damage with reference to

Table 9.1
Institutional interactions of the EU Water Framework Directive

EU Nitrates Directive	• Nitrates Directive supports implementation of Water Framework Directive. • Water Framework Directive is expected to support implementation of Nitrates Directive.
EU Bathing Waters Directive	• Water Framework Directive influences the amendment of Bathing Waters Directive. • Bathing Waters Directive supports implementation of Water Framework Directive. • Water Framework Directive is expected to support implementation of Bathing Waters Directive.
EU IPPC Directive	• IPPC Directive allows the Water Framework Directive to establish explicit link by defining environmental quality standards. • Later Water Framework Directive changes meaning of environmental quality standards protected under earlier IPPC Directive. • IPPC Directive supports implementation of Water Framework Directive by requiring that permits do not lead to breaches of established environmental quality standards.
EU Habitats Directive	• Reference to Natura 2000 included in Water Framework Directive. • Water Framework Directive supports achievement of objectives of Habitats Directive.
EU Directive on Environmental Liability	• Water Framework Directive is used for defining damage under Liability Directive. • Liability Directive is to support implementation of Water Framework Directive.
Convention on Transboundary Watercourses and Lakes	• Convention triggers certain implementing provisions in Water Framework Directive. • Water Framework Directive contributes to achieving the objectives of the Convention.
Oslo and Paris Convention (OSPAR) for the protection of the Northeast Atlantic	• OSPAR triggers certain implementing provisions in Water Framework Directive. • Water Framework Directive supports achieving objectives of/helps implement OSPAR.
International North Sea Conferences	• International North Sea Conferences facilitated/triggered Water Framework Directive.
Aarhus Convention on public participation and access to information/justice	• Aarhus Convention led to enhanced public participation requirements in Water Framework Directive.
Ramsar Convention for the protection of wetlands	• Water Framework Directive supports achieving objectives of/helps implement Ramsar Convention.

other directives, among them the Water Framework Directive. The Water Framework Directive also includes reference to Natura 2000 of the Habitats Directive (see also chapter 10).

Finally, there are several interactions between the Water Framework Directive and the IPPC Directive, which establishes broad requirements for the regulation of industrial installations and is dealt with in more detail in the second half of this chapter. Whereas the IPPC Directive does not explicitly refer to the Water Framework Directive, it requires that regulators should not issue permits for industrial activities that would lead to exceedance of existing EU environmental standards. This obligation was not directly influenced by the Water Framework Directive, because it was negotiated and adopted previous to the latter instrument. However, it constitutes an automatic reference that allows the Water Framework Directive to modify the substance of member states' obligations under the IPPC Directive even after its adoption. Hence, the commitments under the Water Framework Directive automatically influenced the commitments under the IPPC Directive (Interaction through Commitment). Subsequently, implementation of the IPPC Directive helps implement the Water Framework Directive (Behavioral Interaction).

Informal mechanisms, such as the Water Directors' Group (comprising senior officials from member states and the European Commission), have been established to coordinate EU water legislation in detail (Water Directors' Group 2000). This may facilitate rule change, or at least rule adaptation, clarify implementation issues, and stimulate proposals to amend existing institutions if this is seen as necessary. Other informal (nonstatutory) developments, for example integrated coastal-zone management, will also affect the rule development under the Framework Directive (Farmer 1999). However, only detailed analysis following implementation will reveal the full nature of these possible future interactions and responses to interaction.

There are also a number of cases of vertical interaction between the Water Framework Directive and international conventions. In most cases, the conventions were adopted prior to the adoption of the Water Framework Directive, so that the commitments of the former influenced the content of the Directive (Interaction through Commitment). The most significant of these cases are those relating to the regional seas conventions and the Convention on Transboundary Watercourses and Lakes. This Convention has introduced issues such as ecological status and integrated river-basin management, which are central to the Directive. The Oslo-Paris Convention for the protection of the Northeast Atlantic (OSPAR) and the International

North Sea Conferences (see chapter 5), as well as the Helsinki Convention for the protection of the Baltic Sea, have led to the development of specific rule agreements, such as on the discharge of dangerous substances, and significantly influenced the details of the subsequent decision on priority substances that forms Annex X of the Directive. According to the European Commission, the Aarhus Convention on Access to Information, Public Participation in Decision-Making and Access to Justice in Environmental Matters led to enhanced public participation requirements in the Water Framework Directive (Water Directors' Group 2002).

The Water Framework Directive also supports the implementation of several international conventions by providing a stronger legal framework for parties to meet objectives (Behavioral Interaction). This applies in particular to OSPAR and the Convention on Transboundary Watercourses and Lakes. The effect is synergistic, intentional (there being clear reference to these objectives in the Directive), and outcome-based. A similar, though less strong, case can be made for interaction with the Ramsar Convention on the protection of wetlands. Within the Convention on Transboundary Watercourses and Lakes, attempts have been made to enhance these synergistic effects through the development of "soft" implementation rules (as discussed in more detail in the subsequent case study).

Interaction between the Water Framework Directive and the Convention on Transboundary Watercourses and Lakes

This case study focuses on a particular case of vertical interaction between the UNECE Convention on Transboundary Watercourses and Lakes and the Water Framework Directive. It illustrates how the Directive supports the implementation of the Convention (Behavioral Interaction). It highlights the importance of the different nature of institutional development and rules at the international and EU level in this process. It will also be seen that as implementation of the Water Framework Directive has taken place, parties to the Convention have responded to this interaction by elaborating further rules for nonmembers of the EU.

It should be noted that this case is part of a more complex set of vertical interactions between the Water Framework Directive and the Convention on Transboundary Watercourses and Lakes. Initially, the Convention has had a strong and synergistic influence on the development of the Directive (table 9.1). Only in the second stage is the Directive now capable of assisting implementation of the Convention.

The Convention on Transboundary Watercourses and Lakes

Cooperation on water issues has taken place within the framework of the UNECE for around thirty years. In its early stages this led to a series of recommendations relating to issues having a transboundary component, for example recommendations on agriculture in the 1970s. Concerted activity on transboundary waters began with the UNECE decision on principles of transboundary water cooperation in 1987 (Enderlein 2001). It contained the major elements found in the Convention, which was adopted in 1992 and entered into force on October 6, 1996. However, the development of the Convention was not just a transition from "soft law" at the UNECE level to a binding agreement in order to ensure implementation. It also developed out of soft-law agreements at a bi- or multilateral level between countries tackling specific transboundary water problems. The experience of the implementation of such agreements between countries was essential in developing workable solutions within the Convention. The debate leading up to the adoption of the Convention overlapped with the debate on the future of water policy within the EU. All EU member states as well as the EU (legally: the European Community) itself have since ratified the Convention.

The Convention has the aim of strengthening local, national, and regional actions to protect transboundary surface and groundwaters based on maintaining the function of ecosystems. Parties to the Convention are, particularly, required to prevent, control, and reduce pollution of transboundary waters by hazardous substances, nutrients, and microorganisms. The Convention recognizes the precautionary and polluter-pays principles as guiding principles in the implementation of measures as well as the need to sustain water systems for future generations. It establishes the river basin as the unit of management and requests that parties identify the catchments or subcatchments, which are subject to cooperation. Because previous agreements between riparian countries of shared rivers and lakes often resulted in incomplete resolution of the transboundary problems that they sought to address, the Convention specifically obliges parties "to enter into bilateral or multilateral agreement or other arrangements, where these do not yet exist, or adapt the existing ones, where necessary, to eliminate the contradictions with the basic principles of this Convention, in order to define their mutual relations and conduct regarding the prevention, control and reduction of transboundary impact" (Art. 9 of the Convention). The Convention, therefore, represents an important milestone in international cooperation, which is taken further by the Water Framework Directive.

The Case

While the Water Framework Directive is the principal instrument to implement the Convention within the European Union, it changes the situation of the member states significantly. The Directive is not simply an instrument at EU level acting in a "parallel" context to the Convention, it is the legal response of the EU (legally: the European Community) to ratification of the Convention, as a member of that Convention. For the EU member states, however, the Directive has a very different character from the Convention, mainly for two reasons.

First, the Directive is significantly broader in scope than the Convention. While it draws extensively on the general requirements of the Convention, such as ecosystem objectives and integrated river-basin management, in two areas in particular it reaches beyond the Convention. Whereas the Convention covers merely *transboundary* waters and lakes and *relevant parts* of a catchment, the Directive covers all waters, not just those of a transboundary nature. The reality of water management is that a full catchment-based approach is the most effective means of achieving environmental objectives. The treatment of transboundary areas on their own may lead to poor decision making and failures to achieve objectives. Thus the Directive clearly has the potential to enhance the effects of the Convention. Moreover, the Directive obliges member states to take account of a wide scope of issues in achieving its objectives. Hence, member states are subject to additional obligations. The role of EU legislation in this case is particularly important. The Convention requires action to be undertaken within each member country. However, its focus is on transboundary cooperation through joint planning and action. Thus, even if the Convention is translated into "hard" national law (as could be done with country-specific obligations under conventions relating to pollutant reduction), these transboundary elements are difficult to incorporate. In contrast, EU legislation is the perfect vehicle for this.

Second, the Directive reflects particularly "hard" supranational law to be implemented by the member states. The European Commission monitors compliance and, where it considers compliance to be inadequate, it can seek legal action against a member state through the European Court of Justice. None of these "encouragements" to compliance is available under the Convention. While the implementation of the Convention itself in the member states is thus not subject to the detailed scrutiny of the European Commission, its provisions incorporated into the Framework Directive will be.

The EU member states have reacted to the stricter set of obligations enshrined in the Directive in a number of ways. Although it is difficult at this stage to be precise about the additional support that the Directive provides because the Directive still awaits detailed implementation in the member states, the influence of the Directive on transboundary cooperation may be significant. For example, the Rhine Commission has indicated that, in response to the Directive, it will extend its cooperative efforts beyond existing countries (Switzerland and countries downstream) to include all countries in the catchment (e.g., Austria and Italy) (ICPR 2001). There have also been a series of activities within member states and, collectively, by the member states at the EU level. A range of working documents illustrate this, examples being Ireland (Environmental Protection Agency 2000) and the guidance on planning being developed under the Common Implementation Strategy (2002) and by EU nongovernmental organizations (NGOs) (WWF 2001).

Whereas the EU member states are predominantly faced with implementation of the Water Framework Directive, they simultaneously boost implementation of the Convention. The examples of transboundary cooperation just mentioned could, or even should, have taken place through the implementation of the Convention. However, they have not been apparent prior to the Directive. It is the Directive that has taken them forward because its provisions are enforceable as "hard" law. The need for integrated planning is highlighted within the Convention, yet activity has only taken off since the adoption of the Directive. This is also true in other areas where the two institutions overlap, such as in setting ecological objectives. This synergistic vertical interaction and the enforceability of EU legislation will thus result in greater implementation of the Convention.

The case follows the causal mechanism of Behavioral Interaction as illustrated by figure 9.1. It does not affect the rules of either of the two institutions involved, but their performance within the issue areas governed. The Directive implements the Convention at EU level, based on the fact that both the European Union and its member states are parties to the Convention. The Directive incorporates all provisions of the Convention, and it expands its scope significantly. Even more important, it turns them into "hard" supranational EU law. Early indications are that member states are responding to the harder nature of the Directive. Thus, the Convention's new supervisory instrument regarding implementation by EU member states enhances the implementation of the Convention. Given the early stages of the implementation of the Directive, the practical consequences of this interaction at the outcome level are not yet fully known. However, response

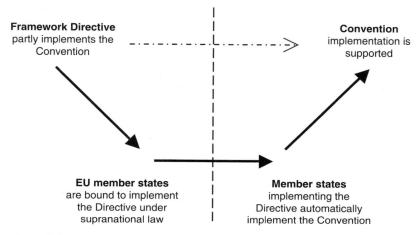

Figure 9.1
Water Framework Directive helps implement Convention on Transboundary Watercourses and Lakes

action within the Convention to enhance and fully exploit existing synergies is under way.

Response Action

The actors operating within the Convention have attempted to enhance the synergistic interaction with the Water Framework Directive as far as possible through deliberate response action and intensified collaboration of the two institutions. This is seen through the direct influence that the Directive is having on pushing forward the development of "soft" rules such as guidelines under the Convention to elaborate its rules. Most particularly, the Convention has taken advantage of this activity to enhance its own guidance for implementation and to seek to improve coordination between the instruments and exploit synergies. While these guidelines would be unlikely to have any additional effect on parties that will implement the Directive, they will influence other parties in the UNECE region.

The implementation of the Convention is supported by the work of a series of working groups addressing issues such as legal and administrative aspects, monitoring and assessment, water and health, and so on. Their responsibility is to draft recommendations, codes of practice and other soft-law instruments, and assist the Conference of the Parties to the Convention and promote the harmonization of rules. A specific task for the working groups is to "avoid, to the extent possible, duplication of effort with other water-related activities of other United Nations bodies and other international organizations" (UNECE 2001). Within the UNECE region, this clearly includes initiatives from the EU.

Guidelines on monitoring of waters under the Convention were published in 1996 (UNECE 1996). In 2000 a review of these guidelines was undertaken that began to establish links with developments at the EU level. The review highlighted that "special attention" (UNECE 2000) had been given to recent developments in EU legislation, especially developments on the Water Framework Directive. The review makes specific recommendations on objectives. These specifically include that "the management of the water environment should aim at sustaining or restoring the good ecological quality of river basins" (UNECE 2000). This objective explicitly refers to the Water Framework Directive and the definitions contained in it.

The links between the two institutions are strongly promoted under the Convention. An important milestone in this regard was a workshop in Bratislava in October 2001. Among its conclusions and recommendations, it stated that "it is recommended that the Bureau of the Meeting of the Parties to the UNECE Water Convention makes arrangements, as appropriate, with the European Commission so that activities under both the UNECE Water Convention and the EC water framework Directive are brought even closer together." Moreover, "the working groups established under the Convention may encourage the water framework regime to be used by non-EU parties." Finally, it is "recommended that Parties to the Convention that are not EU Member States or candidate countries should make appropriate use of the guidance on the economic analysis that is under development in the framework of the EU Common Strategy. A program element aiming at testing this guidance document in countries in transition and adapting it, if required, to the specific conditions of these countries, could be considered for inclusion in the work plan for 2003 to 2006" (UNECE 2001).

The work plan for the Convention for the period 2000–2003 also included coordinating elements between the two institutions. The Meeting of the Parties should provide guidance on the prevention of deterioration of ecosystems and their protection, and the promotion of sustainable water use as stipulated both in the Convention and the (proposal for the) EU Directive. It should also assist countries in environmental management and sustainable development of international lakes, taking account of legal frameworks such as the Convention and the Directive.

The Integrated Pollution Prevention and Control (IPPC) Directive

The Integrated Pollution Prevention and Control (IPPC) Directive (96/61/EC) of 1996 provides a comprehensive approach to the regulation of a wide range of industrial installations in the EU. Prior to the adoption of the Directive, EU legislation provided only a limited framework for industrial regulation. However, the IPPC Directive not only broadens the scope of such regulation, it also makes explicit links to the requirements in other EU legislation in order to provide an integrated approach to delivering environmental objectives. This sets an interesting framework for the examination of interactions between institutions.

The Directive requires regulation of industrial activities grouped into six categories: energy industries, production and processing of metals, mineral industries, chemical industries, waste management, and other activities such as pulp and paper, tanning, food processing, and certain agricultural activities like intensive animal units. The Directive is aimed mostly at large installations, and for the majority of sectors there are production-capacity thresholds that exclude the smaller installations (Emmott and Haigh 1996; Emmott 1999; Gislev 2001).

The objective of the Directive is to attain "a high level of protection for the environment taken as a whole" (Art. 1). In contrast to previous legislation, which dealt with emissions only to air or water, this is to be achieved by preventing or reducing emissions to air, water, and land, and it includes measures concerning waste. Manufacturers and authorities thus have to think about all emissions and their environmental impact in the design of the whole plant ("clean technology") rather than relying on "end-of-pipe" techniques, which frequently solve one environmental problem by creating a new one. Europe's traditional environmental regulation has emphasized end-of-pipe abatement techniques (Gouldson and Murphy 1998; Farmer 2001b). In contrast to most end-of-pipe measures, pollution prevention promoted by the IPPC Directive is not only of environmental benefit. It also represents a significant economic benefit, because the generation of pollution and waste, including heat, reveals inefficiencies within the production process. The basic technology requirement to be reflected in IPPC permits is "best available techniques" (BAT). Within the definition of BAT, "available" is specified as meaning economically and technically viable, taking into consideration costs and advantages. In determining BAT, special consideration must be given to certain factors listed in an annex, including the use of low-waste technology, the use of less hazardous substances, the furthering of recovery and recycling, the consumption of raw materials and water, and energy efficiency. An obligation is placed on member states to ensure that their competent authorities remain informed of BAT developments (Art. 11).

Member states' competent authorities must ensure that installations are operated in such a way that certain general principles are followed. These are: to take all appropriate preventive measures against pollution; to ensure that no significant pollution is caused; to avoid waste production and to recover or safely dispose of waste produced; to use energy efficiently; to take the necessary measures to prevent accidents; and to protect and clean up the site on cessation of the industrial activity. Member states are to ensure that installations covered by the Directive are not operated without a permit (Bohne 2000; Ten Brink and Farmer 2004). Permit holders must be required to advise the competent authorities of any changes in their operations, and any substantial modifications must also be made subject to prior authorization. Furthermore, competent authorities must reconsider and, if necessary, update permit conditions periodically. Reconsideration must be undertaken inter alia when excessive pollution occurs or when developments in BAT allow significant emission reductions without excessive cost (Art. 13).

From November 1999, EU member states have to ensure that no new installation is operated, and that no substantial change is made to the operation of an existing installation, without an IPPC permit. The rules do not immediately apply to unmodified existing installations that have been given an eight-year transition period until 2007, with longer exemptions for certain installations in the new member states (Farmer 2003). Nevertheless, some member states have chosen to require mandatory IPPC permits for existing installations before this deadline.

Overview of Cases of Interaction for the IPPC Directive

The IPPC Directive has interacted both with institutions established prior and subsequent to its adoption. Virtually all these interactions produce synergistic effects. Likewise, interactions across the boundaries of the policy field are virtually absent. Although the Directive regulates some agricultural activities like intensive pig and poultry units, for example, there is no interaction with the Common Agricultural Policy (CAP), because these activities receive no CAP subsidies. The Directive on Emissions Trading for Carbon Dioxide (2003/87/EC) might prove disruptive in procedural terms in its interaction with the IPPC Directive, since carbon dioxide controls from selected industries are no longer subject to BAT assessments. However, it might be synergistic in achieving overall environmental objectives. Precise effects can only be determined as implementation occurs. Table 9.2 provides an overview of important horizontal and vertical interactions.

The IPPC Directive is the target institution in a number of cases of Interaction through Commitment by which its rules are directly or indirectly shaped and molded. The rules of the Directive were explicitly developed to take account of the principles of waste management already established in the Waste Framework Directive (2000/61/EC), such as that of waste avoidance. This was a clear intention of both the Commission and member states. In several other cases, the Directive is deliberately linked to directives that set out their own environmental objectives. The IPPC Directive requires that regulators do not issue permits for industrial activities leading to an exceedence of any EU environmental standard (Art. 9). The Air Quality Framework Directive has developed air-limit values (chapter 12). The Water Framework Directive will identify good ecological status for surface waters (see above in this chapter and table 9.1). The Habitats Directive and the Birds Directive identify favorable conservation status for designated sites (chapter 10). Even without an explicit reference to these instruments, the IPPC Directive adopts their substantive environmental standards. Commitments under the instruments mentioned also become commitments under the IPPC Directive, because the latter allows other instruments to define its substantive environmental standards. Although this particular type of interaction becomes apparent only as individual permit decisions are made, it therefore constitutes a form of Interaction through Commitment.

A further example of such Interaction through Commitment is seen in the interaction between the IPPC Directive and those EU directives that establish standard emission limits for processes across the EU. Examples include the Solvent Emissions Directive (1999/13/EC), which establishes limits for emissions of volatile organic compounds to air, and the Large Combustion Plants Directive (the latter interaction is examined in detail below). Such limits act as minimum standards to be applied by regulators, and the commitments under the instruments mentioned thus affect the material content of the obligations of the IPPC Directive. However, they do not mitigate the necessity to determine BAT, which could result in stricter requirements.

The IPPC Directive is also the source, and occasionally the target, of a number of cases of Behavioral Interaction. Given the absence of independent environmental objectives and strict standards, the crosscutting IPPC Directive is designed to facilitate achievement of the more concrete objectives of the sector-specific instruments. Its implementation will almost automatically assist in achieving the objectives of all

Table 9.2
Institutional interactions of the IPPC Directive

EU Waste Framework Directive	• Has led to the inclusion of the principle of waste avoidance in the IPPC Directive • Benefits from implementation of IPPC Directive that requires waste avoidance in line with the Waste Framework Directive
EU Air Quality Framework Directive	• Is linked to IPPC Directive that requires permits do not lead to breaches of established environmental quality standards • Benefits from implementation of IPPC Directive that requires that permits do not lead to breaches of established environmental quality standards
EU Habitats Directive	• Is linked to IPPC Directive that requires that certified installations do not affect adversely "favorable conservation status" • Benefits from IPPC Directive that requires that certified installations do not affect adversely "favorable conservation status"
EU Birds Directive	• Is linked to IPPC Directive that requires that certified installations do not affect adversely "favorable conservation status" • Benefits from implementation of IPPC Directive that requires that certified installations do not affect adversely "favorable conservation status"
EU Large Combustion Plants (LCP) Directive	• Ensures minimum standards, thus limiting flexibility in issuing permits under IPPC Directive
EU Solvents Directive	• Ensures minimum standards, thus limiting flexibility in issuing permits under IPPC Directive
EU Environmental Management and Auditing Scheme (EMAS Regulation)	• Facilitates implementation of IPPC Directive in that EMAS certificates can be used to simplify permitting procedures • Benefits from implementation of IPPC Directive that provides incentive to establish EMAS
EU Environmental Impact Assessment (EIA) Directive	• Is linked to IPPC Directive that allows use of Environmental Impact Assessment under EIA Directive in permitting procedures • Facilitates implementation of IPPC Directive (in that Environmental Impact Assessment can be used under IPPC)
EU Seveso II Directive on industrial accidents	• Benefits from IPPC Directive that promotes an integrated approach and contributes to a greening of installations so that the impact of any accident would be minimized

Table 9.2
(continued)

Aarhus Convention on public participation and access to information/justice	• Has led to amendments of rules on public participation under IPPC Directive
OSPAR Convention for the protection of the Northeast Atlantic	• Benefits from implementation of IPPC Directive (reduction of pollution of Northeast Atlantic)
Helsinki Convention for the protection of the Baltic Sea	• Benefits from implementation of IPPC Directive (reduction of pollution of Baltic Sea)
ECE Convention on Long-Range Transboundary Air Pollution	• Benefits from implementation of IPPC Directive (reduction of air pollution)
UN Framework Convention on Climate Change	• Benefits from implementation of IPPC Directive (reduction of emissions of greenhouse gases)

EU environmental institutions that regulate matters also regulated under the IPPC Directive. For example, if an IPPC permit requires reduction of industrial wastes, or the limitation of emissions of air and water pollutants, or the protection of a recognized habitat, it simultaneously helps implement the relevant instruments, namely the Waste Framework Directive, the Air Quality Framework Directive (chapter 12), the Habitats Directive (chapter 10), the Birds Directive, or the Water Framework Directive (see earlier in this chapter and table 9.1). The integrated approach pursued by the IPPC Directive also reduces the danger of industrial accidents and thus supports implementation of the objectives of the Seveso II Directive (96/82/EC). In turn, environmental impact assessments required under the Environmental Impact Assessment Directive of 1985 and certificates issued under the Environmental Management and Auditing Scheme (EMAS) Regulation of 2001 may be introduced into the IPPC licensing process and thus help implement the IPPC Directive procedurally.

Implementation of the IPPC Directive also assists implementation of several international environmental regimes. These include global institutions, such as the UN Framework Convention on Climate Change (chapter 3), those at the European level, such as the UNECE Convention on Long-Range Transboundary Air Pollution, and those at a subregional level, such as the regional seas (OSPAR and Helsinki Conventions). Prevention or reduction of pollution to the atmosphere or to surface waters occurs within the issue areas governed, and thus at the outcome level (Behavioral Interaction). There is no interaction at the rule level. The only relevant instance of vertical Interaction through Commitment resulted in the only amendment of the IPPC Directive to date. The Aarhus Convention on public participation and access to environmental information identified a series of occasions on which the public should have access to information and have a right to contribute to decision making (Jendroska and Stec 2001). The IPPC Directive required public consultation on permit applications, but the Convention introduced the requirement for public information of the permit decisions that are made. EU member states and the Commission, in signing the Convention, recognized in advance that this would require an amendment of the IPPC Directive.

Automatic Rule Adaptation: How the Large Combustion Plants Directive Provides a Safety Net for the IPPC Directive

The IPPC Directive and the Large Combustion Plants (LCP) Directive interact according to the causal mechanism of Interaction through Commitment. This revolves around the incorporation, by the IPPC Directive, of emission-limit values set in the framework of the LCP Directive. This type of interaction relates to any EU directive that will set emission limits for activities covered by the IPPC Directive.

The Large Combustion Plants Directive

The fundamental aim of the original Large Combustion Plants Directive (Directive 88/609/EEC; Official Journal L336, 7.12.1988) was to reduce emissions of the gases that form the major contributors to acid rain from their main sources (mostly fossil-fuel power stations). The 1988 Directive was the first EU law to significantly tackle these sources of air pollution. Although these sources were also regulated by other instruments of EU legislation, not least the IPPC Directive, the Directive was renewed in 2001.

The 1988 Large Combustion Plants Directive required that member states take appropriate measures to ensure that all licenses for the existing plants contain conditions that comply with the emission-limit values for SO_2, NO_x, and dust set in Annexes III to VII for new plants (post-1988). Alternatively they could subject them to a national emission-reduction plan,[2] which ought to lead to the same emission level that would have been achieved by applying the emission-limit values individually to the existing plants in operation. In other words, the plan would allow some plants to exceed the limits provided that emissions from other plants were below them. The reduction targets for emissions of SO_2 and NO_x from existing plants were set in Annexes I and II, with which the plan had to comply. The national emission-reduction plan was to include objectives, related targets, and the measures and timetables to reach them.

Directive 88/609 was repealed by Directive 2001/81/EC on November 27, 2002, which has its roots in the Commission's 1997 acidification strategy. It sets stricter emission limits in line with the technological progress that has been achieved in this sector. The 2001 Directive applies to all combustion plants, not just those coming into operation since 1988. During adoption, Germany and the United Kingdom had disagreed over the role of older plants.[3] Germany was unwilling to accept a directive that would not include old plants, whereas the United Kingdom was equally adamant not to include them. According to a compromise reached in June 2000, existing plants were included in the Directive only with a residual life of 20,000 hours after the 2008 deadline. The European Parliament adopted the compromise agreement reached with the Council.[4]

The Case

Whereas implementation of the LCP Directive has resulted in significant reductions of both the emissions of acidifying substances and acid deposition, the IPPC Directive is designed so as to replace sector-specific instruments regulating particular forms of pollution from industrial plants. The clue to this case of interaction is provided by the answer to the question of why the member states and EU decision-making bodies chose to retain the LCP Directive and even bothered to thoroughly revise the instrument.

Retention, or change, of the LCP Directive has the immediate effect of establishing strict and comparatively clear-cut emission-limit values under the IPPC Directive. While the IPPC Directive does not itself set strict emission limits, it incorporates limits established under other EU environmental instruments (Art. 18 of the IPPC Directive). The LCP Directive constitutes legislation setting emission-limit values as under Article 18 of the IPPC Directive (consideration 7 of the renewed LCP Directive). Due to the automatic reference clause in Article 18 of the IPPC Directive, adoption or renewal of the LCP Directive thus results automatically in a simultaneous change of the rules of the IPPC Directive. Practically, it introduces strict emission limits into the murky discussion on the appropriate application of best available techniques. The interaction is illustrated in figure 9.2.

How strong this interaction is depends on exactly how the member states would implement the IPPC Directive and guidelines associated with it in the absence of the

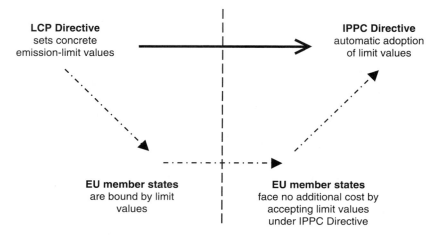

Figure 9.2
Automatic incorporation of rules of Large Combustion Plants Directive into IPPC Directive

LCP Directive. To understand this, we need to consider the basis for implementing the IPPC Directive and for setting emission-limit values under this instrument.

Implementation of the IPPC Directive is closely related to the application of the "best available techniques" (BAT) and immediately depends on the interpretation of this term. BAT is defined in Article 2(11) as follows:

"Best available techniques" shall mean the most effective and advanced stage in the development of activities and their methods of operation which indicate the practical suitability of particular techniques for providing in principle the basis for emission limit values designed to prevent and, where that is not practicable, generally to reduce emissions and the impact on the environment as a whole.

The Directive points out that BAT is not a static concept, but develops over time. As mentioned before, it requires a competent authority to be informed of developments in best available techniques and periodically to reconsider and, under certain circumstances (e.g., improvements in BAT), update permit conditions.

The Directive requires the Commission to organize an exchange of information on BAT (Art 16(2)), which has resulted in the development of BAT reference documents (BREFs; Bär, Kraemer, and Emmott 2000). A BREF explores the available techniques for a particular type of process and sets out options, including emission limits, that should be used by member states in determining BAT on an individual basis. The documents are not binding and require interpretation on a case-by-case basis. The BREF outline and guide under the IPPC Directive states that "a BREF does not interpret the Directive itself, nor does it remove the obligations on operators and Member States under the Directive to make decisions at national, regional or local level including the necessary balanced decisions required by the Directive. BREFs do not prescribe techniques or emission limit values" (Institute for Prospective Technology Studies 2000). The section on BAT of this outline and guide states that "while the BAT reference documents do not set legally binding standards, they are meant to give information for the guidance of industry, Member States and the public on achievable emission and consumption levels when using specified techniques. The appropriate limit values for any specific case will need to be determined taking into account the objectives of the IPPC Directive and the local considerations." It is critical to understand how the "appropriateness" of limit values is determined.

The development of BREFs has not resulted in a single definition of BAT for identical or for different categories of installation. For example, the BREF for refineries discusses various options, listing emission-limit values for NO_x ranging from 70 to 500 $\mu g/m^3$. This is a very wide range. Similarly, the 400-page BREF on LCPs describes a wide range of techniques that can be applied, but does not prescribe emission-limit values for member states to use as BAT. The information contained in the BREFs indicates that while following their recommendations would require stricter conditions on installations in a number of member states, the current requirements on some installations may be likely to meet BAT requirements (although this will only become clear once full BAT determinations are carried out). Member states have to report to the European Commission on the application of BAT. It is likely that these reports will show a wide range of interpretations across the EU, reflecting the variation found in the BREFs (see also Schnutenhaus 1994; Haigh 2000).

The BREF on LCPs has taken account of a wide range of technical developments. It presents a range of options that might be considered BAT. However, not being prescriptive, it has not been subject to the political arguments that took place during the adoption of the 2001 Large Combustion Plants Directive. There are different views on the consequences of this instrument for the IPPC Directive. According to an NGO position, the emission limits of the renewed LCP Directive do not reflect BAT and implementation of the IPPC Directive requires stricter emission limits (James 2001). However, others view the LCP Directive as providing a very strong lead on what is expected at the EU level. Thus, interpretations on what emission-limit values might be required under IPPC on a case-by-case basis vary significantly.

There are likely to be a number of instances where the LCP limits will be set in IPPC permits.

Therefore, the rationale not only for the survival of the LCP Directive, but for its renewal, rests in the concern of actors within the EU over the potential for full implementation of the IPPC Directive. The interpretation of BAT, in terms of which specific emission limits will be applied under the IPPC Directive for large combustion plants, remains uncertain. Only if in the future BREFs are found to be perfect and all member states follow them perfectly should there be no need for specific directives (Haigh 2000). The development of the LCP Directive of 2001 suggests that "imperfection" was expected at some point in the implementation of BAT in the member states. The position of the United Kingdom with regard to existing installations during the negotiations of the LCP Directive, as described above, suggests that concerns about the practical implementation of the IPPC Directive might have been justified.

Implementation of the IPPC Directive (on this issue) is now much easier to monitor than it would have been in the absence of the LCP Directive. The latter requires implementation early in 2008, a few months after the deadline for compliance under the IPPC Directive. Assessing compliance with the specific emission-limit values set under the LCP Directive is relatively straightforward. It is, therefore, relatively easy for the Commission, regulators, or the public to identify whether these limits are being complied with. In the absence of the LCP Directive, member states would (eventually) have had to report on emission-limit values derived from BAT assessments. Given that these were not prescribed, lengthy debates would almost surely ensue over whether the best available techniques have been adequately determined. A challenge of IPPC permits for large combustion plants by the Commission would necessarily take considerable time because a technical assessment would be required. It could, therefore, delay compliance for years.

Whereas the LCP Directive clearly supports the achievement of objectives of the IPPC Directive for protection of the environment in the beginning, the direction of influence, as well as the causal mechanism by which it is driven, might change over time. Requirements of the IPPC Directive include observation of the emission-limit values originating from the LCP Directive, but this is merely a necessary, not a sufficient condition for compliance. After all, the IPPC Directive requires application of best available techniques. "Such compliance may involve more stringent emission limit values, emission limit values for other substances and other media, and other appropriate conditions" (consideration 8). In particular, "best available techniques" is a dynamic concept that envisages continuous adaptation of requirements. Hence, the LCP emission limits constitute minimum standards under the IPPC Directive. As soon as these limits are exceeded, the IPPC Directive will begin to assist (over-)achievement of the objectives of the LCP Directive. This effect will not be a matter of direct or indirect rule change, but purely one of implementation. It will thus constitute Behavioral Interaction.

Overall, the LCP Directive can be viewed as a "safety net" so as to prevent the member states from using the looser framework of the IPPC Directive to undermine current standards of environmental protection. Through the automatic reference clause within the IPPC Directive it is capable of modifying the obligations under this Directive. Thus, the interaction produces, on the surface, a straightforwardly synergistic effect on the IPPC Directive by ensuring that specified emission limits for large combustion plants are complied with. The strict limits in the LCP Directive help achieve the environmental objectives of the IPPC Directive because it also regulates all activities covered by the LCP Directive. However, the synergistic effect is only as strong as the likelihood that, given the chance, member states would have sought to justify weaker emission limits when interpreting the IPPC Directive alone. And it will last only until the European Commission manages to challenge any individual determinations of BAT, which could take many years. Over time, the direction of influence will be gradually reversed, if the obligation to apply BAT under the IPPC Directive results in stronger emission limits than those provided for by the LCP Directive.

Conclusions

The IPPC Directive and the Water Framework Directive represent a type of framework legislation that seeks to trigger interaction with many other legal instruments to increase the effectiveness of EU environmental governance. They form the pinnacles of EU lawmaking in their respective areas, namely water management and industrial pollution control. They are designed to be holistic, to be relatively comprehensive, and to act as frameworks within which other regulatory activities can reside. Thus, both directives not only have many interactions with other EU legal instruments and international institutions, but are specifically designed to do so. Although such an objective could also be developed at the international level, the comprehensive and supranational institutional framework of the European Union is particularly suited for its realization. Having said this, the integration with other

EU institutions is not perfect and those implementing the rules can be frustrated by inconsistencies and lack of coherence between specific rules of the different instruments (see Farmer, Skinner, and Beyer 2003; Farmer and ten Brink 2004).

The inventories of interactions show that almost all of the identified horizontal interactions with other EU instruments are synergistic, and that the two directives considered in this chapter constitute attempts to enhance synergy as far as possible. The virtually exclusively synergistic quality of effects may be attributed to the fact that interaction occurs predominantly with instruments pursuing broadly similar or at least easily compatible objectives. Generally, interaction occurs in two ways. On the one hand, both the IPPC Directive and the Water Framework Directive draw on particular concepts and precise emission-limit values contained in the more specific instruments. Hence, their rules are influenced by the commitments of these specific instruments (Interaction through Commitment). As the case of the Large Combustion Plants Directive and the IPPC Directive demonstrates, influence may originate even from instruments adopted later than the relevant target institution, if the latter contains a general reference clause. On the other hand, the two directives discussed in this chapter are the source of synergy from Behavioral Interaction assisting the implementation of various other instruments.

Interactions in which the two directives are involved demonstrate that some "double work" has been deliberately developed at the EU level. Acting as "frameworks" or "umbrellas," the two directives result in "double work" for EU decision makers and implementing parties. In most cases both directives seek to minimize this effect by encouraging the practical integration of the rules of other institutions within the rule framework of the relevant framework directive. However, the case of the interaction between the IPPC Directive and the Large Combustion Plants Directive illustrates that double work may be desired. The concern of some actors within the EU decision-making process about how well member states will implement the IPPC Directive has led them to adopt a seemingly "unnecessary" directive to ensure that environmental outcomes are met—and to resort to a safety-net approach.

The vertical interaction between the Water Framework Directive and the Convention on Transboundary Watercourses and Lakes demonstrates that interaction is frequently a two-way process composed of two—or more—separate cases. Basic concepts of ecological quality were elaborated initially within the Convention, which influenced the elaboration of the Directive. This case was driven by Interaction through Commitment. After its adoption, the Directive with its encompassing approach and its hard supranational law facilitates implementation of the Convention through Behavioral Interaction. This second interaction is responded to by co-ordination between the two instruments and the adoption of secondary measures within the Convention. Hence, each of the two instruments has pushed the other during one crucial phase of the governance process.

Notes

1. The term *European Union* (EU) will be used broadly throughout this chapter, which includes the period before the Treaty of Maastricht.

2. "Large Combustion Plants Directive-Limits Also for Existing Plants," *Acid News* 3, October 2000, 8–9.

3. "Large Combustion Plants Directive-Limits Also for Existing Plants," *Acid News* 3, October 2000, 8–9.

4. "Ministers and Parliament Agree Air Pollution Directives," *ENDS Report* 319, August 2001, 52; European Environmental Bureau, "National Emission Ceilings and Large Combustion Plants Directives: Conciliation Could Have Been Better," press release, Brussels, July 7, 2001; "Parliament to Press for Tougher Limits on Emissions by Large Combustion Plants," *International Environmental Reporter*, March 28, 2001, 236–237.

References

Bär, Stefanie, Andreas R. Kraemer, and Neil Emmott. 2000. Der Sevilla-Prozess: Motor für Umweltschutz in der Industrie. *Wasser und Abfall* 10/2000: 64–66.

Bloch, Helmut. 2001. EU Policy on Nutrients Emissions: Legislation and Implementation. *Water, Science and Technology* 44 (1): 1–6.

Bohne, Eberhard. 2000. *The Evolution of Integrated Permitting and Inspections of Industrial Installations in the European Union: Report to the European Commission.* Brussels: DG Environment.

Chave, Peter. 2001. *The EU Water Framework Directive—An Introduction.* London: International Water Association.

Common Implementation Strategy. 2002. *Best Practices in River Basin Planning: First Draft.* Common Strategy on the Implementation of the Water Framework Directive. Brussels: Water Directors' Group, DG Environment.

Emmott, Neil. 1999. IPPC and Beyond—Developing a Strategic Approach to Industry for European Environmental Policy. *Journal of Environmental Policy and Planning* 1 (2): 77–92.

Emmott, Neil, and Nigel Haigh. 1996. Integrated Pollution Prevention and Control: UK and EC Approaches and Possible Next Steps. *Journal of Environmental Law* 8 (2): 301–311.

Enderlein, Rainer E. 2001. *The ECE Water Convention: A Powerful Tool to Prevent Conflicts over Transboundary Waters.* Geneva: UNECE.

Environmental Protection Agency. 2000. *Preparation for the Proposed EU Water Framework Directive.* Dublin: Environmental Protection Agency.

European Commission. 1997. *Proposal for a Directive Establishing a Framework for Community Action in the Field of Water Policy*. Doc. COM(1997)49. Brussels: European Commission.

Farmer, Andrew M. 1999. The Proposed EU Water Framework Directive with Particular Reference to the Coastal Zone. *Marine Environmental Management* 6 (1): 41–48.

Farmer, Andrew M. 2000. Integrating the EU's Water Policies. *Inland, Coastal and Estuarine Waters* 2 (1): 6–7.

Farmer, Andrew M. 2001a. The EC Water Framework Directive: An Introduction. *Water Law* 12 (1): 40–46.

Farmer, Andrew M. 2001b. *Industrial Regulation and Sustainable Development*. Brighton: National Society for Clean Air.

Farmer, Andrew M. 2003. The Environmental and Sustainability Implications of EU Enlargement. *Elements* 18 (1): 14–17.

Farmer, Andrew M., Ian S. Skinner, and Peter Beyer. 2003. *Effective Enforcement Needs a Good Legal Base*. Brussels: European Commission, IMPEL.

Farmer, Andrew M., and Patrick ten Brink. 2004. *"Simple is Better": Effective Regulation for a More Competitive Europe: The 1996 EU Integrated Pollution Prevention and Control (IPPC) Directive*. The Hague: The Netherlands Ministry of Housing, Spatial Planning and the Environment.

Farmer, Andrew M., and David Wilkinson. 2001. The EU Sixth Environmental Action Programme: Implications for Water Management. *Water Law* 12 (4): 236–239.

Gislev, Magnus. 2001. The EU IPPC Directive and Its Links to Other Relevant Instruments. Paper presented at a conference on Prevention and Control of Industrial Pollution: International Conference on Policy Approaches. Brussels: DG Environment.

Gouldson, Andrew, and Joseph Murphy. 1998. *Regulatory Realities: The Implementation and Impact of Industrial Environmental Regulation*. London: Earthscan.

Griffiths, Martin. 2002. The European Water Framework Directive: An Approach to Integrated River Basin Management. *European Water Management Online*, 2002. Available at http://www.ewaonline.de/journal/2002_05.pdf.

Haigh, Nigel. 2000. The IPPC Directive and BAT in a Wider Context. Proceedings of European Conference. In Umweltbundesamt, ed., *European Conference—The Sevilla Process: A Driver for Environmental Performance in Industry, Stuttgart, 6–7 April 2000, Proceedings*, 57–60. Berlin: German Federal Environmental Protection Agency.

ICPR. 2001. *Rhine 2020—Program on the Sustainable Development of the Rhine*. Koblenz, Germany: International Commission on the Protection of the Rhine.

Institute for Prospective Technology Studies. 2000. *Guidance on BREFs*. Seville: Institute for Prospective Technology Studies. Available at http://eippcb.jrc.es/pages/Boutline.htm.

James, Lesley. 2001. The NGO Perspective. Paper presented at an international conference titled "Prevention and Control of Industrial Pollution: International Conference on Policy Approaches," Seville, April 25–26, 2002.

Jendroska, Jerzy, and Stephen Stec. 2001. The Aarhus Convention: Towards a New Era in Environmental Democracy. *Environmental Liability* 9 (2): 140–151.

Lanz, Klaus, and Stefan Scheuer. 2001. *EEB Handbook on EU Water Policy under the Water Framework Directive*. Brussels: European Environmental Bureau.

Schnutenhaus, Jörn. 1994. Integrated Pollution Control: New German Initiatives in the European Environment Council. *European Environmental Law Review* 3 (12): 207–220.

Stern, Alex. 1995. *Water in Europe: What to Expect from the EU Policy Review*. Brussels: Club de Bruxelles.

Tanzi, Attila. 2000. *The Relationship between the 1992 UNECE Convention on the Protection and Use of Transboundary Watercourses and International Lakes and the 1997 U.N. Convention on the Law of the Non Navigational Use of International Watercourses: Report of the UNECE Task Force on Legal and Administrative Aspects*. Geneva: United Nations Economic Commission for Europe.

Ten Brink, Patrick, and Andrew M. Farmer. 2004. *Analysing Views, Policies and Practical Experience in the EU of Permitting Installations under IPPC*. The Hague: The Netherlands Ministry of Housing, Spatial Planning and the Environment. Available at http://www2.vrom.nl/docs/internationaal/04%20ENAP%20background%20report.pdf.

UNECE. 1996. *Guidelines on Water-Quality Monitoring and Assessment of Transboundary Rivers*. Geneva: United Nations Economic Commission for Europe.

UNECE. 2000. *Guidelines on Monitoring and Assessment of Transboundary Rivers*. Geneva: United Nations Economic Commission for Europe.

UNECE. 2001. Working Group on Water Management. *Report on the Workshop on Approaches and Tools for River Basin Management: Experience Drawn from the Implementation of the EC Water Framework Directive (Bratislava, 15–16 October 2001)*. Doc. MP.WAT/WG.1/2001/8, December 24, 2001. Geneva: United Nations Economic Commission for Europe.

Water Directors' Group. 2000. *Common Strategy on the Implementation of the Water Framework Directive*. Brussels: DG Environment.

Water Directors' Group. 2002. *Guidance on Public Participation in Relation to the Water Framework Directive*. Brussels: DG Environment.

WWF. 2001. *Elements of Good Practice in Integrated River Basin Management*. Brussels: World Wide Fund for Nature.

10

The EU Habitats Directive: Enhancing Synergy with Pan-European Nature Conservation and with the EU Structural Funds

Clare Coffey

The 1992 EU Directive on the Conservation of Natural Habitats and of Wild Fauna and Flora (Directive 92/43/EEC) represents the cornerstone of EU nature conservation policy.[1] Proposed by the European Commission in the late 1980s, the Habitats Directive sought to respond to the continuing deterioration of European natural habitats and an increasing number of seriously threatened wild species. More than a decade after its adoption, the Habitats Directive remains the single most important EU instrument for safeguarding biodiversity across the EU.

In addition to its importance as a policy instrument, the Directive also provides a rich seam for anyone interested in institutional interaction. The territorial reach of the Directive's network of protected areas and the level of protection to be afforded to these areas make interactions with other EU institutions almost inevitable. In addition, the Directive serves as the EU's main instrument for implementing the 1979 Convention on the Conservation of European Wildlife and Natural Habitats (Bern Convention), as well as key provisions of the Convention on Biological Diversity (CBD). In general, several interactions of the Habitats Directive have generated varied and innovative responses.

This chapter opens with a more extensive introduction of the Habitats Directive, followed by a summary of the main interactions between the Directive and other EU and international institutions. The core of the chapter centers on two of these interactions. The first interaction is between the Habitats Directive and the Bern Convention and focuses on the two ecological networks under the respective regimes—Natura 2000 and the Emerald Network. This interaction is particularly interesting with respect to the way it has evolved over time. The second interaction between the Habitats Directive and one of the EU's main funding mechanisms—the Structural Funds—emphasizes the way attempts have been made to harness the financial muscle of the Funds (at the heart of an initially disruptive interaction) to support better implementation of the Habitats Directive. The chapter closes by drawing out key lessons to inform more general efforts to secure less disruptive and more synergistic institutional interaction.

The Habitats Directive and Natura 2000

The principal aim of the 1992 Habitats Directive is to "contribute towards ensuring bio-diversity through the conservation of natural habitats and of wild fauna and flora in the European territory of the Member States" (Article 2). This is to be achieved by restoring or maintaining natural and seminatural habitats and wild species of EU-wide interest at a "favorable conservation status."

Although the Directive contains important provisions governing the protection of listed species, monitoring, research, and so on, it is probably best known for introducing the "Natura 2000" network. Natura 2000 brings together both Special Protection Areas (SPAs) of bird habitats classified under the 1979 Birds Directive (Directive 79/409/EEC) and Special Areas of Conservation (SACs) designated under the Habitats Directive, which apply to the protection of nonbird species and their habitats. The vision for Natura 2000 is one of an ecologically coherent network of SPAs and SACs, spanning the entire territory of the EU.

The process for establishing and managing Natura 2000 sites is at the heart of the Habitats Directive. As regards the creation of SACs, member states are to propose sites on the basis of their relative national, European, and global significance, most notably by taking into account their biogeographic specificities, their rarity, as well as associated threat levels (Art. 4(1)). Suitable sites were to be included in a European list of "Sites of Community Importance" that was to be adopted by the European Commission by mid-1998 (Art. 4(2)). Subsequently, member states have up to six years to formally designate the sites as SACs (Art. 4(4)). Annex III of the Directive sets out the criteria for the selection of Sites of Community Importance and the subsequent designation of SACs. In contrast to the SAC process, the procedure for the selection and classification of SPAs under the Birds Directive is largely left to the member states (Art. 4).

In most respects, the Habitats Directive establishes a common level of protection for the Natura 2000 network as a whole. The deterioration of sites is to be avoided (Art. 6(2)), in some cases requiring the active management of sites (Art. 6(1)). Any plans or projects likely to have a significant effect on a site's conservation objectives have to be subject to "appropriate assessment" (Art. 6(3)). Such plans and projects should only be granted approval after ascertaining that activities will not "adversely affect the integrity of the site concerned," or if, in the light of a negative assessment and in the absence of alternative solutions, there are "imperative reasons of overriding public interest" (Art. 6(4)). If damaging projects are to go ahead, member states have to take all compensatory measures necessary to ensure the overall coherence of Natura 2000 (Art. 6(4)), for example, by designating suitable alternative areas. Apart from Article 6(1), these provisions apply to all SPAs and all Habitats Directive sites included in the Commission's lists of Sites of Community Importance—in other words, before these sites are formally designated as SACs.

Natura 2000 was described by the former Environment Commissioner Margot Wallström as "the most ambitious initiative ever undertaken at European level,"[2] but practical implementation of the network has "been plagued by difficulties and delays" (Jen 2002). By 2003, the Commission's "Natura Barometer" showed that significant progress had been made, resulting in more than 16 percent of the territory of the then fifteen EU member states being identified for Natura 2000. However, the process of proposing sites under the Habitats Directive was still incomplete in all fifteen member states, seven years after the legal deadline for submitting site proposals under the Habitats Directive. Moreover, just three member states were considered to have completed the classification of bird sites required under the 1979 Birds Directive.[3]

Many different factors contributed to Natura 2000's poor record. The Directive's scope and stringency, local resistance to Natura 2000 (Paavola 2002), the lack of financial and human resources to support site identification, designation and management costs (Jen 2002; European Commission 2002), as well as agricultural and other land-use pressures (European Commission 2004b) are all believed to have contributed to implementation failures. Some of the insufficiencies have resulted from negative interactions with other institutions, of which the one with the EU Structural Funds is analyzed in more detail below.

Living with Other EU and International Agreements

The number of institutional interactions between the Habitats Directive and other EU instruments or international institutions is significant. The territorial focus and reach of the Natura 2000 network, coupled with the more general and non-site-specific species-protection requirements, means that the Habitats Directive has implications for the whole of the EU territory. At the same time, the successful delivery of the Directive's provisions will be influenced by a wide range of human activities and related policies. Based on an initial inventory by Coffey and Shaw (2001), table 10.1 provides an overview of key cases of "horizontal" interaction between the Directive and four other EU environmental and nonenvironmental policies, and "vertical" interaction between the Directive and five international environmental agreements. It should be noted, however, that neither the inventory nor table 10.1 contains all interactions between the Habitats Directive and other instruments. The Habitats Directive interacts with numerous other EU sectoral institutions, including fisheries, agricultural, and transport policies, for instance. Similarly, the type of interaction between the Habitats Directive and OSPAR is to an extent replicated in relation to other European regional seas conventions, covering the Baltic and Mediterranean Seas.

The majority of interactions identified involved EU policy or international agreements in the *environmental policy field.* These interactions involved all three causal mechanisms distinguished in this volume. The Habitats Directive has drawn on concepts, knowledge, and ideas from the Birds Directive and also reflects aspects of the Convention on Biological Diversity (CBD) that was negotiated concurrently with the Directive (Verschuuren 2002) (Cognitive Interaction). Interaction through Commitment is visible from the fact that commitments under the Habitats Directive have led to direct references in the EU Water Framework Directive (2000/60/EC; see also chapter 9), the IPPC Directive (96/61/EC; see chapter 9), and the Environmental Liability Directive (2004/35/EC). Furthermore, the European Court of Justice's interpretation of EU member states' commitments under the Birds Directive eventually resulted in a weakening of the related provisions in the Habitats Directive (Fairbrass and Jordan 2001). The Birds Directive was directly altered by the Habitats Directive, something that is possible in the EU system where one piece of legislation can amend another piece of legislation. In the case of the Bern Convention, the commitment to its implementation in the EU provided an important driving force in the preparation of the Habitats Directive. In turn, the commitment to Natura 2000 contained in the Habitats Directive largely drove the development of the Bern Convention's Emerald program, as is further detailed later on in this chapter. With respect to Behavioral Interaction, the implementation of the Habitats Directive has been supported by the implementation of the Water Framework Directive, the IPPC Directive (see chapter 9), OSPAR, the Agreement on Small Cetaceans of the Baltic and North Seas (ASCOBANS), and the Pan-European Biodiversity and Landscape Diversity Strategy. It should also be supported by implementation of the

Table 10.1
Institutional interactions of the Habitats Directive

EU Birds Directive	• Birds Directive has served as a model for Habitats Directive (in parts). • Habitats Directive has supported achievement of objectives of Birds Directive, including by strengthening certain aspects of protection of bird sites. • Strict interpretation of site protection under the Birds Directive by European Court of Justice results in Habitats Directive being weaker than initially proposed. • Habitats Directive includes provisions that directly weaken level of protection afforded to sites designated under Birds Directive.
EU Water Framework Directive (WFD)	• A reference to Natura 2000 sites was included in the WFD. • WFD supports achievement of objectives of Habitats Directive, in general and specifically by introducing legal deadline for reaching good ecological status in water-dependent Natura 2000 sites.
EU Environmental Liability Directive	• Habitats Directive is used in part for defining damage covered under Liability Directive. • Liability Directive introduces additional incentive for behavior that is compatible with the Habitats Directive.
EU Structural Funds	• Structural Fund projects that conflict with nature conservation objectives undermine implementation of the Habitats Directive. • Cross-compliance rule in the Structural Funds is used to encourage member states to submit site lists under the Habitats Directive, and to avoid damage to sites.
OSPAR Convention for the protection of the Northeast Atlantic	• OSPAR supports implementation of Habitats Directive in the marine environment.
Bern Convention on the Conservation of European Wildlife and Natural Habitats	• Necessity to implement Bern Convention in the Community drives preparation of Habitats Directive. • Habitats Directive supports achievement of objectives of Bern Convention. • Habitats Directive Natura 2000 program provides model/reference point for development of Bern Convention Emerald program.
Convention on Biological Diversity (CBD)	• Habitats Directive has adopted concepts also contained in the CBD, which was negotiated simultaneously. • Habitats Directive supports achievement of objectives of CBD in the EU.

Table 10.1
(continued)

Convention on Migratory Species of Wild Animals (CMS)	• CMS Agreement on Small Cetaceans of the Baltic and North Seas (ASCOBANS) supports achievement of objectives of Habitats Directive at the national level.
Pan-European Biodiversity and Landscape Diversity Strategy (PEBLDS)	• PEBLDS supports implementation of Habitats Directive, particularly through its focus on ecological corridors between sites.

Source: Coffey and Shaw 2001.

Liability Directive, which requires member states to introduce liability for damage caused to Natura 2000 sites. The Habitats Directive has supported the implementation of the Birds Directive, the Bern Convention, and the CBD.

While disruption was the exception rather than the rule in the case of interactions between the Directive and other environmental institutions, it would appear to be more commonplace in interactions with legal instruments related to other, nonenvironmental policy fields. Among the interactions with other environmental instruments, disruption only occurred with the Birds Directive because the Habitats Directive lowered the level of protection afforded to sites classified under the Birds Directive. Table 10.1 contains one exemplary case of disruptive interaction with nonenvironmental instruments concerning the EU Structural Funds that have funded various projects that conflict with the nature conservation objectives of the Habitats Directive (Behavioral Interaction). Although not contained in table 10.1, the relationship between the Habitats Directive and EU policies such as the Common Agricultural Policy (CAP), the Common Fisheries Policy (CFP), and the Common Transport Policy is also problematic. In particular in response to these disruptive interactions, however, nonenvironmental policies have also at times supported the Habitats Directive. The Structural Funds, for instance, have progressively been amended, to allow greater scope to use funds for nature conservation purposes. As discussed later in this chapter, a form of "cross-compliance" has in addition been used in an effort to improve the compatibility between the Habitats Directive and the Funds. Similar examples exist with respect to the CAP (Baldock, Dwyer, and Sumpsi Vinas 2002) and the CFP (e.g., Regulation 602/2004 protecting deep water corals around the Darwin Mounds from deepwater trawling). It has not been the case, however, that disruptive interactions have ceased altogether.

In seeking to promote synergies and reduce disruptions, one question that arises is whether interactions are actually intended or simply incidental. In most of the identified cases of synergistic interaction with the Habitats Directive, whether this involved environmental policies or not, the positive influence was intended either by the source or target of the interaction, or both. The opposite can on the whole be said of disruptive interactions, which were generally found to be unintended at the level of the policy, even if the interaction was predictable. This suggests that potential disruptions, once identified, may be prevented or remedied more easily than would be the case if disruptions were intended by one or other of the institutions. In all cases (including the initially disruptive interactions), a response has been generated that has improved synergies and strengthened the overall coherence of policies in favor of the Habitats Directive and Natura 2000. There is little doubt, however, that efforts to improve synergy can and should be strengthened further.

The Habitats Directive and the Bern Convention: An Evolving Relationship

The Bern Convention came into force on June 1, 1982, six years before the Habitats Directive was formally proposed (European Commission 1988) and ten years prior to the Directive's adoption. This pan-European Convention acknowledges in its preamble "that wild flora and fauna constitute a natural heritage of aesthetic, scientific, cultural, recreational, economic and intrinsic value that needs to be preserved and handed on to future generations." It has been ratified by forty-five European and African states, as well as the European Community (http://www.coe.int).

The Bern Convention was drafted by the Council of Europe, Europe's oldest political organization unrelated to the EU, founded in 1949. Work under the Convention is coordinated by a Standing Committee that is open to all parties to the Convention and meets every year. The Standing Committee, among other things, makes recommendations to the parties and reviews the implementation of the Convention (http://www.coe.int).

As will be demonstrated below, the coevolution of the Habitats Directive and the Bern Convention largely followed the causal mechanism of Interaction through Commitment. First, the commitments accepted by the EU and its member states under the Bern Convention contributed to the emergence of the Habitats Directive. The Directive in large part implements the Convention, but also goes beyond the Convention's provisions, in particular by establishing a coherent network of protected sites (Natura 2000). In a second phase, the commitment to Natura 2000 under the Habitats Directive was a driving force in the establishment of the Convention's Emerald Network. Moreover, the Directive is now driving habitat protection in a pan-European context. While the first phase of the interaction is briefly outlined below, the main focus of this section is on the second phase.

Initial Interaction: A "Simple" Case of EU Implementation?

In 1982, when the Bern Convention entered into force, the 1979 Birds Directive was the only EU (legally then: European Economic Community) directive explicitly addressing nature conservation issues. However, more general ideas on nature conservation had been set out in the early Environmental Action Programs (Haigh 2003), with the second Action Program (1977–1981) including among its objectives to "maintain a satisfactory ecological balance and ensure the protection of the biosphere" (European Commission 1977). The Commission's broader ambitions in the area of nature conservation had thus been outlined.

By having adopted the Birds Directive, the EU had assumed competence to act externally on those issues covered by the Directive. Three months after adoption of the Birds Directive by the Council, the Commission came forward with a proposal to ratify the Bern Convention (European Commission 1979). The proposal was adopted in 1981 (European Commission 1982), and the EU came under pressure from the European Parliament and members of the nongovernmental community to go beyond the Birds Directive and to adopt additional EU implementing legislation (Haigh 2003).

However, opposition among certain member states to further nature conservation legislation, while weakening, persisted. At the time of ratification of the Bern Convention, opponents had been assured that the Convention would not lead to additional EU legislation in those areas not covered by the Birds Directive (personal communication with Commission official). Now, these member states expressed their doubts over the effectiveness, practicality, and desirability of a directive that covered all of the issues provided for under the Convention. It has even been suggested by some that some member states were actively trying to deflect initiatives for an EU instrument on habitat protection, by instead proposing the reinforcement of relevant provisions under the Bern Convention (personal communication with Council of Europe official). This enhanced resistance was, arguably, a sign that pressure on the opponents to a directive was increasing and support for their case weakening. In particular, to the extent that new EU legislation on nature conservation was merely to implement the Bern Convention, it would not introduce new substantive commitments because all EU member states and the EU itself were already bound by the Convention. It thus became increasingly difficult to argue against adopting implementing EU legislation.

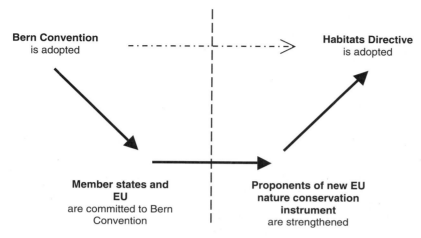

Figure 10.1
EU Habitats Directive implements Bern Convention

Following the establishment of a clear legal basis for EU nature conservation leg-islation through the 1987 Single European Act, the Commission came forward with a proposal for a new directive in 1988 (European Commission 1988). The Habitats Directive was adopted four years later (figure 10.1).

In many respects, the Directive implements the Convention in the EU and thus contains many of the Convention provisions. The Directive, for instance, adopted relevant definitions used by the Convention and more importantly, reinforced the emphasis given to habitat conservation by Recommendations 14 and 16 of the Convention's Standing Committee. A reference to "species [and endangered natural habitats] requiring specific habitat conservation measures" in Recommendation 14 is echoed in Annexes I and II of the Directive, which list natural habitat types as well as animal and plant species of Community interest that require the designation of Special Areas of Conservation (SACs). The phrase "Special Areas of Conserva-tion" was itself inspired by the terminology employed by Recommendation 16 on "Areas of Special Conservation Interest" (Council of Europe 2001). Other provi-sions of the Directive were also influenced by the Convention's provisions on habitat protection[4] (Council of Europe 2001).

Once in place, the Directive provided an additional means, besides the Birds Directive, of implementing and enforcing the Bern Convention in the EU. EU law, unlike international law, imposes legal obligations that are directly applicable in the member states and must be invoked by national courts even if national implementing legislation is lacking or conflicting (Haigh 2003). The provisions relating to Natura 2000 site protection and management are also believed, at least by some EU member states, to have direct effect (Verschuuren 2002). This means that they can confer rights on individuals that can be relied on against the state and other individuals or companies (Haigh 2003). Moreover, the European Commission has powers, resources, and duties to supervise, support, and enforce EU legislation, reaching far beyond those available to the Council of Europe. In accordance with Article 226 of the Treaty of Rome (as amended), the Commission can, for example, start legal proceedings against any member state failing to comply with EU legislation, potentially resulting in member states being referred to the European Court of Justice. Persistent noncompliance can even result in fines being imposed on the guilty member state (Art. 228). Compliance with the Bern Convention, by contrast, is followed up by the opening of case files and "on-the-spot" appraisals (Council of Europe 1999b), a procedure that has no formal legal implications.

Apart from serving as an instrument to implement the Bern Convention in the EU, the Habitats Directive went beyond the Convention's legal provisions and reflected some of the criticisms of the Convention (Haigh 2003). In particular, it was more explicit than the Bern Convention about the need for site protection and a coherent European ecological network, and set a precedent for transboundary coordination in habitat protection by establishing Natura 2000 as a core instrument. In addition, the Directive set a clear time frame for the transposition and implementation of its provisions and clear reporting requirements. The Habitats Directive thus represented more than just a simple case of transposition, if such a thing exists.

Changing the Direction of Influence: The Bern Convention Becomes the New Target

The elements of the Habitats Directive that went beyond a simple implementation of the Bern Convention mark the beginning of a reversal in the direction of influence between the Directive and the Convention, resulting in the Natura 2000 concept being "exported" to the Bern Convention (figure 10.2). While the Habitats Directive was intended to improve the effectiveness of the Convention but not to influence the Convention itself, the Bern Convention secretariat and Standing Committee responded to the newly adopted Habitats Directive. In effect, the Emerald Network emulated and developed in parallel to Natura 2000, extending the network of protected areas beyond the EU and into the territories of the other parties to the Bern Convention.

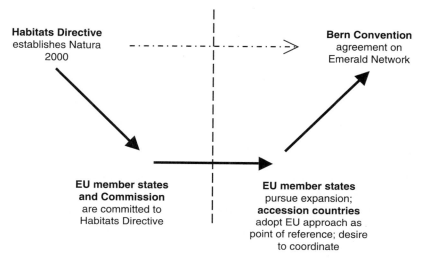

Figure 10.2
Habitats Directive affects regulatory approach of Bern Convention

The change in roles between the two institutions emerged from converging interests among three groups of actors: the EU member states and the European Commission; the countries of Central and Eastern Europe waiting to join the EU; and the Convention secretariat. Being committed to the Habitats Directive and Natura 2000, the EU member states and the European Commission had an interest in ensuring that pan-European commitments would follow a similar route (and certainly not go beyond EU requirements). First, the Council of Europe's endorsement of Natura 2000 meant that EU member states would be considered to be automatically complying with the Bern Convention's site provisions. Second, the effectiveness of Natura 2000 would be improved, if neighboring countries adopted similar approaches. Third, looking ahead to enlargement, the Emerald Network could help pave the way for the quick adoption of the Natura 2000 approach by the accession countries.

For the accession countries of Central and Eastern Europe, the prospect of joining the EU and the related need to implement Natura 2000 was an important motivation. Since they had to comply with the Habitats Directive in due course, establishing the Emerald Network imposed relatively limited additional costs and instead promised to help with the preparations for joining the EU. By 1996, delegates from the Central and Eastern European states were therefore stating their keen interest in the development of an ecological network and calls for an increase in priority awarded to habitat protection under the Bern Convention were being heard (Council of Europe 1996).

The secretariat of the Convention also recognized the potential benefits of synchronizing developments under the Habitats Directive and the Bern Convention, using and building on the approach adopted for Natura 2000. It would not only facilitate preparations for Natura 2000 among accession countries but also provide a comparable ecological network to those countries unable, reluctant, or otherwise unsuitable to join the EU.

Work on the Convention's Areas of Special Conservation Interest had already started in 1989 (Standing Committee Recommendation 16), but was subsequently suspended to await finalization of Natura 2000. The changes in the political map of Europe in the late 1980s and early 1990s contributed to this suspension as the secretariat of the Convention was redirecting its attention toward extending its scope to include the new democracies of Central and Eastern Europe (Council of Europe 2001). By 1996, Natura 2000 was starting to be implemented and preparations for accession to the EU by Central and Eastern European countries were advancing. The political priority awarded to the accession process and associated momentum gained at the national and international level effectively promoted the creation of a preaccession tool, which helped applicant countries meet the requirements for EU accession. The secretariat consequently "revived" the idea of a pan-European network (Council of Europe 2001), and the Standing Committee adopted Resolution No. 3 concerning the setting up of a Pan-European Ecological Network in 1996 (available at http://www.coe.int). In doing this, the Habitats Directive served as the source of inspiration. The regulatory provisions for the Emerald Network were deliberately drafted in such a way that Natura 2000 would effectively constitute a regional unit within the Emerald Network.

The importance of EU enlargement as a driving force for the interaction has been confirmed by efforts to align implementation within the accession countries through the Emerald Network pilot-project scheme (Council of Europe 1999a), offering practical and financial support for the establishment of the network in non-EU member states. Pilot countries benefited from participating in training workshops and obtaining access to the Emerald Network software, which was technically compatible with the respective software used for Natura 2000. Successful completion of the pilot phase required, among other things, the submission of a list of proposed Areas of Special Conservation Interest (ASCIs) to the Standing Committee to the

Bern Convention (Council of Europe 1999a). By 2002, eighteen countries had participated in the pilot-project scheme, including the ten new EU member states and three further accession countries (Council of Europe 2001). The focus had thus been on the countries preparing to join the EU, emphasizing the preparatory role of the Emerald Network and the motivating force of EU membership.

While the Emerald Network might also have been established in the absence of the Habitats Directive and the accession process, it is unlikely to have occurred at the same pace and in the same form. The "network concept" was already a well-established conservation tool within the Council of Europe, which had already launched the European Network of Biogenetic Reserves in 1976. Also, the need for greater emphasis on habitat conservation had been acknowledged previously. However, the operationalization of the network concept in the context of the Emerald program was heavily influenced by Natura 2000. The influence of Natura 2000 is also obvious from the implementation of both networks. For instance, when differences in the lists of habitat types used by the two institutions caused problems, it was informally agreed that accession countries were, for the time being, to concentrate on those habitat types listed in the Habitats Directive.

Continuing Efforts to Coordinate

Beyond the decision to establish the Emerald Network, coordination efforts between the Habitats Directive and the Bern Convention regarding their networks of conservation sites have continued, supported in particular by the European Environment Agency (EEA) and its Topic Centre on Nature Protection and Biodiversity (ETC/NPB), the Convention secretariat, and the European Commission.

The EEA and its Topic Centre have provided scientific and technical support in the development of an integrated regime for nature conservation at the Community and pan-European level. While established under EU law, the EEA serves an extended membership of the Council of Europe. A memorandum of cooperation was signed between the Convention's secretariat and the EEA to ensure the "mutual compatibility of data, information and approaches for measurement, analysis and assessment in the environment field ... and avoid duplication of activities" (Council of Europe 2000). On this basis, the EEA has monitored conservation action across Europe and provided a common database of designated areas. The EEA's role in establishing greater synchrony between various European habitat classification systems, and its input in the development of compatible software, has significantly improved the synergistic development of the two institutions. In particular, it has helped ensure that the scientific and technical aspects of developing Natura 2000 and the Emerald Network are taken forward in a parallel and mutually reinforcing process.

Important, although less central, has been the ongoing contact between the Bern Convention secretariat and the European Commission. The former has generally been, with the help of representatives of certain contracting parties, the driving force in facilitating better coordination between Natura 2000 and the Emerald Network. The European Commission's involvement appears to have fluctuated with personal initiative and individual responsibility. According to officials from the Council of Europe, a change in staff responsible for overseeing work on the Bern Convention led to an improvement of cooperation in the mid-1990s. In 2002, there was nobody directly responsible for the Bern Convention within the Directorate General Environment of the Commission, suggesting that coordinative action may have been given a lower priority.

Perfect Interaction or Room for Improvement?

The relationship between the Habitats Directive and the Bern Convention has been synergistic in both directions. The Bern Convention was a key driver behind the adoption of the Directive that served to strengthen the effectiveness of the Convention. Subsequently, the Directive's concept of Natura 2000 has driven, and continues to drive, the development of the Emerald Network under the Convention. The Habitats Directive generated a significant impetus and incentive for countries preparing to join the EU to participate in the Emerald Network. Non-EU countries have also adapted their habitat site protection to Natura 2000. In consequence, a more effective pan-European system of habitat protection has emerged, facilitated by scientific and technical assistance of the EEA and its Topic Centre as well as coordination of the Convention secretariat and the European Commission.

While this may seem to represent an example of a perfect institutional interaction, there is room for further improvement. Interinstitutional coordination could be strengthened, not least because it has often remained dependent on personal initiative, individual responsibility, and good timing. Improvements could be made, for example, to the harmonization of habitat lists and the establishment of site-management standards. Both the Directive in its Article 11 and the Convention (para. 4(e) of Standing Committee Recommendation 16 of 1989) require their members to monitor the conservation status of sites under protection. Yet guidelines for appropriate monitoring standards at the European level are lacking, and monitoring schemes at the national level diverge considerably. The European Commission was expected to address the issue of ecological monitoring under the Habitats Directive, and was to work in collaboration with the EEA to draw up a set of guidelines for EU member states. Full coordination on such issues with the Council of Europe would appear advisable.

In conclusion, the synergistic development of the two institutions has so far predominantly been successful and ongoing work suggests that this trend should continue. Future progress in creating spatial as well as institutional coherence between the two ecological networks depends on the continued interinstitutional cooperation, and on technical support. This is likely to be enhanced by ongoing activities.

Making the Most of Differing Objectives: Harnessing the Power of the Structural Funds

The long-standing interaction between the Habitats Directive and the EU Structural Funds has been the result of the territorial overlap of the two institutions, combined with differences in objectives: whereas the main objective of the Habitats Directive is to contribute to the conservation of nature and biodiversity, the Structural Funds' objective is to secure social and economic development by supporting regional development and cohesion within the EU. The Structural Funds represent the EU's main expenditure item, aside from the Common Agricultural Policy.

While not necessarily at odds, the two institutions have not generally been implemented in a consistent or mutually supportive way. In particular, projects supported by the Structural Funds have damaged Natura 2000 sites. The response has been twofold. First, reforms of the Structural Funds required EU member states to comply with EU nature conservation objectives. Second, on that basis, the European Commission intervened in a rather innovative way in the late 1990s to "force" the member states to effectively implement the Habitats Directive. As a result, the Natura 2000 site-proposal process was speeded up and the disruptive interaction between Natura 2000 and the Structural Funds improved, although problems persisted. This section outlines the different stages and characteristics of the interaction, with a particular focus on the Commission's initiative to secure a more synergistic coexistence between the two instruments.

The EU Structural Funds

The Structural Funds are one of the EU's two main funding instruments and aim to promote the economic and social development of disadvantaged regions, sectors, and social groups in the EU. There are four Structural Funds. The European Regional Development Fund provides support for productive investment, basic infrastructure, and local development as well as for employment initiatives and small and medium enterprises (Regulation 1783/1999). The European Social Fund is to develop the labor market and human resources (Regulation 1784/1999). The European Agriculture Guidance and Guarantee Fund (Guidance Section) supports agriculture and rural development (Regulation 1257/1999). The Financial Instrument for Fisheries Guidance provides funding for the structural adjustment of the fisheries sector (Regulation 1263/1999).

The overall aim of assistance is to reduce social and economic disparities in Europe, with a significant proportion of funding targeted at Europe's most disadvantaged ("Objective 1") areas, which often also happen to be the EU's most important areas in nature conservation terms. Together the Funds account for approximately one-third of the EU's annual budget, totaling EUR 195 billion over the period 2000–2006. Moreover, since almost all assistance is released only if matched with national and private funds, the Structural Funds have the effect of mobilizing significant additional expenditure beyond the EUR 195 billion (e.g., see European Commission 2004b).

The way assistance is provided has changed considerably over the last thirty years, originally involving the European Commission directly in the process of selecting and funding individual projects. The Commission's remit has since receded, with funding distributed on the basis of multiannual programs. The Funds now represent one of the most devolved policies of the EU. Aid is distributed to the regions and sectors on the basis of seven-year rolling programs. These are drawn up and subsequently implemented by the member states. Within the basic regulatory framework agreed by the EU, the member states decide where to direct aid and how to make it available (Haigh 2003). Member states and regional authorities consequently play a major role in determining the content, use, and eventual impact of assistance. This provides significant scope for tailoring funding to suit specific regional and national priorities and needs. It also increases the chances of funding being used in ways that conflict with EU nature conservation requirements.

Structural Funds Undermine Implementation of Habitats Directive

Even before the Habitats Directive had been adopted, there was evidence of Structural Fund projects contributing to the deterioration of important natural areas, including EU bird sites (SPAs) and other sites of national and international importance (see Baldock and Long 1988). Until the 1990s, Structural Fund regulations did not contain environmental conditions for funding, nor did they explicitly require member states to observe all EU laws or provide for specific safeguards to help ensure that funding was not used in ways that conflicted with other EU laws. Moreover, those responsible for overseeing the implementation of funding programs rarely involved environmental authorities in the programming or project-selection phases (Coffey 1998). The result was that Structural Funds assistance was being used to stimulate infrastructure projects in different parts of the EU, some of which conflicted with the Community's nature policy (Long 1995, after Lenschow 2002).

At the beginning of the 1990s, pressure mounted in favor of a general greening of the Funds, resulting in the incorporation of more effective environmental safeguards in the Structural Funds. The conservation organizations World Wild Fund for Nature (WWF) and the Royal Society for the Protection of Birds (RSPB) organized a well-orchestrated campaign to this end. In July 1993, a year after the adoption of the Habitats Directive, a major revision of the Structural Funds covering the period 1994 to 1999 led to agreement on more extensive environmental provisions, including a requirement for member states to produce environmental profiles of the regions for which they were seeking support. These were to contain state-of-the-environment reports, an evaluation of the environmental impact of programs "in terms of sustainable development, in agreement with the provisions of Community law in force," and a description of arrangements to ensure compliance with EU environmental law (Wilkinson 1994).

Despite these strengthened provisions, the Structural Funds continued to trigger Behavioral Interaction that undermined the effective implementation of the Habitats Directive (see figure 10.3). The Funds created an incentive for regions to attract financial assistance irrespective of the requirements of the Habitats Directive. Accordingly, the member states continued to not always respect agreed environmental commitments and to pursue environmentally problematic projects. Poor compliance with the Habitats and Birds Directives was linked to fear, on behalf of economic authorities, that development or growth objectives would be compromised (Lenschow 2002). In effect, the financial "muscle" of the Structural Funds gave them greater weight when decisions were made at the national, regional, and local level, compared to environmental policies that were supported only with a relatively minor budget at the EU level.[5]

As a consequence, the Habitats Directive was often given second place by member states or regional authorities in Structural Funds programs and in the

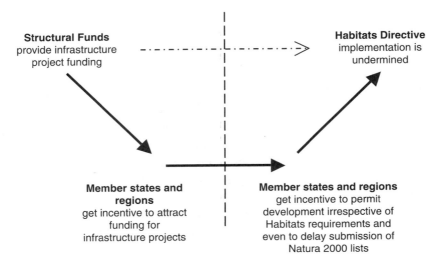

Figure 10.3
EU Structural Funds undermine implementation of Habitats Directive

project-selection process (Lenschow 2002). The higher-profile cases included projects to develop a visitor centre in the Burren in Ireland[6] and to divert the river Acheloos in Greece.[7]

In addition, the process of preparing Structural Funds programs and selecting projects arguably provided an incentive for regions to delay the submission of lists of protected sites. Because designation of sites was associated with the obligation to protect them, nondesignation provided more freedom in the choice of fundable development projects. Hence, designation might have jeopardized chances of securing Structural Funds support. Thus, by June 1998 very limited progress had been made in identifying sites, although member states had been legally required to submit lists of proposed sites to the European Commission by mid-1995 (Art. 4(1) Habitats Directive).

Reforming the Structural Funds and Ensuring Compliance with Their Rules
The failure of member states to implement the environmental safeguards and the disincentive provided by the Structural Funds with regard to compliance with environmental legislation, including the Habitats Directive, reinforced efforts to reform the Structural Funds in the mid-1990s. Following discussions between the Directorate General Environment of the Commission and European Parliamentarians, the

European Parliament's considerable powers in relation to the EU's annual budget were used to underpin calls for a reform of the Funds. In October 1995, the Parliament threatened to freeze 50 percent of the EU's Structural and Cohesion Funds budget unless the Commission produced an environmental code of conduct governing the future use of the Funds (Wilkinson 1998). The Commission responded rapidly by adopting a communication on "Cohesion Policy and the Environment" that set out a ten-point plan for tightening environmental requirements in the current Structural Funds regulations and promised to incorporate strengthened provisions in the 1999 Structural Funds revisions (European Commission 1995).

The main rules governing all four Structural Funds were strengthened in 1999. The new rules provided the legal framework for the Funds for the period 2000–2006. According to Article 12 of Regulation 1260/1999 laying down the general provisions governing the Structural Funds, it became an explicit requirement that "operations financed by the Funds ... be in conformity with the provisions of the Treaty, with instruments adopted under it and with Community policies and actions, including the rules on ... environmental protection and improvement." Plans and programs were to be drawn up and monitored by representative "partnerships" of national and local stakeholders, "taking account of the need to promote ... sustainable development through the integration of environmental protection and improvement requirements" (Art. 8). The implementation of Structural Fund assistance was also to be subject to ex ante, midterm, and ex post evaluations designed to assess their impact and effectiveness (Art. 40).

Despite the requirement for all funding to be in compliance with other EU legislation, problems between the Habitats Directive and the Structural Funds continued. In particular, member states were putting forward new draft EU regional funding programs outlining intended expenditures over the period 2000–2006, without first having complied with the requirement under the Habitats Directive to submit completed lists of proposed Natura 2000 sites. In the absence of proposed site lists, it was virtually impossible for the Commission to assess whether funding programs would or would not have damaging implications for areas suitable for nomination under the Habitats Directive.

Under these circumstances, the new 1999 Structural Funds rules provided a platform for different parts of the Commission to jointly force member states to come forward with Natura 2000 site proposals and details of how they were going to ensure sites were not damaged by Structural Funds expenditure. The Commission initiative took shape in July 1999 when an agreement was made between the two

Commissioners responsible for regional policy and environment, respectively. Following earlier commitments regarding greening the Structural Funds, and continued pressure from the European Parliament and nongovernmental organizations (NGOs), the Commission decided to exercise its powers to withhold Structural Funds unless proposed lists of sites under the Habitats Directive were submitted to it. Each member state's Structural Funds plans and programs were to be examined for their environmental merit, and applications would not be processed "if elements concerning respect for Natura 2000 are insufficient" (Haigh 2001). The Commission was stating that it was unable to assess the environmental impact of new Structural Funds programs unless it had lists of proposed sites at its disposal (European Commission 2000).

In March 2000, the Commission adopted guidelines "concerning the relationship between implementation of the Structural Funds programming for 2000–2006 and the respect of Community environmental policy (Natura 2000 Directives)" (Fischler 2000). The guidelines stated that

programming documents ... must contain clear and irrevocable commitments to guarantee consistency of their programmes with the protection of sites as provided for under Natura 2000. An explicit part of such a commitment should be to send in proposed lists under the "Habitats" Directive (Article 4(1)) together with the related scientific information....

States concerned must also give a formal guarantee that they will not allow sites to be protected under Natura 2000 to deteriorate during operations part-financed by the Structural Funds. They should also commit themselves to providing the Commission, in their programming documents or at least when presenting their programming complement for each operational programme, with information about the steps they have taken to prevent the deterioration of sites to be protected under Natura 2000.[8]

The Commission action was based on the existing provisions of both the Habitats Directive and the relevant Structural Funds Regulation but did not require changes of these instruments themselves. Rule adaptation was limited to interpreting standards. The existence of explicit EU rules requiring "cross-compliance" between Structural Funds expenditure and EU environmental legislation provided a clear legal basis for this way of encouraging member states to adapt their behavior. Without such a legal basis, the Commission would not have been able to take the initiative and threaten withholding EU funding.

The Commission initiative relied on the common interest of the two Commission Directorates General on regional policy and the environment, personal initiative of Commission officials responsible for the Habitats Directive, as well as the Commissioners for Regional Policy and Environment. The environment side saw it as a

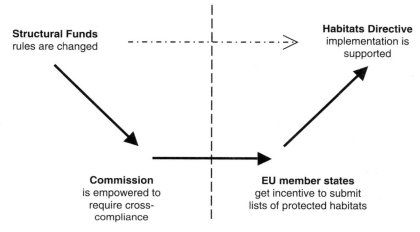

Figure 10.4
Cross-Compliance requirement makes Structural Funds support implementation of Habitats Directive

means of advancing the Natura 2000 site-selection process, while the regional policy side had an interest in applying its earlier commitments regarding greening of the Structural Funds so as to avoid accusations and threats from the European Parliament and NGOs. Despite the pivotal role played by officials and Commissioners, the initiative survived changes in staff and the departure of the two Commissioners in September 1999, when a new Commission was agreed.

The threat of the Commission to withhold financial assistance changed the effect of the Behavioral Interaction on the Habitats Directive quite dramatically (see figure 10.4). The financial strength of the Structural Funds that contributed to the initial disruptive interaction was now used as a powerful lever to secure progress in the Natura 2000 site-designation process. The Structural Funds provided an incentive to member states and their regions to speed up designation of habitats sites and to ensure proper protection of those sites. Specifically, the European Commission warned five countries (Ireland, Germany, France, the Netherlands, and Portugal) that it might not be able to assess certain draft Structural Funds programs covering the 2000–2006 period, unless a sufficient number of proposed Natura 2000 sites had been put forward to the Commission (IEEP 1999).

Since significant funds were at stake, the member states concerned took the threat very seriously and adapted their behavior. For example, following criticism of the

UK list of proposed sites at a meeting in September 1999, and facing the prospect of funding being withheld in certain regions, the United Kingdom announced in summer 2000 that it was forwarding a further list of proposed sites to the Commission (Defra 2001). In addition, further safeguards were put in place to ensure that future Structural Funds expenditure would not undermine sites themselves. This included a requirement for authorities responsible for monitoring Natura 2000 sites to submit a signed declaration as to whether or not projects were likely to have significant negative effects on sites (personal communication with European Commission official). However, the Commission was somewhat reticent to carry through its threat of withholding funds in the case of member states not submitting site lists. Thus, while insufficiencies continued to be noted in relation to all fifteen member states' proposed site lists, funding was actually only blocked in relation to the Wallonia region of Belgium (personal communication with European Commission official).

Overall, as a result of changes of the rules governing the Structural Funds agreed to in the 1990s, the European Commission has been empowered to require cross-compliance by member states with the Habitats Directive's requirements. This provided significant incentives for member states to submit lists of proposed Natura 2000 sites and ensure their proper protection. The Commission thus harnessed the initial cause of the disruptive interaction—the Structural Funds' financial "muscle"—to induce compliance with the Habitats Directive and to ensure compatibility between both institutions. The threat of withholding funding indeed supported the implementation of the Habitats Directive by leading member states to submit lists more rapidly than would otherwise have been expected (figure 10.4). However, an unwillingness to carry through the threat and actually withhold funding may have contributed to the fact that national site lists were still incomplete in all cases by the end of 2003.[9]

Conclusions

The cases of interaction analyzed follow the causal mechanisms of Interaction through Commitment and Behavioral Interaction. The Bern Convention cases center on the changing relationship between the two institutions. A rather "simple" case of regional implementation of the international commitments of the Bern Convention is followed by a spread of Habitats Directive commitments across Europe, well beyond the boundaries of the former fifteen EU member states (Interaction through Commitment). The interaction between the Structural Funds and the Habitats Directive, in contrast, involved modifying the driver of an initially disruptive interaction—funding—so as to make it contribute to nature conservation objectives in a constructive and mutually supportive manner. The existing provisions and tools of the regimes were used together as a means of changing the behavior of actors, thus reducing the level of disruption between the regimes, even if problems persist (Behavioral Interaction).

As demonstrated by the Structural Funds cases, the cause of an interaction does not necessarily tell us anything about the effect. The political (or economic) weight given to each institution can be much more important. It is quite feasible that, endowed with billions of euros per annum, the Habitats Directive would have impeded delivery of the Structural Funds objectives so that the direction of influence between both institutions would have been different. Furthermore, the role of broader political processes and the influence of nongovernmental actors can be critical in generating changes in interactions, in this case redirecting the power of the Funds to work in favor (at least in part) of the Habitats Directive.

Membership issues and associated commitments have been central to the Bern Convention case. This involved not only differences in membership of the two institutions at any given time, but also expected future changes in membership. The prospect of EU enlargement, and its political and legal ramifications, has been particularly significant in generating a strong response to the Habitats Directive, as the new EU member states prepared to take on new commitments under EU law.

In the interactions that were studied in detail, responses to the interactions have always led to improvements in synergy. The strength of responses was influenced by a number of particular factors, including the work of supporting agents (the European Environment Agency) and personal initiative (Commission and Council of Europe officials). Moreover, the interactions analyzed resulted in particularly strong and rather unexpected responses, primarily in the form of behavioral adaptation and adjustments made within the confines of the institution itself.

Several reasons are suggested for the relative lack of responses involving changes to the institutions directly—that is, by collective decision making. First, the collective decision-making process is slow and is not guaranteed to result in an "optimal" outcome. Alternative solutions are therefore often preferable, at least in the short or medium term. Second, the policy framework may not be directly responsible for the disruptive interaction even if policy changes could help to mitigate conflicts. The real problem may lie with governments, agencies, or other actors that are unable to coordinate multiple objectives sufficiently, instead prioritizing one set of objectives over another. This may be particularly problematic in relation to devolved or framework legislation where member states have more scope to decide how objectives are delivered. The challenge in these and other cases is to help or indeed force actors to address trade-offs between objectives. The best way of doing that in the short term may not involve adopting new or adapting existing institutions.

Notes

This chapter is based on an earlier draft by Coffey and Richartz (2002).

1. The term *European Union* (EU) will be used broadly throughout this chapter, to include the period before the Treaty of Maastricht.

2. Margot Wallström, Commissioner for the Environment, *Tenth Anniversary of the Habitats Directive: there is much to celebrate*! Available at http://www.natura2000benefits.org/ireland/carta.htm.

3. *Natura Barometer*. Brussels: European Commission. Available at http://www.europa.eu.int/comm/environment/nature/barometer/barometer.htm.

4. Resolution No. 1 (1989) of the Standing Committee on the provisions relating to the conservation of habitats; Recommendation No. 15 (1989) of the Standing Committee on the conservation of endangered natural habitat types; Recommendation No. 25 (1991) of the Standing Committee on the conservation of natural areas outside protected areas proper; all available at http://www.coe.int.

5. Regulation 1655/2000 Concerning the Financial Instrument for the Environment, Official Journal L192, 28.7.2000.

6. See http://www.iol.ie/~burrenag/hist32000.html for a history of the case.

7. See http://www-penelope.drec.unilim.fr/penelope/cases/greek/leaf1.htm.

8. Quote translated from letter in French with attached guidelines from Commissioners Monika Wulf-Mathies and Ritt Bjerregaard to the Permanent Representative of Ireland. Brussels, June 23, 1999.

9. See note 2.

References

Baldock, David, Janet Dwyer, and José M. Sumpsi Vinas. 2002. *Environmental Integration and the CAP*. Report to DG Agriculture, European Commission. London: Institute for European Environmental Policy.

Baldock, David, and Tony Long. 1988. *The Mediterranean under Pressure: The Influence of the CAP on Spain and Portugal and the IMPs in France, Greece and Italy*. Gland, Switzerland: WWF International.

Ballesteros, Marta. 1996. *Implementation of Recommendation No. 16 on Areas of Special Conservation Interest: Part I Legal Basis for a European Ecological Network*. Doc. T-PVS (96) 5. Strasbourg.

BirdLife International. 1995. *The Structural Funds and Biodiversity Conservation*, PR27/L37. Cambridge: BirdLife International.

Coffey, Clare. 1998. European Community Funding and the Sustainability Transition. In Timothy O'Riordan and Heather Voisey, eds., *The Transition to Sustainability: The Politics of Agenda 21 in Europe*, 130–150. London: Earthscan.

Coffey, Clare, and Saskia Richartz. 2002. The EU Habitats Directive: Generating Strong Responses. Unpublished manuscript.

Coffey, Clare, and Karen Shaw. 2001. *The Habitats Directive 92/43: Inventory of Interactions with Other Institutions*. London: Institute for European Environmental Policy.

Council of Europe. 1996. *Report on the 16th Standing Committee Meeting*. Strasbourg, December 2–6, 1996. Doc. T-PVS (96) 102.

Council of Europe. 1999a. Group of Experts for the Setting up of the Emerald Network of Areas of Special Conservation Interest. *Building up the Emerald Network: A Guide for Emerald Network Country Team Leaders*. Strasbourg, September 18–19, 2000. Doc. T-PVS/Emerald (99) 1 rev.

Council of Europe. 1999b. *Opening and Closing of Files—and Follow-up to Recommendations*. Doc. T-PVS (99) 16, Strasbourg.

Council of Europe. 2000. *Memorandum of Co-operation between the Council of Europe and the European Environment Agency*. Doc. T-PVS (2000) 14. Copenhagen, July 3, 2000.

Council of Europe. 2001. Meeting of the Group of Experts for the Setting up of the Emerald Network. *The Emerald Network*. Istanbul, October 4–6, 2001. Doc. T-PVS (2001) 51, Strasbourg.

Defra. 2001. *First Report by the UK under Article 17 on the Implementation of the EC Habitats Directive*. London: Department of the Environment, Food and Rural Affairs.

European Commission. 1977. *Second Environmental Action Programme*. Official Journal C139, 13.6.77.

European Commission. 1979. *Proposal for a Council Decision Concerning the Conclusion of the Convention on the Conservation of European Wildlife and Natural Habitats*. Official Journal C210, 22.8.1979.

European Commission. 1982. *Council Decision 82/72/EEC Concerning the Conclusion of the Convention on the Conservation of European Wildlife and Natural Habitats*. Official Journal L38, 10.2.1982.

European Commission. 1988. *Proposal for a Directive on the Protection of Natural and Semi-natural Habitats and of Wild Fauna and Flora*. Doc. COM(88)381, Official Journal C247, 21.9.1988.

European Commission. 1995. *Cohesion Policy and the Environment*. Doc. COM(95)509 final, 22.11.1995. Brussels: European Commission.

European Commission. 2002. Article 8 Working Group. *Final Report*. Brussels: European Commission.

European Commission. 2004a. *A New Partnership for Cohesion: Convergence, Competitiveness, Cooperation: Third Report on Economic and Social Cohesion*. Luxembourg: European Communities.

European Commission. 2004b. *Report on Implementation of the Birds Directive: Draft Report*. Brussels: European Commission.

European Commission. n.d. *Composite Report from the Commission on the Implementation of the Directive 92/43/EEC on the Conservation of Natural Habitats and of Wild Fauna and Flora*. Brussels: European Commission.

Fairbrass, Jenny, and Andrew Jordan. 2001. Protecting Biodiversity in the European Union: National Barriers and European Opportunities? *Journal of European Public Policy* 8 (4): 499–518.

Fischler, Franz. 2000. Letter regarding Commission Guidelines on the Relationship between Rural Development Programming and Respect for the Community Environmental Policy. Brussels, May 25, 1999.

Haigh, Nigel, ed. 2003. *Manual of Environmental Policy: The EU and Britain*. Leeds: Maney Publishing and Institute for European Environmental Policy.

IEEP. 1999. *Nature Conservation: Commission Threatens Action over Habitats Directive*. Briefing note. London: Institute for European Environmental Policy.

Jen, Sandra. 1999. The Convention on the Conservation of European Wildlife and Natural Habitats (Bern, 1979): Procedures of Application in Practice. *Journal of International Wildlife Law and Policy* 2 (2): 239–258.

Jen, Sandra. 2002. WWF European Policy Office. WWF Contribution to Minutes of Natura 2000 Conferences. Brussels: World Wide Fund. Available at http://greens-efa.org/pdf/documents/Natura2000/WWF_EN.pdf.

Lenschow, Andrea. 2002. Dynamics in a Multilevel Polity: Greening the European Union Regional and Cohesion Funds. In Andrea Lenschow, ed., *Environmental Policy Integration: Greening Sectoral Policies in Europe*, 193–215. London: Earthscan.

Long, Tony. 1995. Shaping Public Policy in the European Union: A Case Study of the Structural Funds. *Journal of European Public Policy* 2 (4): 672–679.

Paavola, Juoni. 2002. Protected Areas Governance and Justice: Theory and the European Union's Habitats Directive. *Environmental Sciences* 1 (1): 59–77.

Ten Brink, Patrick, Claire Monkhouse, and Saskia Richartz. 2002. *Promoting the Socio-Economic Benefits of Natura 2000*. London: Institute for European Environmental Policy.

Verschuuren, Jonathan M. 2002. Implementation of the Convention on Biodiversity in Europe: 10 Years of Experience with the Habitats Directive (Comments). *Journal of International Wildlife Law and Policy* 5 (3): 235–250.

Wilkinson, David. 1994. Using the European Union's Structural Funds and Cohesion Funds for the Protection of the Environment. *Review of European Community and International Environmental Law* 3 (2/3): 119–126.

Wilkinson, David. 1998. Steps Towards Integrating the Environment into Other EU Policy Sectors. In Timothy O'Riordan and Heather Voisey, eds., *The Transition to Sustainability: The Politics of Agenda 21 in Europe*, 113–129. London: Earthscan.

11

The EU Deliberate Release Directive: Environmental Precaution versus Trade and Product Regulation

Ingmar von Homeyer

The first generation of genetically modified (GM) agricultural products, such as GM seeds, crops, and food, has been commercially available since the mid-1990s. GM maize and soy are the most common products, followed by oilseed rape. A particularly common characteristic of these products is genetically engineered pesticide resistance, which is associated with several possible environmental risks. For example, resistance may be transferred to related wild species through crossbreeding or gene transfer and GM crops may have undesirable side effects on nontarget organisms, such as beneficial insects. In addition to these *primary* effects, there are *secondary* effects caused by the complementary pesticide, rather than the crops themselves. For instance, pesticide use may cause resistance in target weeds or have a negative impact on biodiversity (Sauter and Meyer 2000, 64–75, 221–226).

In 1990 the EU adopted the Directive on the Deliberate Release of Genetically Modified Organisms into the Environment (Deliberate Release Directive, DRD) to address the potential environmental risks of GM products. The DRD is one of the most controversial pieces of EU environmental legislation. Its alleged negative effects on the commercialization of, and trade in, genetically modified organisms (GMOs) have been heavily criticized by the United States and other main producers as well as parts of industry and some scientists working in the field. The Directive interacts with several environmental and nonenvironmental institutions, in particular in the agricultural and food sectors and concerning trade. Politically significant interactions are with EU product-sector legislation, such as rules governing the authorization for Communitywide sale of food, feed, seeds, and pesticides, and various international institutions, in particular the Sanitary and Phytosanitary (SPS) Agreement and the Technical Barriers to Trade (TBT) Agreement of the World Trade Organization (WTO).

This chapter starts with a short overview of the DRD. The next section summarizes the Directive's main interactions. This is followed by more detailed analyses of the interactions with the EU Pesticides Directive (PD) and the WTO SPS Agreement. Both interactions focus on the DRD's precautionary approach. The final section draws some conclusions from the main findings.

The Deliberate Release Directive

The DRD (Directive 90/220/EEC) pursues the twofold aim of European harmonization and protecting human health and the environment (Art. 1). It covers deliberate releases of GMOs for research purposes (Part B) and marketing of GM products (Part C). Releases for research purposes are authorized at the national level in accordance with the Directive. Involvement of EU-level institutions is significantly stronger in product approval than with respect to releases for research purposes. An application is submitted to a National Competent Authority (NCA), but authorization depends on other EU member states that can raise objections in the so-called Article 21 Committee, which oversees the implementation of the DRD. This EU regulatory committee decides on the basis of a Commission proposal, the adoption of which requires a qualified majority of votes held by the member states. Otherwise the matter is referred to the EU Council of (Environment) Ministers. If the Council does not decide by a qualified majority within three months, the Commission may adopt its original proposal. However, Article 16 of the DRD allows an EU member state to provisionally suspend the authorization of a GM product if there are "justifiable reasons to consider that a product ... constitutes a risk."

The DRD is based on a precautionary regulatory approach, which assumes that—given potentially serious environmental or health risks—protective measures may be justified even if there is no clear scientific evidence of harm. Precaution constitutes the DRD's raison d'être and justifies the Directive's technology-specific character. More specifically, the DRD uses characteristics of the production process—that is, use of genetic engineering—as "regulatory trigger." This approach reflects the assumption that GMOs pose potential risks requiring specific regulation because of the way they are produced. The DRD also uses a precautionary approach at the operational level because risk assessment focuses on the evaluation of *potential* environmental risks.

In addition to the default authorization procedure involving the Article 21 Committee, the DRD provides for an alternative procedure based on conventional product-sector legislation. Under sectoral legislation, regulatory oversight is triggered by the kind of product as defined by its intended use (product groups), rather than by technology. Reflecting the DRD's precautionary approach, Article 10(2) of the DRD allows for exclusive authorization under applicable sectoral legislation only if such legislation "provides for a specific environmental risk assessment *similar* to that laid down in this Directive" (emphasis added).

The EU adopted a heavily revised DRD (Directive 2001/18/EC) in March 2001 that is significantly stricter than its predecessor. Among other things, the revised DRD explicitly incorporates the precautionary principle as a rationale for its adoption (Recital 8 and Art. 1) and as a principle of risk assessment (Art. 4 and Annex II). Furthermore, the revised Directive clarifies that precautionary risk assessment covers indirect and long-term effects. It also introduces new requirements for clear labeling and traceability of GMOs (Art. 12 and 14) and makes authorization under sectoral legislation contingent on the application of "equivalent" (rather than "similar") measures, including risk assessment (Art. 12(3)).

Overview of Interactions

Because of the wide range of possible applications of GMOs, there is a large potential for interactions involving the DRD. For example, GMOs are an issue for the Food and Agriculture Organization of the UN (FAO) because they may affect food security (Becker and Hanrahan 2004, 3). GMOs may also aid environmental protection by dissolving toxic chemicals or mitigating climate change by increasing the capacity of plants to absorb CO_2. This may affect international institutions for the protection of water resources and the climate change regime. More worrying are applications in biological warfare—a possibility that could lead to interactions with security and defense regimes. However, for the time being, many of these interactions remain hypothetical, not least because only relatively few nonmedicinal GM products have so far been developed.

The DRD's most intensive and politically important interactions with other EU legal instruments and international institutions are summarized in table 11.1. These interactions focus on three main issues: the DRD's precautionary regulatory approach, and its labeling and traceability provisions. Four clusters of horizontal interactions with other EU legislative instruments can be distinguished. First of all, the DRD's precautionary risk assessment influenced EU sectoral legislation in two ways. First, the DRD added a second regulatory hurdle for GM products that must

Table 11.1
Main interactions of the Deliberate Release Directive

EU sectoral legislation (risk assessment)	• DRD established second regulatory hurdle requiring precautionary risk assessment of GMOs, thus disrupting authorization under sectoral legislation. • DRD requires sectoral legislation to provide for "similar" (original DRD) or "equivalent" (revised DRD) environmental risk assessment.
EU Novel Food Regulation	• DRD required labeling only for certain GMOs and thus undermined the Novel Food Regulation that aimed to introduce more general labeling of GM food.
EU sectoral legislation (labeling)	• Amended DRD allowed for labeling irrespective of actual GMO content, thereby undermining sectoral legislation that aims to introduce unambiguous labeling of GMOs according to certain thresholds of GM content.
EU Pesticides Directive	• Unclear scope of DRD's precautionary risk assessment led to EU decision to evaluate secondary effects under PD, rather than DRD. • As an increasing number of member states pursued evaluation of secondary effects under DRD, authorization of products conforming to PD was negatively affected.
EU Environmental Liability Directive	• Liability of GMOs was not included in revised DRD because it was to be dealt with in upcoming Liability Directive. • Liability Directive refers to DRD and partially covers GMOs. • Liability Directive is expected to have a positive effect on the implementation of the DRD.
WTO SPS Agreement	• DRD's precautionary approach leads to delays in GM product approval or even bans, thereby restricting international trade. • Partial "internationalization" of DRD's precautionary approach may lead to modification of SPS Agreement's concept of precaution. • WTO dispute-settlement mechanism provides SPS Agreement with potentially effective instrument to impose rudimentary precaution on DRD.
WTO TBT Agreement	• DRD's labeling and traceability provisions restrict trade, thereby undermining objective of TBT Agreement. • WTO dispute-settlement mechanism provides TBT Agreement with potentially effective instrument to enforce compliance, possibly undermining the DRD.
UNEP Technical Guidelines on Biosafety	• DRD constituted input for formulation of UNEP Guidelines.

be approved under both sectoral legislation and the DRD (Barling 1997, 1044). The additional hurdle increases regulatory uncertainty, because it may cause delays and result in additional authorization requirements or outright product bans. These behavioral effects disrupt the traditional approval process under sectoral legislation (Behavioral Interaction). Second, by allowing for exclusive approval of GM products under sectoral legislation only if such legislation incorporates a "similar" (original DRD) or even "equivalent" (revised DRD) risk assessment, the DRD committed EU legislators to a precautionary risk assessment and thus put pressure on them to amend sectoral legislation accordingly (Interaction through Commitment).

The second cluster of horizontal interactions concerns the EU Pesticides Directive (PD). It is analyzed in more detail in the next section. Reacting to differing interpretations, the Article 21 Committee decided in 1994 that the evaluation of secondary effects of GM products was to be considered under the Pesticides Directive, rather than the DRD. This interpretation, which was not supported by all member states, was driven by the desire to avoid conflicting interpretations of their commitments by individual member states (Interaction through Commitment). This attempt to settle the dispute was, however, unsuccessful because a growing number of member states defied the Article 21 Committee's decision and requested evaluation of secondary effects under the DRD. They employed Article 16 of the DRD to suspend authorizations and blocked authorizations in the Article 21 Committee. This development contributed to delays in product approval and outright bans and thus undermined the PD at the outcome level (Behavioral Interaction).

Third, the DRD interacted with EU rules on labeling. From 1997 on, the Novel Food Regulation required labeling of food consisting of GMOs. However, the DRD only required labeling of GM products associated with specific health or environmental risks. Therefore, some GM crops that may be used as food ingredients and had already been authorized under the DRD, such as certain GM maize and soy varieties, were not subject to labeling requirements, which undermined the labeling provisions of the Novel Food Regulation (Behavioral Interaction). Reacting to the Novel Food Regulation, the EU amended the DRD to require more general labeling of GMOs. However, for products sold in mixtures that may or may not contain GMOs, the amendment allowed a "may contain GMOs" label. This had the effect of undermining the labeling provisions of several pieces of subsequent sectoral legislation establishing thresholds for GMO content beyond which labeling was required, because the "may contain GMOs" label occurred irrespective of actual GMO content (Behavioral Interaction).

Finally, the DRD also interacted with the EU Environmental Liability Directive (2004/35/EC). Initially, the commitment to elaborate a Liability Directive was successfully employed as a major argument to prevent the inclusion of liability provisions regarding GMOs in the revised DRD (Interaction through Commitment). In its final form, the Liability Directive indeed refers to the DRD and covers GMOs, although to a lesser extent than many supporters of including provisions on liability in the revised DRD may have wished (Interaction through Commitment). Nevertheless, the Liability Directive is likely to assist in the effective implementation of the DRD (Behavioral Interaction).

The DRD's vertical interactions with international institutions frequently involve the WTO SPS Agreement. First, the DRD's precautionary risk assessment led to delays, product bans, and moratoriums, which restricted U.S. exports of GM maize and soy to the EU. These import restrictions undermined the SPS Agreement's objective of trade liberalization (Behavioral Interaction). Second, the SPS Agreement is backed up by WTO dispute settlement, which may reject the DRD's precautionary approach and authorize trade sanctions against the EU. Such trade sanctions would undermine the implementation of the DRD (Behavioral Interaction). Third, the SPS Agreement recognizes certain internationally agreed-on safety standards. Reflecting its commitment to the DRD, the EU was partly successful in promoting the DRD's concept of precaution in several international institutions (Interaction through Commitment). This may eventually lead to a reinterpretation or formal modification of the SPS Agreement's concept of precaution. The interactions between the DRD and the SPS Agreement are examined in more detail below.

Furthermore, the DRD's provisions for extensive labeling and traceability of GMOs tend to restrict trade, in particular because compliance requires potentially costly separation of GM products from conventional products (Becker and Hanrahan 2004, 4–5). Therefore, these provisions undermine the WTO TBT Agreement's main objective of increasing trade flows (Wolff 2003, 7–9) (Behavioral Interaction). Like the SPS Agreement, the TBT Agreement is backed up by the WTO dispute-settlement mechanism. If the latter ruled against the DRD's labeling and traceablity provisions in a possible future case, the resulting trade sanctions would undermine the implementation of the DRD (Behavioral Interaction).

Finally, the DRD also influenced the Technical Guidelines for Safety in Biotechnology adopted by the United Nations Environment Program (UNEP) in 1995, which are partly modeled on the DRD. The United Kingdom and the Netherlands played key roles in preparing draft guidelines, which were subsequently discussed by the Article 21 Committee. At that time, the DRD constituted the most comprehensive and advanced set of rules specifically designed to ensure the safe use and commercialization of GMOs and thus served as an important informational input in the preparation of the UNEP Guidelines (UNEP 1997, sec. III; Cantley 1995, 633–634) (Cognitive Interaction).

Interactions with the Pesticides Directive: Precaution Prevails

The interaction with the Pesticides Directive resulted from conflicting interpretations of the scope of the DRD's precautionary risk assessment. Against some opposing EU member states, the Commission, supported by a majority of member states, decided that secondary effects should be evaluated under the PD. However, once GM crops had been authorized on this basis, several EU member states invoked Article 16 of the DRD and enacted national bans citing, among other things, possible harmful secondary effects of the complementary pesticides. This undermined the PD, according to which the bans were not justified. As a result of these conflicts, the revised DRD explicitly provides for a precautionary risk assessment covering secondary effects.

The Pesticides Directive
The Pesticides Directive (Directive 91/414/EEC Concerning the Placing of Plant Protection Products on the Market) harmonizes authorization criteria and basic approval procedures for pesticides in the EU. First, the Directive establishes approval criteria for national authorities. Second, it bans pesticides containing substances not listed in its Annex I, while also laying down a procedure for adding substances to that Annex. Third, it establishes the principle of "mutual recognition" according to which a product that has been authorized in a member state in accordance with the Directive can be sold throughout the Union. National authorities retain responsibility for product authorizations, but the procedure for adding substances to Annex I involves the Standing Committee on Plant Health, in which member states and the Commission are represented. Decision making is similar to the Article 21 Committee, including qualified majority voting and the possibility of referring decisions to the Council (here: the Agriculture Council). If the Council fails to act, the Commission may adopt its proposal. Scientific advisory committees, in particular the Scientific Committee for Pesticides (later: Scientific Committee on Plants), assist the Commission.

In contrast to the DRD, the Pesticides Directive is not based on the precautionary principle. Its authorization requirements focus on clearly identifiable, actual effects:

pesticides may not have any "harmful effect on plants or plant products, directly or indirectly (e.g. through drinking water, food or feed), or on groundwater and they may not have any unacceptable influence on the environment, having particular regard to the following considerations: its fate and distribution in the environment, particularly contamination of water including drinking water and groundwater; its impact on non-target species" (Art. 4(b(iv, v)), Pesticides Directive). These criteria are less demanding than those of the DRD. In particular, the DRD uses a broader definition of harmful effects, which includes potential effects (Sauter and Meyer 2000, 119). Article 1(3) of the PD acknowledges these differences, calling on the Commission to submit a proposal for an amendment of the Pesticides Directive. The amendment was to provide for a specific environmental risk assessment so as to allow application of Article 10(2) of the DRD on product approval under sectoral legislation. However, such an amendment was not adopted.

Deliberate Release Directive Undermines Pesticides Directive

When the first marketing applications for pesticide-resistant GM crops were discussed in the mid-1990s, secondary effects played a major role. These effects are not caused by the GM crops themselves, but by the complementary pesticide (often a common pesticide that can be used on additional kinds of crops if these crops have been genetically modified to make them resistant to the pesticide). The effects include developing resistance in target weeds or a negative impact on biodiversity. If certain GM crops are not authorized under the DRD due to the potential secondary effects of the complementary pesticide, the DRD restricts the applicability of that pesticide. Consequently, the DRD's precautionary approach restricts the market for that pesticide and undermines the conventional environmental evaluation criteria for pesticides as set out by the PD.

The DRD neither defines the scope of "adverse effects on human health and the environment" (Art. 4) nor provides sufficiently detailed procedures and criteria for risk assessment (Schomberg 1998, 5). Against this background, a minority of member states argued that the precautionary environmental risk assessment required under the DRD covered secondary effects originating from the complementary pesticide. The diverging interpretations primarily reflected differing national agricultural policies and approaches to risk assessment. In 1994, the Commission attempted to clarify the situation. It proposed that secondary effects were not covered by the DRD but by sectoral legislation, specifically the Pesticides Directive (Commission Decision 94/385/EC). However, some member states dissented, not least because

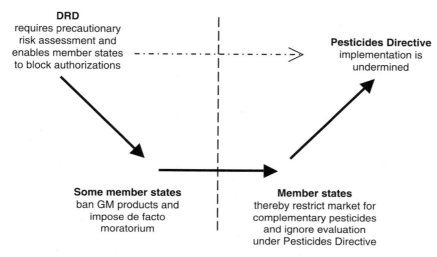

Figure 11.1
Deliberate Release Directive undermines Pesticides Directive

the PD did not provide for a precautionary environmental risk assessment. Despite initial support by most member states for the Commission's restrictive interpretation of the DRD's scope (Torgersen and Seifert 2000, 210–211), a growing number of member states subsequently also included, or called for, an evaluation of secondary effects under the DRD.

Figure 11.1 illustrates how the resulting conflict undermined the implementation of the Pesticides Directive. First, the DRD's vague provisions on risk assessment invited conflicting interpretations, in particular concerning secondary effects.[1] Second, faced with in their view insufficient risk assessments, some member states enacted national bans invoking the DRD's Article 16 emergency clause. They also used the Article 21 Committee procedure—which requires a qualified majority for product approval—to grind the authorization process to a complete halt. Third, in doing so, member states ignored assessments of secondary effects under the PD, which had concluded that such effects were tolerable. Since pesticide-resistant GM crops did not become available, the use of the complementary pesticides was also restricted—for reasons that were invalid according to the criteria of the Pesticides Directive. Thus, the effectiveness of this Directive was undermined.

The controversial approval of Ciba-Geigy's Bt-176 maize had a particularly strong impact on the escalation of conflict. This GM crop variety was engineered to be resistant to certain herbicides and to produce a naturally occurring toxin ("Bt") with insecticidal effects. In 1995 Austria, Denmark, Sweden, and the United Kingdom objected to the marketing application for the Bt-176 maize in the Article 21 Committee. Except for the United Kingdom, these countries argued that, among other things, no assessment of secondary effects originating from the complementary pesticide and the self-produced toxin had been made (Sauter and Meyer 2000, 228–231; Toft 1999, 14). The Commission rejected this view, reiterating its position that these issues were a matter for the Pesticides Directive (Levidow, Carr, and Wield 1999a, 51). After the Council had failed to achieve the qualified majority necessary for approval, the Commission first referred the issue to its scientific advisory committees and then approved the Bt-176 maize in December 1996. This decision was supported by the Scientific Committee on Pesticides, which had argued that secondary effects—for example, Bt-resistance in destructive insects—constituted an agronomic rather than an environmental problem. As with conventional crops, the Committee considered that such problems could be managed using alternative pesticides. Additional effects that might be caused by a switch to alternative pesticides, decreasing effectiveness of Bt as an "environmentally friendly" pesticide, and the possibility of an overall increase in pesticide use were not addressed (Sauter and Meyer 2000, 229–230, 233). Immediately following the Commission's approval of the Bt-176 maize, Austria, Luxembourg, and Italy invoked Article 16 of the DRD, banning cultivation on their territories (Friends of the Earth 1997, 6).

The controversial approval of herbicide-resistant GM oilseed rape (MS1xRF1/RF2) developed by the company Plant Genetics Systems (later: AgrEvo) illustrates how support among EU member states for the prevailing interpretation of the division of competencies between the DRD and the PD waned in the second half of the 1990s. France and the United Kingdom, in particular, reassessed their positions. The company had applied for a broad authorization of its oilseed rape in France. The Commission ignored calls by several member states for an evaluation of secondary effects under the DRD (Levidow, Carr, and Wield 1999a, 29; Schomberg 1998, 17; Fromwald and Strauss 1998, 15) and proposed approval. As with the Bt-176 maize, secondary effects were treated as an agronomic rather than environmental problem (Levidow and Carr 2000, 263; Levidow, Carr, and Wield 1999a, 28; 1999b, 14, 18; Roy and Joly 1999, 19). However, following adoption of the Commission's proposal, France withdrew its support and imposed a general moratorium on the commercialization of pesticide-resistant oilseed rape. This U-turn prevented the final approval of the oilseed rape, which must be granted by the country where the original application was submitted (in this case: France). More generally, it implied that the French government had reassessed its position and now considered secondary effects relevant for risk assessment under the DRD (Roy and Joly 1999, 19–20). France subsequently supported demands to explicitly require evaluation of secondary effects under the DRD (Roy and Joly 2000, 253). British authorities had often been the most outspoken and influential opponents of such demands. However, in 1998 the United Kingdom decided to require risk assessment to cover secondary effects (Levidow, Carr, and Wield 1999b, 14). Additional monitoring and testing requirements eventually culminated in a new British approach combining "managed development" of GM crops with a three-year moratorium on commercial cultivation (Levidow and Carr 2000, 264). Similar measures were subsequently adopted in other member states, such as Germany (Sauter and Meyer 2000, 98). These bans, moratoriums, and modifications of national risk-assessment practices meant that an increasing number of EU member states ignored the evaluation criteria for assessment of secondary effects under the PD.

Response Action to Solve the Conflict: Revision of the DRD

Whereas the early bans and moratoriums reflected the positions of individual member states, a more coordinated approach emerged in 1997 when the Commission proposed to lift national bans of the Bt-176 maize. When the proposal failed to achieve a qualified majority in the Article 21 Committee and, subsequently, the Council in 1998, the Commission refrained from taking legal action against the bans for fear of a political backlash (Winkler 1999, 10). More importantly, the conflicts over the scope of the DRD's risk assessment contributed significantly to the adoption of the de facto moratorium on the approval of GM crops announced by the Environment Council in June 1999 (Sauter and Meyer 2000, 91–93). The moratorium halted new approvals for more than five years. Also in 1999, the Environment Council adopted a legislative Common Position on the revision of the DRD. The Common Position provided the main substantive basis for the adoption of the revised DRD in 2001.

The revised DRD clarifies that risk assessment covers secondary effects. According to its Principles for Environmental Risk Assessment (Annex II, Part A), the risk assessment aims to identify and evaluate "potential adverse effects of the GMO, either direct or indirect, immediate or delayed, on human health and the environment." Such adverse effects may, among other things, occur through "changes in management, including, where applicable, in agricultural practices" (Annex II, Part C.2).

The introduction of market-stage precautionary measures, such as monitoring plans to identify previously unknown or delayed adverse effects (Art. 20) and time-limited authorizations (Art. 17), supports the new provisions on secondary effects.

The adoption of the provisions on secondary effects is remarkable, because the initiative to revise the DRD originally responded to various complaints about exaggerated regulation of GMOs (Homeyer 2002). While this may to some extent be characterized as the result of a learning process (Levidow, Carr, and Wield 2000, 204–206), two other factors help explain why the DRD's risk assessment was extended rather than reduced. First, as a result of the blocking of further commercialization of GMOs in the EU (de facto moratorium) emanating from the insufficient provisions of the original DRD, interested member states were able to put considerable pressure on industry, other member states, and the Commission to reverse the thrust of the revision process and to accept their demands, including the explicit requirement of an evaluation of secondary effects under the DRD. Second, and more importantly, in 1996 the political climate for the revision of the DRD changed markedly when the BSE ("mad-cow" disease) crisis coincided with the first EU imports of GM soy from the United States (Vogel 2001). This event reinvigorated opposition by environmental nongovernmental organizations (NGOs), such as Greenpeace and Friends of the Earth, and others to GM crops and food. In the following years the unfolding new political context hardened the position of member states that had already evaluated secondary effects under the DRD and won over others, such as the United Kingdom and France. Overall, it seems difficult to imagine that a sufficient number of member states would have supported the de facto moratorium in the absence of the heightened public opposition and protests (Homeyer 2003).

Given that risk assessment under the revised DRD clearly covers secondary effects, the new provisions appear to resolve the disruptive interaction with the PD. However, it is unlikely to resolve all issues over the evaluation of secondary effects. For example, the revised DRD's provisions on market-stage precautions (monitoring and so on) may create new conflicts, because it is not clear which factors, including certain secondary effects, need to be assessed *before* a marketing permission is given, and which ones may be assessed later, in the framework of market-stage precautions. To avoid conflicts over this question, it will be necessary to develop common criteria and procedures (Sauter and Meyer 2000, 142–143). Furthermore, there is no consensus among member states on the normative yardstick necessary to define "adverse effects" (Art. 4(1) of the revised DRD), including secondary effects. For example, the reduction of pesticide use is an important agricultural-policy objective in some member states, such as Austria (Torgersen and Seifert 2000, 213–214), but less so in others. Because of this difference, evaluations of relevant secondary effects are likely to continue to differ. A resolution of these conflicts would require agreement on principles of good agricultural practice (Sauter and Meyer 2000, 114–115). Ongoing discussions concerning the reform of the EU's Common Agricultural Policy (CAP), the integration of environmental concerns into the CAP, and sustainable development may offer opportunities to address relevant issues.

Interaction with the WTO SPS Agreement: Trade versus Precaution?

The Deliberate Release Directive subjects all GM products—including imports—to a strict approval procedure. Products approved outside the EU may therefore be subject to delayed EU authorization, additional requirements, or outright bans. Reflecting an increasingly strict interpretation of the DRD's precautionary risk assessment by several EU member states, the 1999 de facto moratorium blocked authorization of GM products that had so far not received EU clearance. As a result, the DRD undermined the free-trade objectives of the World Trade Organization (WTO), in particular of the WTO SPS Agreement. The Agreement seeks to restrict the scope for national safety measures to increase trade in agricultural commodities and food. However, opinions are divided on whether the precautionary approach of the DRD constitutes a formal breach of WTO rules. Ultimately, this question will be decided within ongoing and potential future WTO dispute-settlement cases, which in turn are influenced by various other international forums and agreements.

The WTO Agreement on Sanitary and Phytosanitary Measures
The General Agreement on Tariffs and Trade (GATT) was established in 1947. In 1994 the Uruguay Round of GATT negotiations resulted in the creation of the WTO and the adoption of the SPS Agreement. The main function of the WTO is to ensure that trade flows as smoothly, predictably, and freely as possible. As part of the WTO rules, the SPS Agreement aims to reduce trade barriers created by different national standards to protect human, plant, and animal life and health. Therefore, it introduces restrictions on these standards. In particular, safety measures should not be more trade-restrictive than necessary and their application should not result in arbitrarily different treatment. Measures should not create disguised trade barriers and, with limited exceptions for interim measures, must be based on scientific principles (Art. 2 and 5 of the SPS Agreement).

Rather than emphasizing the precautionary principle, the SPS Agreement not only tends to treat science as a sufficient but—at least in practice—also as a necessary criterion for establishing the legitimacy of relevant trade restrictions (Peel 2004; Wolff 2003, 1, 9–10; Scott 2000, 148–149). According to its Article 2(2), WTO members have the obligation to "ensure that any sanitary or phytosanitary measure ... is based on scientific principles and is not maintained without sufficient scientific evidence." The rudimentary version of the precautionary principle contained in Article 5(7) provides the only exception. This article states that in "cases where relevant scientific evidence is insufficient, a Member may *provisionally* adopt sanitary or phytosanitary measures on the basis of available pertinent information.... In such circumstances, Members shall seek to obtain the additional information necessary for a more objective assessment of risk and review the sanitary or phytosanitary measure accordingly *within a reasonable period of time* [emphases added]." The underlying assumption seems to be that it will be relatively easy to provide conclusive scientific evidence to determine the legitimacy of measures in any given case. The emphasis on science also influences the SPS Agreement's provisions on risk assessment: according to Article 5(1 and 2) of the Agreement, safety standards must be based on an appropriate risk assessment that "shall take into account available scientific evidence."

The SPS Agreement automatically recognizes national measures that conform to international standards. In this context, the Agreement explicitly refers to three international standard-setting bodies: the Codex Alimentarius Commission (CAC; food safety), the International Plant Protection Convention (IPPC; plant health), and the Office International des Epizooties (OIE; animal health). Essentially, except for precautionary interim measures, countries may consequently not introduce or maintain measures that are stricter than internationally agreed-on standards without scientific justification (Art. 3).

Like other WTO rules, the SPS Agreement is supported by comparatively strong enforcement mechanisms. The SPS Committee comprising WTO member countries oversees implementation of the SPS Agreement. The Committee reviews notifications of relevant national measures, keeps contact with other international bodies, and makes proposals for amendments (Art. 12). If member countries disagree on the conformity of national measures with the SPS Agreement, they may take recourse to the WTO dispute-settlement mechanism, which can authorize the damaged party to use trade sanctions against an infringing country.

Deliberate Release Directive Undermines SPS Agreement

The interaction between the DRD's provisions on precautionary risk assessment and the WTO SPS Agreement occurred against the background of a fast rise in the global production of GM agricultural products in the second half of the 1990s and the simultaneous emergence of a highly uneven international pattern of cultivation of GM crops. Starting from a very modest 1.7 million hectares in 1996, six years later GM crops were already grown on a total of 58.7 million hectares. In 2002, the United States—the leading country in the development of agricultural biotechnology—accounted for 66 percent of total agricultural land planted with GM crops worldwide. At 23 percent Argentina was also a significant producer. Canada (6 percent) and China (4 percent) accounted for most of the remaining production (Brack, Falkner, and Goll 2003, 2).

The gap between high levels of cultivation of GM crops in the United States and other countries, and low production in the EU corresponds to some extent to differences in the approach and stringency of safety legislation. First, EU and U.S. laws are built on different assumptions: reflecting the precautionary principle, the EU regulatory approach addresses (bio-)technology as such. In contrast, product characteristics—for example, whether a GM crop is associated with a plant-pest risk—trigger regulation in the United States. As a result, the EU had to elaborate new, specific legislation for GMOs (i.e., the DRD), while U.S. regulatory oversight could largely rely on preexisting laws. Second, following from these differences in approach, product authorization under the revised DRD is generally given for a limited period of time and coupled with monitoring requirements because it is built on the assumption that experience and scientific knowledge about the potential risks of GM products are lacking. While the U.S. approach does not exclude such precautionary measures, they are applied on a much less general basis (Levidow 2001, 8).

Because of the relative stringency of its precautionary approach, the DRD restricts trade, thereby undermining the SPS Agreement (figure 11.2). EU imports originating from countries with less stringent regulations—mainly the United States—face lengthy authorization procedures or may not be approved at all. This compromises the SPS Agreement's main objective of trade liberalization. As early as 1998, the U.S. Department of Agriculture (USDA) estimated that the EU's prolonged approval of U.S. GM maize led to a loss of around U.S.$200 million for U.S. exporters (Kelch, Simone, and Madell 1998, 1). The "American share of European maize ... imports dropped from 86% in 1995 to 12% in 1999," largely because of delays in

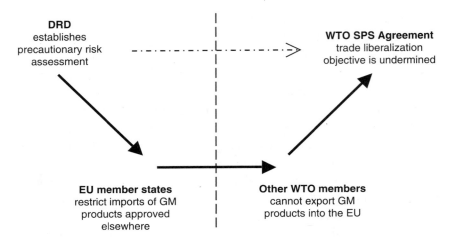

Figure 11.2
Deliberate Release Directive undermines WTO SPS Agreement

EU product approval (Vogel 2001, 14). Regulatory hurdles also contributed to a sharp decline in U.S. soybean exports to the EU between 1995 and 1999. Similar U.S. losses in exports of maize and soybeans to the EU occurred in subsequent years.

However, the losses caused by delays in the EU approval process are likely to be smaller than stated by U.S. authorities. First, because of the widespread rejection of GM food by European consumers and campaigns by environmental NGOs, European retailers and food producers have mostly stopped storing or manufacturing GM products (Levidow and Murphy 2003, 56; USDA 2003, 6). The resulting U.S. export losses cannot be attributed to EU regulations. Second, long delays in the EU authorization process were often caused by the EU de facto moratorium. Although the moratorium was related to the DRD in that it reflected a precautionary approach,[2] it also conflicted with the DRD's approval procedure, which does not provide for a general moratorium but requires a case-by-case evaluation of applications.

Outlook
The conflict between the DRD and the SPS Agreement may be resolved by collective decision making. The EU could adapt the DRD to the SPS Agreement's rudimentary concept of precaution, for example in response to a related finding of the WTO dispute-settlement mechanism. Alternatively, the SPS Agreement could be made compatible with a wider understanding of precaution either by formally changing

or by reinterpreting it. Finally, both institutions could be adapted so as to meet at some middle ground. Whether and to what extent these solutions will be employed depends on at least three partly interrelated factors: the outcome of ongoing and future WTO dispute-settlement proceedings, negotiations in other relevant international organizations, and negotiations within the EU and the WTO. To the extent that the solutions resulted from developments in the EU or WTO, they would constitute new cases of interaction between both.

WTO dispute-settlement proceedings could have an important impact by either increasing the pressure on the EU to adapt the DRD or interpreting WTO rules so as to make them more compatible with the DRD's precautionary approach. A U.S. complaint filed at the WTO in 2003 against the EU de facto moratorium and various national bans provides a first test case because precaution was a key rationale for the moratorium. The United States had previously threatened to file a WTO complaint (Yerkey 1999), but had not done so for a number of reasons, including the risk of losing a WTO case, unfavorable political circumstances such as the final negotiations of the Cartagena Protocol on Biosafety (U.S. Mission to the EU 1999; Kelch, Simone, and Madell 1998), and, subsequently, the Afghanistan and Iraq wars, as well as concerns that too much overt pressure on the EU would further increase consumer and political resistance.[3] Eventually, signs of a growing "internationalization" (Gupta 1999, 28) of the DRD's precautionary approach contributed to the filing of the WTO complaint. In particular, Zambia, supported by other African countries, had rejected U.S. GM food aid in 2003, citing precaution and concerns regarding potential negative implications for agricultural exports to the EU. It has even been argued that the WTO complaint was motivated more by a wish to deter third countries from following the DRD's precautionary approach than by the actual losses of U.S. export opportunities to the EU (Murphy and Chataway 2003, 12).[4] Previous rulings by the WTO Dispute Settlement Body, in particular in the Hormones case, do not provide clear indications as to the outcome of the new case, with some elements seemingly supporting the DRD's precautionary approach and others appearing to speak against it (Peel 2004; Brack, Falkner, and Goll 2003, 9; Murphy and Chataway 2003, 11).

The outcome of this and of potential future WTO dispute-settlement proceedings will be influenced by third international institutions. As mentioned above, the SPS Agreement recognizes trade-restrictive measures conforming to standards originating from some international institutions. Standards developed by two organizations appear particularly relevant with respect to the DRD. The International Plant Protection Convention (IPPC) focuses on plant pests, including environmental effects on biodiversity. Its overall significance for the interaction might be relatively limited because most trade in GMOs concerns GM feed and food. The Codex Alimentarius Commission operating in this field has become increasingly active since the late 1990s. Although it deals with food safety rather than environmental issues, its standards cover GM agricultural products and address relevant issues of scientific uncertainty (Murphy and Chataway 2003; Brack, Falkner, and Goll 2003, 8–9; Genewatch 2003, 6–7). In addition, the Cartagena Protocol on Biosafety adopted in 2000 may influence WTO dispute settlement.

In 2004, the IPPC's governing body, the Interim Commission on Phytosanitary Measures (ICPM), adopted a supplement to the International Standard on Phytosanitary Measures (ISPM) No. 11, which addresses the plant-pest risks of GMOs.[5] As a result of the decision to amend ISPM No. 11 instead of adopting a separate GMO standard, the new IPPC provisions reflect, and build on, those for conventional plants, rather than the SPS Agreement's science-dependent approach. In fact, the United States had called for a separate IPPC standard for GMOs, but had been willing to compromise in order to ensure a quick adoption of IPPC standards that were perceived as an alternative to, or precedent for the implementation of, the Cartagena Biosafety Protocol (USDA 2001). Although the revised standard does not mention precaution, it may support the DRD's approach in several ways. Perhaps most importantly, it is modest as to the role of science. ISPM No. 11 treats scientific uncertainty as an inherent problem of risk assessment that regulation needs to address (Sections 2.4, 3). Also, ISPM No. 11 risk assessment is based on economic, social, and environmental considerations in addition to science (Section 2.3.2.4). Other ISPM No. 11 provisions may also offer support for the DRD. For example, the *potential* to be injurious may be sufficient for a GMO to qualify as a pest (Section 1.1). Direct, indirect, and long-term effects may be assessed (Section 2.3.1). In addition to comparison to similar organisms, other ways of establishing the acceptable level of risk are possible (Section 3.1). Many factors may be indicative of the need to subject a GMO to a complete risk assessment, including lack of knowledge and insufficient information (Annex 3).

The CAC has adopted two particularly relevant standards in 2003. First, the "Working Principles for Risk Analysis for Application in the Framework of the Codex Alimentarius" provide general guidelines. However, because of the implications for the SPS Agreement and the ongoing controversies over the DRD's precautionary approach (Murphy and Chataway 2003, 4, 13; Cosbey 2000), the CAC failed to agree on guidance for cases involving scientific uncertainty. It therefore decided that, rather than adopting an official standard, it would merely adopt a "related text, such as a code of practice" in possible future cases (CAC 2001, 12). Second, the CAC adopted "Principles for the Risk Analysis of Food Derived from Modern Biotechnology," which tend to support the DRD's precautionary approach. First, the Principles are also technology-specific and stipulate that GM food must generally undergo a risk assessment. Second, the standards support an interpretation of "substantive equivalence" (of GM and conventional food) that seems compatible with the DRD's precautionary approach. Traditionally, substantive equivalence used to be invoked to *deny* biotechnology-specific risk assessment of "substantively equivalent" GM products. However, the Codex standard employs the concept primarily as a heuristic tool to *guide* rather than to deny risk assessment of GM products (Levidow and Murphy 2002, 11–12). Finally, scientific uncertainty is recognized as inherent in risk assessment, in particular with respect to allergenicity (Murphy and Chataway 2003, 15–16).

The Cartagena Protocol on Biosafety to the Convention on Biological Diversity (CBD) is also likely to influence the interaction. Like the DRD, the Protocol is technology-specific (Brack, Falkner, and Goll 2003, 3–4). Going beyond IPPC and Codex standards, it explicitly refers to precaution in its Preamble and Article 1 (objectives). In addition, the Protocol suggests a precautionary approach in its operational clauses, stating that "lack of scientific certainty ... shall not prevent ... a decision ... in order to avoid or minimize ... potential adverse effects" (Art. 10(6); see also chapter 8). The Protocol is not recognized as a relevant international standard-setting body under the SPS Agreement, and the contentiousness of the Protocol makes it unlikely that it will be recognized as such anytime soon. Even without formal recognition, however, the Protocol forms part of the wider legal context in which the SPS Agreement must be interpreted (Oliva 2004, 9) and may thus have a—weaker—impact on WTO dispute-settlement proceedings.

The DRD interacts with the SPS Agreement as a result of commitment to the extent that, first, the DRD influenced the ISPM, CAC, and Biosafety negotiations and, second, these institutions contribute to a corresponding reinterpretation of the SPS Agreement. More specifically, the EU member states' commitment to the DRD's precautionary approach seems to have strengthened their resolve to promote similar measures in relevant third institutions. In turn, these institutions affect the interpretation of the SPS Agreement.

Furthermore, relevant decisions have already been made within the EU. The EU in 2003 adopted Regulation 1830/2003 implementing the traceability and labeling requirements of the revised DRD. To reduce negative trade impacts, the Regulation introduces thresholds for accidental or technically unavoidable GM contamination and even allows for contamination by certain GMOs that have not yet been authorized in the EU. Following the adoption of additional pieces of implementing legislation, the EU approved import of a GM maize variety in May 2004, thereby ending the de facto moratorium. Although this decision increases the chances that the moratorium could be deemed a temporary precautionary measure under the SPS Agreement (Brack, Falkner, and Goll 2003, 9–10), it seems unlikely to resolve the wider tensions between the DRD's precautionary approach and the SPS Agreement.

There have also been attempts to address the issue of precaution in WTO negotiations. In the context of the 1999 WTO Ministerial Conference in Seattle, the United States and others proposed unsuccessfully to form a working group to examine GMO-related issues (Wolff 2003, 12; see also chapter 8). Subsequently, several WTO members—including the EU, the United States, South Korea, and Japan—have taken relevant initiatives within the WTO to pursue their varying objectives (European Commission 2000; European Union 2001; WTO 2000; Wolff 2003, 12). Finally, the relationship between the WTO and multilateral environmental agreements became part of the Doha Round of trade negotiations agreed to in 2001. The negotiations could clarify the relationship between the Biosafety Protocol and the SPS Agreement. However, these initiatives have so far made little progress (Brack, Falkner, and Goll 2003, 7).

The interaction may thus eventually be played out by means of the WTO dispute-settlement procedure rather than political decision making. The WTO would, prima facie, appear to be in a strong position to resolve the interaction in favor of the SPS Agreement due to its powerful dispute-settlement mechanism. However, WTO dispute settlement is embedded in other international institutions, in this case primarily the Codex, the IPPC, and the Biosafety Protocol. These institutions approach the role of science and scientific uncertainty in risk assessment in ways that tend to be more similar to the DRD's precautionary approach than to rudimentary precaution enshrined in the SPS Agreement. In particular with respect to the Biosafety Protocol, and to a lesser extent the Codex, this may partly be explained in terms of successful EU efforts to internationalize the DRD's precautionary approach.

Conclusions

Most of the DRD's main institutional interactions involve either EU sectoral legislation or the WTO. This may help explain why most interactions have had the DRD as a source and have resulted in disruption (at the outcome level). Interactions with sectoral legislation often reflect the challenge of coordinating precautionary, technology-specific legislation with more traditional approval procedures. In particular, this holds for the four cases involving the DRD's precautionary environmental risk assessment. The DRD's risk assessment reflects a belief in potentially significant risks of GM products combined with an actual or perceived lack of experience/ knowledge. In contrast, sectoral legislation builds on accumulated experience with various product groups and focuses on assessing product characteristics from the perspective of intended use. Because the DRD challenges the basic assumption underlying sectoral legislation—that regulation on the basis of product groups is generally sufficient—it emerged as a source of disruptive Behavioral Interaction with sectoral legislation. The interaction with the Pesticides Directive exemplifies the tensions: although risk assessment under this instrument addressed the secondary effects of pesticide-resistant GM crops, this was insufficient in terms of the DRD's precautionary approach, which covers a wider range of potential risks.

Interactions with the WTO, in particular the SPS Agreement, are related to similar differences in regulatory approaches. Here, these differences translate into conflicts over the role of science. More specifically, the SPS Agreement's strong reliance on science—which is essentially in harmony with the focus on use-related experience at the base of sectoral legislation because such experience can often be transformed into scientific knowledge—clashes with the core assumptions underlying precautionary regulation: scientific uncertainty and insufficient knowledge. Prima facie, trade restrictions caused by precautionary regulations are therefore more likely to disrupt the implementation of the SPS Agreement than those caused by conventional product-sector legislation.

Coordination to address the DRD's disruptive effects is generally weak. This is remarkable, in particular with respect to EU-level interactions, where coordination could have benefited from a high degree of institutional integration. In fact, the detailed analysis of the interactions with the Pesticides Directive and the SPS Agreement suggests that coordination may have been more relevant at the less integrated global level. Explicitly covering secondary effects, the revised DRD resolved the interaction with the Pesticides Directive. But this solution resulted primarily from the political and economic pressure generated by national bans and the de facto moratorium. In addition, the underlying question of which normative yardstick should be used to evaluate secondary effects has, if anything, only been addressed in an insufficient and indirect way. In contrast, coordination appears to be more relevant for efforts to address the interaction with the SPS Agreement. The standard-setting bodies recognized by the SPS Agreement provide relevant forums. Although negotiations take place "in the shadow of the WTO" (Cosbey 2000), links to other institutions, such as the Biosafety Protocol, and entrenched regulatory traditions seem to provide the CAC and the ISPM with sufficient autonomy to play a mediating role.

Notes

1. In addition to secondary effects, different interpretations regarding other issues—for example, the use of antibiotic-resistant genes—contributed to the escalation of conflicts.

2. For instance, in June 1999 some EU member states supported the moratorium by declaring their intention "to take a thoroughly precautionary approach … [and] not to authorize the placing on the market of any GMOs until it is demonstrated that there is no adverse effect on the environment and human health" (2194th Council Meeting—ENVIRONMENT—Luxembourg, June 24–25, 1999; available at http://ue.eu.int/ueDocs/cms_Data/docs/pressData/en/envir/ACF5B.htm).

3. "US Shifts Tactics in GMO Clash with EU," *Financial Times*, October 15, 2002, 6.

4. "EU Plays for Time over US Threat on GMOs," *Agence France-Press* (AFP), Brussels, January 12, 2003.

5. Using the terminology of the Cartagena Biosafety Protocol, the IPPC refers to living modified organisms (LMOs) rather than GMOs. For the present purpose and in everyday usage the terms can be considered to be the same (see also chapter 8).

References

Barling, David. 1997. Regulatory Conflict and Marketing of Agricultural Biotechnology in the European Community. In Jeffrey Stanyer and Gerrey Stoker, eds., *Contemporary Political Studies*, 1040–1048. Nottingham: Political Studies Association of the U.K.

Becker, Geoffrey S., and Charles E. Hanrahan. 2004. *Agricultural Biotechnology: The U.S.-EU Dispute.* CRS Report for Congress, Code RS21556, updated March 16, 2004. Washington, DC: Congressional Research Service, Library of Congress.

Brack, Duncan, Robert Falkner, and Judith Goll. 2003. *The Next Trade War? GM Products, the Cartagena Protocol and the WTO.* Briefing Paper No. 8. September 2003. London: Royal Institute of International Affairs, Development Programme.

CAC. 2001. *Report of the Twenty-Fourth Session of the Codex Alimentarius Commission*, Geneva, July 2–7, 2001. Doc. ALINORM 01/41.

Cantley, Mark F. 1995. The Regulation of Modern Biotechnology: A Historical and European Perspective. In Hans-Juergen Rehm and Gerald Reed, eds., *Biotechnology Vol. 12: Legal, Economic, and Ethical Dimensions*, 505–579. Weinheim, Germany: VCH.

Cosbey, Aaron. 2000. *A Forced Evolution: The Codex Alimentarius Commission, Scientific Uncertainty and the Precautionary Principle*. Winnipeg: International Institute for Sustainable Development.

European Commission. 2000. *Communication from the Commission on the Precautionary Principle*. Doc. COM (2000) 1, February 2, 2000. Brussels: European Commission.

European Union. 2001. *Food Safety*. Note by the European Communities. Doc. D(2001) (DIVERS/500186 ur), Brussels, July 20, 2001; available at http://europa.eu.int/comm/agriculture/external/wto/document/food_en.pdf.

Friends of the Earth. 1997. Austria Bans Genetech Maize. *Mailout* 3 (1): 6. Friends of the Earth Europe Biotechnology Programme.

Fromwald, Susanne, and Sylvia Strauss. 1998, May. *Genetically Engineered Oil Seed Rape (AgrEvo/PGS): A Critical Assessment and Background Information*. Amsterdam: Greenpeace.

Genewatch. 2003, December. The GM Dispute at the WTO: Forcing GM Food on Europe? *GeneWatch UK*. Briefing No. 25.

Gupta, Aarti. 1999. *Framing "Biosafety" in an International Context: The Biosafety Protocol Negotiations*. ENRP Discussion Paper E-99-10. Cambridge, MA: Kennedy School of Government, Harvard University.

von Homeyer, Ingmar. 2002. Institutional Change and Governance in the European Union: The Case of Biotechnology Regulation. Doctoral dissertation, European University Institute, Florence.

von Homeyer, Ingmar. 2003. *The Revision of the Directive on the Deliberate Release of Genetically Modified Organisms (GMOs) into the Environment*. The European Public Space Observatory (EUROPUB) Project. Case study report (WP 2). Available at ftp://ftp.iccr-international.org/europub/europub-d2-annex2.pdf.

Kelch, David, Mark Simone, and Mary Lisa Madell. 1998. *Biotechnology in Agriculture Confronts WTO Agreements*. Agriculture in the WTO/WRS-98-4. Washington, DC: Economic Research Service, U.S. Department of Agriculture (USDA).

Levidow, Les. 2001. Unsound Science? Trans-Atlantic Regulatory Disputes over GM Crops. National Europe Centre Paper No. 3. Canberra: The Australian National University.

Levidow, Les, and Susan Carr. 2000. UK: Precautionary Commercialisation? *Journal of Risk Research* 3 (3): 261–270.

Levidow, Les, Susan Carr, and David Wield. 1999a. EU Level Report. In *Safety Regulation of Transgenic Crops: Completing the Internal Market? A Study on the Implementation of Directive 90/220*. Centre for Technology Strategy, Faculty of Technology, The Open University, Milton Keynes, UK. Available at http://technology.open.ac.uk/cts/srtc/EU-Levelreport%20update.pdf.

Levidow, Les, Susan Carr, and David Wield. 1999b. United Kingdom: Precautionary Commercialisation. In *Safety Regulation of Transgenic Crops: Completing the Internal Market? A Study on the Implementation of Directive 90/220*. Centre for Technology Strategy, Faculty of Technology, The Open University, Milton Keynes. Available at http://technology.open.ac.uk/cts/srtc/UK-NATReport.pdf.

Levidow, Les, Susan Carr, and David Wield. 2000. Genetically Modified Crops in the European Union: Regulatory Conflicts as Precautionary Opportunities? *Journal of Risk Research* 3 (3): 198–208.

Levidow, Les, and Joseph Murphy. 2002. The Decline of Substantial Equivalence: How Civil Society Demoted a Risky Concept. Paper presented at a conference at the Institute of Development Studies titled "Science and Citizenship in a Global Context: Challenges from New Technologies," University of Sussex, December 12–13.

Levidow, Les, and Joseph Murphy. 2003. Reframing Regulatory Science: Trans-Atlantic Conflicts over GM Crops. *Cahiers d'économie et sociologie rurales* (68–69): 48–74.

Murphy, Joseph, and Joanna Chataway. 2003, October 1. *Science and International Agreements: The Case of Genetically Modified Organisms and Risk*. Written Evidence to the Science and Technology Select Committee of the House of Lords (Sub-Committee I). Available at http://www.innogen.ac.uk/ownImages/Lords%20SCST%20evidence.pdf.

Oliva, Maria Julia. 2004. Science and Precaution in the GMO Dispute: A Brief Analysis of the U.S. Submission. *Bridges* 8 (5): 8–10.

Peel, Jacqueline. 2004. Risk Regulation under the WTO SPS Agreement: Science as an International Normative Yardstick? Jean Monnet Working Paper 02/04. New York: New York University School of Law.

Roy, Alexis, and Pierre-Benoit Joly. 1999. France: Broadening Precautionary Expertise. In *Safety Regulation of Transgenic Crops: Completing the Internal Market? A Study on the Implementation of Directive 90/220*. Centre for Technology Strategy, Faculty of Technology, The Open University, Milton Keynes, UK. Available at http://technology.open.ac.uk/cts/srtc/FR-NATReport.pdf.

Roy, Alexis, and Pierre-Benoit Joly. 2000. France: Broadening Precautionary Expertise? *Journal of Risk Research* 3 (3): 247–254.

Sauter, Arnold, and Rolf Meyer. 2000. Risikoabschätzung und Nachzulassungs-Monitoring transgener Pflanzen. *TAB-Arbeitsbericht Nr. 68*. Berlin: Büro für Technikfolgen-Abschätzung beim Deutschen Bundestag.

von Schomberg, René. 1998. *An Appraisal of the Working in Practice of Directive 90/220 on the Deliberate Release of Genetically Modified Organisms*. Draft Final Report, Scientific and Technological Options Assessment (STOA), European Parliament, Luxembourg.

Scott, Joanne. 2000. On Kith and Kine (and Crustaceans): Trade and Environment in the EU and the WTO. In Joseph Weiler, ed., *The EU, the WTO and NAFTA: Towards a Common Law of International Trade*, 125–167. Oxford: Oxford University Press.

Toft, Jesper. 1999. Denmark: Potential Polarisation or Consensus? In *Safety Regulation of Transgenic Crops: Completing the Internal Market? A Study on the Implementation of Directive 90/220*. Centre for Technology Strategy, Faculty of Technology, The Open University, Milton Keynes, UK. Available at http://technology.open.ac.uk/cts/srtc/DK-NATReport.pdf.

Torgersen, Helge, and Franz Seifert. 2000. Austria: Precautionary Blockage of Agricultural Biotechnology. *Journal of Risk Research* 3 (3): 209–217.

UNEP. 1997, March 18. *Background Document on Existing International Agreements Related to Biosafety.* United Nations Environment Programme. Doc. UNEP/CBD/BSWG/2/3.

USDA. 2001, August 23. *APHIS Public Meeting in the Matter of International Plant Protection Convention (IPPC) Standard on Plant Pest Risks Associated with Living Modified Organisms (LMOs).* Washington, DC: U.S. Department of Agriculture.

USDA. 2003. *United Kingdom Exporter Guide Annual 2003.* GAIN-Report-UK 3031. Washington, DC: U.S. Department of Agriculture Foreign Agricultural Service.

U.S. Mission to the EU. 1999, March 19. *Rominger Press Conference at USEU on Biotechnology.* United States Mission to the European Union. Available at http://www.useu.be/archive/Roming322.html.

Vogel, David. 2001. Ships Passing in the Night: The Changing Politics of Risk Regulation in Europe and the United States. EUI Working Paper RSC No. 2001/16. Florence: European University Institute.

Winkler, Roland. 1999. Legal Aspects at the EU Level. In *Safety Regulation of Transgenic Crops: Completing the Internal Market? A Study on the Implementation of Directive 90/220.* Centre for Technology Strategy, Faculty of Technology, The Open University, Milton Keynes, UK. Available at http://technology.open.ac.uk/cts/srtc/EU-legal-aspects.pdf.

Wolff, Christiane. 2003. *Biosafety, Biotechnology and the WTO: The SPS and TBT Agreements and GATT.* Agriculture and Commodities Division, WTO Secretariat.

WTO. 2000, April 18. WTO Secretariat. *Summary of the Meeting Held on 15–16 March 2000. Committee on Sanitary and Phytosanitary Measures.* World Trade Organization. Doc. G/SPS/R/18.

Yerkey, Gary G. 1999. U.S. Considers Filing WTO Complaint over EU Barriers to GMO Trade, USTR Says. Available at http://www.biotech-info.net/filing_complaint.html.

12

The EU Air Quality Framework Directive: Shaped and Saved by Interaction?

Jørgen Wettestad

Although the development of EU air-quality policy started in the 1980s, the 1996 Air Quality Framework Directive (FD) is an important legal milestone in the EU's fight against air pollution (Wettestad 2002). The Directive itself did not create precise air-quality objectives. The main reason for describing it as a milestone is found in four subsequent daughter directives, which have both broadened the scope of EU policy in this area in terms of substances covered and introduced far more stringent air-quality limit values than previously applied. Because it makes sense to see the 1996 Directive and the subsequent daughter directives as different facets of the same institutional entity, references in the rest of the chapter to the Air Quality FD also encompass the daughter directives.

The FD has interacted and interacts with a number of institutions and processes both outside and within the EU. A main thesis of this chapter is that *to understand both the shaping and future performance of the EU air-quality FD, it is crucial to understand the FD's interaction with external and internal institutions*. Three cases of (potential) interaction are investigated in detail. In terms of vertical interaction with external institutions, the air-quality guidelines produced by the World Health Organization (WHO) seem to have been especially crucial influences on the EU legislation. It is interesting to scrutinize this interaction further for several reasons. First, because there is considerable internal EU expertise in this field, this case of interaction touches on the question of the extent to which EU environmental policy should be a "home brew" and the extent to which it should rely on external expertise. Moreover, the WHO guidelines are nonbinding international "soft law," and hence this case also touches on the question of the extent to which nonbinding instruments can have a profound influence on the development of binding legislation in international (environmental) politics. In addition, because the WHO is very much a scientific organization and the EU is primarily about politics, the case touches on the generally complex, but important, relationship between science and politics in the international environmental arena (e.g., Andresen et al. 2000). Hence, a first central puzzle in this chapter becomes: How can it be explained that the binding EU Air Quality FD has seemingly been heavily shaped by the nonbinding and external WHO guidelines?

Horizontal interaction within the EU is distinctly different from the relationship between EU legislation and the policies of other international institutions. Within the EU, the different strands of (environmental) policy should ideally be compatible. But separate decision making processes may in practice easily lead to uncoordinated and fragmented decision making. Given the central role of cleaner fuel and lower emissions from vehicles for the improvement of air quality, there is an obvious link to the revised fuel standards and vehicle-emission limits emanating from the Auto-Oil I process. After being founded in 1992, the Auto-Oil I Program led to directive proposals in 1996 on stricter fuel standards and tighter emission limits, and these directives were adopted in 1998. Hence, the air-quality directives and the Auto-Oil I Program and directives were debated and adopted during roughly the same period. They also partly targeted the same substances, such as nitrogen oxides (NO_X), benzene, and carbon monoxide. But the fact that the EU launched an air-policy integration program in 2001—called the Clean Air for Europe (CAFÉ) Program—could be a sign that integration and coordination of air-quality and vehicle-emissions reduction policies had been lacking so far. So, a second central question in this chapter becomes: To what extent have the air-quality and Auto-Oil policymaking processes interacted and how well have they been coordinated?

However, this is not necessarily the only or the most important process of interaction between these strands of legislation. Given the obvious role of cleaner fuel and lowered emissions for achieving better air quality, there is a distinct possibility that the *really* important interaction effects take place at the stage of outcomes—that is, when the focused directives are implemented. Hence, a third central question addressed in this chapter becomes: Will the most important interaction between EU Auto-Oil standards and air-quality standards take place when the former standards are implemented? In other words, will the Air Quality FD's fate and performance be "saved" by the Auto-Oil directives?

The next section sums up the main elements of the Air Quality FD and the four subsequent daughter directives. This is followed by a summary of how the Air Quality FD has interacted with various institutions and processes within and outside of the EU. The major emphasis of the chapter is then on the interactions with the

WHO air-quality guidelines and the Auto-Oil directives, including an assessment of the CAFÉ response. The chapter concludes with some more general observations and lessons.

The Air Quality Framework Directive

The Framework Directive is part of the air-quality policy of the EU. Instruments of this policy set binding or recommendatory air-quality standards for particular pollutants, while they do not specify the pollution-abatement measures that member states might apply to achieve the stipulated limits. The first EU air-quality directives were adopted in the early 1980s. In 1980, Directive 80/779/EEC on air-quality limit values and guide values for sulfur dioxide and suspended particulates was adopted. This was the first piece of Communitywide legislation to lay down mandatory air-quality standards. The next air-quality directive targeted lead and was adopted in 1982 (Directive 82/884/EEC on limit value for lead in the air). The lead directive was followed by Directive 85/203/EEC on air-quality standards for nitrogen dioxide. The EU's fourth Environmental Action Program, launched in 1987, placed more emphasis on the problem of photochemical pollution and particularly ground-level ozone. The Commission described this as "one of the major environmental problems" of the century (Haigh 2003, sec. 6.15, 2). Moreover, in the early 1990s, increasing concentrations of ground-level ozone were a source of concern for many European countries. Against this background, Directive 92/72/EEC on air pollution by ozone was adopted in 1992. The directive required member states to develop a network for the collection of information on ozone levels.

According to Elsom (1999, 106), a revision of EU air-quality policy was spurred by WHO's decision in 1993 to review and revise its 1987 air-quality guideline values for Europe. By the spring of 1993, early drafts of a framework directive on air quality were discussed in meetings between the Commission and national officials. More than twenty substances were targeted[1] and a system consisting of different types of quality objectives was envisaged. "Alert thresholds" were related to the top three pollutants; "guide values" recommended by international expert groups such as WHO were to be established for all the pollutants; and "limit values" (i.e., obligatory environmental quality standards to be met) were to be set for the pollutants in stages.

As indicated, the 1996 Air Quality FD (i.e., EU Council Directive 96/62/EC on Ambient Air Quality Assessment and Management) itself did not create any precise air-quality objectives, but rather set out a framework and basic principles for ambient-air-quality monitoring and management. These were to go into effect once daughter directives for specific pollutants had been adopted. At the same time that ambient standards were set, criteria were to be established for the assessment of air pollution. These criteria were to include details on the location, number, and type of sampling sites, as well as on the use of other techniques such as modeling. Once daughter directives had been adopted, member states would have to assess ambient air quality in accordance with the provisions specified.[2] A key ingredient in the Directive was a requirement for all EU countries to adopt monitoring systems in accordance with common standards (both in terms of the location of monitoring sites and measurement techniques), and to report the results regularly to the Commission.

As the next step, several groups of experts, consisting of representatives from the European Commission, the European Environment Agency, the World Health Organization, EU member states, industry, and environmental nongovernmental organizations (NGOs), developed proposals for daughter directives. The first one concerned standards for sulfur dioxide, nitrogen dioxide, particulate matter, and lead. In June 1998, a common position on this daughter directive was obtained in the EU Council of Ministers, signaling an overall tightening of standards, but also with standards for particulates and NO_X "significantly diluted" from those originally proposed by the Commission.[3] The first daughter directive was then formally adopted as EU Council Directive 99/30/EC (Directive Relating to Limit Values for Sulfur Dioxide, Nitrogen Dioxide and Oxides of Nitrogen, Particulate Matter and Lead in Ambient Air) in April 1999. A second daughter directive was proposed by the Commission in December 1998, targeting benzene and carbon monoxide. It was adopted in November 2000 (EU Council Directive 2000/69/EC Relating to Limit Values for Benzene and Carbon Monoxide in Ambient Air).

A third daughter directive has targeted the issue of ground-level ozone. As indicated, this issue was given specific emphasis in EU air-pollution policymaking from the early 1990s on. The formal proposal for a directive on ozone in ambient air was presented in June 1999. The proposed daughter directive contained aspirational, nonbinding target values for ozone by 2010, which were "widely seen as ambitious".[4] Agreement was reached in November 2001 and the resulting Directive 2002/3/EC (Directive relating to ozone in ambient air) adopted in February 2002, with member states being obliged to meet the 2010 targets "save where not achievable through proportionate measures."

In December 2001, it was reported that the Commission had delayed proposing a fourth daughter directive, which was supposed to target polyaromatic hydrocarbons (PAHs), cadmium, arsenic, and nickel. This was due to vocal industry protests.[5] In October 2002, it was announced that the Commission was planning to launch a directive with nonbinding instead of mandatory limits.[6] The EU Council and the European Parliament reached a final compromise in April 2004 on "stricter, though still not strictly binding, targets".[7]

Main Horizontal and Vertical Interactions of the Air Quality Framework Directive: An Overview

The FD has interacted and interacts with a number of other EU policy instruments and international institutions. We have provided an inventory of such interaction elsewhere and only provide a brief summary here (Wettestad and Farmer 2001). The relevant interactions are summed up in table 12.1.

With regard to other EU policy instruments, the Air Quality FD has in particular interacted with five processes and instruments at the level of implementation (Behavioral Interaction). First of all, the establishment of the Single Market in the EU has

Table 12.1
Interactions of the EU Air Quality Framework Directive

EU Single Market	• Has amplified a trend of increasing transport emissions and hence disruptively affected the process of improving air quality
EU National Emission Ceilings (NEC) Directive	• Sets emission ceilings, which will help achieve air-quality targets
EU Auto-Oil I Directives	• Set stricter fuel standards and vehicle-emission limits, which will help achieve air-quality targets
EU SAVE Program	• Contributes to increased energy efficiency, which helps reduce emissions and improve air quality
EU Renewable Energy Directive	• Contributes to enhanced use of renewable-energy sources, which helps reduce emissions and improve air quality
Convention on Long-Range Transboundary Air Pollution (CLRTAP)	• Developed the critical-loads concept, which facilitated the EU process of setting air-quality standards
World Health Organization (WHO)	• Produces air-quality guidelines, which have heavily influenced EU air-quality standards

led to a growth of emissions of air pollutants in particular in the area of traffic, which has negatively affected air quality. In contrast, other EU legislative instruments have directly and indirectly contributed to emission reductions and thus have supported the objectives of the Air Quality FD. These are in particular the Acidification Strategy and the National Emission Ceilings (NEC) Directive, the EU's SAVE Program entailing directives on minimum energy-efficiency standards and related labeling, the Renewable Energy Directive promoting the use of renewable sources of energy, and the Auto-Oil I Program and related directives on fuel standards and vehicle-emission limits. The EU's Directive on Integrated Pollution Prevention and Control (IPPC Directive) has had a similar effect (chapter 9).

Regarding vertical interaction with international institutions, two cases are particularly relevant. First, the so-called critical-loads concept developed in the context of the Convention on Long-Range Transboundary Air Pollution (CLRTAP) under the UN Economic Commission for Europe (UNECE) facilitated the setting of air-quality standards in the framework of the Air Quality FD. A critical load can be defined as a quantitative estimate of an exposure to one or more pollutants below which significantly harmful effects on specified sensitive elements of the environment do not occur according to present knowledge (Wettestad 2002). Second, the air-quality guidelines produced by the WHO influenced the air-quality standards of the FD, as further detailed in the next section. Both these interactions have operated at the output level in that agreements reached under CLRTAP and the WHO influenced the design and content of the Air Quality FD (Interaction through Commitment).

Vertical Interaction with the WHO: External Air-Quality Guidelines as Ambitious Benchmarks for EU Policy Entrepreneurs?

The WHO Air-Quality Guidelines

The WHO recognized as early as 1958 that air pollution was a global threat to health. In 1972, initial guidelines regarding the levels of ambient air pollutants that constitute hazards to health were formulated for the "classic" compounds sulfur dioxide (SO_2), solid particulate matter, carbon monoxide (CO), and photochemical oxidants. The next major step in this process was the publication of the *Air Quality Guidelines for Europe* for a much broader set of air pollutants in 1987. These guidelines were based on evidence from the epidemiological and toxicological literature published in Europe and North America. Work on making the guidelines globally applicable started in 1997. With regard to the health significance of air pollution, a new database of time-series studies was developed, first in the United States and later in Europe and other areas.[8]

The revision of the guidelines during the 1990s involved a more elaborate process and several stages. First, a planning group composed of national experts outlined the structure of the revised report. Then experts in various countries were asked to produce drafts for various sections of the report. These drafts were reviewed by WHO working groups, and subsequently sent out for a final round of peer review by other experts.[9] With regard to the specific role of the EU, a funding agreement between the European Commission and the European Regional Centre of WHO, resulting in WHO's 2000 Air Quality Guidelines for Europe, should be noted (European Commission 2001, 14). As guidelines for EU and national policymaking, they constitute nonbinding soft law.

Negotiating the Daughter Directives: The Heyday of the WHO Guidelines
The EU's fifth Environmental Action Program, adopted in 1992, called for the effective protection of everyone from recognized health risks caused by air pollution. As a central "action," proposals for amendments of existing legislation were pinpointed. A central target for 2000 was that "WHO values [should] become mandatory at EU level" (European Commission 1993, 8).

While the work on the Air Quality FD was spurred by the revision of the WHO guidelines, the processes of producing the daughter directives have been characterized as "the heyday of the WHO guidelines" with regard to the use of expertise.[10] In the explanatory memorandum to the proposal for the first daughter directive (European Commission 1997), the Commission justified each of the proposed limit values by reference to the most recent WHO guidelines. In the case of sulfur dioxide, WHO guidelines established a maximum concentration limit averaged over ten minutes. The Commission then "translated" this guideline into suggestions for hourly and daily limit values. The suggested hourly limit was 350 micrograms per cubic meter (μ/m^3), and the suggested 24-hour limit was 125 μ/m^3. As proposals were developed in expert groups with member-state representation, the proposals for limit values were accompanied by political modifications in the form of allowed exceedances per year and deadlines for compliance. For instance, the 350 μ/m^3 hourly limit was not to be exceeded more than twenty-four times a year. Because Commission proposals already included central member-state opinions, they were not much altered in the legislative process. For example, the Commission proposal for SO_2 was adopted unaltered by the Council.

Even though this was not always the case, the WHO values were generally maintained throughout. For example, WHO's advised maximum hourly limit for NO_X was 200 μ/m^3, complemented by an annual 40 μ/m^3 limit, and a vegetation limit of 30 μ/m^3. The Commission's proposal for the first daughter directive of the Air Quality FD closely followed the WHO with regard to all these limit values, but included an opening for eight exceedances of the hourly limit per year. The final directive maintained all the WHO limit values (i.e., 200/40/30), but increased the allowed exceedances of the hourly limit to eighteen times per year (to be met as of 2005). In the case of particulate matter, the number of allowed exceedances was increased from twenty-five to thirty-five. As indicated above, some saw this as a "significant dilution" of environmental ambitiousness.[11]

In the case of the second daughter directive, targeting benzene and carbon monoxide, the connection to the WHO guidelines was somewhat weaker. This had to do in particular with the fact that WHO could not come up with a recommended safe level of exposure for benzene (WHO 2000, chap. 5.2). However, in the case of carbon monoxide, the maximum daily eight-hour mean of 10 mg/m^3 recommended by WHO (2000, chap. 5.5) was proposed by the Commission and adopted by the Council.

To protect human health, the June 1999 proposal for a third daughter directive on ground-level ozone took its lead from the WHO guidelines, which called for a limit on ambient ozone concentrations of 120 μ/m^3. Based on stakeholder and expert input, the Commission then suggested that this limit could be breached up to twenty days per calendar year (Amann and Lutz 2000, 9). According to Amann and Lutz (2000, 18), a higher 160 μ/m^3 limit value with fewer allowed exceedances was discussed in the preparatory work. However, the Commission saw it as important to maintain the connection to the WHO guidelines and hence the 120 μ/m^3 limit value (with somewhat more allowed exceedances) was chosen. Cutting a long story short, agreement was finally reached in November 2001, with member states being obliged to meet the 120 μ/m^3 target by 2010 "save where not achievable through proportionate measures." The final agreement also allowed twenty-five exceedances per year, hence diluting the connection to the WHO guidelines a little further.[12] Overall, the agreement constituted a typical EU compromise by creating more than aspirational, nonbinding targets, but still with a certain flexibility in terms of bindingness.

Assessment and Outlook

The WHO guidelines have been the most important scientific reference point in EU policymaking on air quality. As soon as WHO's work in this area started in 1987, it became an important benchmark in the EU context. Already in the 1992 ozone directive, the threshold values were directly derived from the WHO guidelines. In the same year, the EU's fifth Environmental Action Program established as a target that WHO values should become mandatory within the EU by 2000. This can be interpreted through the lenses of Cognitive Interaction. The WHO guidelines of 1987 constituted information that influenced the perceptions of EU decision makers and made them adopt these Guidelines as a template for EU policy. The broad-based international character and participation of high-quality experts clearly gave and continue to give WHO's processes a high-quality stamp within the EU.

The interaction between WHO and the Air Quality FD can primarily be interpreted through the lenses of Interaction through Commitment. Actors within the EU became committed to the WHO guidelines through the fifth Environmental Action Program of 1992. Although the Action Programs did not become legally binding until 1993, targets in the earlier Programs represented strong political signals for EU policymaking. As pointed out by Weale et al. (2000, 58), all five Action Programs provided important indications of policy orientation. Hence, actors within the EU have used the scientific and politically undiluted WHO guidelines as benchmarks, from which it was difficult to diverge because of the existing general commitment to them. Marking "the heyday of the WHO guidelines," the Commission utilized WHO target values as the foundation for its proposals for Air Quality daughter directives whenever an appropriate WHO guideline existed. Even though the WHO targets were always politically softened during the preparatory work on the Commission proposals, mostly by introducing a number of allowed days of exceedance, they still closely reflected the WHO guidelines. This also holds true for the occasions on which the softening was increased further in the Council (figure 12.1).

The interaction has been intentional and has had synergistic effects. The WHO guidelines have been produced in order to influence other actors such as the EU. There are strong reasons to assume that the EU has, as a result, adopted more ambitious policies than would have come about without the WHO benchmarks. For instance, all the summaries of the preparatory processes published in the Commission's directive proposals include information about some member states and industrial stakeholders reacting negatively to the high level of policy ambition stemming

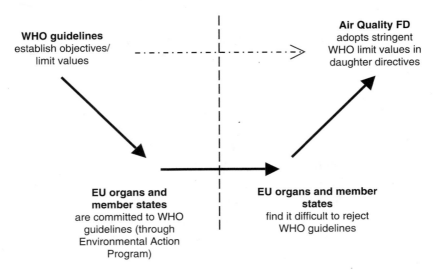

Figure 12.1
WHO guidelines strengthen EU air-quality legislation

from the WHO input. However, to measure this effect more precisely, more detailed knowledge about the relevant negotiation processes and the exact degree of member-state resistance overcome with the help of the WHO guidelines would be required.

Because of the synergistic effects so far, it may not be surprising that the WHO and its air-quality guidelines are likely to continue to play a significant role in EU policymaking in the years ahead. As mentioned in the introduction, in 2001, the Commission's Environment Directorate launched an initiative to incorporate the various aspects of EU air-quality policy into a unified framework under the banner of *Clean Air for Europe* or CAFÉ (European Commission 2001). CAFÉ can hence be seen as providing an important EU response to the interaction and (lack of) coordination between subissues in the issue area of air-pollution control. So how does the EU assess the interaction with WHO? Overall, the response is positive. According to the 2001 CAFÉ Communication, during the consultation process leading to the launch of CAFÉ, it became clear that a large majority of national representatives and stakeholders supported the use of WHO guidelines as the fundamental advice on risk (European Commission 2001, 14). This seems also to some extent to be the position of the Commission, although the picture is somewhat ambiguous.[13]

Accordingly, the Commission signed a contract with WHO on a revision of the "Guidelines for Europe."[14] Due to delays in getting the contract going, it was uncertain whether these guidelines could be ready for the next main round of revision of EU air-quality policy. Moreover, the process of producing the WHO guidelines has been criticized for lack of transparency. Hence, there seems to be a need to rethink the way the EU organizes its scientific advisory process in this issue area. In a reappraisal process, several options could be evaluated, including a possible lower-cost option of producing the relevant knowledge "in-house" in the EU.

Horizontal Interaction with the EU Auto-Oil Legislation: Limited Policy Coordination, but Crucial Implementation Effects?

EU internal interaction is distinctly different from the relationship between EU legislation and international institutions. Within the EU, the different strands of (environmental) policy should ideally interact and be compatible. In the air-quality context, measures to curb vehicle emissions are of central interest. In this field, the Auto-Oil I process was the most important EU process in the 1990s. Since discussions on the air-quality directives and the Auto-Oil I Program and related directives proceeded roughly in parallel and partly targeted the same substances, an interesting first question becomes: How closely have these "functionally" related processes and directives interacted at the level of outputs? This issue is discussed in the next subsection. Subsequently, interaction at the level of outcomes is assessed since cleaner fuel and stricter emission limits contribute to better air quality, and the most important interaction effects may thus emanate from the implementation of the Auto-Oil directives. This is followed by a discussion of the EU system's main response to the interaction, before a concluding summary and interpretation of this horizontal interaction.

Output Interaction: The Evolution of Auto-Oil I

Two main phases in the Auto-Oil I process can be distinguished: a preparatory phase, from 1992 to 1996, and a policymaking phase, from 1996 to 1998.

The Auto-Oil Preparatory Phase (1992–1996)   The Auto-Oil process was initiated by the Commission in 1992. The adoption of the strengthened 1990 U.S. Clean Air Act, WHO's air-quality guidelines for Europe, and growing frustration in industry circles over a policymaking approach paying too little attention to costs in relation to benefits, have all been identified as contributing factors (Weale et al. 2000; Young and Wallace 2000, chap. 2; Haigh 2003, sec. 6.8, 8). There was thus an interest in finding more cost-effective solutions.[15] As a response to these various concerns, a symposium on vehicle-emission standards for the year 2000 was organized and attended by a wide range of participants (Friedrich, Tappe, and Wurzel 1998, 105). A central theme of this symposium was the development of cost-effective measures based on ambient-air-quality standards.

The Commissioners for Environment, Industry and Energy then invited the European Automotive Manufacturers Association (ACEA) and the European Petroleum Industry Association (EUROPIA) to collaborate in a technical research program. It was decided to launch three independent but interrelated projects:

• Urban ambient-air-quality studies. The aim here was to predict the air quality of seven European cities (Athens, Cologne, The Hague, London, Lyon, Madrid, and Milan) and ground-level ozone across the EU for the year 2010, and on this basis derive emission-reduction targets.
• A "European Program on Emissions, Fuels and Engine Technologies," focusing on the effect of vehicle technology and fuel characteristics on emissions.
• A cost-effectiveness study, calculating the costs and emission impact for different emission-reduction measures.

While legislation proposals were originally to be ready by the end of 1994, this was delayed,[16] and the Commission did not put forward the first two proposals for directives to take effect in the year 2000 until June 1996, when the main policy-making phase of this process started.

To what extent did EU air-quality legislation and the Auto-Oil I process influence each other? Given the early stage of development of EU air-quality legislation, its influence on the developing fuel-standard and vehicles-emission legislation was almost inevitably weak. Instead, the Auto-Oil legislation was directly influenced by the WHO air-quality guidelines that acquired additional force because of the expected EU air-quality legislation. As noted by Goodwin (1999, 11), "The levels of air pollution that were used as the target levels came from the emerging guidelines being developed by the World Health Organization. These were stricter than the standards that applied in the Member States and the EU but were used because they were expected to form the basis for future legislation." Influence was also weak the other way around. Given the general character of the FD and its main focus on monitoring, it is not surprising to find no formal reference to the developing Auto-

Oil legislation in it. Article 7 only mentions the possible need for measures targeting motor-vehicle traffic in the air-quality action plans to be drawn up by member states.

The Auto-Oil Policymaking Phase (1996–1998)   The Auto-Oil I study was ready in the spring of 1996. Although the Commission had used target levels based on WHO guidelines as yardsticks for assessing the acceptability of future levels of pollution, it was still noted that "Article 4 of Directive 94/12/EC on Motor Vehicle Air Pollution Control requires that measures to reduce emissions from road traffic shall be designed to meet the requirements of the Community's air quality criteria and related objectives" (European Commission 1996, sec. 3).

In June 1996 the Commission then formally put forward the first two proposals for directives arising from the Auto-Oil I Program. Central components in this initial package of proposals consisted of tighter emission standards for passenger cars and fuel specifications for petrol and diesel. First, by 2000 petrol was to contain no more than 200 parts per million (ppm) of sulfur (down from the estimated market average of 300 ppm), and diesel 350 ppm of sulfur (down from the estimated market average of 450 ppm). Second, a proposal to strengthen the existing emission limits for passenger cars (these being based on Directive 70/220/EEC on Motor Vehicle Air Pollution Control, last amended by Directive 94/12/EC) contained emission limits for 2000 and lower "indicative" limits for 2005. These limits related to carbon monoxide (CO), hydrocarbons (HC), NO_X, and—only for diesel cars—particulates. According to then Environment Commissioner Ritt Bjerregaard, the proposals were "extremely ambitious," and she emphasized again that the proposed new standards should help the EU to achieve WHO air-quality standards.[17] The proposed measures were to be followed by an Auto-Oil II phase, specifying requirements for the year 2005.

After several rounds of inputs from the European Parliament and the Council, and a final round in a conciliation committee, somewhat tightened directives were agreed to in June 1998. EU Council Directive 98/69/EC relating to passenger cars and light commercial vehicles tightened existing emission limits in two stages (2000 and 2005). In EU Council Directive 98/70/EC relating to the quality of petrol and diesel fuels, key targets for the year 2000 were petrol with 150 parts per million (ppm) and diesel with 350 ppm of sulfur. For 2005, the petrol sulfur target was 50 ppm (see Haigh 2003, secs. 6.8 and 6.20, for more information about these directives). Since the conciliation agreement settled many of the 2005 standards intended to be specified in an Auto-Oil II Program, this latter Program was redesigned as a more analytic Program aiming at improved modeling and knowledge.

So what role did EU air-quality legislation in this field play in this phase of the Auto-Oil I process? Air-quality *considerations* functioned as a central contextual factor, while the specific links between EU air-quality legislation and the Auto-Oil I legislation remained weak. Although the main controversies were fought over technological possibilities and the costs of different options, all sides in the debate continually referred to the implications of these possibilities and options for air quality and health. The final agreement was hailed by members of the European Parliament, member states, and the Commission as a major breakthrough in the effort to fight urban air pollution. For instance, according to Environment Commissioner Ritt Bjerregaard, "We shall see cleaner air in our cities, and we shall have fewer ozone episodes in the summer".[18] However, EU air-quality legislation, including the 1996 Framework Directive, was only referred to as a general parameter for Auto-Oil legislation, while a specific influence is not detectable. As in the preparatory phase, decision makers instead used WHO's air-quality guidelines as central benchmarks. This is hardly surprising because none of the daughter directives had yet been adopted by June 1998 and hence Auto-Oil I decision makers had few recent, specific EU air-quality standards available.

All in all, it is also hard to find clues indicating that the influence the other way around from Auto-Oil I legislation on the preparation and negotiation of air-quality legislation was very strong. The negotiation of the ground-level ozone directive was closely related to the processes of producing an EU ozone strategy and a directive on national emission ceilings (NECs), as further discussed elsewhere (Wettestad 2002). Hence, interpolicy coordination was taking place, and it is reasonable to assume that the relationship between Auto-Oil I and air-quality legislation was included as a topic in the interpolicy coordination efforts that took place in the period from 1997 to 1999. This coordination, however, primarily involved processes other than Auto-Oil I. Furthermore, as described by Amann and Lutz (2000), a central analytic tool in the EU's work on revising its ozone legislation was the RAINS model developed by the International Institute for Applied Systems Analysis (IIASA) in Laxenburg, Austria. Among the key inputs to this model was a summary of emission-control policies within the transport sector regarding NO_X and volatile organic compounds (VOCs), including recent policies adopted within the Auto-Oil I context. Hence, this modeling work represented one way the Auto-Oil legislation influenced air-quality legislation. However, given the multitude of relevant policies to be included, this influence was rather indirect and probably not very strong.

Outcome Interaction: Auto-Oil Implementation Will Undoubtedly Help the Achievement of Air-Quality Targets

We must first recall here that the Auto-Oil I directives were adopted relatively recently. As noted above, revised fuel standards and vehicle-emission requirements were adopted in June 1998. Moreover, for instance the United Kingdom did not put the necessary fuel-standard implementing legislation into place until December 2001 (Haigh 2003, sec. 6.20, 4). This makes it hard to find clear effects of Auto-Oil implementation on the achievement of the EU's revised air-quality targets under the FD.

Although it is not possible to find clear evidence so far of synergistic interaction effects, it is clear that such synergistic effects will occur in the years ahead (figure 12.2). For instance, in 1996 the Commission estimated that emissions of NO_x from road traffic would decline by 65 percent by 2010 from 1995 levels, and those of VOCs, carbon monoxide, and urban particulate matter by 70 percent. Between a third and a half of these reductions would be attributable to the Auto-Oil Program.[19] Moreover, in the 2002 *Environmental Signals* report of the European Environment Agency, transport measures from Auto-Oil I and II are one of the factors expected to lead to reduced emissions of particulate matter (European Environment Agency 2002, 77). The main available evidence is related to the implementation of Auto-Oil I Directive 98/70/EC on the quality of petrol and diesel fuels. In April 2004, the first annual implementation report was published (European Commission

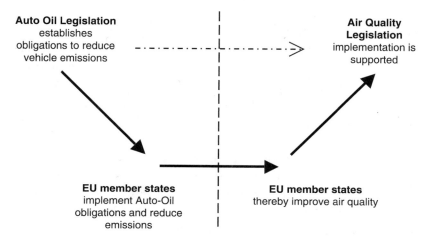

Figure 12.2
Auto-Oil legislation supports implementation of EU air-quality legislation

2004). Falling EU motor-fuel sulfur levels were reported. For instance, by 2002, low-sulfur fuels had already attained a market share of 47 percent for petrol and 43 percent for diesel. The report noted that the specifications laid down in Directive 98/70/EC were generally met (European Commission 2004, 2). This development is of course good news for European air quality, although it is hard to measure the precise effect and the precise contribution of the Auto-Oil directive.

However, various worrisome trends and signals make it highly questionable whether the synergy has been strong enough and the relationship between transport and air quality has been handled optimally so far. For instance, in the Commission's review of Auto-Oil II, only modest reductions in exposure to particulate matter were expected by 2010 (European Commission 2000, 11). Moreover, in September 2001, on the basis of a preliminary assessment of the follow-up of the first air-quality daughter directive, the Commission's Environment Directorate issued clear warning signals. Urban areas all over Europe would likely fail to meet the limits on NO_X and particulates set in the 1999 directive. A central reason pinpointed was the volume of road transport growing out of control.[20] This disturbing picture is reinforced in the European Environment Agency's *Environmental Signals* reports (European Environment Agency 2002, 2004). In these reports, the assessments of urban air-quality exceedances for both ground-level ozone and particulates reveal unfavorable trends. So, the time has come to take a closer look at the response of the EU system in the form of the CAFÉ Program. How will the relationship between these activities and strands of legislation be handled in the future?

Outlook: Improved Interaction through CAFÉ?

Two of the central, stated objectives of CAFÉ are to ensure that measures in different sectors needed to achieve air-quality objectives are taken in a cost-effective manner at the relevant policy level through the development of effective structural links with the relevant policy areas; and to develop an overall integrated strategy to achieve air-quality objectives in a cost-effective way.[21] Particulate matter and ozone are specifically targeted issues.

It makes sense to see CAFÉ as confirming inadequate EU integration of transport and air-quality policies so far. On the one hand, the CAFÉ Communication points out that considerable achievements have been made in terms of putting into place various pieces of legislation to improve fuel standards and bring down emissions from transport. Hence, the integration of vehicle and transport policies and air-quality policies has not been a total failure. On the other hand, the two targeted issues of particulate matter and ozone are closely linked to emissions from transport. As mentioned in the previous section, various worrisome trends continue to exist and serious air-quality problems remain. As a result, the Auto-Oil II Program singled out particulate matter and ozone as remaining air-quality problems. So, despite significant progress, there is still room for improvement.

In terms of addressing these integration challenges, CAFÉ has utilized several organizational devices.[22] First, the program has been developed under the leadership of a permanent secretariat housed within the Commission's Environment Directorate, assisted by an interservice group composed of all relevant Commission departments. The mandate of this group, chaired by the Environment Directorate, is to foster strategic discussion and consensus between the services and ensure that Commission policy in this area is fully coordinated. Second, a steering group composed of representatives of the member states, the European Parliament, stakeholders, and relevant international organizations has met two or three times a year to advise the Commission on the strategic direction of the program. This has meant the active involvement of a broader range of actors than those involved in the Auto-Oil context, especially Auto-Oil I.[23] Third, in terms of more specific coordination between sectors, a sectoral coordination group has been set up with the objective of ensuring full communication between CAFÉ and sectoral policies, including the development of source-based measures.

Are the measures announced in CAFÉ an adequate response? It is too early to determine this conclusively. CAFÉ has been criticized for unclear financing of the program,[24] and for lacking specification of the work program that must be rapidly established in order to meet the 2004 deadline.[25] With regard to the coordination efforts, it has been noted that "most if not all the key sectoral areas of policy making required to build the strategy remain the responsibility of those same parts of the Commission that ran them previously. They have not been brought into the grasp of policy makers running the CAFÉ program, so it remains to be seen if the requisite linkages can be made to work in practice as well as they may look in theory" ("Commission Launches Clean Air for Europe Programme").[26]

A Summary and Interpretation of the Interaction
Although this study has not been able to reveal the complex coordination processes within the Commission in detail, the distinct impression is one of a quite limited interaction at the level of outputs. The Auto-Oil process and outputs mainly used WHO guidelines as benchmarks. The air-quality process included Auto-Oil effects

in the modeling input, but more effort was seemingly made in coordinating with other policies, such as the NEC Directive. The explanation may be simple: because the Auto-Oil and air-quality directives inevitably interact when they are implemented, the challenge for policymakers was much more to achieve the strongest outputs possible than to spend time and resources on coordination.

The strongest interaction between these two strands of legislation will take place at the level of outcomes. In terms of interaction mechanisms, this is thus a case of Behavioral Interaction. The Auto-Oil directives establish obligations of EU member states to implement fuel standards and emission limits for vehicles. As the member states implement these obligations, this is bound to lead to emission reductions that improve air quality and thus support the implementation of the air-quality legislation (figure 12.2). The EU has estimated that without the Auto-Oil directives, the emissions of NO_X, carbon monoxide, and particulate matter from transport by 2010 would be almost twice as high. Hence, the implementation of these directives and the reduced emissions will make it considerably easier for the EU to attain targets established in the air-quality daughter directives for concentrations of NO_X and the other pollutants mentioned. However, given the many processes both within and outside the transport sector that contribute to air quality, it is difficult to be more precise with regard to the *specific* synergistic effects of the Auto-Oil directives. This interaction at the level of outcomes has been intentional, since a central aim for the Auto-Oil directives was to improve air quality and hence the performance of EU air-quality directives.

The overall management of the interaction so far must be characterized as moderately positive. On the one hand, the Auto-Oil and air-quality directives mean that the gap within the EU between transport activities and air-quality ambitions has been narrowed. Therefore, a concern is now that sectors other than transport are lagging behind in reducing emissions. On the other hand, the "transport-air-quality" gap has in no way been closed, and the CAFÉ Program is launching improved interinstitutional coordination as a central instrument to come up with stricter policies to narrow the gap further in the years ahead.

Some Concluding Notes on the Role of Non-EU Expertise, Soft-Law Instruments, and Timing

How much should EU environmental policy be a "home brew" and how much should it rely on external expertise? With regard to the vertical, strongly synergistic interaction with the WHO guidelines, it was noted that the overall response to the interaction within the EU system has been positive, and the CAFÉ Program signals a continuation of interaction practices. But in a policymaking climate where cost-effectiveness is increasingly emphasized as a guiding principle for the work of the Commission and the EU as a whole, an increasing interest in more low-cost, in-house expertise was also noted. This forms the basis for a more general dilemma for the EU, with far wider relevance than only the air-pollution context, and for a possible lesson to be learned. On the one hand, the ability to point to highly authoritative external expertise may provide EU actors with a sort of undisputable, "distant" authority. On the other hand, in line with the considerable development of EU environmental policy, the EU has built up considerable in-house national and EU-wide expertise. Relying on this expertise will often be cheaper than using external expertise. However, the use of national expertise may also potentially be more controversial if suspicions of a "politicization" of science arise. This case holds no clear answer to this dilemma, but given the constructive role played by the WHO guidelines in a number of EU processes, a shift toward more use of in-house expertise should be carefully considered before a decision is made.

Another general lesson emanating from this vertical case has to do with the discussion of the role of nonbinding instruments in international environmental politics. Are they toothless paper tigers or are they flexible instruments for pushing up environmental standards? This case offers further evidence that nonbinding instruments can have a profound influence on the development of binding legislation in international and European (environmental) politics. The crucial factor in this case seems to be the high legitimacy surrounding the guideline-producing processes within the WHO.

With regard to the horizontal, EU-internal interaction between the air-quality directives and the stricter fuel standards and vehicle-emission limits being developed under the banner of Auto-Oil I, there is clearly an interesting timing dimension involved.[27] When the Commission put forward the fuel-standard and emission-limit proposals in June 1996, none of the air-quality daughter directives (which laid out the more specific air-quality requirements) had been presented or adopted. It is reasonable to assume that if they had been adopted prior to the fuel-standard and vehicle-emission proposals, they could have functioned more as explicit reference points in the debate on the need for stricter policies. However, in this specific context, the lack of EU legislation was to a large extent compensated for by a direct reference to the WHO guidelines. But it may be more of an exception than a rule that such external, authoritative reference points are available, and then the timing of internal EU policymaking processes becomes more critical.

Notes

The author would like to express special thanks to Andrew Farmer, IEEP, for valuable inputs to the initial work on this chapter.

1. The top fourteen were sulfur dioxide, nitrogen oxides, ozone, particulates, black smoke, lead, carbon monoxide, cadmium, acid deposition, toluene, benzene, benzopyrene, formaldehyde, and peroxyacetylnitrate (PAN) (European Commission 2001, 14).

2. Measurement is mandatory in so-called agglomerations—zones where the population concentration exceeds 250,000 inhabitants—and in zones where pollution exceeds some proportion of the limit values.

3. "Air Quality-Some Standards Ready," *Acid News* 3, October 1998, 7; "Ministers Agree Air Pollution Rules, Lengthy Deadline on Water Quality," *ENDS Report* 281, June 1998, 47.

4. "Executive Finalizes EU Proposals on Emissions Ceilings," *Environment Watch*, June 18, 1999, 7–9 (here: 7).

5. "Fourth EU Air Quality Directive Delayed," *ENDS Environment Daily*, December 20, 2001.

6. "Commission Back-Pedals on Metals in Air Limits," *ENDS Environment Daily*, October 30, 2002.

7. "Fourth EU Air Quality Directive Agreed," *ENDS Environment Daily*, April 14, 2004; "Agreement on Air Quality Directive for Heavy Metals, PAHs," *ENDS Report* 351, April 2004, 53–54.

8. The time-series approach takes a day as the unit of analysis and relates the daily occurrence of events such as deaths or admissions to hospital to daily average concentrations of pollutants, while taking careful account of confounding factors such as season, temperature, and day of the week. Powerful statistical techniques have been applied and coefficients have been produced that relate the daily average concentrations of pollutants to their effects. For more information, see http://www.who.int/environmental_information/Air/Guidelines.

9. Personal communication with Per Schwarze, Department Director within the Norwegian Institute of Public Health and participant in the process of producing the revised WHO guidelines.

10. Interview with Commission official, February 13, 2002.

11. See note 3.

12. "Council and MEPs Agree on Ozone in Ambient Air," *Europe Environment* 601, December 4, 2001, 1.

13. Interviews with Commission official, February 13, 2002.

14. According to M. Krzyzanowski, WHO, the EU's financial contribution to this revision process is much more significant than the contribution in the mid-1990s. Personal communication, December 11, 2002.

15. Interview with Matthew Ferguson, Institute for European Environmental Policy, November 1999.

16. "Car Industry Lashes Out at Auto-Oil Proposals," *ENDS Report* 257, June 1996, 41–43 (here: 41).

17. "Auto-Oil: Commission Proposes New Emission and Fuel Standards," *Europe Environment* 480, June 27, 1996, 1.

18. "Legislation Setting Auto Emission, Fuel Quality Standards Approved by Union," *International Environment Reporter*, July 8, 1998, 671.

19. "Full Package Revealed," *Acid News* 4: 1, October 1996, 3.

20. "EU Likely to Miss Air Quality Goals," *ENDS Environment Daily*, September 24, 2001.

21. The other main objectives are to develop, collect, and validate scientific information concerning air pollution, including projections, inventories, integrated assessment modeling, and cost-effectiveness analysis studies, leading to the development of air-quality and deposition objectives and indicators and identification of measures required to reduce emissions; to support the implementation of legislation and develop new legislation, especially the Air Quality Framework Directive daughter directives, and contribute to the review of international protocols; and to disseminate widely (including to the public) information and results from the program (European Commission 2001).

22. This section relies heavily on information provided by the CAFÉ website. See http://europa.eu.int/comm/environment/air/cafe.htm#Organisationalstructure.

23. This can be seen as a response to and balancing of Auto-Oil's heavy industry involvement. Interview with Commission official, February 13, 2002.

24. "Editorial: Should Have Learnt," *Acid News* 2, June 2001, 2.

25. "Commission Launches Clean Air for Europe Programme," *Environment Watch*, May 11, 2001, 5–6.

26. See note 25 (here: 6).

27. See Wettestad 2002 for a discussion of how unfortunate timing with other processes influenced the process of developing a National Emission Ceilings Directive.

References

Ammann, Markus, and Martin Lutz. 2000. The Revision of the Air Quality Legislation in the European Union Related to Ground-Level Ozone. Working paper. Laxenburg, Austria, and Brussels: International Institute for Applied Systems Analysis (IIASA)/European Commission, DG-ENV.

Andresen, Steinar, Arild Underdal, Tora Skodvin, and Jørgen Wettestad. 2000. *Science and Politics in International Environmental Regimes: Between Integrity and Involvement.* Manchester: Manchester University Press.

Elsom, Derek M. 1999. Development and Implementation of Strategic Frameworks for Air Quality Management in the UK and the European Community. *Journal of Environmental Planning and Management* 42 (1): 103–121.

European Commission. 1993. *Towards Sustainability—A European Community Programme of Policy and Action in Relation to the Environment and Sustainable Development*. Brussels: Commission of the European Communities.

European Commission. 1996. *Communication from the Commission to the European Parliament and the Council on a Future Strategy for the Control of Atmospheric Emissions from Road Transport Taking into Account the Results from the Auto/Oil Programme*. Doc. COM (1996) 248, June 18, 1996. Brussels: European Commission.

European Commission. 1997. *Explanatory Memorandum to the Proposed First Daughter Directive*. Doc. COM(1997) 500, October 8, 1997. Brussels: European Commission.

European Commission. 2000. *Communication from the Commission: A Review of the Auto-Oil II Programme*. Doc. COM(2000) 626, October 5, 2000. Brussels: European Commission.

European Commission. 2001. *The Clean Air for Europe (CAFÉ) Programme: Towards a Thematic Strategy for Air Quality*. Communication from the Commission. Doc. COM (2001) 245, May 4, 2001. Brussels: European Commission.

European Commission. 2004. *Quality of Gasoline and Diesel Fuel Used for Road Transport in the European Union: First Annual Report*. Doc. COM (2004) 310, April 27, 2004. Brussels: European Commission.

European Environment Agency. 2002. *Environmental Signals*. Copenhagen: EEA.

European Environment Agency. 2004. *EEA Signals 2004*. Copenhagen: EEA.

Friedrich, Axel, Matthias Tappe, and Rüdiger Wurzel. 1998. *The Auto-Oil Programme: Missed Opportunity or Leap Forward?* Research paper 1/98. Hull: University of Hull.

Goodwin, Frazer. 1999. *Controlling Traffic Pollution and the Auto Oil Programme*. Paper 99/8. Brussels: European Federation for Transport and Environment.

Haigh, Nigel, ed. 2003. *Manual of Environmental Policy: The EU and Britain*. Leeds: Maney Publishing and Institute for European Environmental Policy.

Weale, Albert, Geoffrey Pridham, Michelle Cini, Dimitrios Konstadakopulos, Martin Porter, and Brendan Flynn. 2000. *Environmental Governance in Europe*. Oxford: Oxford University Press.

Wettestad, Jørgen. 2002. *Clearing the Air—European Advances in Tackling Acid Rain and Atmospheric Pollution*. Aldershot: Ashgate.

Wettestad, Jørgen, and Andrew Farmer. 2001. *The EU Air Quality Framework Directive: EU Pitcher; International Catcher*. Inventory paper. Lysaker, Norway, and London: Fridtjof Nansen Institute and Institute for European Environmental Policy.

WHO. 2000. *WHO Air Quality Guidelines*. 2nd ed. WHO Regional Publications, European Series 91. Geneva: World Health Organization.

Young, Alasdair R., and Helen Wallace. 2000. *Regulatory Politics in the Enlarging European Union: Weighing Civic and Producer Interests*. Manchester: Manchester University Press.

13

Comparative Empirical Analysis and Ideal Types of Institutional Interaction

Thomas Gehring and Sebastian Oberthür

The empirical chapters of this volume demonstrate that interaction between international and EU environmental institutions matters for the development and the performance of these institutions. The eleven core institutions included in our study (i.e., six environmentally relevant international institutions and five environmental EU directives) have significantly influenced the functioning and effectiveness of other governance instruments, and have themselves been the subject of similar influence. Policymakers are therefore well advised to take into account interaction effects when designing international agreements and EU legal instruments. Analysts who want to understand the development and performance of institutions will have to take into account the network of international and EU institutions in which these institutions are embedded.

The wealth of empirical information gathered in this study provides a unique opportunity to push the exploration of institutional interaction a step further. The inventories contained in chapters 3–12 comprise more than 160 cases of interaction in which (at least) one of our eleven core institutions has been involved, either as the source of influence or as its target. Cases were identified independently from their political salience, from the degree of intentionality of interested actors, and from their effects on the target. This sample of cases not only provides, for the first time, a broader picture of the realm of institutional interaction; it also allows us to explore systematic patterns of institutional interaction in a comparative perspective.

To this end, this chapter proceeds in three steps. First, we examine the overall contours of the phenomenon of institutional interaction as reflected in our sample of cases. Cases are analyzed according to some variables that we believe to be important for advancing the understanding of institutional interaction. In this effort, the effect of a case of interaction on the target institution constitutes the key dependent variable. While our methodology of case selection does not ensure the generalizability of our results, the empirical analysis produces a number of interesting findings that may easily be tested against other samples of cases from environmental affairs and beyond. Second, we develop a number of Weberian ideal types of institutional interaction, which subdivide and specify the general causal mechanisms developed in chapter 2, and elaborate their distinctive features. In doing so, we develop a framework for a more sophisticated analysis of institutional interaction so as to be able to better understand and explain the strikingly different properties of cases of interaction driven by the same causal mechanism. Cases of Cognitive Interaction follow one of two distinct ideal types, whereas Interaction through Commitment occurs in three variants. In contrast, it proved difficult to identify ideal types of Behavioral Interaction. Since their inherent logics are deductively generated, the Weberian ideal types of institutional interaction are independent from our empirical sample. Finally, we examine certain more complex phenomena of institutional interaction that reach beyond the occurrence of cases, and look ahead to the future of the study of institutional interaction.

A Sample of 163 Cases of Institutional Interaction

In this section, we engage in a comparative analysis of institutional interaction based on a database that contains the core characteristics of all cases of our sample. Data gathering involved three steps. First, we selected eleven core institutions so as to ensure that relevant patterns of interaction are not accidentally excluded, and that the core institutions address the full spectrum of international and EU environmental governance and include well-known cases of institutional interaction. No relevant area of governance is systematically excluded. Moreover, the institutions were to be important in order to support the relevance of our findings. Second, case-study authors identified the important cases of institutional interaction in which these institutions have been involved, either as the source or as the target, and that have a significant impact on the effectiveness of governance. They focused on cases with shorter rather than longer causal chains to keep the analytic effort within manageable limits. The inventories that are part of chapters 3–12 of this volume contain a total of 163 cases of institutional interaction. Third, case-study authors coded the cases of our sample according to a number of variables assumed to be important for institutional interaction. These variables refer to dimensions along which we may expect actual cases of interaction to vary. The resulting data are reflected in the database included in the appendix to this book.

In the following, we introduce the core characteristics of cases of institutional interaction on which the empirical analysis of this chapter is founded. On this basis, we subsequently examine the universe of the case-specific data comparatively and identify a number of interesting findings about patterns of interaction in our sample.

Core Characteristics of a Case of Interaction

For the systematic analysis of institutional interaction, we need variables that allow us to characterize and distinguish interaction cases in meaningful ways. Human beings generally recognize and structure their living environment through self-constructed distinctions, internal models, "paradigms," or "theories." For example, "cars" remains an amorphous category, unless we introduce further distinctions, for example between vans, limousines, and station wagons.

In this subsection, we introduce six important variables that may serve to distinguish and characterize cases of institutional interaction. These variables are not necessarily the only ones that could be explored fruitfully. However, they illuminate core characteristics of cases of interaction, refer to categories well established in standard institutional analysis, and embody critical factors relevant to the causal pathways of institutional interaction (Gehring and Oberthür 2004). The variables and their range of potential values are listed in table 13.1.

Table 13.1
Variables of institutional interaction and relevant distinctions

Variable	Relevant Distinctions
Quality of effect (within the target institution)	• Synergy • Disruption • Neutral or unclear
Policy fields (of source and target institution)	• Same policy field • Different policy fields
Intentionality (of the triggering action of the source institution)	• Intentional • Unintentional
Key differences	• Objectives of source and target • Memberships of source and target • Means of source and target
Policy responses	• Collective response • No collective response
Potential for further improvement	• Significant potential • No significant potential

In line with our overall interest in the effectiveness of governance, the effects of, and policy responses to, institutional interaction are in the center of our interest as dependent variables, while the other core characteristics serve as independent variables. As an offspring of research on the effectiveness of international and EU institutions, the study of institutional interaction is particularly interested in the consequences of interaction for the effectiveness of governance and in its political management. We want to know which kinds of interaction can be expected to produce beneficial or detrimental effects on governance and how these effects may be influenced through targeted policy responses. In introducing the variables, we point out what we may learn from investigating them empirically and derive hypotheses about the empirical results we may expect to find, focusing in particular on the effectiveness of governance.

Quality of Effect: Synergy or Disruption   The objective of the target institution represents the major yardstick for assessing the consequences of a case of institutional interaction. An institution's objective indicates the direction of collectively desired change, or the aim of maintaining a desired status quo against some collectively undesired change (Gehring 1994, 433–449). Every institution established for purposes of governance has such an objective, even though some of its members might not fully support its active pursuit. The objective of a given international institution has also been the major yardstick for assessing its consequences in the established research on the effectiveness of international institutions. The effects of a case of institutional interaction are generally felt within the target institution, be it in its decision-making process or in the issue area governed by it (chapter 2).

The effects of a case of institutional interaction may be synergistic, disruptive, or neutral/unclear for the target institution. If the effects support the objectives of the target institution, they create synergy between the two institutions involved. If they contradict the target's objective, they result in disruption. The effects of an interaction may also be indeterminate or neutral, if they do not clearly hamper or reinforce the target institution's pursuit of its objective (chapter 2). The empirical chapters of this volume provide various illustrations of the differing quality of effects.

Perhaps the most fundamental empirical issue concerning the effects of institutional interaction relates to the question of whether synergy or disruption dominates the realm of institutional interaction. Given that the existing literature on institutional interaction has put particular emphasis on problematic interaction (chapters

1 and 2), conventional wisdom may expect disruption to prevail. However, policy-makers may also be expected to strive to avoid disruption to the extent possible. Moreover, it will be interesting to know whether the distribution of synergy and disruption varies between our general causal mechanisms.

Policy Fields   Interaction may take place within a single policy field or between institutions belonging to different policy fields. For example, an environmental institution may interact either with another environmental institution or with an institution belonging to the field of transportation or agriculture. In the policy debate on the increasing potential for interinstitutional conflict and the growing need for inter-institutional coordination, interaction between institutions belonging to different policy fields plays a particularly prominent role—as witnessed by the debate on the relationship between the World Trade Organization (WTO) and multilateral environmental agreements (chapter 8).

The policy field to which an institution belongs is determined by ministerial competences within countries. Our assignment of an institution to a policy field does not depend on our own views or on the perspectives of scientific observers. Whether two international and/or EU institutions belong to the same or different policy fields depends on whether the same or different ministries are generally responsible for representing state interests in these institutions. Hence, the 1995 UN Fish Stocks Agreement aiming at the sustainable use of the world's fish resources and their precautionary protection may be characterized as an environmental institution by some scientific observers, while the EU Common Fisheries Policy might be considered economic in nature because of the prevalence of economic, or regional, considerations (chapter 6). However, in most countries both institutions belong to the portfolio of fisheries ministers, so that they are assigned to the same policy field despite their diverging objectives.

We may hypothesize that institutions from different policy fields are likely to disrupt each other, while institutions from the same policy field may tend to create synergy. Ministries may be more inclined to avoid inconsistencies between institutions belonging to their portfolio than with respect to other institutions, the performance of which they will not be held accountable for. Environment ministers may, for example, be expected to be less inclined to avoid inconsistencies with economic institutions. We may also expect that policy responses to institutional interaction within one policy field will tend to be more effective than with respect to interaction between institutions in different policy fields. This would correlate with the view that current interaction problems, to a large extent, reflect problems of policy consistency and coordination at the national level (Victor 1999).

Intentionality   Actors within the source institution may trigger a particular instance of institutional interaction intentionally or not. For example, the EU Directive on Integrated Pollution Prevention Control (IPPC Directive) was adopted *in order to* improve the performance of a number of other EU environmental instruments (chapter 9). In contrast, trade rules agreed within WTO were not intended to interfere with a number of environmental regimes, but to liberalize international trade (chapter 8).

For our purposes, intentionality refers to the action within the source institution that triggers a case of institutional interaction. It does not refer to the target institution because it is not an appropriate variable to characterize effects. Only in the case of Cognitive Interaction are actors within the target institution completely free to decide on the interaction. In contrast, the effects of Behavioral Interaction are felt within the target institution irrespective of the intentions and wishes of its members. In the case of Interaction through Commitment, members of the target institution have to decide under pressure.

Intentionality must be kept separate from anticipation (Martin and Simmons 1998). While all unanticipated cases of interaction are also unintended, not all anticipated cases are intended. If interaction effects are known to the actors within the source institution, they may still occur as unintentional side effects of the pursuit of some other objective. If the effect is disruption, actors may choose not to avoid unintended but anticipated interaction because they consider the costs of doing so higher than the benefits. In contrast, the effects of unanticipated interaction come about as a surprise, although it might have been possible to anticipate them on closer inspection.

We may expect intentional disruption to occur rarely in the realm of institutional interaction involving environmental institutions. It is difficult to imagine environmental ministers intentionally making decisions in one forum that are at odds with rules of another environmental institution. And even across the borders of different policy fields, intentional disruption might be the exception rather than the rule because it would undermine the functioning of the system of international and EU institutions. Also, policy coordination within governments may be assumed to work against the making of conflicting decisions in international and EU forums.

We may expect that intentional disruption will occur particularly rarely within the EU because of the comparatively sophisticated institutional framework.

Key Differences   There must be situation-specific drivers that provide a basis for interinstitutional influence to occur. Such problem-specific drivers constitute an important part of what is occasionally referred to as problem structure (Miles et al. 2002; Hasenclever, Mayer, and Rittberger 1997). We seek to identify them in the form of key differences between institutions. This effort is based on the following consideration: If two institutions were very similar or even identical in all important respects, it would be difficult to see how one of them could exert significant influence on the other. If two institutions were so different in all relevant aspects that they did not touch on each other's areas of activity, interaction would be improbable. Therefore, interacting institutions will differ in some important respects, while being similar in others.

We suggest that for interaction to occur two institutions must differ significantly with respect to at least one of three key factors, namely their objectives, their memberships, or their means of governance. Institutions may interact because they pursue different *objectives*, while memberships and means of governance are similar. All specific international and EU institutions are focusing on a limited issue area and a limited set of objectives. States establish such issue-area-specific institutions to enable them to focus on some relevant issues at one time instead of being overwhelmed by complexity. From negotiation analysis, we know that actors will adjust their preferences according to the delimitation of issue areas. Modification of issues to be negotiated will influence the constellation of interests (Sebenius 1983, 1992). Hence, an identical group of states may pursue different interests in institutions governing different issue areas and may thus maintain institutions with starkly diverging objectives. Furthermore, *memberships* of two institutions can be so clearly distinct from each other that we may expect their interaction to rely on this variation. From negotiation analysis, we know that adding or subtracting actors will change the constellation of interests. Hence, two institutions with similar objectives and means may develop differently because their memberships vary significantly, and their interaction may be a result of the difference in memberships. Finally, two institutions may have largely similar objectives and identical memberships, while the *means* employed to realize their objectives differ. Some institutions operate with soft-law instruments, while others employ hard law (Abbott and Snidal 2000). Some institutions have powerful sanctions at their disposal, while others comprise financial mechanisms or lack sanctioning power. Hence, interaction may matter even if the institutions involved are established and maintained by the same group of actors for the same purpose.

The variable of key differences seems theoretically very promising, but it proved difficult to codify. Codification difficulties originated from the fact that interacting institutions frequently differ in two, occasionally even all three respects. Identifying the most significant key difference in a given case is far from trivial. As a result, the classification of some cases proved contentious, and for several cases it was not possible to clearly determine one key difference. For this reason, we do not analyze the data of this category quantitatively. However, we found the three key differences particularly useful as empirical points of reference for the theoretical development of ideal types of Interaction through Commitment (see the next section). The appendix contains data of this category only for cases of Interaction through Commitment.

Policy Responses and Potential for Further Improvement   From the perspective of international and EU governance, we are interested in *collective* policy responses in the framework of the interacting institutions. A case of interaction may be responded to either within the source institution or within the target institution, or within both institutions (or even within a third institution) in order to mitigate disruption or to enhance synergy. Such "interplay management" (Stokke 2001; also Stokke 2000) involves the "politics of institutional design and management" (Young 2002, 23). One of the institutions involved may take appropriate decisions separately. A policy response will be coordinated, if it results from a communication process overarching the two institutions, for example in the form of an exchange of the relevant secretariats or of negotiations between the two groups of actors. In this case, the interacting institutions create a "political linkage" that arises "when actors decide to consider two or more arrangements as parts of a larger institutional complex" (Young et al. 1999, 50).

Response action must be carefully distinguished from the original interaction effect in the target institution that constitutes an essential element of every case of institutional interaction. Response action is always additional and not a necessary element of the interaction. It may or may not occur depending on whether relevant actors recognize a case of interaction, how they assess the benefits of a response, whether a suitable response is available, and so on. The original interaction effect is particularly easily confused with response action in the case of output-level interaction, because both may consist of collective decision making within the target institution. For example, air-quality standards adopted by EU member states under the Air Quality Framework Directive were heavily influenced by relevant guidelines of the World Health Organization (WHO). The decision to rely on the guidelines constituted the main effect of the interaction. In contrast, the subsequent decision of the European Commission to provide funding for the revision of the WHO guidelines was a policy response. It did not form part of the original causal pathway and was not a direct effect of the WHO guidelines (chapter 12).

The examination of policy responses is particularly interesting from a governance perspective because policy responses enable actors to react to institutional interaction and influence its effects. There are many aspects of policy responses that deserve scientific attention. For example, few approaches to classifying and systematizing responses to institutional interaction exist (see King 1997, 18, 23). We may, for instance distinguish between collective decision making by the target institution and by the source institution, coordinated decision making by the two institutions, administrative coordination between their secretariats, and an exchange of information. On the basis of an appropriate categorization, it might also be worth investigating in more detail the level of success and effectiveness of different (kinds of) policy responses in varying interaction situations. However, these questions are beyond the scope of our study. We limit ourselves to investigating (1) whether or not collective policy responses have occurred and (2) whether or not a significant potential for further improvement through collective policy responses continues to exist.

The assessment of the potential for further improvement relies on the subjective expert judgment of the case-study authors. Data reflect the situation in 2001 and 2002 that may have changed as a result of subsequent developments. Data do not reflect cases of merely marginal potential for improvement. In cases of Behavioral Interaction, we took the core obligations of the source institution as a given that could not be altered in order to modify the effect on the target. The disruptive influence of the Convention on International Trade in Endangered Species of Wild Fauna and Flora (CITES) on the WTO (chapter 7), for example, could in principle be ended if CITES stopped restricting international trade. However, this would in effect mean dissolving CITES.

We may expect that collective policy responses occur more frequently in cases of disruptive effects than in cases producing synergy. Experimental psychology has found that people react more strongly to the risk of losses (conflict) than to the promise of additional benefits (Tversky and Kahnemann 1981, 1984). Moreover, disruptive interaction creates aggrieved actors who will struggle to remedy the situation, while synergistic interaction produces merely winners, even if the opportunities for cooperation gains are not fully exploited. Accordingly, actors in both institutions involved may tend to consume the additional benefit without engaging in further efforts, while disruptive effects will attract their attention more easily.

With respect to the potential for further improvement, it may be particularly interesting to explore whether or not such a potential exists more frequently in cases that have or have not led to a collective response yet. Given our expectation that in particular a number of synergistic cases may not have been responded to at all, we may on the one hand expect a potential for further improvement in particular in cases that have not drawn a collective response yet. On the other hand, existing responses may have easily left unexploited the potential for improvement.

Key Insights from the Analysis of 163 Cases of Institutional Interaction

In the following pages, we present key findings from the empirical analysis of the 163 cases of institutional interaction of our sample. After providing a brief overview of the sample, we present and analyze key findings in three areas: synergy and disruption, policy responses, and potential for future improvement. Given the methodology of case selection, we are confident that our results at least approximate and roughly reflect the overall situation in international and EU environmental governance, although the figures may be expected to differ to some extent for other samples drawn from this area. However, our insights are evidently tied to our specific sample. We caution that the sample is not statistically representative and therefore does not allow for the generalization of insights to other populations of cases. In particular, we do not claim that the empirical results hold for interaction phenomena beyond international and EU environmental governance.

The Universe of Cases of Our Sample   Table 13.2 provides aggregate information on our dataset in total and according to the three kinds of horizontal and vertical interaction. The cases of the sample are roughly evenly distributed across the three dimensions of interaction: our sample contains fifty-eight cases of horizontal interaction between international institutions, forty-nine cases of horizontal interaction between EU legal instruments, and fifty-six cases of vertical interaction between international and EU instruments.

As can be seen in table 13.2, more than two-thirds of our cases of institutional interaction occurred within one policy field, namely environmental protection. In

Table 13.2
The sample of cases of institutional interaction

Variables	Horizontal international		Horizontal EU		Vertical		Total	
	No.	%	No.	%	No.	%	No.	%
Totals	**58**	**100**	**49**	**100**	**56**	**100**	**163**	**100**
Synergy	27	46.6	34	69.4	41	73.2	102	62.6
Disruption	19	32.8	9	18.4	13	23.2	41	25.2
Neutral/unclear	12	20.7	6	12.2	2	3.6	20	12.3
Same policy field	27	46.6	38	77.6	45	80.4	110	67.5
Different policy fields	31	53.4	11	22.4	11	19.6	53	32.5
Intentional	18	31.0	18	36.7	25	44.6	61	37.4
Unintentional	39	67.2	28	57.1	30	53.6	97	59.5
Uncertain	1	1.7	3	6.1	1	1.8	5	3.1
Response	33	56.9	14	28.6	15	26.8	62	38.0
No response	25	43.1	35	71.4	41	73.2	101	62.0
No further potential	14	24.1	12	24.5	20	35.7	46	28.2
Further potential	21	36.2	13	26.5	19	33.9	53	32.5
Unclear	23	39.7	24	49.0	17	30.4	64	39.3

Source: Own compilation from database reflected in the appendix.

slightly less than one-third of the cases, the interaction crossed the border separating two policy fields. Interaction between institutions belonging to different policy fields is more frequent at the international level than both at the EU level and vertically.

Although the majority of cases occurred unintentionally, policymakers in the source institution collectively employed institutional interaction as a means to pursue their objectives in a significant share of cases. Nearly two-fifths of all identified cases of interaction were triggered intentionally by the source institution. Intentional interaction was somewhat more common at the EU level than internationally, which may reflect the comparatively integrated framework of EU policymaking. Vertical interaction was even more frequently triggered intentionally, partly because implementation of international commitments at the EU level has been coded as intentional throughout. In any event, policymakers in international and EU environmental governance already exploit opportunities arising from institutional interaction at least partially.

Data on the quality of effect, policy responses, and the potential for further improvement related to the aggregate of our sample are discussed in more detail in the next subsection. More detailed information about the distribution of our sample across the general causal mechanisms is presented in the context of the discussion of ideal types of institutional interaction later in this chapter.

Quality of Effects: Synergy Dominates, but Disruption Occurs   Institutional interaction was found to lead to synergy with the target institution and thus improve the effectiveness of international and European governance in more than 60 percent of our cases. Only about one-quarter of the cases identified resulted in clear disruption. The balance is made up of twenty cases in which the effect was neutral or in which scientific uncertainty or uncertainty about the relationship between the effect and the target institution's objective prevented a clear-cut assessment. Disruption appears to be somewhat more frequent at the international level (nearly one-third). However, synergistic effects dominate at all three levels of interaction, namely interaction between international institutions, between EU legal instruments, and vertically between international and EU institutions (table 13.2).

This finding suggests that institutional interaction may not primarily be a bad thing that ought to be diminished as much as possible. It contrasts with conventional wisdom, as reflected in the relevant literature that has so far emphasized the problems rather than the opportunities arising from the interaction of international and EU legal instruments. Higher political salience of disruptive cases may be explained by the fact that people generally react more strongly to the risk of losses (conflict) than to the promise of additional benefits (Tversky and Kahnemann 1981, 1984). The predominance of synergistic interaction also casts doubt on the widespread belief that institutional interaction is a phenomenon of institutional overflow ("treaty congestion," Brown Weiss 1993), which threatens to lead to dysfunctional duplication of work and conflict in international and EU environmental affairs. Our sample suggests that institutional fragmentation may also provide a valuable asset for skilful policymaking to enhance environmental governance. Policies to minimize allegedly undesirably interaction could risk sacrificing this asset.

Whereas our finding calls to mind that synergy must not be neglected, it does not suggest that synergy is necessarily more important than disruption, or that everything is all right with international and EU environmental governance. Although we do not have supporting evidence, we cannot exclude that the aggregate effects of the less numerous disruptive cases weigh more heavily than the aggregate effects of the more numerous synergistic cases. To calculate the net effects of institutional interaction, one would have to aggregate cases and assign a particular weight to every single case (Underdal 2004; Gehring 2004), which is beyond the scope of our analysis. There may also be more scope to reduce disruption than to enhance synergy.

The distribution of synergy and disruption across our general causal mechanisms provides few additional insights. For all three causal mechanisms, synergy by far outweighs disruption. It is noteworthy that disruption appears to be comparatively rare and neutral/unclear effects rather frequent in cases of Cognitive Interaction. Overall, however, there is no strong correlation between the quality of effect and the causal mechanisms of institutional interaction. Accordingly, Cramer's V describing the strength of the correlation between the two nominal variables as a value between 0 (no correlation) and 1 (complete correlation) is 0.255 and thus comparatively low (table 13.3).

Distinguishing interaction staying within the same policy field from interaction involving different policy fields is more revealing (table 13.4). As expected, synergy is much more frequent in the former case, accounting for more than 80 percent of the cases of interaction within the same policy field. In contrast, a majority of about 57 percent of the cases of institutional interaction transcending the borders of a policy field have resulted in disruption. Also, 30 of the 41 cases of disruption occurred between institutions located in different policy fields. In contrast, about 9 out of 10 synergistic cases (91 of 102) were found to be within one policy field. With some

Table 13.3
Quality of effect and causal mechanisms

	Cognitive interaction		Interaction through commitment		Behavioral interaction		Total	
	No.	%	No.	%	No.	%	No.	%
Synergy	10	62.5	36	54.5	56	69.1	102	62.6
Disruption	1	6.3	16	24.2	24	29.6	41	25.2
Neutral/unclear	5	31.3	14	21.2	1	1.2	20	12.3
Total	16	100	66	100	81	100	163	100
Cramer's V				0.255				

Source: Own compilation from database reflected in the appendix.

Table 13.4
Quality of effect, policy fields, and intentionality

Quality of effect	Horizontal international Same PF		Horizontal international Different PFs		Horizontal EU Same PF		Horizontal EU Different PFs		Vertical Same PF		Vertical Different PFs		Total Same PF		Total Different PFs	
	No.	%	No.	%	No.	%	No.	%	No.	%	No.	%	No.	%	No.	%
Synergy	20	74.1	7	22.6	31	81.6	3	27.3	40	88.9	1	9.1	91	82.7	11	20.8
Disruption	4	14.8	15	48.4	2	5.3	7	63.6	5	11.1	8	72.7	11	10.0	30	56.6
Neutral/unclear	3	11.1	9	29.0	5	13.2	1	9.1	0	0.0	2	18.2	8	7.3	12	22.6
Total	27	100	31	100	38	100	11	100	45	100	11	100	110	100	53	100
Cramer's V	0.516				0.632				0.736				0.605			

Quality of effect	Horizontal international Intentional		Horizontal international Unintentional		Horizontal EU Intentional		Horizontal EU Unintentional		Vertical Intentional		Vertical Unintentional		Total Intentional		Total Unintentional	
	No.	%	No.	%	No.	%	No.	%	No.	%	No.	%	No.	%	No.	%
Synergy	11	61.1	15	38.5	15	83.3	17	60.7	21	84.0	20	66.7	47	77.0	52	53.6
Disruption	0	0.0	19	48.7	2	11.1	6	21.4	3	12.0	10	33.3	5	8.2	35	36.1
Neutral/unclear	7	38.9	5	12.8	1	5.6	5	17.9	1	4.0	0	0.0	9	14.8	10	10.3
Total	18	100	39	100	18	100	28	100	25	100	30	100	61	100	97	100
Cramer's V	0.498				0.244				0.282				0.312			

Source: Own compilation from database reflected in the appendix; assessment of intentionality excludes five cases in which intentionality remained uncertain; PF = policy field.

variation, the picture is similar for all three dimensions of interaction. Whether an interaction occurs between institutions within the same or across different policy fields is far more relevant for the quality of the effect. The value for Cramer's V of more than 0.5 for all dimensions provides a strong indication of the relevance of the correlation (table 13.4).

Also confirming our expectations, disruption has in most cases occurred as an unintended side effect. According to our sample, policymakers in international and EU environmental governance apparently employ institutional interaction primarily to create synergy. Intentional disruption appears to be the exception rather than the rule. Only 1 out of 8 disruptive cases was triggered intentionally by the source institution (5 of 40) as compared with nearly half of the synergistic cases (47 of 99). More than three-fourths of the cases of intentional interaction resulted in synergy, while this was only the case for less than 55 percent of the unintentional cases (disruption: less than 10 percent and more than 35 percent, respectively). Although with a Cramer's V of 0.312 the correlation of the quality of effect with intentionality is noticeable, it is less relevant than the correlation with the policy-field variable. Whereas there is hardly any relevant correlation for horizontal interaction between EU instruments and for vertical interaction, Cramer's V of 0.498 indicates a comparatively strong correlation between quality of effect and intentionality at the international level, which may be traced back to a comparatively high number of disruptive cases that are exclusively unintentional (table 13.4).

Our figures do not confirm the expectation that intentionally created disruption is particularly rare at the EU level (due to the comparatively integrated legislative process). While the limited number of cases does not allow us to draw any firm conclusions, it may be observed that both cases of intentional disruption between EU legal instruments contained in our sample followed the causal mechanism of Behavioral Interaction. A preliminary explanation for their occurrence is offered in the section on Behavioral Interaction in this chapter.

Policy Responses: Frequent in Case of Disruption, Rare in Case of Synergy   Collective policy responses were identified in less than 40 percent of the cases of interaction contained in our sample (table 13.2). While this share may appear low, it needs to be taken into account that more than 60 percent of our cases had a synergistic effect. In line with our expectations, more than 80 percent of these synergistic cases were not responded to at all but were "consumed" without further action (table 13.5). At all three levels of interaction, response action focused on cases of disruptive

Table 13.5
Policy responses, quality of effect, and potential for further improvement

Policy response	Horizontal international						Horizontal EU						Vertical						Total					
	Synergy		Disruption		Neutral/unclear		Synergy		Disruption		Neutral/unclear		Synergy		Disruption		Neutral/unclear		Synergy		Disruption		Neutral/unclear	
	No.	%	No.	%	No.	%	No.	%	No.	%	No.	%	No.	%	No.	%	No.	%	No.	%	No.	%	No.	%
Response	9	33.3	16	84.2	8	66.7	3	8.8	9	100	2	33.3	5	12.2	9	69.2	1	50.0	17	16.7	34	82.9	11	55.0
No response	18	66.7	3	15.8	4	33.3	31	91.2	0	0.0	4	66.7	36	87.8	4	30.8	1	50.0	85	83.3	7	17.1	9	45.0
Total	27	100	19	100	12	100	34	100	9	100	6	100	41	100	13	100	2	100	102	100	41	100	20	100
Cramer's V	0.462						0.770						0.550						0.593					

Policy response	Horizontal international						Horizontal EU						Vertical						Total					
	Further potential		No further potential		Unclear		Further potential		No further potential		Unclear		Further potential		No further potential		Unclear		Further potential		No further potential		Unclear	
	No.	%	No.	%	No.	%	No.	%	No.	%	No.	%	No.	%	No.	%	No.	%	No.	%	No.	%	No.	%
Response	16	76.2	5	35.7	12	52.2	8	61.5	0	0.0	6	25.0	7	36.8	1	5.0	7	41.2	31	58.5	6	13.0	25	39.1
No response	5	23.8	9	64.3	11	47.8	5	38.5	12	100	18	75.0	12	63.2	19	95.0	10	58.8	22	41.5	40	87.0	39	60.9
Total	21	100	14	100	23	100	13	100	12	100	24	100	19	100	20	100	17	100	53	100	46	100	64	100
Cramer's V	0.321						0.492						0.369						0.364					

Source: Own compilation from database reflected in the appendix; calculation of Cramer's V for further potential does not take into account unclear cases.

effects that accounted for a majority of the identified responses (34 of 62). At the EU level, all disruptive cases were responded to in one way or the other. At all levels, there is a strong correlation between the variables of quality of effect and policy response (Cramer's V for total: 0.593).

Response action occurred in about 57 percent of the cases located at the international level and thus far more frequently than at the EU level and with respect to the vertical cases (both between 25 and 30 percent; table 13.2). This imbalance can be traced back to two factors. First, disruptive cases that are generally responded to more frequently are more abundant at the international level. Second, synergistic cases appear more likely to be responded to internationally (more than 30 percent) than at the other levels of interaction (table 13.5). We may speculate that this latter difference may be accounted for by the greater prominence of a formal exchange of information between institutions at the international level. This type of response may be less likely to occur vertically as well as at the EU level, where an information exchange may not be formally established between different EU legal instruments but occurs through the European Commission.

Potential for Further Improvement Is Widespread   In a significant number of cases, a potential for further improvement by means of additional policy responses was identified. Experts saw a potential for further improvement in about 30 percent of the cases of interaction, while they found no such potential in roughly another 30 percent of the cases. In about 40 percent of the cases, the situation remained unclear (table 13.2). Overall, there is a significant and widespread potential for enhancing EU and international environmental governance to be exploited by a more systematic "interplay management" (Stokke 2001).

Somewhat counterintuitive, potential for further improvement appears to exist in particular where response action has already been taken. The Cramer's V of 0.364 points to a comparatively weak but still relevant correlation. Hence, in a majority of cases in which a potential for improvement exists, actors have already attempted to improve the situation by means of collective action, but have not realized the full potential in most of these cases. Only in the case of vertical interaction had a majority of cases in which experts identified a significant potential not drawn a collective political response. This may be due to the hierarchical relationship between international and EU law, so that it may be particularly difficult to pursue collective action to enhance existing synergy or mitigate conflict. However, there are cases at all levels of interaction in which an existing potential for improvement has not yet been attempted to be realized by means of collective action (overall twenty-two cases, accounting for nearly 15 percent of the cases of our sample) (table 13.5).

From our data, it appears that significant benefits from enhancing synergy have been neglected so far and remain to be reaped. Whereas synergistic cases of interaction more rarely display a potential for further improvement than disruptive cases, existing opportunities for enhancing synergy have received far less attention than the threat of disruption. A potential for further improvement was found in all except one of the twenty-seven disruptive cases that allowed for a clear assessment, as compared with twenty-four of the sixty-four synergistic cases (table 13.6).[1] Also, two-thirds (twenty-one of thirty-one) of the cases that have been responded to and still have further potential were disruptive. However, about three-fourths of the cases (sixteen of twenty-two cases) that have *not* been responded to but possess a potential for further improvement were synergistic. Accordingly, Cramer's V indicates a less relevant correlation between further potential and quality of effect for cases that have not been responded to than for those that have (table 13.6).

A number of interesting questions may be explored in the future. For example, is existing potential for improvement through targeted policy responses more easily exploited in cases of interaction within the same policy field than in interaction across different policy fields, as one might expect? There are only six cases in which policy responses appear to have led to a full exploitation of the potential for im-

Table 13.6
Quality of effect, policy responses, and potential for further improvement

	Response				No response				Total			
	Further potential		No further potential		Further potential		No further potential		Further potential		No further potential	
Quality of effect	No.	%	No.	%	No.	%	No.	%	No.	%	No.	%
Synergy	8	25.8	2	33.3	16	72.7	38	95.0	24	45.3	40	87.0
Disruption	21	67.7	0	0.0	5	22.7	1	2.5	26	49.1	1	2.2
Neutral/unclear	2	6.5	4	66.7	1	4.5	1	2.5	3	5.7	5	10.9
Total	31	100	6	100	22	100	40	100	53	100	46	100
Cramer's V	0.645				0.336				0.525			

Source: Own compilation from database reflected in the appendix, excluding cases with unclear potential for further improvement.

provement (table 13.6). Of these six cases, two involved institutional interaction within the same policy field (not reflecting the distribution within our overall sample). This is not in line with our expectation that interaction within the same policy field should be more conducive to creating synergy and mitigating disruption. However, the limited number of cases does not allow us to draw any firm conclusions. Moreover, our analysis did not allow us to assess *to what extent* a potential for improvement has been realized through policy responses.

Weberian Ideal Types of Institutional Interaction

In chapter 2, we introduced three causal mechanisms that provide the analytic framework of this study. Cognitive Interaction reflects a learning process and relies on the transfer of information. Interaction through Commitment is based on the commitment of some members of the target institution to the obligations of the source institution and an ensuing change of their preferences. Behavioral Interaction occurs within the issue areas but outside the decision-making processes of either of the institutions involved. The basic causal mechanisms reflect the causal pathways through which influence is channeled from the source institution to the target institution.

In the following, we move beyond these three basic causal mechanisms and develop more specific ideal types of institutional interaction that help us understand how interaction operates and why some cases generate disruptive effects, while others create synergy. We do not attempt to modify, change, or replace the basic causal mechanisms. Instead, we endeavor to identify patterns of interaction that elucidate systematically the different forms and effects of varying cases of interaction following the same causal mechanism. Chapters 3–12 of this volume have illustrated the variance of forms and effects of different cases of interaction. To take account of this variance, we further specify and differentiate the general causal mechanisms by developing ideal types of institutional interaction.

The construction of models or ideal types is a well-known method of social-science inquiry. However, types and classes have explanatory power only if their existence is based on a distinct logic (Weber 1976, 1–11). Mere grouping or classification of empirical cases according to certain individual properties does not explain anything. Instead, an abstract, theoretical reconstruction of their inherent logics is needed. Weberian ideal types are abstract models of social interaction phenomena, to which real-world cases can be compared.

While Weberian ideal types are by definition mutually exclusive, real-world cases may reflect aspects of more than one model at the same time. Ideal types are necessarily mutually exclusive because they follow their own distinct rationales. They are constructed to elucidate the important components of these rationales. As abstract models, ideal types reflect the basic pattern of a real-world situation appropriately, or they do not, but they cannot be empirically right or wrong (Snidal 1985). However, they grossly reduce the complexity of real-world cases, and are not intended to provide precise descriptions of all properties of these cases. "Mixed cases" that are concurrently driven by two or more of the basic rationales and therefore difficult to classify may exist.

We constructed Weberian ideal types of institutional interaction in an iterative three-step process oscillating between inductive and deductive reasoning. First, we systematically assessed our sample of 163 cases of institutional interaction. On the basis of the coding of these cases as reflected in the database in the appendix, we grouped the cases of our sample following the same causal mechanism in numerous different ways in accordance with the variables spelled out above in order to identify systematic patterns. Second, we constructed distinct rationales of the resulting groups of cases. In essence, this step was a matter of deductive reasoning directed at reconstructing the basic logic driving a number of cases. It aimed to identify groupings that are based on systematic differences in their underlying logics. As a result, we identified two ideal types of Cognitive Interaction and three types of Interaction through Commitment. In contrast, it proved difficult to identify ideal types of Behavioral Interaction. Third, we sought to assign the cases of Cognitive Interaction and Interaction through Commitment within our sample to the corresponding ideal types. This exercise put our families of Weberian ideal types to a first empirical test. That all our cases of Cognitive Interaction and Interaction through Commitment could be assigned to the two families of ideal types indicates that our ideal types cover a broad range of existing interaction phenomena.

This process of deriving ideal types of institutional interaction revealed that few possible groupings of cases lend themselves to constructing distinct rationales. While cases could be grouped in various ways, most groups did not allow for the deductive development of consistent underlying logics. For example, one could group cases of Interaction through Commitment according to their effects (synergistic versus disruptive) or the intentionality of action on the part of the source institution, but it proved impossible to identify an abstract model of the underlying rationale fitting the relevant cases. Likewise, cases of horizontal interaction at the EU level are not systematically different from those at the international level, or from the vertical cases between international and EU institutions. Ideal types of Cognitive Interaction eventually identified vary with respect to the variable intentionality, while ideal types of Interaction through Commitment possess distinct key differences.

Although our ideal types of interaction are based on our specific sample of cases, they are relevant for other samples both from international and EU environmental affairs and beyond. The types are generally applicable, because they do not originate from mere classification of the cases within our sample of cases. Instead, they are the result of deductive reasoning that addresses the question of what drives the cases of a particular class. There is no reason to assume that cases beyond our sample cannot reasonably be analyzed by comparing them with our ideal types of interaction. Hypotheses derived from these abstract models can well be tested against other samples of cases. However, our ideal types are linked to our specific sample in two ways. First, we could only identify types of interaction that occur within our sample. Consequently, there might be cases that do not fit these types and require the development of additional ones. Second, the empirical cases and their properties as well as the distribution of cases between types of interaction can be assumed to change between samples. We submit that our ideal types also provide a useful framework of analysis of institutional interaction beyond our sample of cases.

Ideal Types of Cognitive Interaction

Cognitive Interaction can be conceived of as a form of learning across the boundaries of institutions. Cases driven by this causal mechanism are based on the transfer of information alone. Members of the target institution must voluntarily change their perceptions in response to new information provided by the source institution. Cognitive interaction is the least intrusive causal mechanism because it depends completely on the voluntary acceptance of the members of the target institution. The source institution does not exert significant pressure on the target to adapt. It does not establish obligations or otherwise change preferences of the members of the target institution against their conviction.

Intentionality is the crucial distinction between types of Cognitive Interaction. While "learning" cannot be imposed, it may or may not be intentionally triggered by the source institution. If the source institution intentionally requests the target to change in a certain respect, the attention of the members of the target institution is deliberately drawn to the effects of their decisions on the source institution. If

Cognitive Interaction is not intended by the source institution, members of the target institution use an institutional arrangement or policy idea of the source institution as a model. Hence, intentionality determines whether the center of activity rests with the source institution or the target institution.

Other possible distinctions did not provide a solid foundation for the development of distinct rationales. For example, there is no reason to believe that learning with synergistic effects for the target institution is founded on a rationale that is fundamentally different from that of learning with a disruptive effect on the target. Likewise, learning across the boundaries of policy fields or among institutions with different objectives does not seem to be fundamentally different from learning within the same policy field or between institutions with similar objectives, although the latter might be somewhat more frequent.

Policy Model

If Cognitive Interaction is unintentionally triggered, members of the target institution voluntarily use some aspect of the source institution as a Policy Model. For example, the compliance system under the Montreal Protocol for the protection of the ozone layer influenced the negotiations on the compliance system under the Kyoto Protocol on climate change because it provided a model of how to supervise implementation and deal with cases of possible noncompliance (Oberthür and Ott 1999, 215–222; Werksman 2005; chapter 3). The members of the Montreal Protocol did not establish the model *in order* to influence the Kyoto Protocol. They did also not have the ability to impose their model on the target. Instead, the Montreal Protocol presented an institutional arrangement that the members of the Kyoto Protocol conceived of as a useful precedent in developing solutions for their problem.

In the Policy-Model type of Cognitive Interaction, action seems to concentrate in the target institution. This impression is due to two characteristics of these cases. On the one hand, members of the source institution will find it difficult to foresee which kind of information or decision originating from their collective decision-making process might prompt interaction of this kind. Any institutional arrangement, decision, or scientific or technological information from the source institution might serve as a Policy Model. And numerous types of actors might pick up the information or idea and feed it into the decision-making process of the target institution. This may be done, for example, by one or more member states, by an interested nongovernmental organization, by the secretariat of the target institution, or even by relevant individuals. These actors may, but do not have to be active within the source institution, because information and ideas can also be obtained by surveying the field, reading reports, or examining institutional arrangements from outside. On the other hand, it is the actors making the institutional decisions within the target institution (usually the member states) whom the new information must convince so that they change their preferences. Only then can we expect a new constellation of interests to emerge, which might lead to modified decisions within the target institution.

Learning from a Policy Model is not limited to the unchanged acceptance of a policy model developed elsewhere. Frequently, a model is not simply copied into the target institution ("simple learning"), but it is modified and adapted so as to fit the particular needs of the target. "Learning" is thus regularly a complex process of the collective examination and appraisal of the model followed by its modification and development ("complex learning"; see Haas 1990).

Interaction of the Policy-Model type can be expected to strengthen the effectiveness of the target institution, while being indifferent to the effectiveness of the source institution. Effects will be largely supportive of the target's objectives, because the interaction can materialize only if the target members collectively consider the policy model to be useful. Actors cannot be forced to learn and they will not pick up alleged models that they are not convinced of. However, it cannot be entirely excluded that actors learn "wrong" lessons that prove to hamper rather than enhance effectiveness. If learning from a policy model leads to better decisions in the target institution, this will (at least potentially) strengthen the target's influence on the behavior of relevant actors within its issue area (outcome level), which will (possibly) also enhance the effects at the impact level. In contrast, the source institution will usually not be significantly affected, because learning within the target institution and its effects at the outcome and impact levels could only accidentally feed back onto the original source institution.

The Policy-Model type of interaction highlights that members of an institution can enhance the effectiveness of their governance efforts by learning from occurrences taking place within other institutions. Any institution—be it international or European, environmental or other—may learn in this way from any other institution that displays appropriate precedents and deals with relevant problems. Frequently, negotiators operating in the framework of international and EU institutions already look for precedents. However, this process is so far frequently ad hoc and incidental. Especially in international institutions, learning processes may be further promoted by mandating secretariats and conferences of the parties to systematically look for and investigate models existing in other institutions. Elaborating and institutionalizing routines and mechanisms for doing so may enhance the potential of interinstitutional learning so as to foster effective governance.

Request for Assistance

Cognitive Interaction may also take the form of an intentional request by the source institution for assistance from the target institution. The attention of actors within the target institution is thereby drawn to a particular aspect of the outside world that they had so far not taken due account of—at least in the eyes of the source institution. The source institution still has little ability to force the target to adapt without the latter's consent and remains completely dependent on the goodwill of the target. For example, several wildlife-protection treaties have asked the Convention on International Trade in Endangered Species of Wild Fauna and Flora (CITES) for assistance. And CITES itself requested assistance from specialized international institutions such as the World Customs Organization (WCO) and Interpol to reinforce the effectiveness of its trade restrictions (chapter 7).

In contrast to learning from a Policy Model, the source institution largely frames the learning process in cases of Request for Assistance. It intentionally triggers the interaction by a decision without which interaction of this type would not occur. Moreover, a Request for Assistance will usually be formally transferred by the secretariat of the source institution to the secretariat of the target institution, and it will be officially fed into the decision-making process of the latter. Evidently, the source institution cannot force the target institution to adapt. Some learning in the form of an adaptation of preferences to new information is necessary to produce a reaction within the target institution. Actors learn either that their institution produces side effects that the source institution considers undesirable or that an adaptation of their institution could further strengthen the effectiveness of the source institution.

Its rationale suggests that a Request for Assistance will generate synergistic or at least neutral effects for the target institution. We cannot expect to find cases with disruptive effects on the target institution, because a successful Request for Assistance requires that actors operating within the target institution voluntarily take action in response. It is hardly conceivable that these actors would adopt measures in response to a Request for Assistance that are detrimental for the target's policy objectives. Even if "negative" learning is unlikely to occur, Requests for Assistance will not necessarily reinforce the effectiveness of the target institution. Considering frequent overlaps in membership between the institutions involved, the target institution might find it difficult to reject a request even if it does not benefit from responding. Hence, we may well expect to find cases in which the effects on the target institution are indeterminate.

Whereas the Request for Assistance is directed at the target institution, it is ultimately intended to further the effectiveness of the source institution by triggering a feedback case of Behavioral Interaction. If CITES asks the World Customs Organization to adapt the international customs codes to its needs, it first of all asks for a corresponding decision of the WCO. However, CITES members issue the request because they expect the application of adapted customs codes to facilitate the effective implementation of CITES obligations. This second case of interaction occurs within the issue areas governed by the institutions involved outside their decision-making apparatuses, when customs officers in the port of Hamburg or at the John F. Kennedy Airport in New York check imported goods.

Requests for Assistance provide an instrument for furthering effective international and EU governance. Although the source institution cannot force the target institution to adapt its rules, a Request for Assistance enables an institution to draw on other institutions in order to enhance its own effectiveness. To this end, members of international and possibly also of EU institutions might actively search for opportunities to instigate learning processes within other institutions. Since the success of a Request for Assistance largely depends on the positive reaction by the target institution, the endeavor will be particularly promising if the requested adaptation is easily compatible with the objectives of the target institution, or, even better, if it supports them.

Cases of Cognitive Interaction in the Sample

Significant Cognitive Interaction seems to be a comparatively rare phenomenon. Only 16 of the 163 cases of our sample (9.8 percent) fall into this category. They are evenly divided between the two types of Policy Model and Request for Assistance (see table 13.7). The reasons may be assumed to differ between the two types. Clear-cut Policy-Model cases with significant effects are difficult to detect. Learning from a Policy Model is a ubiquitous, gradual, and frequently tacit phenomenon that does not always produce traceable evidence. Since we focused on cases of clear and significant influence, some Policy-Model cases may have evaded identification. In contrast, Requests for Assistance are readily observable because they are usually reflected in a formal decision of the source institution. While opportunities for requesting assistance may be limited, interested actors may also fail to seize further

Table 13.7
Cases of Cognitive Interaction in our sample

	Policy model		Request for assistance		Total	
	No.	%	No.	%	No.	%
Totals	8	100	8	100	16	100
Horizontal international	5	62.5	8	100	13	81.3
Horizontal EU	1	12.5	0	0.0	1	6.3
Vertical	2	25.0	0	0.0	2	12.5
Synergy	6	75.0	4	50.0	10	62.5
Disruption	1	12.5	0	0.0	1	6.3
Neutral/unclear	1	12.5	4	50.0	5	31.3
Same policy field	7	87.5	4	50.0	11	68.8
Different policy field	1	12.5	4	50.0	5	31.3
Response	1	12.5	3	37.5	4	25.0
No response	7	87.5	5	62.5	12	75.0

Source: Own compilation from database reflected in the appendix.

opportunities that exist in environmental governance. Our sample comprises eight cases of Request for Assistance, seven of which involve CITES either as the source or as the target institution. The CITES Secretariat has actively pursued this type of interaction (see chapter 7). Similar requests have been reported in the literature, for example with respect to the Montreal Protocol asking the World Customs Organization (WCO) to adapt (Oberthür 2001).

Our sample suggests that Request for Assistance is particularly relevant to the horizontally structured realm of international institutions. All our cases of this type involve horizontal interaction between international institutions, while none of the horizontal interactions between EU institutions and vertical interactions between international and EU institutions fit this model (table 13.7). There are reasons for this concentration of cases. Horizontal requests for assistance are less likely in the more integrative institutional framework of EU decision making. Having the exclusive competence within the EU to initiate legislative proposals, the European Commission may be expected to address emerging issues of coordination between institutions in the process of preparing such proposals. "Interservice consultations" are designed to involve, and get agreement of, all relevant Commission services. As a result, formal requests for assistance possess less relevance within the EU. They are also unlikely to occur vertically between international institutions and EU legal instruments because of the status of the EU as a subject of international law that concludes international agreements alongside nation-states (Schweitzer 2003; see also Oberthür 1999). The EU is a party to most international treaty systems dealt with in this study and pursues its interests in changes of an international regime in the same way as any other party, namely in the relevant international negotiations. Where international regimes and organizations, in turn, ask the EU to adapt, the EU is not totally free but is usually required to implement internationally agreed-on rules in much the same way as any other party. Such a request would thus initiate a different causal mechanism, namely "Interaction through Commitment."

Our sample demonstrates that learning from a Policy Model is possible across all formal boundaries and levels, so that it occurs within and across policy fields as well as at all levels of interaction (table 13.7). We found cases between international institutions, between EU institutions, and, vertically, between international and EU institutions. Moreover, learning from a Policy Model is possible across policy fields, although the fact that this occurred in only one of our eight cases suggests that it might be easier and more probable between institutions operating within the same policy field. The fact that response action was rare may be attributed to the fact that source institutions remain totally unaffected by the interaction, while target institutions already exploited the learning opportunities inherent in the case.

As expected, cases of the Policy-Model type are primarily about creating synergy. We identified two deviant cases (table 13.7). One case had disruptive effects. In the mid-1990s, several parties to the climate change regime wanted to employ the model of the technology and economic assessment panels of the Montreal Protocol (on the latter see Parson 1993, 2003) for feeding scientific advice into the political decision-making process. Other parties blocked the adoption of a similar arrangement precisely because of its effectiveness. From the "model" of the Montreal Protocol, they had learned which features of the science-policy interface should be avoided in order to limit the effectiveness of scientific advice. On the basis of the consensus principle that prevails in many international institutions, minorities may thus "learn" to block certain decisions. The quality of the effect of this type of interaction therefore depends on whether the lessons learned from the Policy Model benefit the leaders or the laggards within the target institution. The other deviant case is simply difficult to judge. The Montreal Protocol provided to the WTO a model for admissible trade restrictions for environmental protection in a multilateral framework, which takes interests of nonparties duly into account. It is difficult to determine whether this is conducive to the objectives of WTO (because it mitigates conflict over environmentally motivated trade restrictions) or not (because it leads to acceptance of such restrictions under certain circumstances).

None of the Requests for Assistance in our sample resulted in disruption. Four of our eight cases created synergistic effects for the target institution. These cases related to interaction between CITES and other wildlife treaties. The other four cases had neutral or insignificant effects on the policy objectives of the target institutions. Three of them related to CITES' Requests for Assistance to institutions located in other policy fields (WCO and Interpol). It may not be surprising that Requests for Assistance occur both within the same policy field and across different policy fields. That response action appears to occur more frequently in cases of Request for Assistance than in the Policy-Model cases may be due to the fact that Requests for Assistance per se establish some kind of contact between the source and the target institution that may lead to further coordination or joint activities. However, the number of cases is too small to draw any firm conclusions.

Ideal Types of Interaction through Commitment

It is characteristic of cases of Interaction through Commitment that commitments entered into by the members of the source institution change the constellation of interests within the target institution tangibly. Actors have an interest in being consistent and developing a reputation of keeping their promises. They may also be interested in subjecting others to costly obligations that they have already accepted. Options that are in conformity with the obligation of the source institution are therefore adopted with a higher probability, while agreement on options that are in conflict with obligations of the source institution is less likely. Being aware of the binding force of obligations, actors may even gain an interest in adopting commitments in one institution in order to frame the policy choices available in another institution. As a result, commitments of the source institution may be exported to the target institution or may serve to prevent adoption of contradicting decisions in the target. In contrast to Cognitive Interaction, Interaction through Commitment does not rely on a transfer of information and learning, but on the binding force of obligations. While only the source institution can initiate Interaction through Commitment, it is still not capable of *determining* the action of the target institution.

The causal mechanism of Interaction through Commitment covers a broad range of phenomena. Some of them create disruption, like the pending conflict between the WTO and several multilateral environmental agreements (chapter 8), while others generate synergy. Some of the synergistic cases of interaction reach across the boundaries of policy fields, while some disruptive ones remain within a single policy field. Some are intentionally created, while others occur unintentionally. All these criteria might lend themselves to creating a typology, but they do not support abstract model types that rely on a clear rationale and cover all relevant cases of our sample.

While cases of Interaction through Commitment require a significant overlap of the memberships and the issue areas of the institutions involved, institutions must differ in some important dimension to create momentum for interaction. In contrast to Cognitive Interaction, Interaction through Commitment presupposes that some countries are members of both institutions. Otherwise, no actors within the target institution would be committed to obligations originating from the source institution. Likewise, issue areas must overlap somewhat. Otherwise, no commitment of the source institution could matter directly for the decision-making process of the target institution. However, a significant difference between the institutions is also a prerequisite for Interaction through Commitment. In the hypothetical situation of two identical institutions, we could not expect significant interaction between them.

The three ideal types of Interaction through Commitment developed in the following paragraphs vary with respect to their values of the variable "key differences" introduced in the first part of this chapter. Cases of the ideal type of Jurisdictional Delimitation are driven by different objectives of the interacting institutions. Cases of the type of Nested Institutions are driven by significantly different memberships of the two institutions involved. Cases of the type of Additional Means gain their relevance from significantly different means of the institutions involved. In each of these ideal types, institutions are assumed to be congruent as to the other two potential key differences. As a result, the underlying rationales of these three types of interaction can be expected to differ profoundly because interinstitutional influence relies on exactly one distinct key difference for each ideal type. To avoid confusion, it is repeated here that real-world cases of institutional interaction may well be driven by more than a single rationale. These "mixed" cases do not require separate ideal types.

Jurisdictional Delimitation

Cases of Interaction through Commitment driven by differences in objectives create a demand for the delimitation of jurisdictions. We call this ideal type of interaction

"Jurisdictional Delimitation." In the ideal type, the same group of member states addresses the same issue by identical means within two institutions with different objectives. As a result, actors are confronted with the prospect of conflicting obligations concerning the same subject. Consider that international trade is regulated within the WTO for the purpose of liberalizing trade and thus removing obstacles to international trade. At the same time, the Cartagena Biosafety Protocol to the Convention on Biological Diversity (CBD) governs international trade in genetically modified organisms (GMOs) predominantly for the purpose of protecting the environment of the importing countries. In practice, the WTO protects the interests of exporting countries, whereas the Biosafety Protocol guards the interests of importing countries (chapter 8). While it is perfectly possible that a group of states simultaneously aims at liberalizing trade and at protecting their environment, a country cannot at the same time restrict trade to protect its environment and remove these trade obstacles. Conflicting commitments may lead to ambiguity because actors cannot sincerely implement both of them simultaneously. To resolve the conflict, jurisdictions of the institutions involved must be separated from each other, so that the substantive overlap of the two issue areas diminishes. Hence, cases of Jurisdictional Delimitation create a demand for the clear allocation of exclusive regulatory authority.

In some cases, it may be possible to delimit the jurisdictions involved so clearly that interdependence of governance disappears completely, whereas it continues to exist on a less contentious basis in other cases. Diverse regional seas regimes minimize interdependence of their governance activities through territorial separation of their issue areas. In contrast, delimitation of the jurisdictions of the regime for the protection of the ozone layer and the climate change regime is founded on a subject-by-subject approach. Chlorofluorocarbons (CFCs) and other ozone-depleting substances regulated by the Montreal Protocol are excluded from regulation by the climate change regime, even though most of these substances are also greenhouse gases. In spite of a gradual delimitation of their jurisdictions, the WTO and environmental regimes with trade restrictions remain more interdependent. While international trade is generally governed by the WTO, it is increasingly recognized that the details of certain trade restrictions established for purposes of environmental protection fall within the authority of international environmental institutions. In these latter cases, some contentious issues are assigned to one institution, although they remain of interest to the other institution involved. Consequently, the regulating institution must take the competing regulatory objectives duly into account.

Jurisdictional Delimitation cases demonstrate that the issue areas governed by international or EU institutions are not "given," but socially constructed. In cooperation theory, it is usually assumed that the boundaries of an institution's issue area are largely preexisting, or externally "given." While negotiation analysis emphasizes that constellations of interests can be modified by adding or subtracting actors and issues (Sebenius 1983, 1992; also Haas 1975), Jurisdictional Delimitation cases point to the need for occasional manipulation of the boundaries of relevant issue areas to avoid conflict or fruitless competition between institutions.

Due to their underlying rationale, Jurisdictional Delimitation cases will usually restrain the effectiveness of both institutions involved. The probability of conflicts and trade-offs will be high, if two institutions with significantly different objectives regulate the same issue, because regulatory considerations differ. The target institution's effectiveness will almost inevitably be undermined, if the source institution encroaches on its jurisdiction. By creating conflicting obligations the source institution enlarges the room for national and subnational actors to interpret the obligations to their liking and thus to disregard the target's commitments at least partially. At the same time, conflicting obligations make it also easier for national and subnational actors to disregard the commitments of the source institution so that they regularly also jeopardize the effective implementation of obligations under the source institution. Under these circumstances, synergy between the institutions involved will be rare or totally absent. It can only be expected if one of the institutions dominates the situation and a delimitation of issue areas occurs amicably.

The delimitation of issue areas tends to be a matter of conflict and of the distribution of power between the institutions involved, rather than of amicable problem solving. The model type of Jurisdictional Delimitation elucidates when and why overlapping jurisdictions create a demand for their separation, but not where the balance will or should lie (nor how and when it will be achieved). The regulatory competition between the institutions can usually be solved in different ways. Authority for regulating imports of GMOs could be exclusively allocated to the WTO that would presumably give priority to free-trade considerations, or to the Cartagena Protocol, which can be expected to prioritize environmental protection. In reality, the balance in this case is struck somewhere in between these extremes (chapter 8). How it is struck is eventually a matter of the political process based on interests of varying strength, with all uncertainties and attractions inherent in this process.

The members of both the source institution and the target institution are in a "mixed-motive" situation that resembles the game-theoretic constellation of the Battle of the Sexes (Stein 1982; Keohane 1984). On the one hand, they possess a common interest in some sort of separation of jurisdictions in order to avoid fruitless regulatory competition and a reduced effectiveness of their respective institutions. Neither side will be served if the institutions involved mutually undermine their effectiveness. On the other hand, the constituencies of the institutions have conflicting preferences that make it notoriously difficult to find a mutually acceptable solution. In the aforementioned conflict between the WTO and the Cartagena Protocol on the regulation of GMOs, neither side can be content with a conflict that disturbs both international trade and environmental protection. However, actors favoring free trade will advocate regulation by the WTO, while countries struggling for far-reaching domestic environmental regulation will prefer enlarged jurisdiction of the Cartagena Protocol. The conflict might even extend to different constituent groups (ministries, advocacy groups) within member states.

The governance challenge consists in arriving at a delimitation of jurisdictions that balances the diverging interests and realizes the common interests. Conflict management will tend to identify measures that honor the basic objectives of each institution, while being least intrusive into the objectives and operation of the other institution. It does not necessarily require an overarching institutional structure. Only in the EU are supranational actors such as the European Commission and the European Court of Justice available to assist in striking the right balance in accordance with general principles. Balancing of competing political objectives such as free trade and environmental protection or sustainable development can occur within either of the institutions pursuing them. Actors that are members of both institutions are likely to play a major role, because they will usually have the strongest interest in making contradictory demands compatible.

In Battle-of-the-Sexes situations, an equilibrium found is assumed to be fairly stable, because neither side can expect to gain from resumption of conflict. This standard conclusion from game theory suggests that, if the conflicting institutions are established consecutively, the earlier institution will posses a "first-mover advantage" (Héritier 1996; Mattli 2003). Commitments of the earlier institution will almost automatically limit the room for maneuver within negotiations of the later institution by strengthening the actors preferring the earlier institution's objectives.

Hence, it will be difficult to change the balance by establishing a new institution that encroaches on the issue area of the old one.

Occasionally, it may nevertheless prove useful as a political strategy to deliberately raise (potential) jurisdictional conflict—even by creating new institutions. For example, this may be the case if new regulatory objectives such as environmental protection are to be promoted in a field already governed by an existing institution. Consider that the world trade regime (GATT/WTO), having developed since the late 1940s, principally covers all international trade issues. Whenever international environmental regimes established since the 1970s have restricted trade for environmental purposes, they have almost automatically encroached on the established jurisdiction of the trade regime. However, environmental trade restrictions agreed on within multilateral environmental agreements are today widely acknowledged as legitimate, if sufficiently adapted to the needs of the world trade regime (chapter 8). Hence, raising jurisdictional conflict is not per se futile or negative for the effectiveness of international governance. To be successful, it requires a sufficiently high capacity to seriously endanger the jurisdictional authority of the target. The force of such threats will depend on their credibility and thus on the ability and political will of source-institution members to follow up on their initial action, if the target proves unwilling to adapt.

Nested Institutions

Interaction through Commitment may take place between two institutions that differ exclusively with respect to their membership, while pursuing identical objectives and employing the same means. These cases follow the ideal type of Nested Institutions. Even if addressing identical problems, institutions with divergent memberships may arrive at differing obligations because the relevant constellation of interests depends on the set of actors involved (Sebenius 1983, 1992). However, the causal mechanism of Interaction through Commitment requires that memberships overlap somewhat. In the absence of any overlap, such as between two regional seas conventions in different parts of the world, no state would be motivated to adapt its preferences within the target institution to the obligations of the source institution. The two conditions of difference in and overlap of memberships of two institutions will be fulfilled in their clearest form if the membership of one institution forms part of the membership of another institution. In this case, two formally independent institutions with similar objectives and regulatory means are "nested" into each other (Aggarwal 1983; Young 1996). Nested-Institution cases gain their momentum in particular from the tension between EU legislation or other regional arrangements on the one hand and larger, in particular pan-European or global, agreements on the other hand. For example, the decision of the regional regime for the protection of the Northeast Atlantic (Oslo and Paris Conventions, OSPAR) to ban dumping and incineration of waste at sea led to the adoption of similar measures within the global London Dumping Convention (chapter 5; Meinke 2002).

Interaction between Nested Institutions rests on three related mechanisms. First, it is typically easier to reach agreement within a smaller (e.g., regional) than in a larger (e.g., global) institution because a higher number of participants usually implies a greater heterogeneity of interests (Snidal 1994). In international legal systems, the prevailing consensus principle complicates decision making, and even in the European Union a comparatively small minority can block a decision by the Council of Ministers. As a consequence, the rejection of a decision by an interested actor or subgroup of actors is the more probable, the larger a group is. It may be noted that a greater homogeneity of interests within an institution may also follow from other factors such as a greater homogeneity of economic or political conditions of the members. Consequently, a similar momentum could in principle develop between institutions of a similar size but with partially overlapping memberships.

Second, commitments agreed within the smaller institution will streamline the preferences of its members in two dimensions. Internally, accepted obligations will bind members of the institution, where heterogeneous preferences might have prevailed before. Hence, accepted commitments remove options that existed before. Externally, the members of the smaller institution may develop a common interest in extending the agreed-on commitments to third parties that benefit from the smaller agreement like free riders. Thus, even members of the smaller institution who accepted the commitment only grudgingly can be expected to gain an interest in its wider application, because they have to implement it. This interest will be particularly strong if implementation of the agreed-on commitments is costly and lessens the competitiveness of sincere cooperators (Gehring 1997).

Third, streamlined preferences reinforce the position of a smaller group as compared to the necessarily more heterogeneous individual negotiation positions. Based on their common commitment, members of the group form a coalition. It will be more difficult to convince a whole group of negotiators than a single country to change its preagreed negotiation position. Likewise, it will be easier to offer a single country a side payment that makes it change its position than a whole group of countries. Hence, the probability increases that the coordinated position of the coalition constitutes some "focal point" (Schelling 1995, 100) around which expectations for an agreement converge. This does not ensure that diffusion of the policy measure from the smaller to the larger institution is successful. Although they are also members of the larger institution, the members of the smaller institution cannot impose their measures on the broader membership of the target institution. If resistance against the measure is too strong, the diffusion process will stop and interaction will fail.

Influence from Interaction between Nested Institutions can only originate from the smaller institution and affect the larger institution. If the smaller institution took over an obligation from the larger one, no additional actor would become subject to the obligation, so that this transfer would not be relevant for the effectiveness of governance. The transfer of an obligation to a smaller institution could affect the effectiveness of governance only if it activated an additional means of implementation. As we will see in the next subsection, such a transfer belongs to a further type of Interaction through Commitment that is characterized by the difference in means available for governance within the two institutions rather than the difference of their memberships.

The rationale of interaction between Nested Institutions suggests that effects will largely support the effectiveness of the target institution, and occasionally also of the source institution, while disruption is unlikely to occur. The assumption of identical objectives renders disruptive effects on target institutions highly improbable if not impossible. It is difficult to imagine how the transfer of a policy measure from a smaller to a larger institution with identical objectives might lead to disruption. It will most probably contribute to increasing the effectiveness of the target. Interaction will only exceptionally produce disruptive effects, if the policy measure adopted has unintended negative consequences or interferes with other policy measures existing within the target institution. However, this result would not any more be an immediate consequence of the rationale underlying cases of Nested Institutions. In the latter case, it presupposes a certain difference of means between the two institutions involved. The effectiveness of the source institution will not be affected by interaction between Nested Institutions, even though the resulting transfer of commitments promotes other interests of the members of the source institution (otherwise this type of interaction would not come about). If the objectives and governance means of the two institutions do not differ, positive feedback is difficult to conceive of, but it is not entirely excluded. Consider that, if the European Union decided to commit member states to taxing air transport in order to reduce pollution, it might not be possible to subject planes from third states to similar rules. Under the circumstances, diffusion of the obligation to a global institution with larger membership would support the effectiveness of the regional institution.

Interaction between Nested Institutions constitutes a mechanism for policy diffusion within the same policy field and provides opportunities for forum shopping. Where possible, actors striving for regulation of a particular issue may choose whether to promote their proposals predominantly in a smaller or in a larger institution. If they choose the smaller one, they may actively employ it as a "pilot institution" to exercise "leadership by example" (Grubb and Gupta 2000, 21; also Young 1991) to subsequently expand an obligation to a larger membership. To do so, they can create provisions in the smaller institution as a catalyst for change in the broader institution operating in the same issue area. Whereas regional agreement may not suffice to bring about broader international change, it can help tip the balance. Thus, policymakers within the EU and regional agreements should be conscious of the rationale of interaction between Nested Institutions because passing of ambitious standards may drive broader international and global agreement.

Additional Means

Interaction through Commitment may also take place between two institutions with an identical membership and the same objective, if the governance instruments (means) available within these institutions differ significantly. After adoption of an obligation within one institution, a given group of actors will comparatively easily agree on the same obligation within a second institution governing the same issue area with the same objectives because of their previous agreement. However, such simple diffusion of an obligation cannot be assumed to change the situation significantly for actors that are members of both institutions unless incorporation of the obligation into the target institution mobilizes an additional instrument (means) of implementation. In this case, the diffusion will matter for the effectiveness of environmental governance, because it will make it more difficult for addressees to sidestep or ignore the obligation.

Frequently, international and EU institutions do not control the full spectrum of possible governance instruments but differ in the means available to them. For example, an institution combating freshwater pollution may set standards that limit the emission of particular pollutants from particular sources. It may also employ water-quality standards that provide addressees with considerable freedom of how achieve them. Moreover, an environmental institution may not define specific limit values but set procedural obligations such as the requirement to conduct an environmental impact assessment prior to the implementation of certain projects or to open the permission procedure to the public (chapter 9). Likewise, one institution may rely almost exclusively on "soft" international law, while another institution resorts to "hard," legally binding international law (Abbott and Snidal 2000). The European Union even controls supranational law that is, under certain conditions, directly applicable within the legal systems of the member states and supported by the particularly stringent supervisory and judiciary mechanism of the EU (Burley and Mattli 1993; Alter 2000; Craig and de Búrca 2002). Finally, some institutions are capable of linking sincere implementation of environmental obligations to the granting of financial or other benefits, while others are not.

Interaction of the Additional-Means type will regularly raise the effectiveness of both institutions involved. If the diffusion of an obligation from one institution to another one with identical objectives and memberships activates an additional means of implementation, it will support the effectiveness of the target institution at the behavioral and impact levels. Without the influence of the source institution, the target would neither have adopted nor implemented the obligation. Since the new obligation is, by definition, in line with the target institution's own objective, implementing the obligation will support this objective by activating the target's means of implementation in addition to the means of the source institution. At the same time, activating an Additional Means automatically contributes to a more effective implementation of the source institution. An increased effectiveness of one institution will simultaneously reinforce the effectiveness of the other institution, because, according to the ideal type, objectives, and memberships of the two interacting institutions are similar or identical. The adoption of the obligation in the target institution can thus be expected to trigger a case of Behavioral Interaction that feeds back on the source institution. The interaction between the regime for the protection of the Northeast Atlantic (OSPAR) and the International North Sea Conferences established in the 1980s may serve as an illustration. While relying on declarations that were formally nonbinding, the Conferences took place at a high political level and generated political pressure. Having politically agreed on the phaseout of certain substances and activities, it became difficult for the same countries to resist the adoption of substantively identical hard-law obligations within the framework of OSPAR. These hard-law obligations provided a more effective basis for the protection of the Northeast Atlantic. Their implementation, in turn, automatically helped achieve the goals of the North Sea Conferences declarations (chapter 5).

Because of its synergistic effects on the source and the target institution, interaction activating Additional Means allows actors operating within the source institution to enhance the effectiveness of international and EU governance. This type of interaction may have its highest potential within the same policy field where objectives of source and target institution are most likely to coincide, but its occurrence across the boundaries of policy fields is not excluded. Actors and groups of actors in international and EU institutions can employ the mechanism intentionally to further and reinforce their objectives. As in the case of Nested Institutions, interaction activating Additional Means provides opportunities for forum shopping because actors can choose in which of the institutions available to launch a particular regulatory initiative. As the interaction between the North Sea Conferences and OSPAR illustrates, actors may even establish an institution in an area already governed by another institution for the sole purpose of triggering interaction activating Additional Means (chapter 5). In principle, synergistic effects may also be enhanced through direct coordination between the interacting institutions.

Cases of Interaction through Commitment in the Sample

Our sample comprises sixty-six cases of Interaction through Commitment. Most of them fall into the category of Additional Means (forty-two), while roughly one-third are Jurisdictional Delimitation cases (twenty-one) and only three are of the Nested Institutions type. Partly, this distribution is due to the fact that the many vertical cases of implementation of international obligations into EU law were counted as interaction activating Additional Means because they mobilize particularly hard supranational law.

In line with the logic of the ideal types, disruption prevails in cases of Jurisdictional Delimitation, while the other two types predominantly produced synergistic effects on the target institution. The relevance of the correlation between quality of effect and type of Interaction through Commitment is confirmed by a Cramer's V of 0.483. Cases of Jurisdictional Delimitation did primarily involve institutions from different policy fields, while the types of Additional Means and Nested Institutions appear to have their highest potential within the same policy field where objectives of source and target institution are most likely to be synergistic. This finding is in line with the logics of the ideal types, but it also reflects the overall correlation between the variables quality of effect and policy field. In light of the overall quantitative results presented in the first part of this chapter, it is also hardly surprising that policy responses occurred far more frequently in the case of Jurisdictional Delimita-

Table 13.8
Cases of Interaction through Commitment in our sample

	Jurisdictional delimitation		Nested institutions		Additional means		Total	
	No.	%	No.	%	No.	%	No.	%
Totals	**21**	**100**	**3**	**100**	**42**	**100**	**66**	**100**
Horizontal international	16	76.2	1	33.3	7	16.7	24	36.4
Horizontal EU	4	19.0	0	0.0	14	33.3	18	27.3
Vertical	1	4.8	2	66.7	21	50.0	24	36.4
Synergy	1	4.8	3	100	32	76.2	36	54.5
Disruption	13	61.9	0	0.0	3	7.1	16	24.2
Neutral/unclear	7	33.3	0	0.0	7	16.7	14	21.2
Intentional	4	19.0	0	0.0	25	59.5	29	43.9
Unintentional	16	76.2	3	100	17	40.5	36	54.5
Uncertain	1	4.8	0	0.0	0	0.0	1	1.5
Same policy field	2	9.5	3	100	37	88.1	42	63.6
Different policy field	19	90.5	0	0.0	5	11.9	24	36.4
Response	16	76.2	1	33.3	8	19.0	25	37.9
No response	5	23.8	2	66.7	34	81.0	41	62.1

Source: Own compilation from database reflected in the appendix.

tion than in cases of the other two types of Interaction through Commitment (see table 13.8).

Of our twenty-one cases of Jurisdictional Delimitation, thirteen had disruptive effects, seven produced neutral or unclear effects on the target institution, and only one generated synergy (table 13.8). Many of the disruptive cases involved interaction between the WTO and international environmental institutions, which is intensely discussed in the literature (see the overview in Brack 2002). They refer to the pending conflict regarding the admissibility of trade restrictions employed by environmental agreements either as sanctions to reinforce compliance, as in the case of the Montreal Protocol for the protection of the ozone layer, or as direct instruments for the protection of the environment, such as in the case of the Cartagena Biosafety Protocol on genetically modified organisms (chapter 8). The only synergistic case of Jurisdictional Delimitation in our sample can be attributed to exceptional circumstances, namely a common interest of both institutions paired with grossly asymmetric power relations between them. The climate change regime requested the Global Environment Facility (GEF) to operate its financial mechanism (Werksman 1996;

Fairman 1996). Because financial assistance was part of the package that developing and developed countries agreed on under the climate change regime, there was a need to determine a financial mechanism through which resources would be channeled. Assigning the financial mechanism to the GEF was beneficial for both institutions involved. The GEF acquired a new task within its area of competence, while the climate change regime spared the task of establishing a separate funding mechanism. The situation was dominated by the climate change regime, where the financial mechanism was negotiated, while the GEF could merely offer its assistance, with no leverage at all to support this offer. Under these circumstances, conflict could not arise.

Jurisdictional Delimitation issues appear to arise more rarely within the EU than at the international level. While sixteen of the twenty-one Jurisdictional Delimitation cases are located at the international level, only four cases occurred at the EU level (table 13.8). As in the case of Requests for Assistance, this may be due to the particular institutional structure of the EU. The existence of central actors that oversee the legislative processes as a whole—most importantly the European Commission, but also the Council of Ministers and the European Parliament—allows the EU to address these issues in a more centralized and coordinated fashion already in the process of elaborating legislation. Many Jurisdictional Delimitation issues may thus be expected to be resolved before they reach the level of open conflict. Nevertheless, such conflicts occur even within the highly integrated institutional framework of the EU. A particularly intense political conflict characterized the interaction between the EU Deliberate Release Directive on genetically modified organisms and EU product sector legislation as well as the EU Pesticides Directive regarding the authority to apply specific risk-assessment procedures (chapter 11). Also, the revised Deliberate Release Directive did not contain any liability regime because this aspect was expected to be covered in a separate EU directive on environmental liability, whereas the liability approach of the latter instrument proved to be significantly less stringent than was originally assumed (chapter 11). In the last case, new legislation was used to change existing one, when a strict interpretation of the 1979 Birds Directive by the European Court of Justice led EU member states to soften the relevant provisions through the Habitats Directive (chapter 10).

Vertical cases of Jurisdictional Delimitation occur even more rarely (table 13.8). This may be explained by the fact that the EU is a subject of international law alongside nation states. We did not consider tensions between EU legal instruments and international institutions as a struggle over competences but instead as implementation difficulties on the side of the EU as a member of the international institution. Consequently the only case in our sample has very particular characteristics. EU policymakers attempted to export the precautionary approach towards genetically modified organisms enshrined in the EU Deliberate Release Directive to other international institutions that are capable of indirectly influencing the interpretation of WTO rules (chapter 11).

Whereas most cases of Jurisdictional Delimitation were triggered unintentionally by the source institution, some were intentionally employed in order to affect decision making of the target institution (table 13.8). All cases involving the WTO occurred unintentionally. The WTO does not support free trade *in order to* interfere with a number of environmental regimes. Some of the intentional cases of Jurisdictional Delimitation closely resemble Requests for Assistance. Members of the climate change regime requested the International Civil Aviation Organization (ICAO) and the International Maritime Organization (IMO) to regulate greenhouse gas emissions from international aviation and shipping. While an open conflict over jurisdictional competence has not yet arisen, this case differs from the model of a Request for Assistance in that it is not driven by information but by the capacity of the climate change regime to pass relevant (competing) legislation. This implicit threat has been a significant motivation for the efforts of ICAO and IMO so far (chapter 3; Oberthür 2003).

Over time, a delimitation of jurisdictions was achieved in most cases of Jurisdictional Delimitation contained in our sample. The institutions succeeded in balancing their competing objectives to a large extent. For example, parties to the Montreal Protocol and other environmental agreements waived trade restrictions for nonparties that undertook to comply with the international regulations so as to avoid conflict with WTO rules. How, and in favor of which of the institutions involved, the balance was struck was a function of the power relation between the institutions, as reflected in the credibility of their threats, the relevance of the "sticks" available to them, and the general importance and political weight of their issue areas and underlying objectives.

The small number of three cases of interaction between Nested Institutions in our sample renders the results of a general evaluation highly preliminary. Although our sample does not contain intentionally triggered cases of this ideal type, their occurrence cannot be excluded. In line with the logic of the type we found only cases with synergistic effects on the target institution. Our three cases also illustrate that interaction between Nested Institutions can occur either between a regional and a global institution or between an EU legal instrument and an international institution. The nesting of the EU Habitats Directive in the pan-European Bern Convention on the Conservation of European Wildlife and Natural Habitats is analyzed in detail in chapter 10. Here, the development of the Natura 2000 program of natural protection sites under the EU Habitats Directive contributed significantly to the incorporation of the concept into the Bern Convention in the form of the pan-European Emerald Network.

While it is not accidental that our sample does not contain a case of interaction between Nested Institutions at the EU level, this type might become more relevant within the European Union in the future. So far, all EU legal instruments apply to all member states so that their memberships do not differ. However, since the Amsterdam Treaty of 1998 an opportunity exists for smaller groups of member states to accelerate and deepen their cooperation within the institutional framework of the EU in the form of the so-called "enhanced cooperation" (originally "closer cooperation"), which has not been employed to date (Bär, Homeyer, and Klasing 2002). Principally, a subset of EU member states could "enhance" their cooperation in order to broaden the acceptance of a measure over time, if it is not acceptable to all member states at once.

Cases of interaction activating Additional Means occurred at all three levels (table 13.8). At the international level, legally binding treaty law provided guidance to the generation of influential scientific advice. The inclusion of the precautionary principle in the UN Fish Stocks Agreement (FSA) enabled the biologists involved in the International Council for the Exploration of the Sea (ICES) to use this principle as the basis of their advice on sustainable yield of fish stocks, on which domestic protection measures are based. Furthermore, the fact that the global fisheries regime had identified fisheries subsidies as a problem leading to undesired fishing overcapacity helped place the issue on the agenda of the WTO, which has particular enforcement mechanisms at its disposal (chapter 6). Examples at the EU level primarily consist in an outright referral to obligations enacted elsewhere. For example, the IPPC Directive refers to a number of environmental standards established in other instruments. As a result, the IPPC Directive provides an additional means of supervision and enforcement of these existing obligations (chapter 9). Likewise, the EU Environmental Liability Directive defines environmental damage with reference to existing instruments of EU environmental law such as the Habitats Directive and the Water Framework Directive (chapters 9–10). While these Directives facilitated the elaboration of a definition of damage under the Liability Directive, the latter adds another means (liability) for their enforcement.

Vertical interaction of the Additional-Means type is particularly frequent, accounting for 50 percent of the cases in our sample (table 13.8). This comparatively large figure includes cases related to the implementation of international agreements by the EU, which is, together with the EU member states, a party to many international (environmental) agreements. For example, the Bern Convention prompted preparation of the Habitats Directive (chapter 10), the Aarhus Convention on public participation led to expanded public participation under the IPPC Directive (chapter 9), and the EU passed a regulation restricting trade in endangered species to implement CITES, even though it is, in contrast to its member states, not (yet) a full member of CITES (chapter 7). Also, air-quality guidelines of the World Health Organization have been incorporated into the daughter directives of the EU Air Quality Framework Directive (chapter 12). Such domestic implementation by members of an international regime may not appear particularly relevant for the study of institutional interaction. In all these cases, however, transferal of international obligations into supranational European law activates the particularly stringent supervisory and enforcement mechanism of the EU.

While interaction activating Additional Means resulted in synergy in three-fourths of our cases, it may also lead to neutral or even disruptive effects on the target institution (table 13.8). Especially where international commitments are implemented in EU legal instruments belonging to other policy fields or pursuing different policy objectives, tensions may occur. For example, international fisheries rules support a "greening" of EU fish-import rules and a reduction of EU fisheries subsidies that are hardly compatible with the original objectives of these EU policies (chapter 6). Furthermore, the Convention on Biological Diversity required restrictions on the ability to grant patents for living organisms that were at odds with the original objectives of the EU Patent Directive and resulted in manifest conflict (chapter 4). While no transfer of an obligation would presumably occur under these circumstances horizontally at the international level, the EU is more constrained because, to the extent that it acts as a subject of international law, it is obliged to implement international rules.

Behavioral Interaction

Behavioral Interaction is characterized by the fact that one institution directly influences the effective implementation of another institution it its issue area, rather than its decision-making process. Whereas the two causal mechanisms of Cognitive Interaction and Interaction through Commitment operate at the rule-making (output) level, Behavioral Interaction is located within the issue areas governed by the institutions involved (outcome level). It will occur, if behavioral changes triggered by the source institution are also relevant for the performance of the target institution within its issue area.

Behavioral Interaction is characterized by a high ability of the source institution to influence the target unilaterally. In contrast to interaction at the output level, it occurs through the adaptation of actors' behavior beyond the decision-making process of the source institution and does not depend on a decision within the target institution. The effect on the target might even come about unnoticed by the members of either or both institutions, because it emerges as the aggregate result of the uncoordinated behavior of actors within the two issue areas involved. A collective decision adopted within the target institution, or the source institution, in response to the effects of Behavioral Interaction is possible but does not constitute an essential element of this causal mechanism, because the effect will also occur without a policy response.

It proved difficult to identify Weberian ideal types of Behavioral Interaction that are characterized by distinct logics. One could group the cases of Behavioral Interaction within our sample into classes distinguished by certain of our core characteristics introduced in the first part of this chapter. Cases vary as to whether or not they have been triggered intentionally by the source institution, whether they resulted in synergy or disruption for the target institution, and so on. Unfortunately, none of these groupings revealed distinct underlying rationales or distinct appearances of Behavioral Interaction. For example, whether a case of Behavioral Interaction is triggered intentionally by the source institution or not, does not significantly affect the causal pathway through which influence must pass, nor its result.

Our inability to identify meaningful ideal types of Behavioral Interaction is related to the fact that cases driven by this causal mechanism are almost entirely controlled by the source institution. Cases of Cognitive Interaction and of Interaction through Commitment require activity on *both sides* of the causal pathway, including a decision of the target institution. Cognitive Interaction requires that the source institution produces some information that influences decision making in the target institution, while in cases of Interaction through Commitment an obligation collectively agreed on in the source institution affects decision making in the target. In both cases, the distinction between ideal types is based on systematic variation in factors that determine how action on both sides of the causal pathway relates and comes about. In contrast, Behavioral Interaction depends exclusively on activity at the source side of the causal pathway, while the effect does not need any particular activity at the target side to occur. Therefore, all cases are based on the same fundamental rationale, so that it is unlikely that different ideal types can be identified.

However, the universe of cases of Behavioral Interaction might reveal different rationales if considered in connection with other cases of interaction that are regularly located at the output level. Three of the five types identified above, namely the Request for Assistance, Jurisdictional Delimitation, and Additional Means, are meant to trigger subsequent, or respond to preceding, cases of Behavioral Interaction. Hence, many, though not all, cases of Behavioral Interaction constitute parts of longer causal chains comprising at least two separate cases of interaction. We discuss this broader phenomenon in the next section.

To be sure, we cannot exclude that the core characteristics developed in the beginning of this chapter might simply not be the appropriate ones for identifying meaningful ideal types of Behavioral Interaction. Other core characteristics might have provided a more fruitful foundation in this respect. For example, we did not elaborate systematically on the different types of actors that may be involved in the causal pathways. Interaction may involve behavioral changes of member states of the institutions involved, other states, nonstate actors like nongovernmental organizations, or relevant economic actors like companies. However, we do not have any positive indication that these differences might generate distinct rationales.

In contrast to the five ideal types of institutional interaction at the output level developed above, Behavioral Interaction is indifferent to the quality of its effects. As the mechanism does not indicate *how precisely* interaction affects the performance of the target institution within its own domain, we cannot derive any meaningful hypotheses about whether we might expect predominantly synergistic or disruptive effects. We might speculate whether intentionally created Behavioral Interaction produces a systematically different quality of effects than unintentionally triggered interaction, or whether interaction across the boundaries of policy fields is different from interaction within a single policy field. However, all these assumptions are not derived from the causal mechanism. Hence, we may expect that Behavioral Interaction will produce significant synergistic effects on the target institution in some cases and disruptive effects in others, with no systematic pattern to be derived from the rationale of the causal mechanism.

While Behavioral Interaction may be employed intentionally to influence the effectiveness of another institution, it rarely needs to be accepted as given and can regularly be influenced by political decision making. In many instances, the members of the source institution will endeavor to create synergy, if only because they are simultaneously members of the target institution. This will be generally true for a policy field like EU and international environmental governance. However, the causal mechanism may equally well be employed to undermine the effectiveness of the target institution. This will be predominantly the case if mutually incompatible objectives are pursued and a conflict over jurisdictional authority prevails. Intentionally created disruption is likely to result in conflict with the members of the target institution. Options for enhancing synergy or mitigating disruption will in most cases exist within the source institution that triggered the interaction. Actors operating within the target institution may also be able to take effective action, because the institution possesses regulatory authority over its own affected domain. Depending on the quality of the effect, they can attempt to reduce or increase the susceptibility of their institution for external influence.

Cases of Behavioral Interaction in the Sample

Behavioral Interaction is a widespread phenomenon at all levels of interaction. It drives about half of our cases. Virtually all of the institutions explored in our project are both the source of behavioral effects on other institutions and the target of such effects originating from other institutions. Moreover, the cases of Behavioral Interaction in our sample are roughly evenly divided between horizontal interaction at the international level, horizontal interaction at the EU level, and vertical interaction between EU instruments and international institutions (table 13.9).

Intentionally triggered Behavioral Interaction is particularly frequently used as a governance instrument at the EU level, resulting in a network of mutually reinforcing sectoral legal systems (table 13.9). This may be due to the important strides toward policy integration that EU environmental policymaking has made in recent years (Lenschow 2002). As a result, more encompassing instruments such as the Water Framework Directive as well as crosscutting instruments, such as the Environmental Liability Directive and the IPPC Directive, integrate environmental legislation in a specific sector or add supervision and enforcement mechanisms applicable across several instruments. Consequently, many cases of intentional Behavioral Interaction at the EU level in our sample concern these more encompassing and crosscutting instruments. For example, the Water Framework Directive is partially intended to assist implementation of the Nitrates and Bathing Water Directives. The IPPC Directive is partially intended to assist implementation of the Water Framework Directive, Air Quality Framework Directive, Habitats Directive, and

Table 13.9
Cases of Behavioral Interaction in our sample

	Intentional		Uninten-tional		Unclear intention-ality		Total	
	No.	%	No.	%	No.	%	No.	%
Totals	24	100	53	100	4	100	81	100
Horizontal international	4	16.7	16	30.2	1	25.0	21	25.9
Horizontal EU	15	62.5	12	22.6	3	75.0	30	37.0
Vertical	5	20.8	25	47.2	0	0.0	30	37.0
Same policy field	19	79.2	35	66.0	3	75.0	57	70.4
Different policy field	5	20.8	18	34.0	1	25.0	24	29.6
Synergy	22	91.7	31	58.5	3	75.0	56	69.1
Disruption	2	8.3	21	39.6	1	25.0	24	29.6
Neutral/unclear	0	0.0	1	1.9	0	0.0	1	1.2
Response	6	25.0	26	49.1	1	25.0	33	40.7
No response	18	75.0	27	50.9	3	75.0	48	59.3

Source: Own compilation from database reflected in the appendix.

Birds Directive (chapter 9). Also, the Environmental Liability Directive is intended to support implementation, inter alia, of the Deliberate Release Directive, the Habitats Directive, and the Water Framework Directive (chapters 9–11). Relevant efforts at the international level are less advanced and may meet with more difficulties than in the institutionally relatively coherent EU framework.

Intentional Behavioral Interaction is less common at the international level and in vertical interaction in our sample (table 13.9). All vertical cases concern EU legislation implementing international obligations; generally, they follow from previous interaction of the Additional Means type. For example, the Habitats Directive supports performance of the Bern Convention (chapter 10), the Water Framework Directive deliberately supports the performance of both the Convention on Transboundary Watercourses and Lakes and OSPAR (chapter 9), and several EU legal instruments are designed to support implementation of the climate change regime (chapter 3). The cases at the international level also follow from earlier interaction at the output level. For instance, activities of Interpol and the World Customs Organization in relation to trade in endangered species were entirely designed to assist implementation of CITES—and as such had themselves been the result of a Request for Assistance (chapter 7).

The quality of effect varies significantly with intentionality. In the case of both intentional and unintentional Behavioral Interaction, synergistic cases in our sample outnumber cases with disruptive effects on the target. However, about 40 percent of the cases of unintentional Behavioral Interaction resulted in disruption, while the ratio was less than 10 percent for the intentional cases (table 13.9). This may reflect the deep-rooted interdependence of international and EU environmental institutions, which makes it difficult to avoid side effects. At the same time, deliberately undermining other institutions might be exceptional as far as environmental protection is concerned. The only two cases of intentionally disruptive Behavioral Interaction in our sample occurred at the EU level. While this might be surprising at first glance, disruptive behavioral effects may be created deliberately as a substitute for the amendment of the target institution in particular within the institutionally dense and integrated framework of the EU. EU member states used the EU Habitats Directive of 1992 to weaken the implementation of the 1979 Birds Directive following a ruling of the ECJ that established a rather strict interpretation of the Birds Directive not intended by the member states (chapter 10). The EU Deliberate Release Directive intentionally requested application of a more stringent risk-assessment procedure under EU product-sector legislation that disrupted the latter's objectives in a politically charged situation concerning the marketing of genetically modified products (chapter 11). In both cases, it appeared easier to integrate the desired changes into the new directives that were under discussion anyway than to initiate amendments of the target institutions. Members of source and target were identical and influence occurred hardly against the will, or at least with the knowledge, of the members of the target institution. Intentional Behavioral Interaction with disruptive effects may thus reflect the integrative character of the legal framework of the EU rather than a higher potential for conflict.

As expected, Behavioral Interaction does not have a clear-cut pattern as to the quality of effects produced. Roughly reflecting the distribution of cases in our overall sample, more than two-thirds of the cases of Behavioral Interaction display synergistic effects on the target institution, while about 30 percent are disruptive. The differences between the three levels of horizontal and vertical interaction largely correspond to the differences with respect to intentionality. Thus, both unintentional and disruptive Behavioral Interaction is more frequent vertically and at the international level than at the EU level (compare tables 13.9 and 13.11). Variation between Behavioral Interaction occurring within the same policy field and across different policy fields also largely reflects the situation with respect to our overall sample.

Table 13.10
Cases of Behavioral Interaction in the same and in different policy fields

	Same policy field		Different policy fields		Total	
	No.	%	No.	%	No.	%
Synergy	49	86.0	7	29.2	56	69.1
Disruption	7	12.3	17	70.8	24	29.6
Neutral/unclear	1	1.8	0	0.0	1	1.2
Total	57	100	24	100	81	100
Cramer's V			0.586			

Source: Own compilation from database reflected in the appendix.

Table 13.11
Quality of effect of the cases of Behavioral Interaction in our sample

	Synergy		Disruption		Neutral/unclear		Total	
	No.	%	No.	%	No.	%	No.	%
Totals	56	100	24	100	1	100	81	100
Horizontal international	13	23.2	7	29.2	1	100	21	29.5
Horizontal EU	23	41.1	7	29.2	0	0.0	30	37.0
Vertical	20	35.7	10	41.7	0	0.0	30	37.0
Response	11	19.6	21	87.5	1	100	33	40.7
No response	45	80.4	3	12.5	0	0.0	48	59.3

Source: Own compilation from database reflected in the appendix.

More than 80 percent of the cases of Behavioral Interaction within a single policy field resulted in synergy, while about 70 percent of the cases involving different policy fields had disruptive effects. The Cramer's V of 0.586 indicates a relevant correlation between both variables (table 13.10).

The frequency of responses to cases of Behavioral Interaction varies with the quality of effects. In accordance with our general empirical findings, the target institution tends to reap the benefits without taking further action, especially in the case of synergy (table 13.11). This helps us understand the higher level of policy responses to unintentional Behavioral Interaction, which results in disruption more frequently than intentional Behavioral Interaction (table 13.9). Response action might improve the situation and may even transform originally disruptive effects into (at least partially) synergistic ones. For example, the EU Structural Funds originally under-mined the effectiveness of the Habitats Directive because they funded development projects that encroached on protected natural habitats. Therefore, Structural Fund rules were adapted so as to make funding dependent on the proper designation of habitat-protection sites. The threat to withhold funding now serves as an implicit sanction to enforce the Habitats Directive (chapter 10).

Where to Go from Here?

Apparently, this volume has not resolved all the issues of institutional interaction; it may even have raised more questions than it was able to answer. Given the state of development of research in the field so far, our project had to be in large measure exploratory. It has in particular made three contributions to the study of institu-tional interaction. First, the conceptual approach can be employed to analyze and compare interaction involving both international institutions and EU sectoral legal instruments at large. Second, we have developed causal mechanisms and ideal types that drive institutional interaction in general. Third, the project has produced empir-ical findings on the nature of institutional interaction that may be checked by future studies. Overall, institutional interaction has turned out to be a more multifaceted phenomenon than the existing literature suggested. But many interesting research questions are still waiting to be addressed. In this section, we identify two strands of promising future research on institutional interaction. The first relates to the fur-ther development of the analytic approach presented in this volume. The second im-portant area for future research is the systematic analysis of more complex settings of institutional interaction.

Toward Further Refinement of the Analytic Approach of This Volume

Future research may be directed at deepening our understanding of particular ele-ments of institutional interaction, of which we highlight four here. First, future studies may investigate in more detail the conditions under which the causal mecha-nisms of institutional interaction are triggered and become operational. Our own research focused on actual cases of interaction, because we were interested in enhancing our knowledge of how interaction operates and how it is dealt with po-litically. We did not delve into the issue of under which conditions interaction occurs and does not occur. This question may be particularly relevant for interac-tion at the output level, because the target institution must be motivated to adopt a decision in order to establish a case of interaction. We can expect to identify situations in which a potential for interaction exists but in which the target does not respond, so that there are no effects to be observed. Comparing noncases with actual cases of interaction may help specify under what conditions a potential for interaction is realized. These conditions may vary between the different causal mechanisms and ideal types.

Second, more detailed studies might investigate the factors that influence the success or failure of managing cases of institutional interaction politically. In this respect, a first task will consist in developing a clear distinction between, and indicators for, the more or less successful political management of different kinds of institutional interaction. It might be explored under which conditions an issue of Jurisdictional Delimitation or a case of unintentional Behavioral Interaction can be said to have been dealt with successfully. A related subject of relevance both for analysts and policymakers is the exploration of the role of different kinds of actors, such as governments, nongovernmental organizations, intergovernmental organizations, entities like the European Commission, and secretariats of international institutions, in triggering, and responding to, issues of institutional interaction. Studying how institutional interaction is managed at the EU level may provide useful lessons for the management of interaction at the international level. We observed that the EU has developed particular mechanisms for addressing and managing potential interaction issues. We have also been able to link these particularities to the specificities of the supranational governance system of the EU, in particular to the existence of the European Commission. A closer exploration of Commission activities might reveal the specific functions that are relevant for the successful management of particular types of interaction issues. In a second step it might be possible to identify functional equivalents that may be employed at the international level—given that the creation of supranational actors appears to be out of reach for most, if not all, international institutions.

Inquiry into the conditions under which interaction occurs and its political management is more or less successful can be based either on a bottom-up or a top-down approach. Research may start from empirical cases and noncases of interaction, trying to generalize empirical conditions under which particular causal mechanisms become operational and political management is effective (bottom up). Research may also be based on deductive reasoning to identify the relevant conditions and restrictions in theory, which may subsequently be tested by empirical analysis (top down).

Third, future research might attempt to assess the precise impact of institutional interaction on the ultimate target of governance, in our case the environment. This volume focused on cases of interaction with a significant impact on the environment, or at least the potential for creating such an impact. We refrained from determining this impact in more detail due to the immense additional research effort involved in such an assessment as well as the methodological challenges to be addressed and the uncertain outcome. As in the case of research on the effectiveness of international and EU institutions (Underdal 2004), however, assessing the impact on the environment (or other ultimate targets of governance), possibly from a comparative perspective, is of obvious relevance for the selection of political priorities in addressing issues of institutional interaction. It would also enable us to weigh the impact of varying cases of institutional interaction and to address the question of whether the aggregate effect of all or a specific subset of interaction cases is positive or negative (see Hovi, Sprinz, and Underdal 2003).

Finally, empirically robust knowledge about institutional interaction will require the systematic expansion of the empirical basis on which results rest. The empirical basis of our project has remained limited. Future research may corroborate or modify our findings on the basis of more interaction cases involving other environmental institutions. Reliability of results may also be supported by exploring cases of interaction relevant for the efficiency of governance or having longer, more indirect causal chains—taking into account the concomitant methodological challenges in demonstrating causality. Expanding the empirical research base to other policy fields might prove particularly fruitful. While interaction phenomena occur in all areas of an increasingly densely populated realm of international and EU institutions, institutional frameworks, actors, objectives, and governance approaches differ. In security relations or in the development-aid sector, for example, governance relies less on regulation and rule making than on collective action and financial assistance. In other fields such as international trade, the institutional landscape is far less fragmented than in environmental policy. Future research may explore the relevance of these varying conditions for institutional interaction.

Toward Systematic Analysis of More Complex Interaction Phenomena

Complexity raises a totally new set of issues. Single cases of interaction do not occur in isolation from each other. Frequently, interaction situations will be more complex than the analysis of single cases suggests. Eventually, we will not be content with knowing how and why a particular case of institutional interaction matters. Complex situations raise the problem of "emergent" properties. They may be affected by so many cases of interaction in such unexpected ways that new properties emerge that are not inherent in the single cases. There may be a forest to examine in addition to the many trees it is made of. Therefore, emergent properties will be difficult to grasp by exclusive analysis of the units.

The analytic concept of this volume can be employed to systematically explore more complex settings and their emergent properties by recombining individual cases. While the emergent properties of the forest are related to the coexistence of the many trees and to their mutual influence on each other's existence, possible emergent properties of complex interaction situations will originate from the coexistence of several, or many, cases of interaction. In essence, the investigation of institutional interaction in this volume is based on the analytic disaggregation of complex situations into separate cases with a limited scope and a clear-cut direction of influence (chapter 2). This approach assumes that complex situations will usually not only be composed of several cases, but that these cases also differ in some respect (e.g., regarding source and target institution, causal mechanism, quality of effect, and so on). The systematic recombination of cases would allow us to retain the single case of interaction as our principal unit of analysis, while exploring more complex interaction situations and their typical patterns.

In the following, we explore two particular ways individual cases may be related so as to form more complex interaction situations, namely causal chains and clusters. Cases of interaction may form sequential chains so that an individual case gives rise to a subsequent case that feeds back on the original source institution or influences a third institution. Cases of interaction may also cluster around certain issues and institutions. In this case, several institutions jointly address a particular problem and contribute to the effectiveness of governance of a certain area.

Causal Chains   Two or more cases of interaction will form a causal chain, if one case triggers one or several subsequent cases. For this effect to occur, it is not sufficient that two or more institutions influence each other in more than one case. The original case must have changed the situation within the original target institution sufficiently, so that the latter becomes the source of a further case of interaction directed at the original source institution or at a third institution. Causal chains draw attention to the fact that interaction processes in more complex settings may acquire a momentum of their own, so that the actors and institutions involved are drawn into an autonomous process that they do not fully control any more.

As a first step, we can identify several ideal types of causal chains of interaction between two institutions, which have their own logics and restrictions. First, cases of interaction at the output level may give rise to further cases of output-level interaction in the reverse direction and thus start sequential coevolution processes. Whereas we might think of numerous combinations, in particular two typical patterns involving the ideal types of Interaction through Commitment can be expected to develop.

Coevolution processes may lead to a mutually reinforcing and synergistic development of the normative structure of the institutions involved. Such chains will most probably be composed of cases of Nested Institutions and Additional Means. These types are in significant respects complementary and mostly create synergistic effects between the institutions involved. They cannot be expected to prompt a second case of interaction in the reverse direction, however, as long as the target merely adapts to the normative change originating from the source institution. Only if they give rise to more far-reaching innovations within the target institution can a feedback case influencing the original source institution occur. For example, the Bern Convention drove the preparation of the EU Habitats Directive. As the Directive was elaborated within the EU, the concept of the Natura 2000 network of natural protection sites was developed, which subsequently triggered the adoption of a similar concept (Emerald Network) within the Bern Convention (chapter 10). Whereas the first case of this chain is one of Additional Means, the second is one of Nested Institutions. An Additional-Means case may also lead to a second Additional-Means case, or it may follow from a Nested Institutions case.

Causal chains composed of two or more cases of Interaction through Commitment may also lead to the gradual separation of the jurisdictions of two or more institutions. These chains will typically be composed of Jurisdictional Delimitation cases, which regularly produce disruptive effects on the target institution. Think of a decision within the source institution, which interferes with the governance activities of the target institution. The case will be complete once the target institution reacts to the changed situation. Once again, this reaction will not set off a feedback case as long as it merely consists of an adaptation to the jurisdictional claim of the original source institution. However, if the reaction is sufficiently far-reaching, it may change the constellation of interests within the original source institution so that the latter makes a further decision. For example, the WTO, especially through its Agreement on Sanitary and Phytosanitary Measures (SPS Agreement), constrained the use of trade measures related to genetically modified organisms under the Cartagena Protocol on Biosafety. Negotiations on the Cartagena Protocol, in turn, precluded that detailed rules on the appropriate risk assessment for genetically modified organisms were developed within the WTO (chapter 8; see also Oberthür and Gehring, forthcoming). Whereas this chain will ideally develop over time, its component cases might also occur simultaneously, if *anticipated* changes within one institution are immediately responded to by action within another institution, which creates a feedback.

It is quite improbable that Cognitive Interaction would give rise to causal chains, although this cannot be excluded. In cases of learning from a Policy Model, influence is very diffuse and nontargeted. Since the target institution may learn from otherwise totally unrelated institutions, it would be completely incidental if this learning were to cause immediate effects on the original source institution or on a third institution. Requests for Assistance will usually be all too targeted to trigger coevolution at the output level. Requests tend to focus on very specific and comparatively minor adaptations by the target institution, short of triggering broad changes capable of causing feedback effects on the original source institution.

Second, in another family of causal chains, interaction at the output level causes subsequent Behavioral Interaction. In these chains, the source institution causes normative change within the target institution, which induces behavioral changes of relevant actors within the target's issue area, and these changes affect the performance of the original source institution within its own domain. Three of our types of output-level interaction—namely a Request for Assistance, interaction activating Additional Means, and Jurisdictional Delimitation cases—are particularly suited to triggering this kind of causal chain. An institution issues a Request for Assistance not merely to induce a decision of the target institution, but ultimately to generate a subsequent case of Behavioral Interaction to support performance within its own domain. Whereas the first of these cases might have a neutral or indeterminate effect on the original target institution, the second case will usually be synergistic for the original source institution. For example, CITES asked Interpol and the World Customs Organization for adaptations that subsequently helped improve the effectiveness of its own implementation (chapter 7).

Interaction activating Additional Means is also likely to create subsequent Behavioral Interaction. The major difference vis-à-vis Requests for Assistance is that adaptation is not entirely based on cognition and conviction, but on the commitment of actors to obligations originating from the source institution. Like a Request for Assistance, interaction of the Additional-Means type will be meaningful only if the additional means controlled by the original target institution helps improve the performance of the original source institution. For example, OSPAR had the effect of supporting the implementation of the declarations of the International North Sea Conferences because the soft-law-based North Sea Conferences had previously accelerated the development of hard obligations under OSPAR (chapter 5). The International Council for the Exploration of the Sea (ICES) was able to support the performance of the UN Fish Stocks Agreement (FSA), because the FSA had previously motivated ICES to base its estimates of sustainable fish catch on the precautionary principle (chapter 6). In a vertical direction, CITES induced the adoption of the EU Regulation on trade in endangered species, which subsequently supported the performance of CITES (chapter 7). In all these instances, a synergistic (or at least neutral) interaction at the output level causes a synergistic interaction at the outcome level.

Although less obvious, Jurisdictional Delimitation cases may also create feedback effects at the outcome level. Ideally, we may think of two rather different consequences of a Jurisdictional Delimitation case on the target institution. Interaction may lead to normative adaptation, which accommodates the two institutions and, accordingly, mitigates existing or anticipated disruptive Behavioral Interaction. In this case, *subsequent* Behavioral Interaction is not to be expected. However, Jurisdictional Delimitation may also lead to normative adaptation within the target institution, which does not completely separate the jurisdictions of the institutions involved. As a result, it is likely to cause Behavioral Interaction, which undermines the performance of the original source institution within its own domain. For example, the Cartagena Biosafety Protocol was adapted to the needs of the WTO, especially the SPS Agreement, in a way that exploits the remaining room for interpretation to a large extent. Thus, the implementation of the Protocol might undermine the effectiveness of the WTO in the future (Oberthür and Gehring, forthcoming; see also chapter 8).

The remaining two types of interaction at the output level are unlikely to trigger subsequent Behavioral Interaction. The Policy Model is once again too diffuse to trigger feedback cases of Behavioral Interaction in any systematic way. While a causal chain starting with a Policy Model case cannot be totally excluded, it would be merely incidental. Cases of the Nested Institutions type will also rarely be capable of triggering Behavioral Interaction. If members of a regional institution transfer obligations to a global institution, this cannot be expected to affect the behavior of relevant actors at the regional level significantly, because these actors are already bound by the same obligations. Feedback through Behavioral Interaction could arise only if the transfer led to innovation in the target institution (e.g., the adoption of stricter rules than in the regional institution) or if the behavior of nonregional actors within the region could not be controlled by the regional institution itself.

Third, Behavioral Interaction may trigger subsequent interaction at the output level. In this causal chain, the second case originates from a collective decision made within the original target institution in response to a preceding Behavioral Interaction. For the feedback to occur, this decision has to influence decisions of the original source institution. It can in particular take the form of a Request for Assistance or raise a Jurisdictional Delimitation issue. While this causal chain is absent from our sample, its occurrence is possible. Consider that the Kyoto Protocol undermines the Convention on Biological Diversity (CBD) by providing incentives for establishing fast-growing tree plantations. If the CBD responded by adapting its own rules to mitigate this effect, this would not initiate a second case of interaction. However, if the CBD asked the climate change regime to change its rules or if it set strict new rules in order to gain comprehensive jurisdictional competence over the management of forests, it would create a subsequent case.

These types of causal chains certainly do not exhaust the possibilities of recombining cases to form more complex settings. Thus, causal chains may involve more than two cases. For example, the causal chains operating entirely at the output level are rarely independent from Behavioral Interaction. For example, the Bern Convention not only drove the preparation of the EU Habitats Directive and was later affected by the Directive's concept of the Natura 2000 network of natural protection sites. Because the Habitats Directive mobilized the additional means of supranational law with its particularly strong enforcement arrangements, the Bern Convention's effective implementation was also supported (chapter 10). Likewise, mutual adaptation of the norms enshrined in the Cartagena Protocol and the WTO (including relevant interpretations by the WTO's dispute settlement bodies) are accompanied by mutual influence of the two institutions on each other's performance within their issue areas.

Causal chains that relate three or more institutions in systematic ways will also be of interest. For instance, regulatory competition between WTO-TRIPS and the biodiversity regime has influenced a third institution, the Food and Agriculture Organization (FAO) (see chapter 4; Andersen 2002). Over time, the "Regime Complex for Plant Genetic Resources" involves even more institutions (Raustiala and Victor 2004). Also, the conflicts between the WTO SPS Agreement and the EU Deliberate

Release Directive on genetically modified organisms regarding application of the precautionary principle have affected the decision-making process within other relevant international institutions that set standards that are relevant for the interpretation of the SPS Agreement, including the Codex Alimentarius Commission (chapter 11). The systematic recombination of appropriate causal chains of limited scope may help develop a more rigorous analysis of such complex settings.

The analysis of causal chains of cases of institutional interaction points to the fact that interinstitutional influence is not merely driven by the interests and action of the actors involved. Institutional interaction can itself become an important driver. If cases of interaction influence subsequent or parallel cases, institutional interaction gains momentum. Thus, our approach of disaggregating complex settings into a suitable number of cases and then recombining cases so as to "reconstruct" the more complex setting is not confined to the mere aggregation of properties of the units. It may also enable us to reveal typical patterns and ideal types of more complex interaction situations that possess their own logics and rationales. These logics would not be located within the units, but in the particular forms of their coexistence, and would therefore allow us to grasp the emergent properties of the larger situation. Admittedly, this issue has not been central to the empirical investigation of the present volume and needs further elaboration.

Clusters   Single cases of interaction can also cluster around certain issues and institutions. In this case, several institutions commonly address a particular problem and contribute to the effectiveness of governance within a certain area. While causal chains address causation between cases of interaction, clusters address settings of parallel interaction without causation between cases. Problem areas may comprise a considerable number of institutions, which separately address parts of the larger problem. For example, the marine environment of the North Sea and the North Atlantic is subject to the regulation of numerous institutions, including OSPAR, the North Sea Conferences, the global London Dumping Convention, the MARPOL Convention of the International Maritime Organization on marine pollution from ships, institutions governing pollution of particular rivers such as the Rhine, as well as a number of pertinent EU directives on water and air pollution. Likewise, the problem area of the protection of nature and wildlife is populated by numerous different institutions, including CITES, the CBD, the Convention on Migratory Species, the Bern Convention, and several EU instruments. We may identify similar clusters in the area of air pollution (UNECE Convention on Long-Range Transboundary Air

Pollution, EU directives, IMO regulations, and so on) and beyond. Each single instrument focuses on a limited fraction of the overall problem, obliges varying groups of states, and employs its own means. While this is beyond our effort here, in a broader perspective the analysis may even extend to interaction with national-level institutions.

While such clusters will usually be related to underlying problems as well as relevant actors and their interests, they may follow typical patterns that reflect core characteristics related to the cluster, not the single cases they are composed of. We found deliberately created interaction clusters supported by crosscutting institutions that were established in order to influence other specific institutions. For example, the EU IPPC Directive, introducing an integrated scheme for the authorization of large-scale industrial plants and comparable installations, cuts across numerous issue areas governed by other EU directives, including the Water Framework Directive, the Air Quality Framework Directive, the Solvent Emissions Directive, and the Habitats Directive. The IPPC Directive expressly relates to several of these instruments by its very wording, while it directly affects others or is affected by them (chapter 9). At the international level, the International North Sea Conferences have been established not least to provide for a coordinating mechanism for various institutions relevant for the protection of the North Sea and to set priorities for future activities (chapter 5). The Global Environment Facility (GEF) also constitutes the core of an intentionally created cluster of interacting international institutions. It is designed to provide for a coordinated approach to the financial mechanisms of global environmental agreements (Fairman 1996; Werksman 1996), including the climate change regime, the CBD, and the 2001 Stockholm Convention on Persistent Organic Pollutants.

Other clusters develop over time so that one of the institutions involved gradually acquires a lead function. Such clustering around an emergent lead institution may provide the opportunity for more centralized management of the system of international institutions. However, it also creates an informal hierarchy of institutions that is voluntarily accepted by those involved. For example, CITES has gradually developed to become the center of a cluster of institutions dedicated to the protection of wildlife. In this process, CITES even reached beyond its original mandate, for example by calling on members to join the subagreement on the protection of the houbara bustard of the Convention on Migratory Species, even though this subagreement is unrelated to CITES and does not address international trade in the species. In other cases, CITES responded to requests of other international institutions by addressing the protection of whales or the vicuña, a species of Andean llama. CITES itself requested assistance from nonenvironmental institutions in implementing its rules, in particular Interpol and the World Customs Organization (chapter 7). In the 1990s, the CBD developed a similar approach by coordinating programs and activities with pertinent regimes such as the Ramsar Convention for the protection of wetlands (chapter 4). This cluster is even larger and includes CITES.

Our approach provides a basis for capturing emergent properties of such interaction clusters. Recombining individual cases of interaction into clusters enables us to discover typical patterns and derive their emergent properties. For this purpose, typical patterns and ideal types of the clusters would have to be developed from the examples identified above, or from other suitable constellations of cases. Because this is beyond the scope of our effort here, we have to leave this task to future research efforts.

Toward the Study of Interlocking Structures of Governance Institutions

Eventually, we may want to study the broader consequences of institutional interaction for international society at large, especially within the decentralized international system. If governance within the international system, as well as within the European Union, is not merely the product of more-or-less rationally designed sector-specific institutions (Koremenos, Lipson, and Snidal 2001), but *emerges* from interaction among numerous international, European, and even domestic institutions, established issues of international and European governance arise anew.

Over time, we may gain a clearer picture of the interlocking structure of international governance institutions and EU legal instruments beyond causal chains, clusters, and limited "regime complexes." Analysts of European integration have been more aware of the fact that the many EU legal instruments form parts of larger policies. The study of institutional interaction reveals that international institutions also constitute parts of institutional networks that operate in broad problem areas. Underdal and Young (2004) relate the concern for interlocking structures of governance institutions to the new institutionalism in the study of political economy. Douglass North has argued that a network of institutional arrangements, including property rights, contractual procedures, liability rules, and credit systems, promoted the growth of the dynamic markets of the West in the past several hundred years (North and Thomas 1973). Mancur Olsen (2000) explains the superior economic performance of democratic over authoritarian systems in a similar way.

The recognition of interlocking structures of governance institutions has important ramifications especially for the study of international governance. Although it may be assumed that every single international institution is established and maintained purposively by its respective members, the broader institutional structures within the international system emerge spontaneously without explicit coordination between the discrete institutions involved. Purposive and skillful efforts to enhance the effectiveness of international governance in one sector may be jeopardized by parallel efforts in other sectors. Eventually, institutional interaction may turn out to be as important for the overall effectiveness of governance within the decentralized international order as the skillful design of single institutions. The comparative perspective demonstrates that even in the relatively well-organized institutional setting of the European Union coordination failures and disruption between instruments occur, while the deliberate use of interaction to promote desired policies is more advanced than in international relations.

This volume on institutional interaction constitutes a first step toward the comprehensive analysis of the broader consequences of international and EU institutions and their interlocking structure. It demonstrates that international institutions have effects beyond their domains. These effects might generate even broader consequences for international and domestic society, the legitimacy of international governance, and the actors entitled to participate in decision-making processes or capable of doing so. Whereas our study has hardly been able to delve into pertinent aspects of these broader consequences, it has made a start that demonstrates the potential of the effort. The study of interaction between international and EU institutions thus provides a rich and fascinating research agenda for those interested in international and European governance.

Note

1. This may help explain why a potential for further improvement was particularly frequently identified at the international level, for disruption also figured particularly prominently at that level (table 13.2).

References

Abbott, Kenneth W., and Duncan Snidal. 2000. Hard and Soft Law in International Governance. *International Organization* 54 (3): 421–456.

Aggarwal, Vinod K. 1983. The Unraveling of the Multi-Fiber Arrangement, 1981: An Examination of International Regime Change. *International Organization* 37 (4): 617–646.

Alter, Karen J. 2000. The European Legal System and Domestic Policy: Spillover or Backlash? *International Organization* 54 (3): 489–518.

Andersen, Regine. 2002. The Time Dimension in International Regime Interplay. *Global Environmental Politics* 2 (3): 98–117.

Bär, Stefani, Ingmar von Homeyer, and Anneke Klasing. 2002. Overcoming Deadlock? Enhanced Cooperation and European Environmental Policy after Nice. *Yearbook of European Environmental Law* 2: 241–270.

Brack, Duncan. 2002. Environmental Treaties and Trade: Multilateral Environmental Agreements and the Multilateral Trading System. In Gary P. Sampson and W. Bradney Chambers, eds., *Trade, Environment, and the Millennium*, 2nd ed., 321–352. Tokyo: United Nations University Press.

Brown Weiss, Edith. 1993. International Environmental Issues and the Emergence of a New World Order. *Georgetown Law Journal* 81 (3): 675–710.

Burley, Anne-Marie, and Walter Mattli. 1993. Europe before the Court: A Political Theory of Legal Integration. *International Organization* 47 (1): 41–76.

Craig, Paul, and Gráinne de Búrca. 2002. *EU Law: Text, Cases, and Materials*. 3rd ed. Oxford: Oxford University Press.

Fairman, David. 1996. The Global Environment Facility: Haunted by the Shadow of the Future. In Robert O. Keohane and Marc A. Levy, eds., *Institutions for Environmental Aid: Pitfalls and Promise*, 55–87. Cambridge, MA: MIT Press.

Gehring, Thomas. 1994. *Dynamic International Regimes: Institutions for International Environmental Governance*. Frankfurt/Main: Peter Lang.

Gehring, Thomas. 1997. Governing in Nested Institutions: Environmental Policy in the European Union and the Case of Packaging Waste. *Journal of European Public Policy* 4 (3): 337–354.

Gehring, Thomas. 2004. Methodological Issues in the Study of Broader Consequences. In Arild Underdal and Oran R. Young, eds., *Regime Consequences: Methodological Challenges and Research Strategies*, 219–246. Dordrecht: Kluwer.

Gehring, Thomas, and Sebastian Oberthür. 2004. Exploring Regime Interaction: A Framework for Analysis. In Arild Underdal and Oran R. Young, eds., *Regime Consequences: Methodological Challenges and Research Strategies*, 247–269. Dordrecht: Kluwer.

Grubb, Michael, and Joyeeta Gupta. 2000. Leadership: Theory and Methodology. In Joyeeta Gupta and Michael Grubb, eds., *Climate Change and European Leadership: A Sustainable Role for Europe?*, 15–24. Dordrecht: Kluwer.

Haas, Ernst. 1975. Is There a Hole in the Whole? Knowledge, Technology, Interdependence, and the Construction of International Regimes. *International Organization* 29 (3): 827–876.

Haas, Ernst. 1990. *When Knowledge is Power: Three Models of Change in International Organizations*. Berkeley: University of California Press.

Hasenclever, Andreas, Peter Mayer, and Volker Rittberger. 1997. *Theories of International Regimes*. Cambridge: Cambridge University Press.

Héritier, Adrienne. 1996. The Accommodation of Diversity in the European Policy-Making Process and its Outcomes: Regulatory Policy as a Patchwork. *Journal of European Public Policy* 3 (2): 149–167.

Hovi, Jon, Detlef Sprinz, and Arild Underdal. 2003. The Oslo-Potsdam Solution to Measuring Regime Effectiveness: Critique, Response, and the Road Ahead. *Global Environmental Politics* 3 (3): 74–96.

Keohane, Robert O. 1984. *After Hegemony: Cooperation and Discord in the World Political Economy*. Princeton, NJ: Princeton University Press.

King, Leslie A. 1997. *Institutional Interplay—Research Questions*. Paper Commissioned by Institutional Dimensions of Global Change and International Human Dimensions Programme on Global Environmental Change. Environmental Studies Programme, Burlington VT. School of Natural Resources, University of Vermont.

Koremenos, Barbara, Charles Lipson, and Duncan Snidal. 2001. The Rational Design of International Institutions. *International Organization* 55 (4): 761–799.

Lenschow, Andrea, ed. 2002. *Environmental Policy Integration: Greening Sectoral Policies in Europe*. London: Earthscan.

Martin, Lisa L., and Beth A. Simmons. 1998. Theories and Empirical Studies of International Institutions. *International Organization* 52 (4): 729–757.

Mattli, Walter. 2003. Setting International Standards: Technological Rationality or Primacy of Power. *World Politics* 56 (1): 1–42.

Meinke, Britta. 2002. *Multi-Regime-Regulierung: Wechselwirkungen zwischen globalen und regionalen Umweltregimen*. Darmstadt, Germany: Deutscher Universitäts-Verlag.

Miles, Edward L., Arild Underdal, Steinar Andresen, Jørgen Wettestad, Jon Birger Skjærseth, and Elaine M. Carlin. 2002. *Environmental Regime Effectiveness: Confronting Theory with Evidence*. Cambridge, MA: MIT Press.

North, Douglass, and Robert P. Thomas. 1973. *The Rise of the Western World*. Cambridge: Cambridge University Press.

Oberthür, Sebastian. 1999. The EU as an International Actor: The Case of the Protection of the Ozone Layer. *Journal of Common Market Studies* 37 (4): 641–659.

Oberthür, Sebastian. 2001. Linkages between the Montreal and Kyoto Protocols: Enhancing Synergies between Protecting the Ozone Layer and the Global Climate. *International Environmental Agreements: Politics, Law and Economics* 1 (3): 357–377.

Oberthür, Sebastian. 2003. Institutional Interaction to Address Greenhouse Gas Emissions from International Transport: ICAO, IMO and the Kyoto Protocol. *Climate Policy* 3 (3): 191–205.

Oberthür, Sebastian, and Thomas Gehring. Forthcoming. Disentangling the Interaction between the Cartagena Protocol and the World Trade Organisation. In W. Bradnee Chambers and Joy A. Kim, eds., *Institutional Interplay: The Case of Biosafety*. Tokyo: United Nations University.

Oberthür, Sebastian, and Hermann E. Ott (in collaboration with Richard G. Tarasofsky). 1999. *The Kyoto Protocol: International Climate Policy for the 21st Century.* Berlin: Springer.

Olsen, Mancur Jr. 2000. *Power and Prosperity: Outgrowing Communist and Capitalist Dictatorships.* New York: Basic Books.

Parson, Edward A. 1993. Protecting the Ozone Layer. In Peter M. Haas, Robert O. Keohane, and Marc A. Levy, eds., *Institutions for the Earth: Sources of Effective International Environmental Protection,* 27–73. Cambridge, MA: MIT Press.

Parson, Edward A. 2003. *Protecting the Ozone Layer: Science, Strategy, and Negotiation in the Shaping of a Global Environmental Regime.* Oxford: Oxford University Press.

Raustalia, Kal, and David G. Victor. 2004. The Regime Complex for Plant Genetic Resources. *International Organization* 58 (2): 277–309.

Schelling, Thomas C. 1995. *The Strategy of Conflict.* 15th ed. Cambridge, MA: Harvard University Press.

Schweitzer, Michael. 2003. Überblick zum Verhältnis: Völkerrecht–Europäisches Gemeinschaftsrecht–nationales Recht. In Hans-Werner Rengeling, ed., *Handbuch zum europäischen und deutschen Umweltrecht,* 679–704. Cologne: Carl Heymanns.

Sebenius, James K. 1983. Negotiation Arithmetics: Adding and Subtracting Issues and Parties. *International Organization* 37 (2): 281–316.

Sebenius, James K. 1992. Challenging Conventional Explanations of International Cooperation: Negotiation Analysis and the Case of Epistemic Communities. *International Organization* 46 (1): 323–365.

Snidal, Duncan. 1985. The Game Theory of International Politics. *World Politics* 38 (1): 25–57.

Snidal, Duncan. 1994. The Politics of Scope: Endogenous Actors, Heterogeneity, and Institutions. *Journal of Theoretical Politics* 6 (4): 449–472.

Stein, Arthur. 1982. Coordination and Collaboration: Regimes in an Anarchic World. *International Organization* 36 (2): 299–324.

Stokke, Olav Schram. 2000. Managing Straddling Stocks: The Interplay of Global and Regional Regimes. *Ocean and Coastal Management* 43 (2–3): 205–234.

Stokke, Olav Schram. 2001. *The Interplay of International Regimes: Putting Effectiveness Theory to Work.* FNI Report 14/2001. Lysaker, Norway: Fridtjof Nansen Institute.

Tversky, Amos, and Daniel Kahnemann. 1981. The Framing of Decision and Rational Choice. *Science* 211: 453–458.

Tversky, Amos, and Daniel Kahnemann. 1984. Choices, Values, and Frames. *American Psychologist* 39 (4): 341–350.

Underdal, Arild. 2004. Methodological Challenges in the Study of Regime Effectiveness. In Arild Underdal and Oran R. Young, eds., *Regime Consequences: Methodological Challenges and Research Strategies,* 27–48. Dordrecht: Kluwer.

Underdal, Arild, and Oran R. Young. 2004. Research Strategies for the Future. In Arild Underdal and Oran R. Young, eds., *Regime Consequences: Methodological Challenges and Research Strategies,* 361–380. Dordrecht: Kluwer.

Victor, David G. 1999. The Market for International Environmental Protecting Services and the Perils of Coordination. Paper prepared for the International Conference on Synergies and Coordination between Multilateral Environmental Agreements, United Nations University, July 14–16, 1999, Tokyo. Available at http://www.geic.or.jp/interlinkages/docs/online-docs.html.

Weber, Max. 1976. *Wirtschaft und Gesellschaft: Grundriss der verstehenden Soziologie.* 5th ed. Tübingen, Germany: J.C.B. Mohr.

Werksman, Jacob. 1996. Consolidating Governance of the Global Commons: Insights from the Global Environment Facility. *Yearbook of International Environmental Law* 6: 27–63.

Werksman, Jacob. 2005. The Negotiation of a Kyoto Compliance System. In Olav Schram Stokke, Jon Hovi, and Geir Ulfstein, eds., *Implementing the Climate Regime: International Compliance*, 17–38. London: Earthscan.

Young, Oran R. 1991. Political Leadership and Regime Formation: On the Development of Institutions in International Society. *International Organization* 45 (3): 281–308.

Young, Oran R. 1996. Institutional Linkages in International Society: Polar Perspectives. *Global Governance* 2 (1): 1–24.

Young, Oran R. 2002. *The Institutional Dimensions of Environmental Change: Fit, Interplay, and Scale.* Cambridge, MA: MIT Press.

Young, Oran R., Leslie A. King, Arun Aggarval, Arild Underdal, Peter H. Sand, and Merrilyn Wasson. 1999. *Institutional Dimensions of Global Environmental Change (IDGEC): Science Plan.* Bonn: International Human Dimensions Programme on Global Environmental Change.

Appendix: Overview of Identified Cases of Institutional Interaction

Column "No."	gives the number of the case of interaction in the table.
Column "Brief description of case"	provides a very brief characterization of the case of interaction, including indication of other institution.
Column "Core: T or S"	indicates whether the core institution was the source of the interaction (S) or the target (T).
Column "Hor. or vert."	provides information on whether the interaction is horizontal (H) or vertical (V = between an international and an EU institution).
Column "Quality of effect"	denotes whether the effect on the target institution was synergistic, disruptive, or neutral/uncertain.
Column "Policy fields"	denotes whether the interacting institutions belong to the same or different policy fields.
Column "Intentional"	indicates whether the source institution was assessed as having triggered the interaction intentionally or unintentionally (Yes/No); in some cases, the entry is "uncertain."
Column "Key difference"	provides, for cases of Interaction through Commitment, the key difference of the interaction (O = Objectives; M = Membership; Ma = means).
Column "Policy response"	indicates whether or not a collective policy response occurred (in the source institution, in the target institution, or in both) (Yes/No).
Column "Further potential"	indicates whether case-study authors identified a further potential for improving the situation by targeted policy action (Yes) or not (No), or whether such a further potential was deemed to be uncertain.
Column "Interaction type"	denotes the ideal type of interaction to which the case belongs as derived from the other variables: Model = Policy Model; Request = Request for Assistance; JD = Jurisdictional Delimitation; Nested = Nested Institutions; Means = Additional Means; Behavioral = Behavioral Interaction (see chapter 13 for the ideal types).

Notes: Cases of implementation of international rules within the EU have always been coded as "intentional." Cases that could have shown up twice in the list (with the source or the target institution as the core) have only been included once. Some cases constitute a chain (i.e., need to be seen together). The assessment of policy responses and future potential may change over time.

Climate Change Regime (UNFCCC and Kyoto Protocol: Chapter 3)

No.	Brief description of case	Core: T or S	Hor. or vert.	Quality of effect	Policy fields	Intentional	Key difference	Policy response	Further potential	Interaction type
1.	Compliance procedure of MONTREAL PROTOCOL ON SUBSTANCES THAT DEPLETE THE OZONE LAYER has served as a model for the elaboration of the compliance system of the Kyoto Protocol.	T	H	Synergy	Same	No	no entry (n.e.)	No	No	Model
2.	Following the MONTREAL PROTOCOL, establishment of technology and economic assessment panels under UNFCCC was blocked by a minority.	T	H	Disruption	Same	No	n.e.	No	Yes	Model
3.	MONTREAL PROTOCOL has helped phase out ozone-depleting substances that are also potent greenhouse gases (GHGs).	T	H	Synergy	Same	No	n.e.	No	No	Behavioral
4.	MONTREAL PROTOCOL has supported use of fluorinated GHGs regulated under Kyoto Protocol (hampering climate protection).	T	H	Disruption	Same	No	n.e.	Yes	Yes	Behavioral
5.	CONVENTION ON BIOLOGICAL DIVERSITY may suffer from establishment of monocultural tree plantations induced by climate change regime.	S	H	Disruption	Same	No	n.e.	Yes	Yes	Behavioral

6.	Ramsar Convention on Wetlands may benefit from additional resources for wetland management or suffer from conversion of wetlands for carbon sequestration induced by climate change regime.	S	H	Neutral/uncertain	Same	No	n.e.	Yes	Yes	Behavioral
7.	Convention to Combat Desertification may benefit from forestry activities promoted under the climate change regime that help combat desertification.	S	H	Synergy	Same	No	n.e.	Yes	Yes	Behavioral
8.	Kyoto Protocol has asked International Civil Aviation Organization to address GHG emissions from international aviation.	S	H	Uncertain (disruption)	Different	Yes	O	Yes	No	JD
9.	Kyoto Protocol has asked International Maritime Organization to address GHG emissions from international shipping.	S	H	Uncertain (disruption)	Different	Yes	O	Yes	No	JD
10.	World Trade Organization is used as a major argument against elaboration of trade-relevant climate protection measures ("chill effect").	T	H	Disruption	Different	No	O	Yes	Yes	JD
11.	World Bank has greened its operations to some extent in response to climate change regime.	S	H	Synergy	Different	No	Ma	No	No	Means
12.	Climate change regime has asked the Global Environment Facility to operate its financial mechanism.	S	H	Synergy	Different	Yes	O	Yes	Yes	JD

No.	Brief description of case	Core: T or S	Hor. or vert.	Quality of effect	Policy fields	Intentional	Key difference	Policy response	Further potential	Interaction type
13.	EU LANDFILL DIRECTIVE results in reductions of methane emissions and thus helps implement the Kyoto Protocol.	T	V	Synergy	Same	No	n.e.	No	Uncertain (no)	Behavioral
14.	EU RENEWABLE ENERGY DIRECTIVE is to lead to increasing use of non-GHG emitting energy sources and thus helps implement the Kyoto Protocol.	T	V	Synergy	Different	Yes	n.e.	No	Yes	Behavioral
15.	EU DIRECTIVE ON THE INTERNAL MARKET FOR ELECTRICITY is expected to result, inter alia, in lower energy prices, counteracting efforts to save energy and reduce GHG emissions.	T	V	Disruption	Different	No	n.e.	Yes	Yes	Behavioral
16.	EU DIRECTIVES ON CAR EMISSION STANDARDS require cars to be equipped with catalytic converters, leading to increases of GHG emissions.	T	V	Disruption	Same	No	n.e.	Yes	Yes	Behavioral
17.	EU GHG MONITORING MECHANISM responds to international monitoring and reporting requirements under the Kyoto Protocol.	S	V	Synergy	Same	Yes	Ma	No	No	Means
18.	EU BURDEN-SHARING AGREEMENT of 1997 facilitated agreement on strengthened targets under the Kyoto Protocol.	T	V	Synergy	Same	No	M	No	No	Nested

No.	Description									
19.	Kyoto Protocol triggered the codification of EU BURDEN SHARING in supranational EU law.	S	V	Synergy	Same	Yes	Ma	No	No	Means
20.	EU BURDEN SHARING helps implement the Kyoto Protocol by strengthening enforcement in the EU.	T	V	Synergy	Same	No	n.e.	No	No	Behavioral
21.	Kyoto Protocol contributed to the emergence of an EU REGULATORY FRAMEWORK ON FLUORINATED GHGS (Regulation and Directive).	S	V	Synergy	Same	Yes	Ma	No	Yes	Means
22.	EU REGULATORY FRAMEWORK ON FLUORINATED GHGS is expected to lead to reduction of GHG emissions.	T	V	Synergy	Same	No	n.e.	No	Yes	Behavioral
23.	Climate change regime triggered adoption of the EU EMISSIONS TRADING DIRECTIVE.	S	V	Synergy	Same	Yes	Ma	No	No	Means
24.	EU EMISSIONS TRADING DIRECTIVE is expected to lead to reduction of GHG emissions.	T	V	Synergy	Same	No	n.e.	No	Yes	Behavioral

Convention on Biological Diversity (CBD: Chapter 4)

No.	Description									
25.	Implementation of RAMSAR CONVENTION ON WETLANDS helps CBD achieve its targets.	T	H	Synergy	Same	No	n.e.	Yes	Uncertain (yes)	Behavioral
26.	Implementation of CONVENTION ON MIGRATORY SPECIES (CMS) helps CBD achieve its targets.	T	H	Synergy	Same	No	n.e.	Yes	Uncertain (yes)	Behavioral
27.	CBD has facilitated talks in the UN FORUM ON FORESTS (and its predecessors), which could build on agreements reached under it.	S	H	Synergy	Same	No	Ma	No	No	Means

No.	Brief description of case	Core: T or S	Hor. or vert.	Quality of effect	Policy fields	Intentional	Key difference	Policy response	Further potential	Interaction type
28.	WTO TRIPS Agreement affected negotiations of the CBD on equitable sharing/access to genetic resources.	T	H	Disruption	Different	No	O	Yes	Yes	JD
29.	Rules of WTO TRIPS Agreement on patenting engender behavior at odds with CBD objectives on equitable sharing/access to genetic resources.	T	H	Disruption	Different	No	n.e.	Yes	Yes	Behavioral
30.	CBD objectives on equitable sharing/access to genetic resources lead to cumbersome patent protection at odds with WTO TRIPS Agreement.	S	H	Disruption	Different	No	n.e.	Yes	Yes	Behavioral
31.	FAO Undertaking on Plant Genetic Resources for Food and Agriculture influenced negotiations on CBD regarding property rights and access to genetic resources.	T	H	Disruption	Different	No	O	Yes	Uncertain (no)	JD
32.	CBD influenced FAO Treaty on Plant Genetic Resources for Food and Agriculture regarding access to genetic resources.	S	H	Neutral/uncertain	Different	No	O	No	Uncertain (no)	JD
33.	CBD objectives on equitable sharing and access to genetic resources influenced preparation of the EU Patent Directive of 1998.	S	V	Disruption	Different	Yes	Ma	Yes	Yes	Means
34.	EU Patent Directive may undermine the implementation of the CBD objectives on equitable sharing/access to genetic resources.	T	V	Disruption	Different	No	n.e.	No	Yes	Behavioral

International Regime for the Protection of the Northeast Atlantic (OSPAR/INSCs: Chapter 5)

		T	H	Synergy	Same	Yes	Ma(M)	No	No	Means
35.	INTERNATIONAL NORTH SEA CONFERENCES (INSCs) have facilitated and sped up development of the OSPAR Convention for the protection of the Northeast Atlantic.	T	H	Synergy	Same	Yes	No	No	No	
36.	OSPAR has expanded the scope of INSCs and helped implement INSC Declarations on marine pollution.	S	H	Synergy	Same	Uncertain (yes)	n.e.	No	No	Behavioral
37.	MONTREAL PROTOCOL ON SUBSTANCES THAT DEPLETE THE OZONE LAYER helped implement INSC commitments on carbon tetrachloride and methyl chloroform.	T	H	Synergy	Same	No	n.e.	No	No	Behavioral
38.	The CLIMATE CHANGE REGIME may provide an incentive for CO_2 sequestration in North Sea oil fields, which may violate OSPAR prohibition of dumping at sea.	T	H	Disruption	Same	No	n.e.	No	Yes	Behavioral
39.	LONDON DUMPING CONVENTION benefited from OSPAR that facilitated agreement on global ban on dumping and incineration at sea within London Convention.	S	H	Synergy	Same	No	M	No	No	Nested
40.	Implementation of RHINE CONVENTION helps achieve objectives of OSPAR.	T	H	Synergy	Same	No	n.e.	Yes	Uncertain (yes)	Behavioral
41.	UNECE CONVENTION ON LONG-RANGE TRANSBOUNDARY AIR POLLUTION contributes to achieving the objective of OSPAR on nutrients and eutrophication (NO_X).	T	H	Synergy	Same	No	n.e.	Yes	No	Behavioral

No.	Brief description of case	Core: T or S	Hor. or vert.	Quality of effect	Policy fields	Intentional	Key difference	Policy response	Further potential	Interaction type
42.	INSC Declaration facilitated/triggered EU NITRATES DIRECTIVE.	S	V	Synergy	Same	Yes	Ma(M)	No	No	Means
43.	EU NITRATES DIRECTIVE helps implementation of INSC objectives on nutrients.	T	V	Synergy	Same	No	n.e.	No	No	Behavioral
44.	INSC Declaration facilitated/triggered EU URBAN WASTE-WATER DIRECTIVE.	S	V	Synergy	Same	Yes	Ma(M)	No	No	Means
45.	EU URBAN WASTE-WATER DIRECTIVE helps implementation of INSC objectives on nutrients.	T	V	Synergy	Same	No	n.e.	No	No	Behavioral
46.	OSPAR triggered/facilitated inclusion of an obligation to phase out sewage-sludge dumping in EU URBAN WASTE-WATER DIRECTIVE.	S	V	Synergy	Same	Yes	Ma(M)	No	No	Means
	Global Fisheries Regime (UN Fish Stocks Agreement/FAO: Chapter 6)									
47.	The regional INTERNATIONAL COUNCIL FOR THE EXPLORATION OF THE SEA (ICES) has implemented the precautionary approach following its formal adoption in the global Fish Stocks Agreement (FSA).	S	H	Uncertain (synergy)	Same	Yes	Ma	Yes	Uncertain (yes)	Means
48.	ICES contributed to improved conservation in line with FSA by introducing greater safety margins in its catch recommendations and requesting rapid recovery of troubled stocks.	T	H	Synergy	Same	Yes	n.e.	No	Uncertain (yes)	Behavioral

49.	ICES modified its communication and terminology in response to criticism by FAO and regional regimes.	S	H	Uncertain (synergy)	Same	Yes	n.e.	No	Uncertain (yes)	Request
50.	The NORTHEAST ATLANTIC FISHERIES COMMISSION (NEAFC) responded to the transparency rules of the FSA by adopting new provisions on access to meetings and reports.	S	H	Synergy	Same	Yes	M/Ma	No	Uncertain (no)	Means
51.	FSA supports implementation of the precautionary approach in the EU COMMON FISHERIES POLICY (CFP) (through ICES), which requires pre-agreed decision rules within recovery/management plans.	S	V	Synergy	Same	Yes	Ma(O)	No	Yes	Means
52.	FSA rules support inclusion of management considerations in EU FISH IMPORT REGULATIONS.	S	V	Disruption	Same	Yes	Ma(O)	No	Uncertain (yes)	Means
53.	FAO International Program of Action on fishing capacity (IPOA-Capacity) contributes to reform of related EU RULES AIMING AT A REDUCTION OF SUBSIDIES.	S	V	Disruption	Same	Yes	Ma(O)	No	Yes	Means
54.	FAO IPOA Capacity contributed to reduction of FISHERIES SUBSIDIES in the EU and its member states.	S	V	Disruption	Same	No	n.e.	Yes	Yes	Behavioral
55.	EU FISHERIES SUBSIDIES still undermine conservation and management of fish stocks required by global fisheries regime.	T	V	Disruption	Same	No	n.e.	No	Yes	Behavioral

No.	Brief description of case	Core: T or S	Hor. or vert.	Quality of effect	Policy fields	Intentional	Key difference	Policy response	Further potential	Interaction type
56.	WTO SUBSIDIES RULES improve information flows and bindingness and may therefore help reduce or limit fisheries subsidies and capacity.	T	H	Uncertain (synergy)	Different	No	Ma/O	Yes	Yes	Means
57.	The global fisheries regime helped place fisheries subsidies on the formal WTO AGENDA (Doha Round).	S	H	Synergy	Different	No	Ma/O	Yes	Yes	Means
58.	CONVENTION ON INTERNATIONAL TRADE IN ENDANGERED SPECIES OF WILD FAUNA AND FLORA (CITES) has contributed to the emergence of FAO International Program of Action on the Conservation and Management of Sharks (IPOA-Sharks).	T	H	Synergy	Different	Yes	n.e.	Yes	Yes	Request
59.	CITES benefited in its implementation from improved national reporting procedures and records of shark catches resulting from IPOA-Sharks.	S	H	Synergy	Different	Yes	n.e.	No	Uncertain (yes)	Behavioral
60.	NORTHWEST ATLANTIC FISHERIES ORGANIZATION facilitated adoption of FSA provisions on inspection, detention, and arrest of fishing ships.	T	H	Synergy	Same	No	n.e.	No	Yes	Model
61.	CENTRAL BERING SEA DOUGHNUT HOLE AGREEMENT facilitated adoption of FSA provisions on inspection, detention, and arrest of fishing ships.	T	H	Synergy	Same	No	n.e.	No	Yes	Model

Convention on International Trade in Endangered Species of Wild Fauna and Flora (CITES: Chapter 7)

No.	Description									
62.	The CONVENTION FOR THE CONSERVATION AND MANAGEMENT OF THE VICUÑA (CCMV) has asked CITES for help in limiting trade in Vicuña products and CITES has responded positively with a COP Resolution.	T	H	Synergy	Same	Yes	n.e.	No	Uncertain (no)	Request
63.	The INTERNATIONAL CONVENTION ON THE REGULATION OF WHALING (ICRW) asked CITES for help in limiting trade in whale products and CITES has responded positively with a COP Resolution.	T	H	Synergy	Same	Yes	n.e.	No	Uncertain (yes)	Request
64.	In response to a call for action by the CONVENTION ON MIGRATORY SPECIES (CMS), CITES passed a COP Resolution in support of CMS concerning the houbara bustard.	T	H	Synergy	Same	Yes	n.e.	No	Uncertain (no)	Request
65.	Implementation of CITES helps CONVENTION ON BIOLOGICAL DIVERSITY achieve its objectives (several decisions and resolutions in both institutions).	S	H	Synergy	Same	No	n.e.	Yes	Uncertain (no)	Behavioral
66.	CITES restricts free international trade and thus is in potential conflict with the WORLD TRADE ORGANIZATION (WTO); it allows for trade with nonparties complying with its obligations.	S	H	Disruption	Different	No	n.e.	Yes	Yes	Behavioral
67.	CITES asked the WORLD CUSTOMS ORGANIZATION (WCO) for help in implementation.	S	H	Neutral/uncertain	Different	Yes	n.e.	Yes	Uncertain (no)	Request

No.	Brief description of case	Core: T or S	Hor. or vert.	Quality of effect	Policy fields	Intentional	Key difference	Policy response	Further potential	Further Interaction type
68.	WCO supports implementation of CITES by helping coordinate CITES enforcement and training via national customs organizations.	T	H	Synergy	Different	Yes	n.e.	No	Uncertain (no)	Behavioral
69.	CITES asked WCO to change customs codes (e.g., for shark products).	S	H	Neutral/uncertain	Different	Yes	n.e.	No	Uncertain (no)	Request
70.	CITES asked INTERPOL for help in implementation and enforcement.	S	H	Neutral/uncertain	Different	Yes	n.e.	Yes	No	Request
71.	INTERPOL supports implementation of CITES (e.g., memorandum of understanding on cooperation).	T	H	Synergy	Different	Yes	n.e.	No	Uncertain (no)	Behavioral
72.	The EU adopted a REGULATION TO CONTROL WILDLIFE TRADE in 1982 in response to CITES, although it was not a party to CITES.	S	V	Synergy	Same	Yes	Ma	Yes	Yes	Means
73.	CITES concerns about abolition of internal border controls caused the EU to strengthen its CITES REGULATION in 1997 (revised 2001).	S	V	Synergy	Same	Yes	Ma	Yes	No	Means
74.	CITES REGULATION OF THE EU supports the implementation of CITES.	T	V	Synergy	Same	Yes	n.e.	Yes	Uncertain (no)	Behavioral
75.	Abolition of intra-EU border controls for goods and persons in the wake of the EU SINGLE MARKET PROGRAM endangers effective implementation of CITES trade restrictions in the EU.	T	V	Disruption	Different	No	n.e.	Yes	Uncertain (no)	Behavioral

World Trade Organization (WTO: Chapter 8)

No.	Description									
76.	Montreal Protocol on Substances that Deplete the Ozone Layer granted exemptions from trade restrictions to nonparties complying with it in response to WTO rules.	S	H	Disruption	Different	No	O	Yes	Uncertain (no)	JD
77.	Montreal Protocol did not apply planned restrictions on trade in products produced with ozone-depleting substances, partly in response to WTO rules.	S	H	Disruption	Different	No	O	Yes	Yes	JD
78.	Montreal Protocol has provided a model for WTO of admissible trade restrictions for environmental purposes in a multilateral framework.	T	H	Uncertain (synergy)	Different	No	n.e.	Yes	No	Model
79.	Montreal Protocol did not restrict trade in used products relying on ozone-depleting substances, to a large extent due to WTO disciplines.	S	H	Disruption	Different	No	O	Yes	Yes	JD
80.	WTO disciplines affected implementation of the Montreal Protocol by limiting parties' use of trade measures with respect to used products relying on ozone-depleting substances.	S	H	Disruption	Different	No	n.e.	Yes	Yes	Behavioral
81.	Cartagena Protocol on Biosafety was used to block attempts to regulate biosafety under the WTO.	T	H	Disruption	Different	No	O	No	No	JD
82.	Cartagena Protocol includes preambular language attempting to reconcile tensions with WTO.	S	H	Neutral/uncertain	Different	No	O	No	No	JD

No.	Brief description of case	Core: T or S	Hor. or vert.	Quality of effect	Policy fields	Intentional	Key difference	Policy response	Further potential	Further Interaction type
83.	CARTAGENA PROTOCOL has adapted its risk-assessment procedure from WTO's SPS Agreement, which potentially constrains its use of trade measures.	S	H	Disruption	Different	No	O	Yes	Uncertain (yes)	JD
84.	In response to WTO rules, BASEL CONVENTION ON THE CONTROL OF TRANSBOUNDARY MOVEMENTS OF HAZARDOUS WASTES AND THEIR DISPOSAL granted exemptions from trade restrictions to nonparties complying with it.	S	H	Disruption	Different	No	O	Yes	Uncertain (no)	JD
85.	In response to WTO rules, INTERNATIONAL COMMISSION FOR THE CONSERVATION OF ATLANTIC TUNAS granted exemptions from trade restrictions to nonparties complying with it.	S	H	Disruption	Different	No	O	Yes	Uncertain (no)	JD
86.	In response to WTO rules, CONVENTION ON THE CONSERVATION OF ANTARCTIC MARINE LIVING RESOURCES granted exemptions from trade restrictions to nonparties complying with it.	S	H	Disruption	Different	No	O	Yes	Uncertain (no)	JD
	EU Water Framework Directive (Chapter 9)									
87.	EU NITRATES DIRECTIVE supports implementation of Water Framework Directive.	T	H	Synergy	Same	No	n.e.	No	Yes	Behavioral

No.	Description									
88.	EU Water Framework Directive is expected to support implementation of Nitrates Directive.	S	H	Synergy	Same	Yes	n.e.	No	Uncertain	Behavioral
89.	EU Water Framework Directive influences the amendment of the Bathing Waters Directive.	S	H	Uncertain (synergy)	Same	No	Ma	No	Uncertain	Means
90.	EU Bathing Waters Directive supports implementation of Water Framework Directive.	T	H	Synergy	Same	No	n.e.	No	Yes	Behavioral
91.	EU Water Framework Directive is expected to support implementation of Bathing Waters Directive.	S	H	Synergy	Same	Yes	n.e.	No	Uncertain	Behavioral
92.	EU IPPC Directive allows the Water Framework Directive to establish explicit link by defining environmental quality standards.	T	H	Synergy	Same	No	Ma	No	No	Means
93.	Later EU Water Framework Directive changes meaning of environmental quality standards protected under earlier IPPC Directive.	S	H	Synergy	Same	Yes	Ma	No	No	Means
94.	EU IPPC Directive supports implementation of Water Framework Directive by requiring that permits do not lead to breaches of established environmental quality standards.	T	H	Synergy	Same	Uncertain (yes)	n.e.	No	Uncertain	Behavioral
95.	EU Water Framework Directive was used for defining damage under Directive on Environmental Liability.	S	H	Synergy	Same	No	Ma	No	No	Means
96.	EU Liability Directive is to support implementation of the Water Framework Directive.	T	H	Synergy	Same	Yes	n.e.	No	Uncertain (no)	Behavioral

No.	Brief description of case	Core: T or S	Hor. or vert.	Quality of effect	Policy fields	Intentional	Key difference	Policy response	Further potential	Interaction type
97.	CONVENTION ON TRANSBOUNDARY WATERCOURSES AND LAKES triggers certain implementing provisions in Water Framework Directive.	T	V	Synergy	Same	Yes	Ma	No	Uncertain (no)	Means
98.	Water Framework Directive contributes to achieving the objectives of the CONVENTION ON TRANSBOUNDARY WATERCOURSES AND LAKES.	S	V	Synergy	Same	Yes	n.e.	No	Uncertain	Behavioral
99.	OSPAR CONVENTION for the protection of the Northeast Atlantic triggers certain implementing provisions in Water Framework Directive.	S	V	Synergy	Same	Yes	Ma	No	Uncertain (no)	Means
100.	Water Framework Directive contributes to achieving the objectives of OSPAR CONVENTION.	S	V	Synergy	Same	Yes	n.e.	No	Uncertain	Behavioral
101.	INTERNATIONAL NORTH SEA CONFERENCES facilitated/triggered Water Framework Directive.	T	V	Synergy	Same	Yes	Ma	No	No	Means
102.	AARHUS CONVENTION on public participation and access to information/justice led to enhanced public participation requirements in Water Framework Directive.	T	V	Synergy	Same	Yes	Ma	No	Uncertain (yes)	Means
103.	Water Framework Directive supports achieving objectives of/helps implement RAMSAR CONVENTION ON WETLANDS.	S	V	Synergy	Same	No	n.e.	No	Uncertain	Behavioral

EU Directive on Integrated Pollution Prevention and Control (IPPC Directive: Chapter 9)

104. EU IPPC Directive adopts principle of waste avoidance from WASTE FRAMEWORK DIRECTIVE.	T	H	Synergy	Same	No	Ma	No	No	Means
105. EU WASTE FRAMEWORK DIRECTIVE benefits from implementation of IPPC Directive that requires waste avoidance in line with the former.	S	H	Synergy	Same	Yes	n.e.	No	Uncertain	Behavioral
106. EU IPPC Directive establishes link to AIR QUALITY FRAMEWORK DIRECTIVE by requiring that permits do not lead to breaches of established environmental quality standards.	T	H	Synergy	Same	No	Ma	No	No	Means
107. Implementation of IPPC Directive supports implementation of AIR QUALITY FRAMEWORK DIRECTIVE by requiring that permits do not lead to breaches of established environmental quality standards.	S	H	Synergy	Same	Yes	n.e.	No	Uncertain	Behavioral
108. EU IPPC Directive establishes link to HABITATS DIRECTIVE by requiring that certified installations do not adversely affect "favorable conservation status."	T	H	Synergy	Same	No	Ma	No	No	Means
109. Implementation of EU IPPC Directive supports implementation of HABITATS DIRECTIVE by requiring that certified installations do not adversely affect "favorable conservation status."	S	H	Synergy	Same	Yes	n.e.	No	Uncertain	Behavioral

No.	Brief description of case	Core: T or S	Hor. or vert.	Quality of effect	Policy fields	Intentional	Key difference	Policy response	Further potential	Interaction type
110.	EU IPPC Directive establishes link to Birds Directive by requiring that certified installations do not adversely affect "favorable conservation status."	T	H	Synergy	Same	No	Ma	No	No	Means
111.	Implementation of EU IPPC Directive supports implementation of Birds Directive by requiring that certified installations do not adversely affect "favorable conservation status."	S	H	Synergy	Same	Yes	n.e.	No	Uncertain	Behavioral
112.	Emission limits under EU Large Combustion Plants Directive (incl. revision) ensure minimum standards, thus limiting flexibility in issuing permits under IPPC Directive.	T	H	Uncertain (synergy)	Same	No	Ma	No	Uncertain (no)	Means
113.	Emission limits under EU Solvents Directive ensure minimum standards, thus limiting flexibility in issuing permits under IPPC Directive.	T	H	Uncertain (synergy)	Same	No	Ma	No	Uncertain (no)	Means
114.	EU Environmental Management and Auditing Scheme (EMAS Regulation) facilitates implementation of IPPC Directive in that EMAS certificates can be used to simplify permitting procedures.	T	H	Synergy	Same	No	n.e.	No	Uncertain	Behavioral
115.	IPPC Directive supports implementation of EMAS Regulation by providing incentive to establish EMAS.	S	H	Synergy	Same	No	n.e.	No	Uncertain (no)	Behavioral

No.	Description									
116.	EU IPPC Directive establishes link to ENVIRONMENTAL IMPACT ASSESSMENT (EIA) DIRECTIVE by allowing use of impact assessment under EIA Directive in permitting procedures.	T	H	Uncertain (synergy)	Same	No	Ma	Yes	Uncertain (no)	Means
117.	EU EIA DIRECTIVE facilitates implementation of IPPC (in that impact assessment can be used under IPPC).	T	H	Synergy	Same	No	n.e.	No	Uncertain (no)	Behavioral
118.	EU SEVESO II DIRECTIVE on industrial accidents benefits from IPPC Directive that promotes an integrated approach and contributes to a greening of installations so that the impact of any accident would be minimized.	S	H	Synergy	Same	Uncertain	n.e.	No	No	Behavioral
119.	AARHUS CONVENTION on public participation and access to information/justice has led to amendments of rules on public participation under IPPC Directive.	T	V	Synergy	Same	Yes	Ma	No	No	Means
120.	OSPAR CONVENTION for the protection of the Northeast Atlantic benefits from implementation of IPPC Directive (reduction of pollution of Northeast Atlantic).	S	V	Synergy	Same	No	n.e.	No	No	Behavioral
121.	HELSINKI CONVENTION for the protection of the Baltic Sea benefits from implementation of IPPC Directive (reduction of pollution of Baltic Sea).	S	V	Synergy	Same	No	n.e.	No	No	Behavioral
122.	CONVENTION ON LONG-RANGE TRANSBOUNDARY AIR POLLUTION benefits from implementation of IPPC Directive (reduction of air pollution).	S	V	Synergy	Same	No	n.e.	No	No	Behavioral

No.	Brief description of case	Core: T or S	Hor. or vert.	Quality of effect	Policy fields	Intentional	Key difference	Policy response	Further potential	Interaction type
123.	UN FRAMEWORK CONVENTION ON CLIMATE CHANGE benefits from implementation of IPPC Directive (reduction of emissions of greenhouse gases).	S	V	Synergy	Same	No	n.e.	No	No	Behavioral

EU Habitats Directive (Chapter 10)

No.	Brief description of case	Core: T or S	Hor. or vert.	Quality of effect	Policy fields	Intentional	Key difference	Policy response	Further potential	Interaction type
124.	EU BIRDS DIRECTIVE has served as a model for Habitats Directive (in parts).	T	H	Synergy	Same	No	n.e.	No	No	Model
125.	EU Habitats Directive has supported achievement of objectives of BIRDS DIRECTIVE, including by strengthening certain aspects of protection of bird sites.	S	H	Synergy	Same	Yes	n.e.	Yes	Yes	Behavioral
126.	Strict interpretation of site protection under the EU BIRDS DIRECTIVE by European Court of Justice results in Habitats Directive being weaker than initially proposed.	T	H	Uncertain (disruption)	Same	No	O	No	Uncertain	JD
127.	EU Habitats Directive includes provisions that directly weaken level of protection afforded to sites designated under BIRDS DIRECTIVE.	S	H	Disruption	Same	Yes	n.e.	Yes	Yes	Behavioral
128.	A reference to Natura 2000 was included in the EU WATER FRAMEWORK DIRECTIVE.	S	H	Synergy	Same	No	Ma	No	Uncertain (no)	Means

129. EU WATER FRAMEWORK DIRECTIVE supports achievement of objectives of Habitats Directive.	T	H	Synergy	Same	Yes	n.e.	No	Uncertain (no)	Behavioral
130. Habitats Directive is used in part for defining damage covered under EU ENVIRONMENTAL LIABILITY DIRECTIVE.	S	H	Synergy	Same	No	Ma	No	No	Means
131. EU ENVIRONMENTAL LIABILITY DIRECTIVE introduces additional incentive for behavior that is compatible with the Habitats Directive.	T	H	Synergy	Same	Yes	n.e.	No	Uncertain (no)	Behavioral
132. EU STRUCTURAL FUND projects that conflict with nature conservation objectives undermine implementation of the Habitats Directive.	T	H	Disruption	Different	No	n.e.	Yes	Yes	Behavioral
133. Cross-compliance rule in the EU STRUCTURAL FUNDS is used to encourage member states to submit site lists under the Habitats Directive, and to avoid damage to sites.	T	H	Synergy	Different	No	n.e.	No	Yes	Behavioral
134. OSPAR CONVENTION for the protection of the Northeast Atlantic supports implementation of Habitats Directive in the marine environment.	T	V	Synergy	Same	No	n.e.	No	Uncertain (yes)	Behavioral
135. Necessity to implement BERN CONVENTION ON THE CONSERVATION OF EUROPEAN WILDLIFE AND NATURAL HABITATS in the EU drives preparation of Habitats Directive.	T	V	Synergy	Same	Yes	Ma	No	No	Means

No.	Brief description of case	Core: T or S	Hor. or vert.	Quality of effect	Policy fields	Intentional	Key difference	Policy response	Further potential	Interaction type
136.	Habitats Directive supports achievement of objectives of BERN CONVENTION.	S	V	Synergy	Same	Yes	n.e.	No	Yes	Behavioral
137.	EU Habitats Directive Natura 2000 program provides model/reference point for development of BERN CONVENTION Emerald program.	S	V	Synergy	Same	No	M	Yes	Uncertain (yes)	Nested
138.	Habitats Directive has adopted concepts from the CONVENTION ON BIOLOGICAL DIVERSITY, which was negotiated simultaneously.	T	V	Synergy	Same	No	n.e.	No	Uncertain (no)	Model
139.	Habitats Directive supports achievement of objectives of CONVENTION ON BIOLOGICAL DIVERSITY in the EU.	S	V	Synergy	Same	No	n.e.	Yes	Uncertain (yes)	Behavioral
140.	AGREEMENT ON SMALL CETACEANS OF THE BALTIC AND NORTH SEAS (ASCOBANS) under the Convention on Migratory Species supports achievement of objectives of Habitats Directive at the national level.	T	V	Synergy	Same	No	n.e.	No	Yes	Behavioral
141.	PAN-EUROPEAN BIODIVERSITY AND LANDSCAPE DIVERSITY STRATEGY supports implementation of the Habitats Directive, particularly through its focus on ecological corridors between sites.	T	V	Synergy	Same	No	n.e.	No	Yes	Behavioral

EU Deliberate Release Directive (DRD): Chapter 11)

142. EU Deliberate Release Directive (DRD) established second regulatory hurdle requiring precautionary risk assessment of genetically modified organisms (GMOs), thus disrupting authorization under EU SECTORAL LEGISLATION.	S	H	Disruption	Different	Yes	n.e.	Yes	Yes	Behavioral
143. DRD requires EU SECTORAL LEGISLATION to provide for "similar" (original DRD) or "equivalent" (revised DRD) environmental risk assessment.	S	H	Uncertain (disruption)	Different	Yes	O	Yes	Uncertain (yes)	JD
144. DRD required labeling only for certain GMOs and thus undermined the EU NOVEL FOOD REGULATION that aimed to introduce more general labeling of GM food.	S	H	Disruption	Different	No	n.e.	Yes	Uncertain (no)	Behavioral
145. Amended DRD (1997) allowed for labeling irrespective of actual GMO content, thereby undermining EU SECTORAL LEGISLATION that aims to introduce unambiguous labeling of GMOs according to certain thresholds of GM content.	S	H	Disruption	Different	No	n.e.	Yes	Uncertain (yes)	Behavioral
146. Unclear scope of DRD's precautionary risk assessment led to EU decision to evaluate secondary effects under PESTICIDES DIRECTIVE, rather than DRD.	T	H	Disruption	Different	No	O	Yes	Uncertain (yes)	JD

No.	Brief description of case	Core: T or S	Hor. or vert.	Quality of effect	Policy fields	Intentional	Key difference	Policy response	Further potential	Interaction type
147.	As an increasing number of member states pursued evaluation of secondary effects under DRD, authorization of products conforming to PESTICIDE DIRECTIVE was negatively affected.	S	H	Disruption	Different	Uncertain (yes)	n.e.	Yes	Uncertain (yes)	Behavioral
148.	Liability of GMOs was not included in revised DRD because it was to be dealt with in upcoming EU ENVIRONMENTAL LIABILITY DIRECTIVE.	T	H	Disruption	Same	No	O	Yes	Yes	JD
149.	EU ENVIRONMENTAL LIABILITY DIRECTIVE refers to revised DRD and partially covers GMOs.	S	H	Synergy	Same	Yes	Ma	No	Yes	Means
150.	EU ENVIRONMENTAL LIABILITY DIRECTIVE is expected to have a positive effect on the implementation of the DRD.	T	H	Synergy	Same	Yes	n.e.	No	Yes	Behavioral
151.	DRD's precautionary approach leads to delays in GM product approval or even bans, thereby restricting international trade (at odds with WTO SPS AGREEMENT).	S	V	Disruption	Different	No	n.e.	Yes	Yes	Behavioral
152.	Partial "internationalization" of DRD's precautionary approach may lead to modification of WTO SPS AGREEMENT's concept of precaution.	S	V	Uncertain (disruption)	Different	Uncertain	O/M	No	Yes	JD

153. WTO dispute-settlement mechanism provides WTO SPS Agreement with effective instrument to impose rudimentary precaution on DRD.	T	V	Disruption	Different	No	n.e.	Yes	Yes	Behavioral
154. DRD's labeling and traceability provisions restrict trade, thereby undermining objective of WTO TBT Agreement.	S	V	Disruption	Different	No	n.e.	Yes	Uncertain (yes)	Behavioral
155. WTO dispute-settlement mechanism provides WTO TBT Agreement with effective instrument to enforce compliance, possibly undermining the DRD.	T	V	Disruption	Different	No	n.e.	Yes	Uncertain (yes)	Behavioral
156. DRD constituted input for formulation of UNEP Technical Guidelines on Biosafety.	S	V	Synergy	Same	No	n.e.	No	No	Model
EU Air Quality Framework Directive (Chapter 12)									
157. EU Single Market has amplified a trend of increasing transport emissions and hence disruptively affected the process of improving air quality.	T	H	Disruption	Different	No	n.e.	Yes	Yes	Behavioral
158. EU National Emission Ceilings Directive sets emissions ceilings, which will help achieve air-quality targets.	T	H	Synergy	Same	Yes	n.e.	Yes	Yes	Behavioral
159. EU Auto-Oil I Directives set stricter fuel standards and vehicle-emission limits, which will help achieve air-quality targets.	T	H	Synergy	Same	Yes	n.e.	Yes	Yes	Behavioral

No.	Brief description of case	Core: T or S	Hor. or vert.	Quality of effect	Policy fields	Intentional	Key difference	Policy response	Further potential	Interaction type
160.	EU SAVE PROGRAM (directives on minimum standards of energy efficiency and related labeling) contributes to increased energy efficiency, which helps reduce emissions and improve air quality.	T	H	Synergy	Different	No	n.e.	No	No	Behavioral
161.	EU RENEWABLE ENERGY DIRECTIVE contributes to enhanced use of renewable energy sources, which helps reduce emissions and improve air quality.	T	H	Synergy	Different	No	n.e.	No	No	Behavioral
162.	CONVENTION ON LONG-RANGE TRANSBOUNDARY AIR POLLUTION developed the critical-loads concept, which facilitated the EU process of setting air-quality standards.	T	V	Synergy	Same	No	Ma	No	No	Means
163.	World Health Organization (WHO) produces air-quality guidelines that have heavily influenced EU air-quality standards.	T	V	Uncertain (synergy)	Different	Yes	Ma	Yes	Uncertain (no)	Means

Index

Global Environmental Accord: Strategies for Sustainability and Institutional Innovation
Nazli Choucri, series editor

Nazli Choucri, editor, *Global Accord: Environmental Challenges and International Responses*

Peter M. Haas, Robert O. Keohane, and Marc A. Levy, editors, *Institutions for the Earth: Sources of Effective International Environmental Protection*

Ronald B. Mitchell, *Intentional Oil Pollution at Sea: Environmental Policy and Treaty Compliance*

Robert O. Keohane and Marc A. Levy, editors, *Institutions for Environmental Aid: Pitfalls and Promise*

Oran R. Young, editor, *Global Governance: Drawing Insights from the Environmental Experience*

Jonathan A. Fox and L. David Brown, editors, *The Struggle for Accountability: The World Bank, NGOs, and Grassroots Movements*

David G. Victor, Kal Raustiala, and Eugene B. Skolnikoff, editors, *The Implementation and Effectiveness of International Environmental Commitments: Theory and Practice*

Mostafa K. Tolba, with Iwona Rummel-Bulska, *Global Environmental Diplomacy: Negotiating Environmental Agreements for the World, 1973–1992*

Karen T. Litfin, editor, *The Greening of Sovereignty in World Politics*

Edith Brown Weiss and Harold K. Jacobson, editors, *Engaging Countries: Strengthening Compliance with International Environmental Accords*

Oran R. Young, editor, *The Effectiveness of International Environmental Regimes: Causal Connections and Behavioral Mechanisms*

Ronie Garcia-Johnson, *Exporting Environmentalism: U.S. Multinational Chemical Corporations in Brazil and Mexico*

Lasse Ringius, *Radioactive Waste Disposal at Sea: Public Ideas, Transnational Policy Entrepreneurs, and Environmental Regimes*

Robert G. Darst, *Smokestack Diplomacy: Cooperation and Conflict in East-West Environmental Politics*

Urs Luterbacher and Detlef F. Sprinz, editors, *International Relations and Global Climate Change*

Edward L. Miles, Arild Underdal, Steinar Andresen, Jørgen Wettestad, Jon Birger Skjærseth, and Elaine M. Carlin, *Environmental Regime Effectiveness: Confronting Theory with Evidence*

Erika Weinthal, *State Making and Environmental Cooperation: Linking Domestic and International Politics in Central Asia*

Corey L. Lofdahl, *Environmental Impacts of Globalization and Trade: A Systems Study*

Oran R. Young, *The Institutional Dimensions of Environmental Change: Fit, Interplay, and Scale*

Tamar L. Gutner, *Banking on the Environment: Multilateral Development Banks and Their Environmental Performance in Central and Eastern Europe*

Liliana B. Andonova, *Transnational Politics of the Environment: The European Union and Environmental Policy in Central and Eastern Europe*

David L. Levy and Peter J. Newell, editors, *The Business of Global Environmental Governance*

Dennis Pirages and Ken Cousins, editors, *From Resource Scarcity to Ecological Security: Exploring New Limits to Growth*

Ken Conca, *Governing Water: Contentious Transnational Politics and Global Institution Building*

Sebastian Oberthür and Thomas Gehring, editors, *Institutional Interaction in Global Environmental Governance: Synergy and Conflict among International and EU Policies*